ANYTHING GOES:

The World of Popular Music

ANY THING GOES:

The World of Popular Music

DAVID DACHS

 THE **BOBBS-MERRILL** COMPANY, INC.
A SUBSIDIARY OF HOWARD W. SAMS & CO., INC.
Publishers • INDIANAPOLIS • NEW YORK

To Ethel, Jennie, Joshua, and Julie

First printing, 1964
Copyright © 1964 by David Dachs
All rights reserved
Library of Congress Catalog card number 63-18993

Printed in the United States of America

CONTENTS

ACKNOWLEDGMENTS

I would like to acknowledge the aid of a number of persons in acquiring information, arranging interviews, the securing of recordings, and photographs. None, however, are responsible for the thoughts, ideas, and conclusions which appear.

They are: Peter Reilly, Columbia Records; Irv Lichtman, associate editor of *Cash Box;* Sol Handwerger, MGM Records; Herb Helman, RCA Victor Records; Brown Meggs, Capitol Records; Bud Katzel, Roulette Records; Henry Brief, Record Industry Association of America; Richard Prather, NBC Photo File; Sid Rechetnik, NBC; Rick Ward, ABC-Paramount Records; Arnold Farber, *Home Entertainment Retailing;* Dick Gersh and Howard Cook, Colpix Records; Marshall Robbins, Commander Publications; Mike Berman, Paramount Pictures; Bob Altschuler, Atlantic Records; Paul Baumgarten, Elvis Presley Music; Jay Mark, Luldlow Music; Siegfried Eisgrau, Screen Gems-Columbia Music; Lloyd Leipzig, United Artists Records; Jesse Gross, *Variety;* Dick Frolich, ASCAP; Leonard Salidor, Decca Records; Laura Bell, *Life.*

Also, Erwin Frankel, Gloria Rosenberg (artwork), Iz Fiedler (artwork), Nat Hentoff, Johnny Friedkin, Cy Nicholson, Alan Siegel, Sol Jacobson, David Powers, Max Eisen, Selma Broidy, Art Kaplan, the late Mack Discant and Dick Maney.

ANYTHING GOES:
The World of Popular Music

1 · THE FABULOUS WORLD OF POPULAR MUSIC

> The innocent but highly pervasive culture which is now being
> strewn like fertile seed today across the world by records,
> performing artists, Telstar, TV, radio, and song-of-mouth.
> —Herbert Brean, The Music of *Life*

"I don't think that "Star Dust" would be recorded in today's climate," said the song's lyricist, Mitchell Parish, recently. In his Beekman Place workshop-apartment on New York's East Side, furnished in contemporary décor and filled with books and original art, including an Utrillo, he spoke quietly, but—as they say on sheet music—"with feeling." A skilled writer for more than three decades, sixty-four-year-old Parish, a former admitting clerk in a New York hospital, has crafted the words for hundreds of songs, including such "standards" as "Hands Across the Table," "Deep Purple," "Sweet Lorraine," and "Sleigh-Ride." His most popular song is "Star Dust" (music by Hoagy Carmichael.) It is, of course, one of the most danced to, performed, sung, and recorded songs in the history of American popular music.

"Star Dust" has an orthodox thirty-two-bar structure, but its harmonies are fresh. There is a tremendous nostalgic sweetness in the music, and in the lyric. Jewelry, luggage, air flights have been named after it, and writers have used it as a symbol for romance in short stories and novels with such phrases as "and the band across the lake was playing 'Star Dust.'" Today, this song might be considered "uncommercial" by many "pop" record producers. Yet "Star Dust" became popular *three decades ago.*

"If 'Star Dust' were a new song, a brand new song, freshly written, it would be very difficult to have it exposed," says Parish. "Many songwriters go to a record company with a good song and they are told that it's too good. The public, i.e., teenagers, don't want to spend money on good songs. They want 'Blue Suede Shoes' or some other gibberish. And without getting a record the song is dead. It's dead before it's born. I'm amazed at the obtuseness of many of the teen-

1

agers. They seem to want the monotonous stupid songs with the same deadly beat. They accept it, they like it."

A cartoonist portrays a record shop with bins of records marked "Symphonic," "Opera," "Band," and "Trash." The British recording sensations, The Beatles, appear on Ed Sullivan's TV program. A multiple version of Elvis Presley, the group gyrates in true pelvic rock 'n' roll style, eleven years after Elvis Presley first appeared, to remind us that the good works we do can come back to haunt us.

Fortune magazine, in an economic analysis of the record industry which covered classical music as well as popular, found its folkways "murderous." Sidney Ascher, veteran publicist (Andy Russell, Vic Damone, Tony Bennett) says of the "pop" record business: "It's no business. It does not follow general principles. I think the biggest wheelers and dealers are in the record business."

Criticism of popular music, like that of the Wagnerian "Ring" cycle, goes on and on. The stars who sing, and their styles, are satirized by comedians Jack Benny, Sid Caesar, and Danny Kaye. But somehow, "pop" music keeps to its comic-strip,·honking, self-pitying ways. Some of the criticism may be less than accurate, but it has its roots in the undisguised disenchantment with U.S. popular music, once a proud and attractive art, for more than a decade.

Mitchell Parish may be wrong about not getting a song like "Star Dust" recorded these days; perhaps Tony Bennett might do it, or Ella Fitzgerald. But the facts remain that practically a Who's Who of popular music-makers has been equally gloomy about what has occurred. Bing Crosby, Leonard Bernstein, Ethel Merman, Richard Rodgers have all felt impelled to assail what passes for popular music and lyrics. Frank Sinatra has characterized rock 'n' roll, the "sound" of the past decade, as "the martial music of every sideburned delinquent on the face of the earth."

Scores of editorial writers, journalists, columnists, critics, and essayists have been stunned equally by the luxuriant growth of this cheap, juke-box culture. Referring to current popular music, the *Saturday Evening Post* recently published an article entitled "Dumb Music."

Millions who have hitherto accepted a tradition of good popular music as a fact of life similar to their morning cup of coffee, have wondered what has happened. Why has there been such a flood of poor songs sung by puny talents doing unison kicks during the so-called cultural explosion? What has happened to disembowel the great heritage of Gershwin, Porter, Kern, Youmans, and Duke Ellington? Show songs aside, why is Tin Pan Alley now "teen-alley"? Why do the moguls of AM broadcasting, who are so tigerish in defense of their freedom from government interference by the FCC, cravenly cater to what Mitch Miller has called "the popsicle set"?

And is the teenager incapable of appreciating the quality brand of popular music and musicianship that his counterpart enjoyed during the big band era of Benny Goodman, Glenn Miller, Tommy Dorsey, and Harry James?

The problem is audible, omnipresent, and enduring. Since the early 1950's there has been a decade of musical disquiet, a creative malaise that has injured every section of the population—the public, the composers and lyricists, the musicians, the more responsible elements in the record business, and those engaged in the business of record retailing and distribution.

The past decade has seen (1) the rise of cheap songs to an unrivaled degree; (2) an enormous payola scandal involving many popular disc jockeys; (3) the decline of the Hollywood musical; (4) the emergence of teenage dominance in the conception of music and in the marketing of records; (5) a chaotic sales structure in which you can buy the same recording at five different prices.

All this has occurred within a radically changed Tin Pan Alley. The physical face of popular music has changed. The land of the thirty-two-bar song has experienced a profound marketing revolution, a distributing revolution, and a technical revolution. It is bigger than ever, and possesses a wider frame of reference—the country's population keeps going up and so does the demand for American popular music in the world market.

To shed some light on the decline in the aesthetic standards of popular music, and on its abnormal patterns of marketing, it would be useful to quote Paul Ackerman, editor of *Billboard*, music industry trade paper. At the sensational payola hearings conducted by Congressman Oren Harris during 1959, Ackerman said: "The music business, whose products—songs and records—touch the lives of so many people, is unique in the sense that laymen know so little of its inner workings."

A close scrutiny of popular music's inner workings should provide a clearer idea of the dynamics of a cultural phenomena which is part art form, part "show biz."

Popular music is largely a frantic, neurasthenic, multi-billion-dollar-a-year business. Its ethics may not be the kind taught at the Harvard School of Business Administration, but it is a big business which pays taxes, lobbies in Washington, and is highly unionized. Even disc jockeys are members of AFTRA (American Federation of Television and Radio Artists).

It embraces many types—musically sensitive multimillionaires like Richard Rodgers, Harlem youngsters trying to break out of a black ghetto with a song, Ivy League eggheads like Alan Jay Lerner, and high school dropouts. In its ranks you will find country and western stars who know more about turning equalizing knobs in the record studio than they do about riding a horse. You will find folk music balladeers who know all about Schoenberg and twelve tone; and rock 'n' roll stars like Neil Sedaka ("Oh, Carol, Stupid Cupid") who studied musical theory at the Juilliard School of Music.

In musical content and lyric, it combines elements of all music— Broadway theater music, folk, jazz, gospel, symphonies (themes are recast), the assembly-line single song, rhythm and blues, country and western, Latin-American materials, and lots more. Its lyrics are from every genre—Gilbert and Sullivan, minstrel shows, vaudeville, and folkforms. Allan Sherman's "My Son, the Folk Singer" consisted of folksong parodies, chopped liver style, on a bed of Jewish lettuce. In the lyrics, too, you find new mutations, such as the latest teenage vernacular, or pseudo teenage vernacular, and such Hegelian philosophic statements as "Oh, Yeah."

U. S. popular music has seldom been more nakedly commercial, more money-hungry. Or, if it has always been this way, it has never possessed the superb technology of our times, the marketing skills, and consumption-minded social milieu in which to put its products across.

Popular music is a big, brassy, amoral business. Its modern malpractices would make "Mack the Knife" turn in his *messer* for parochialism. Macheath only looked upon the City of London as his domain. Those who are wheeling and dealing in popular music affect the U. S. and the world—particularly those least able to protect themselves from cultural seduction—the teenagers.

One former record executive has characterized the record business around which most of popular music spins in this way: "One-quarter show business, one-quarter consumer packaging, one-quarter ego, and one-quarter some of the worst mores in the country."

Popular music is a sturdy art even though it is often unpopular and inartistic. We bathe in popular music, do our banking to it, conduct our romances to it. Sometimes we listen to it. And we have had a good track record in creating it. In less than half a century, America gave birth to the finest popular music of the world. This may be excessive nationalism, but no country could match our George Gershwin, Irving

Berlin, Cole Porter, Jerome Kern, Duke Ellington, Rodgers and Hart, Rodgers and Hammerstein, Harold Arlen, Lerner and Loewe, E. Y. Harburg, the best of our jazz, and our country and western music.

The U. S. led the world in creating a modern musical theater. Our fine show songs, our instrumentals, our movie songs, our way of setting colloquial speech to music, exhibited the highest standards of craftsmanship.

These were created within a commercial context. But this commercial context is getting more oppressive, and has already wreaked havoc for more than a decade. But you can't prove it by the "kids."

Popular music has had a thunderous impact upon the folkways, tastes, sensibilities, and inner psyche of all Americans, particularly the young people. These days teenagers do their homework to popular music and dance to its varied genres—the cha-cha-cha, the foxtrot (a reactionary step), the twist, the bossa nova, the mashed potatoes, the hully gully, the limbo rock.

The songs, dances, and juke-box idols of Tin Pan Alley have a global reach. Here is a list of the five most popular recordings in Japan as listed in *Cash Box* on October 20, 1962:

1. The Young World/Ricky Nelson
2. Good Luck Charm/Elvis Presley
3. I Can't Stop Loving You/Ray Charles
4. The Man Who Shot Liberty Valance/Gene Pitney
5. King of the Clown/Neil Sedaka

In Israel that same week, the No. 1 song was a Pat Boone recording. It is hard to conceive of young Israelis on the *kibbutzim* listening to Boone sing this unflattering portrait of a Latin-American:

"Speedy Gonzales"*
La-la-la-la-la-la-la-la-la-la-la
La-la-la-la-la-la-la-la
La-la-la-la-la-la-la-la
Consuela she say
You better come home Speedy Gonzales
Away from Cannery Row
Stop all of your drinkin'
With that floozy named Flo

*Copyright © 1961 and 1962 by Budd Music Corp. Words and music by Buddy Kaye, Ethel Lee, David Hill.

Popular music is the basis of much of the massive structure of American entertainment and show business. Like a giant clover-leaf feeder, popular music channels its products and artists into recordings, radio, TV (from variety shows to that medical melodrama, "Ben Casey," with background music to operate by), Broadway, movies, juke boxes, restaurants, banks, and night clubs. You can name practically every type of entertainment, and except for straight dramatic plays the accents of "pop" music are audible. And even here canny Broadway producers turn to title songs of their shows for promotion purposes on the airwaves.

Popular music is a formidable part of the United States record industry. Of the $641 million spent by Americans in 1962 on recordings of all types—from Stravinsky and Prokofiev to Peter, Paul, and Mary and Frank Sinatra—much of it can be traced to the popular music spectrum. For example, approximately $160 million worth of 45-rpm singles were sold in 1962, or approximately 210 million records. In the long-playing record field, popular music, jazz, folk, show music, country and western, also accounted for much of the industry's volume. A reported $75 million is spent by American consumers on classical music. The remaining record sales are children's discs, and spoken-word recordings of poetry, prose, plays. Undoubtedly, most of the turntables of the nation spin popular music.

But record sales do not begin to disclose the lush financial side of popular music. The professional theater (Broadway, the "road," strawhat, off-Broadway) grosses approximately $70 million a year. Certainly it is the big musicals that provide the biggest grosses, for they play the largest theaters, and they charge more. Current radio income (AM) is estimated at $700 million a year by a Harvard Business School study. What would radio be without popular music? Probably mute.

Imagine television without background music or theme music, without Perry Como or Andy Williams, or without the "standards." Or Dick Clark's televised "dance party" displaying artists "lip-syncing" their hit records. In 1961 TV profits alone were $1,318,300,000, of which 10 to 20 per cent can be traced to TV shows employing musical personalities and record stars, such as Ed Sullivan's program.

There are also approximately 500,000 juke boxes, many of them stereophonic, out of whose electronic insides shoot the "top tunes"—an ironic phrase—to the tune of approximately $500 million a year. A million-dollar background music business also sweetens the pot. And large sums are received from abroad, through the popularity of American recording artists, songs, touring packages, Broadway and movie musicals.

Nor does this exhaust the interlocking popular music structure. In allied fields—at state fairs, college concerts, in-person shows, folk festivals—popular music's appeal (both for the music and the artists) is undeniable. The Golden Express (often it is a plane or a bus) rides day and night, often with William Morris or GAC at the throttle.

Tony Bennett, for example, played the American Shakespeare Festival Theater at Stratford, Connecticut one winter. He received $5,000 for two performances, singing in the same playhouse that offers summertime performances of the classics. In a single college concert, the Kingston Trio can bring in approximately $15,000 at the box office for one hootenanny. "Hootenanny" is reportedly an English word, made popular by Pete Seeger. But it took the U. S. A. to make it pay off at the box office.

Because of this interrelatedness, young Chubby Checker, who as Ernest Evans was an ex-butcher's helper from the new Salzburg—Philadelphia (cradle of many new record artists, including Bobby Rydell, Frankie Avalon, Fabian, James Darren, the Dovells, the Orlons)—has been an outstanding money-maker. To date, he has made more money than Bach, Beethoven, and Palestrina did in their lifetimes. In 1962, in Philadelphia Orphan's Court, (although Checker isn't an orphan, such courts hold jurisdiction over the earnings of show business personalities not yet twenty-one) Chubby Checker reported earnings of $822,459 for the three-year period from 1960-62. His earnings came from diverse sources. Largely they derived from royalties paid by Cameo-Parkway Records for his best-selling "hit single," "The Twist," and for such LP's as "Your Twist Party With the King of the Twist" and "Twist With Chubby Checker" (photograph of Chubby against a checkerboard). He also has earned excellent fees from TV, night clubs, and in-person shows. And he has starred in that didactic motion picture *Don't Knock the Twist*.

Oddly enough, the crest of Cameo-Parkway is in sharp contrast to its rocking, twisting, limboing records: it is the silhouette of the old-fashioned cameo that mother used to wear. In the tangential sense, popular music figures largely in the lucrative radio-TV jingle business. Broadway's Richard Adler, presently a Madison Avenue tune laureate ("Let Hertz put you in the driver's seat") is a key figure in this constricted form which sets the sponsor's message to music. For a man of Mr. Adler's talents, this would seem to be quite a decline from *Pajama Game*, but perhaps it is hard to turn down the money between shows. He is one of several well-known composers and lyricists who function in this cash-register music. He also had been active as a producer of shows for the late President John F. Kennedy and the Democratic National Committee.

The economic reach of popular music is endless. There are the dance studios, the record hops, the entertainment-oriented resorts, and the clothes to twist in. Tomorrow some other dance fad will sire a fashion gimmick. And then there are those teenage song magazines: *Song Hits, Rhythm and Blues, Rock and Roll Songs, Country Song Round-Up.* Built on the popularity of the new teen singers, they feature everything from semi-sociological pieces on the origin of the blues to such traditional articles as the one by Annette, a graduate from Walt Disney's "Mouseketeers," entitled "Things That A Girl Never Tells A Guy."

Annette has grown up, and this is equally true, in a more fundamental sense, of the popular music industry, which is no longer a penny-candy affair. The incomes of thousands of Americans are dependent on the success of popular singers, thirty-two-bar songs (now sometimes sixteen bars), "pop" singles that do not weigh more than two ounces, and LP's that weigh about five ounces. No authoritative breakdown is available on how many persons are employed in the entire field—from songwriter and recording artist to the packer of records at the manufacturing plant. But among those who depend on popular music for a living are the following:

Composers and lyricists
Record company executives and employees
Singers
Musicians
Record manufacturing employees
Disc jockeys
Record distributors
Distributor salesmen
Night club bands
Printers (covers, labels, promotional displays)
Recording studio technicians
Trade paper reporters
Music publishers
Juke box manufacturers
Juke box servicemen and technicians
Talent agents
Record retailers

In the primary group, too, there may be as many as 100,000 persons. In this amalgam are the steadily rising groups of record club employees—clerical workers, "fulfillment experts" (in charge of servicing club members), pressing plants, shipping departments, producers of promotional literature and magazines for the record clubs. Begun in 1955, the Columbia Record Club is the world's largest. During its brief seven years of existence, it has sold millions of LP recordings, a large portion of which were popular music, jazz, and scores from shows. Its acting head is a lawyer, Cornelius ("Neil") Keating.

Small in number but exceptionally influential are the buyers for department stores and discount chains. They include little-known but key individuals, like David Rothfeld. Rothfeld is a dark-eyed, slim, intense man who can handle three phones at once, and he buys for more than twenty Korvette stores. He is one of the single most powerful figures in the record retail field, for Korvette's sells a lot of records.

Another important record-buyer is balding, nervous Sam Goody, who is noted for his willingness to sue. His life has been one long litigation. He has asserted that he is discriminated against by record manufacturers, He hates record clubs; he sells quantities of records by mail order. A pioneer in record discounting, Goody is being pincered by the Korvette-type operations and department stores, which use recordings as "loss-leaders," where Goody is only in one basic business— selling recordings and audio equipment. And, in many ways, Goody is right.

Equally important, but in another way, are the "rack jobbers." They operate somewhat like concessionaires. They function within department stores, dime stores, supermarkets, and other "heavily trafficked" retail outlets. They supply the records, stock the "racks," and pay the store a percentage of the profits. One of the most important figures in this area is millionaire Dave Handleman of Detroit.

To this list may be added the few functioning producers of Broadway musicals—David Merrick, Leland Hayward, Harold Prince, Cy Feuer, and Ernest Martin. And then there are the several hundred employees who work for the American Society for Composers, Authors and Publishers (ASCAP) and Broadcast Music Inc. (BMI)—as tabulators, indexers of songs, station relations aides, field men. Owners of rehearsal halls, voice coaches, musical copyists, and free-lance recording engineering round out the work force that feeds daily off popular music.

Thousands more earn vast sums as a "secondary bloc" within the music-record complex. In this group you will find accountants, musician's union business agents, music contractors, producers of summer tent shows such as St. John Terrell of the Lambertville (Pa.) Music Circus, choreographers, and dancers. Among others whose incomes flow in some degree from the music business are show-business lawyers like Howard Reinheimer, attorney for many of the key musical comedy writers. Further, many agents, personal managers, and night club owners would be technologically unemployed if it weren't for popular music.

Interestingly enough, this mammoth music structure rests upon slender foundations: about three minutes (frequently less) of musical material, compact enough to be printed on two pages of music manuscript.

Keeping the superstructure afloat, if not in an uneasy equilibrium because of the "hit" and "flop" mystique pattern, is the Great American Public. The public has a huge stake in popular music. It has spent millions of dollars on radios, TV sets, transistor affairs that can fit into a coat pocket, and hi-fi sets that can capture an anemic sigh. Many people buy stereo playback equipment and stereo tape. The public feeds the juke boxes and buys the whirling 45's and the 33⅓ long-playing discs.

Aside from the money involved, what is at stake in the "Battle of the Brill," is the musical taste of millions, and along with it, the elevation of certain moods, idols, lyrical themes that bear close watching. The stakes are high, and the struggle for quality is fierce, although it is covered up with *décolletage* and slit-to-navel polo shirts.

And there is even more at stake than the music, although this is of crucial aesthetic importance. There is the public "image." For if the "public" supposedly hates "good things," it feeds the psychology that the "public" is stupid. It deepens anti-democratic attitudes and feelings and builds up an unhealthy gap between the two generations, the teen-agers and the adults, on spurious issues.

Amateurishness and musical illiteracy today are no barriers to success in the teen-oriented popular music. As *Cash Box,* a record industry weekly, once put it:

Rock and Roll is essentially a teenage music, does not require a professional approach as we used to think of it. There is no slickness or smoothness in Rock and Roll. It is an expression of teenage emotion. Therefore, very often, the less professional it appears to be, the more attractive it is to an audience.

And so whereas formerly to get a good sounding record, you had to gather a group of skilled musicians, a top arranger, and an experienced singer, today that is no longer necessary. A publisher can go into a tiny studio with the author usually singing his own songs, accompanied by himself or a small group and come out with a "side" which, while it might not measure up to mature musical standards, nevertheless has the appeal to sell—and sell in large quantity to the teenage market.

Perhaps the most devastating critique of today's Tin Pan Alley was voiced by Alan Livingston, vice-president of one of the largest record companies, Capitol Records. He told *Variety:*

It's a dirty business influenced today less by creativity than by selling techniques, price-cutting, and promotion. Years ago it was a business dependent on creative brain-power and companies interested in improving the quality. In those days we had release dates and the company that put out the best got the majority of the sales. Creativity was the major factor.

The situation today is influenced by selling techniques, price-cutting, distribution, air time, and enough malpractices by smaller labels to warrant federal investigation. How did payola come about if it wasn't for so much over-production that good quality discs couldn't even get a hearing?

Today's records are sold like crackers with big campaigns on how many discounts you'll give and what free merchandise accompanies the good quality product. It's opposed to what the public wants except in dribbles.

A skeptical observer might reply that Tin Pan Alley has never been angelic in its business tactics, and that cheap, hack popular music has always flourished. And yet there are some new factors, and they require as close scrutiny as that lavished by Sherlock Holmes on his opponent, the evil genius Professor Moriarity. Years ago, there was the great tradition of Hollywood musicals, and from them came some of America's loveliest, more rhythmically interesting, inventive, funny, sentimental popular music. Today, this field is practically nonexistent; about the only musicals now being made are remakes of Broadway hits and the Elvis Presley "musicals." In place of the old musicals has grown the title-song industry and the sound tracks of films (nonvocal music), which is rather restrictive.

Broadway is singing the blues, too. High budgets and the public's desire to see nothing but "smash hits" make this genre a tougher proposition. Consequently, there are fewer and fewer musicals being produced on Broadway as contrasted with the 1930's and 1940's. And it has always been musical theater—literate, inventive, more panoramic in content, and free of the teenage market demands—that gave U. S. popular music its greatest quality. If you imagine the popular music of the 1950's without *My Fair Lady, West Side Story, Pajama Game, Gypsy,* and *King and I,* you will realize the profound contributions made by much-maligned Broadway.

In this decade there has been an interweaving of forces—some economic, some technological, some visible, some hidden—that have subtly worked together to subvert the bright promise of popular music. One of these was the payola situation, which in the 1950's made Tin Pan Alley the land of "anything goes." "Funny money," as it is sometimes called, in the crafty hands of music publishers, record companies, promotion men, record distributors, and record librarians helped put across and overexpose poor material performed by poor artists. A certain "sound" was sold. A certain type of artist was elevated. Young taste buds were sensitized to enjoy these "sounds."

Influential disc jockeys in key cities softened up the adolescents, the subteens—the growing teen market—by "laying it on." For a price. In this atmosphere rock 'n' roll and similar musical gems flourished like orchids in the tropics.

And beyond that, there was the song war between the American Society of Composers, Authors and Publishers (ASCAP) and Broadcast Music Inc. (BMI). This continuing battle has incited still more feverish competition, more ruthless business tactics, and—as performance moneys got to be more important—more payola.

In any event, the decline of Hollywood and Broadway as major sources of fresh popular music, the emergence of payola on a ferocious level, and the popular music civil war have caused much woe on the nation's turntables. And America is still suffering from it.

In the 1930's there were three major producers of popular recordings—Victor (its label was then called "Just Victor"), Columbia, and Decca. Perhaps two dozen other independents—or fewer—were active. From the movies, Broadway, Tin Pan Alley, and the swing bands poured forth what many have termed "The Golden Age of Popular Music."

These days there are approximately 1,500 record companies, of which perhaps 300 are fairly active on a regular basis. But all produce recordings. Some 100 to 200 pop "singles" are pressed a week, and some 75 to 100 long-playing albums. This is quite a flood of grooved vinyl.

Everybody is producing records—Philadelphia fruit peddlers, songwriters, plastics manufacturers, home builders. *Surface Noise*, issued by the National Academy of Recording Arts and Sciences, recently carried this note: "Newest label in L. A. is Dimex, headed by a Baltimore hotel headwaiter, Dmitri Davila, and featuring the voice of Baltimore food checker, Jose Alberto, and Biltmore pianist, Ed Greenberg."

Does this mean a musical renaissance? Hardly. Some of the chief characteristics of the popular music of the 1950's and early 1960's might be as follows:

1. *Timeliness.* Derived from a close study of the recordings listed in *Billboard's* "Hot 100."
2. *Stickler for tradition.* Never use a fresh chord or musical phrase when a cliché is close at hand.
3. *Emergence of countless vocal groups.* They are afraid to sing alone.
4. *Experimentation in dynamics.* Turning up the electric guitar to 50-watt capacity.

All in all, there seems to be a narrowing of the creative flow. One "singles" hit breeds 1,000 imitators. Sometime, somewhere, somebody produced the first album with the word "soul" in it. Since then there has been a virtual "soul" industry; "soul jazz," "soul show music," "soul singers." There has been a lot of "soul searching" on Tin Pan Alley.

Besides, there's a living off the past, of recording and re-recording and re-re-recording the "standards." There is a timidity in trying new things, new forms. Most of the thinking goes on in terms of "gimmicks"; having singers sound like instruments, working up lyrics to fit jazz solos, echo-chambered sounds, doing rock 'n' roll with strings, having a Negro singing group sound "white" and a white group imitate Negro inflections, or having Ray Charles superimpose jazz flavors on country music.

Though the dark ages of popular music have been with us for perhaps a decade now, it has not been all black. It's been occasionally deep purple, charcoal gray, and navy blue. And there have been some undeniable bright spots. During the past decade, there have been some superb musicals on Broadway, some imaginative products off-Broadway, and some finely crafted single songs. Some excellent new talent in performing has also surfaced. Here is a rough rundown:

BROADWAY: *Guys and Dolls* (1950), *The King and I* (1951), *Candide* (superb score, 1956), *Music Man* (1957), *Most Happy Fella* (1956), *My Fair Lady* (1956), *Pajama Game* (1954), *Damn Yankees* (1955), *West Side Story* (1957), *Gypsy* (1959)

FILMS: *Seven Brides for Seven Brothers* (1954)
      A Star Is Born (1954)

OFF BROADWAY: *The Fantasticks* (1960)

SONGS: "Witchcraft" (originally written for an unproduced
                revue)
                "Misty" (fine instrumental with awful lyric)
                "Fly Me to the Moon" (originated in night club sector)
                "Sixteen Tons" (first done on TV by Ernie Ford)
                "Cry Me a River"
                "Wee Small Hours"
                "Blowin' in the Wind"

From this necessarily opinionated list, a pattern emerges; the healthiest sector has been the Broadway musical theater. Further the film-
writers accounted for several of the other top songs, including Johnny
Mercer's and Henry Mancini's "Moon River." From the strictly "pop
field," very little of enduring quality has surfaced. The folk singers
stick pretty much to the past, and new folk songs always sound derivi-
tive musically. But in range of subject matter, the modern folk song
is far superior to Tin Pan Alley. Contemporary jazz has much musical
freedom, but it still has not come up with composers with as much
talent and communicative power as Duke Ellington.

Of course, there have been other good, well-constructed songs and
instrumental compositions. But much of the material has been of a
sorry sort bearing such titles as "Sh-Boom," "Be Bop a Lula," "Dance
with Me Henry," "Tweedle Dee," "How Much Is that Doggie in the
Window?," "Don't Say Nothin' Bad About My Baby," "Let's Limbo
Some More," "Diana," "Half Heaven—Half Heartache," "Your Used To
Be," "Ruby Baby." The preceding laundry list of linty tunes has domi-
nated the air time of much of American commercial radio. These tunes
are rich in what is known as a "nowadays sound"—the sound of triads,
the "big beat," of low horizons, lyrically and musically.

While there seems to be constriction in the quality of contemporary
popular music, the popular music business seems to be expanding commercially. It is more sleekly organized, more tigerishly competitive,
and more complaining than ever.

Going down the line, complaints are as loud and clear as a rusty
fog horn. The record companies grumble about intense competition,
price-cutting, and the ineptness of record salesmen and record distributors, many of whom they assert are nothing but "order takers."
The record stores are up in arms, for they are being bushwacked by
the department stores and discount houses. They cannot compete
against the department stores selling records as "loss leaders." The
bulk of the songwriters, composers, and lyricists (and they are the
creators, allegedly the backbone of the industry) complain that cheap
songs dominate. The poor musicians are increasingly being pushed to

the wall, for fewer and fewer of them are making more records. "Live music" opportunities are dwindling. The "Thirty Years' War" which began in 1940 between ASCAP and BMI is still going on. The older, professionally trained singers blanch at the field and gag. Quite a few still record, but largely for the album market. They keep to the old songs. They hate to see what has happened to the field they love, with badly trained voices and inferior material winning over.

And since the emphasis is on merchandising, on reaching the disc jockey, and on new gimmicks, little thought is given to the essential problem facing all the arts, popular and unpopular—its function in our world. Should popular music somehow produce a romantic glow alone, or should it be entertaining? Should it exist to produce good dance music with a beat? Is the audience able to enjoy new musical material, new thoughts, fresh harmonies, rhythmical textures, bright rhyming? Should popular music somehow reflect the world, the crazy world we live in? Is it to be increasingly a mass media for the dissemination of predominately teenage, comic-strip music and lyrics? Is our heritage of superb popular music to be glossed over and crafted into new gimmicky arrangements?

In his play, *Roots*, one of England's new voices, Arnold Wesker, seems quite aware of the problem of the popular arts. In the last act, a character, Beatie Bryant speaks:

. . . So you know who come along? The slop singers and the pop writers and the film makers and the women's magazines and the Sunday papers and the picture strip love stories—that's who come along, and you don't have to make no effort for them, it comes easy. "We know where the money lies," they say, "hell we do! The workers've got it so let's give them what they want. If they want slop songs and film idols, we'll give 'em that then. If they want words of one syllable, we'll give 'em that then. If they want the third-rate, blust, we'll give 'em that then. Anything's good enough for them cos they don't ask for no more!" The whole stinkin' commercial world insults us and we don't care a damn!—it's our own bloody fault! We want the third-rate, we got it.

2 · THE FACE OF MODERN TIN PAN ALLEY

Decentralization: To deprive of centralization; esp., to divide
and distribute (what has been united or concentrated).
—Webster's Collegiate Dictionary

In the 1929 Ring Lardner and George Kaufman comedy, *June Moon*,
which portrayed the comparatively innocent flavor of the Tin Pan Alley
of the 1920's, Fred, the would-be songwriter, is on a train bound for
New York and says to the girl he meets:

"Well, he happened to be playing in Schenectady in vaudeville, and
I happened to meet him and I happened to show him some of my
lyrics. And he said a man like I with the songwriting gift was a sucker
not to go to New York, because that's where they have the Mecca for a
man if you got the songwriting gift."

Perhaps the man with the "songwriting gift" isn't too welcome in
many places any more, but one thing is sure: Manhattan's Tin Pan Alley
is no longer the exclusive citadel of popular music.

There are about seven "Tin Pan Alleys"—New York, Philadelphia,
Chicago, Detroit, Nashville, Los Angeles, and the seventh could be
lumped together as "the rest of the world," for songs and hit recordings
have emerged from London, Italy, Japan, Germany, and Latin America.

For example, the Broadway cast album of *How to Succeed in Busi-
ness Without Really Trying* was taped off-Broadway in New York's
Webster Hall on East 11th Street, once a stronghold of the partisans
of Karl Marx and Prince Peter Kropotkin, the anarchist. Chubby
Checker's recordings are made by Cameo-Parkway in Philadelphia.
Mercury cuts many records in Chicago, its home base. Hillbilly com-
posers and record artists whack out country hits in Nashville. Frank
Sinatra uses California studios to tape his latest Reprise recordings.

Though most of the recording goes on in the cities mentioned above,
voices, orchestras, folk singers are everywhere with portable equipment. One of the big "single" hits of 1962, Stan Getz's version of a

16

South American instrumental, "Desafinado," was tape-recorded by Verve in the All-Souls Unitarian Church in Washington, D.C. And the Kingston Trio, the classic example of what is known as a "popular-folk" group, as opposed to "ethnic-folk" (Leadbelly), have recorded at a San Francisco night club, the hungry i.

Since World War II, the writing, marketing, performing, and recording of music, records, and shows has swirled in all directions from the Brill Building. The reasons for this decentralization are varied, but they are tied up with the expansion of the record industry, the importance of regional centers where hits "break out," and to some extent, payola. The combination of inexpensive recording costs and access to money hungry disc jockeys is not to be discounted.

A guide to New York's popular music milieu could start anywhere in the city, for there are record companies on New York's posh East Side (Kapp), folk-flavored Village coffee houses (The Bitter End, Village Gate) where recordings are taped "live"; cardboard album manufacturers in Queens, "demo" (demonstration discs) recording studios in Brooklyn, and Broadway musical producers in the Sardi building on West 44th Street (David Merrick).

For the sake of tradition, it might be worth starting with the weary-looking Brill Building, 1619 Broadway, a slowly declining architectural landmark of the music business. It is still largely rented. But for a long time there has been a tropism by music-business people toward the more fashionable East Side.

Many artists hate the Brill Building, because they see in the new invasion of the teenagers—artists and composers alike—a triumph of mediocrity. One veteran of the music business lamented recently:

"Do you know that I shrink each time I have to go into the Brill Building. One of my publishers happens to be in that building and I just dread going into it because you see all sorts of flotsam and jetsam all over the sidewalk and in the hallway and in the elevators. It's enough to make you want to throw up."

Interestingly enough, although the building is inhabited by firms and tenants who are 90 per cent in the music business, the realty management does not permit full-blown musical rehearsals. "No band can rehearse there. Singers can go over a song with a piano, or a vocal combo can learn a new song there, but blasting rehearsals are out," says a Brill Building spokesman.

Ten per cent of the Brill Building inhabitants have no visible connection with anything resembling a musical note. These outlanders are attorneys, small film companies, and movie exhibitors. But the thirteen-story Brill, completed in 1932, caters largely to the music business and services connected with the music and recording field, such as photo-copying of sheet music, recording studios for the making of "demos." And if you get tired of running in and out of the offices there is a podia-trist on the premises, who proudly hawks his trade in a bronze plaque fronting glamorous Broadway: Dr. Peter Mogull.

The Brill was always a song factory, but in its golden years it was a lively factory where fine songs were composed and worked on, and where music publishers did work on single songs they had faith in, instead of carrying a large attaché case of demonstration discs to record companies and asking, peddler-like, "Which one do you like?"

The Brill, or "1619 Broadway" as it is sometimes referred to, is still an active establishment, and many hit recordings and singers come from its many offices and cubbyholes. Here are tradition-encrusted firms such as Mills Music with a fat catalog of "standards" (Ellington, Car-michael, Leroy Anderson) and an excellent educational and classical music department. And here are the such newcomers as the Aberbach Brothers (Jean and Julius), the empire builders of the nowadays "pop music," with about a dozen publishing companies including the highly lucrative Elvis Presley Music. Their little thirty-two-bar barony em-braces Hill and Range Songs, Valley Music, and another enticing com-pany, 11th Floor Music, and in ads in trade papers they take on a cor-porate stance and call themselves, "The Aberbach Group."

Daily you can stand there, in front of the Brill, and see young male vocal groups with duck-billed coiffures and teenage girls in saddle shoes, carrying school loose-leaf books. Young record singers, wear-ing that new teen style, Continental or Ivy League slacks shortened to three inches above the shoes, dart in and out with the inevitable brown paper envelope containing a demonstration disc of a new song.

Through the doors of the Brill, golden in shade but dulled by time, also pass the hard-core professionals—businesslike general professional managers, record promotion people, trade-paper reporters, music ar-rangers. You can see thin, graying Johnny Marks, college-educated publisher of a single copyright that has made him wealthy—"Rudolph, the Red-Nosed Reindeer," which has sold more than 37,500,000 records since 1949. Marks focuses attention on Christmas-type songs, and he bends with the time, as can be noted by his recent hit, "Rock around the Christmas Tree" (which has sold over a million records since 1960). His firm is St. Nicholas Music.

Redd Evans, an articulate musician turned music publisher, has a sense of history. A sharp-tongued antagonist within his own organiza-tion, ASCAP, over certain methods of logging and voting procedures, he once had embedded in his reception area a linoleum silhouette of

Thomas Jefferson. He owns Jefferson Music. His big songs are "Wee Small Hours of the Morning," "Dance, Ballerina, Dance," and "Too Young."

You constantly hear occupational jargon in the Brill:

"It's on the *charts!*" (It may be 99th on a listing of the 100 most popular songs, and the subject of an artificial boom, known in the trade as a "hype" from the word hypo. But it is on the "charts," and paradise is possible.)

Or "Columbia is interested." (Translated this may mean that a Columbia Records A & R man has acknowledged that the song came in the mail.)

Tin Pan Alley is not without its traumatic experiences. Not too long ago, in the Turf Restaurant, once the unofficial hub of the popular music fraternity, which existed on the ground floor of the Brill Building, a songwriter came down from an odyssey upstairs with a music publisher. Anguished, he lay down on the floor and, to an audience of songwriters, music publishers, and singers, sobbed: "They're crucifying me! They're crucifying me."

These days the songwriter can be crucified uptown, too. The music business has gone in heavily for the upper West Fifties, particularly the 57th Street area, formerly the habitat of classical music, the ballet, and the Art Students League. Here are music press agents, vocal coaches, managers of talent, and music business attorneys all conferring with each other and scurrying about in the rat race to fame. 119 West 57th Street is an unassuming building, wedged between a record and audio store and a hamburger shop. But in it are many music publishers and one of the key independent record companies, Cadence Records. Cadence, guided by Archie Bleyer, put out the all-time best-selling album in phonograph record history, the LP that has sold more than four million discs, "The First Family."

And in the same building there is a rising music publishing empire developed after World War II by Frank Loesser and his trusted legal watchdog, Harold Orenstein. Loesser's strength is show scores (his own and others), but he has many other valuable single-song copyrights, such as "Cry Me A River." The fifty-four-year-old composer-lyricist of *Guys and Dolls* and *Most Happy Fella* has multiple music publishing entities including Frank (named after himself), Saunders, and Empress. A woodworking hobbyist, Frank also guides with the firmness of a slide rule, Frank Productions, which participates in theater producing.

In 1954, together with Broadway arranger Don Walker, Loesser established Music Theatre, Inc., since re-named Music Theatre International. It sells production rights of top musicals, including *Guys And Dolls* and *Damn Yankees,* to straw-hat theaters, music tents, night clubs, drama societies, PTA's, and schools. Mrs. Loesser is Jo Sullivan, who played the bride, Rosabella, in *Most Happy Fella.*

In the sleek midtown area, where the tan attaché cases can be seen bumper to bumper, there is Show Music Inc., Chappell & Co, 609 Fifth Avenue. Max Dreyfuss, now in his eighties, Gershwin's mentor, helped build up Chappell to its present eminence. It represents the great tradition of show music—Rodgers and Hart, Rodgers and Hammerstein, Cole Porter, and Jule Styne. With offices in principal cities of the world, Chappell operates with efficient éclat, modern office machines, and a quiet, thickly carpeted, un-music businesslike air.

Another building that resembles the Brill in a miniaturized way is 1650 Broadway. Its blue-tinged fluorescent-lit lobby makes it more cheerful to enter than its downtown counterpart. But it is equally nondescript as buildings go. On the second floor there used to be a dimly lit gold mine, Irving Berlin Music. (Now, Helmy Kresa, Berlin's general manager, keeps a watchful eye on such Berlin copyrights as "White Christmas," "Blue Skies," and "Cheek To Cheek," from the shiny, Sperry-Rand Building on the Avenue of the Americas, a fitting home for the author of so many wonderful examples of musical Americana.)

In "1650," you have something rather rare, perhaps the only woman who runs and owns a popular music record company and publishing firm. The stereo-headed companies—Scepter Music and Scepter Records—focused on rock'n'roll—are guided by Florence Greenberg, who got into the business when her son wrote a song that some record company recorded but never released.

Here, too, are music publishers, vocal coaches, disc jockey mailing services, lively popular music record companies such as Amy-Mala and Hi-Life, which puts out ninety-nine-cent LP records, known as massmerchandising "Budget lines." The building sits atop an Arthur Maisel restaurant, a sort of garish Howard Johnson's.

Further East on Madison Avenue, in the *Look* Building, across from CBS headquarters, is the Music Publishers Holding Corp. (MPHC) owned body and soul by Warner Brothers Pictures. Its head, Herman Starr, recently reported that four companies that function under the MPHC umbrella (Harms, Witmark, Remick, New World) control more than thirty thousand copyrights. Among the most valuable annuities there are the Gershwin works, Kern songs, and Porter songs. Some MPHC copyrights are "S'Wonderful," "All Through the Night," "April in Paris," "Birth of the Blues," and the Gershwin satire, "Blah-Blah-Blah." A recent addition to its catalog are the songs of Bob ("Blowin' in the Wind") Dylan, who reportedly named himself after Dylan Thomas.

Of the Warner Brothers combine, a singer says: "It's one of the few remaining music publishers where you can go with a pianist and rehearse. And even get messages from the switchboard."

As to recording companies, they stick pretty much to the stony midriff of Manhattan. But unlike Wall Street or the liquor industry, none can boast of a single building of architectural distinction. Practically all the record companies inhabit dull buildings. One of the world's largest, Columbia Records, 799 Seventh Avenue, is in a squat building edged by a Chinese restaurant. A small glass showcase in the lobby of the building offers visitors an idea of the latest product which is marked by excellent art work, design, and packaging. Here, too, are Epic Records and Harmony (low-cost label), which are related to Columbia by corporate marriage.

In 1964, Columbia Records will move into a multimillion-dollar, thirty-eight-story building designed by Eero Saarinen, who helped design the Lincoln Center for the Performing Arts. To this building will come practically all of the CBS divisions—radio, TV, record club, electronics, recordings—now scattered throughout the midtown area. It will occupy the East Side block from 52nd Street to 53rd Street on the Avenue of the Americas.

Fronting Broadway is Roulette Records, a name redolent of Las Vegas. It has green-monsterish signs telling passersby of its artists, notably Joey Dee, who helped make the nation conscious of the twist by his appearances at the Peppermint Lounge. In midtown, too, is Riverside Records, a hyperactive, jazz-slanted company that is nudging into the popular-music sector. It occupies a cocoon of offices that curl around the mezzanine of the Hotel Paramount on West 45th Street. And then there are those that don't fit into any pattern. Joe Carlton, of Carlton Records, works out of an apartment house.

The East Coast wing of Capitol Records, which guides considerable recording and marketing activity for that firm, used to be on the ground floor of the Mutual Life Insurance Company, 1740 Broadway. This street-level location enabled Capitol to place its new records and best-selling albums in the windows to whip up consumer interest. Now it is ensconced in the modernistic Sperry-Rand Building, along with Irving Berlin.

The movie-connected record firms are close to their celluloid umbilical cords. Colpix Records is in the Columbia Pictures Building, at 711 Fifth Ave. ABC-Paramount Records and its allied labels, Impulse and Command, are in the Paramount Building, 1501 Broadway, which of course, also houses that big barn of a 1920's baroque movie palace, the New York Paramount. 20th Century Fox Records works out of the movie headquarters of 20th Century Fox. Decca is now entrenched on Park Avenue with its corporate kinfolk, Revue Productions (the old MCA group) and Universal Pictures in one of the first glass-and-aluminum postwar structures. It is a clean twenty-one-story building and its nonentertainment business neighbors are Five-Day Deodorant Pads and Tussy Cosmetics.

Way out of the Tin Pan Alley orbit is RCA Victor Records, on West 24th Street, located in an unprepossessing businesslike structure, opposite a post office and adjacent to a garage. It is a *shashlik* away from the Armenian restaurants on Lexington Avenue. Not too far from Victor is London Records, noted mostly for its classical music, but active as merchandiser and distributor for many independent A & R producers. On the edge of Greenwich Village is Vanguard Records, which has produced approximately two thousand LP's since 1950. Run by two brothers, Seymour and Maynard Solomon, it has made a modest dent in the popular music sweepstakes largely through the folk music recordings of Joan Baez. It mostly issues classical music.

"Food, glorious food," is a line in the musical, *Oliver*, but it is also a way of life among those in the music business. In Manhattan, a lot of intratrade talk and romancing of record executives and singers takes place in Al and Dick's Steak House, a midtown restaurant. A sort of a Café Royale of the "pop" music hierarchy, one former music executive sourly described it thusly: "They sit down at Al and Dick's and know the other guy's success, demeaning it and diminishing it, instead of analyzing it." Another reports: "Guys line up at the bar at six and seven P.M. They want to see who is with whom, and who's whispering to whom."

The lower-echelon music fraternity that cluster around the Brill Building used to frequent the Turf Restaurant, now closed. The Turf was once the "establishment," where young writers and singers congregated and got to meet people. It had a slogan, "3,000 cups of coffee a day. It has to be good." It sold deep-dish fruit pies, franks, and good hot coffee.

Philadelphia, hitherto noted for its Liberty Bell, the *Saturday Evening Post*, and the *Ladies Home Journal*, is now known for Bobby Rydell, Fabian, and Frankie Avalon. It is a record-conscious town. In the past decade top teen idols have emerged from here, including such groups as the Dovells and a vocal combo that apparently derived its name from a synthetic yarn, the Orlons.

The key record man in Philadelphia is an ex-musician, songwriter Bernie Lowe of Cameo-Parkway. He is also the Lowe Music Publishing Company which owns the publishing rights to many of the songs recorded by Cameo-Parkway.

Much of Philadephia's status in the record business seems to rest on shaky grounds. It arose chiefly on the heels of Dick Clark's success with his TV dance party shows where high school youngsters danced and TV cameras peeped. The most prominent companies are Cameo-Parkway, which is the largest, Swan, Chancellor, Jamie, and Newtown. Philadelphia has lesser-known disc producers. One—it is listed in *Billboard*—is a record company called Ruthie.

With Dick Clark's daily ABC-TV show pruned in the fall of 1963 to one Saturday afternoon program, there will be less national promotion emanating from Philadelphia. (Clark has a widely syndicated radio program now, which he sells himself.) But the few firms there are teen-slanted, and Philadelphia is considered a key record market, so perhaps the future is not so bleak. Particularly if they can come up with counterparts of Chubby Checker.

South of Tin Pan Alley is Nashville, which produces an enormous amount of recordings in the C & W genre, better known as country and western. Much of Nashville's popularity may be traced to that continuing institution, the "Grand Ole Opry" radio program.

Modernism is strikingly apparent in Nashville. There are superb new, ranch-style recording studios there put up by RCA Victor and Columbia Records. ASCAP has also sent officials to establish a beachhead in what used to be strictly a BMI preserve. There, too, are found many Tin Pan Alley music publishers. There is increasing airline traffic between Nashville and New York. Equally apparent is the fact that Nashville is getting closer and closer to orthodox "pop" music, but with a country twang.

In and around Nashville are many homegrown recording companies like Starday and Hickory, as well as important music publishers like Acuff-Rose, the Chappell of the South. Acuff-Rose publishes most of the late Hank Williams' songs, including "Jambalaya" and "Cold Cold, Heart."

In Nashville there's the Ernest Tubb Record Shop (after the C & W star). The most complex twentieth-century techniques are here in abundance. Electronic equipment worth a fortune, acoustically engineered recording studios, and complex mixing boards, all combine to get the old-fashioned, uncomplicated, rural "Nashville Sound."

Chicago, "hog butcher of the world" (Carl Sandburg) and the capital of the *Playboy* empire ("Bunny" czar, Hugh Hefner), is the home of Mercury Records, a big "semi-major," and its subsidiary labels, Smash and Philips, all located at 35 East Wacker Drive. It was unprepossessing Philips which issued the best-selling long-playing record featuring a European nun singing songs of her own composition, "The Singing Nun." A trio of other related record companies—Chess, Checker, Argo—make their headquarters in the Windy City. Vee-Jay, predominantly rock 'n' roll with a smattering of folk-blues, has moved from Chicago, where it had enjoyed considerable success, to the West Coast.

A heavily weighted local rock 'n' roll recording firm dominates the Detroit scene. It is Tamala-Motown. Berry Gordy, Jr. is the producer of many recordings there; he writes the ditties and publishes them, too (Jobete). It might be worth noting that the auto city is a key "record market," and its heavy Negro population provides a ready market for Negro artists and Negro-oriented "pops."

In Houston, Texas, there is Peacock Records, which is quite active in rock 'n' roll and gospel-spiritual recordings, along with its allied labels, Duke and Back Beat.

Moving northwest, the second biggest record and music publishing center is California, now the most populous state in the union with upward of eighteen million people. A leading producer of oranges, jet aircraft, space-electronics, and films, California has long been involved with popular music. In the mid-twenties, Brunswick and RCA led the way with recordings of live band music. This was the vogue. Says one informant, "Recording engineers used to travel to San Francisco and Seattle to catch those popular bands."

In 1927 the West Coast music scene picked up when Al Jolson sang in *The Jazz Singer,* a film that proved that movies could speak and sing. There followed a wave of musical films, and this nudged into being music publishing branch offices of New York firms. Since many of the big stars of musicals were there, they began making discs for the popular music market and appearing on radio. Remember Dick Powell and "The Hollywood Hotel"?

In 1942 Johnny Mercer and a record retailer, Glenn Wallichs, were walking down the street. "We were walking down the street and thinking that there was a lot of talent around that wasn't doing too much. Nat Cole was around. Others, too. So we decided to start a record company," Mercer once recalled.

From that stroll developed the idea of a new company, Capitol Records. Asked to join was the songwriter-movie producer, Buddy De Sylva. Within a few years Capitol Records began to become a major force in the field, developing such stars at Nat Cole, Kay Starr, Stan Kenton, and Johnny Mercer himself. By the fifties, the firm had become a giant, and in 1956 Capitol Towers was built, an unorthodox, thirteen-story building, shaped somewhat like a pyramid of recordings. It cost $2 million and was designed by a West Coast architect. Because of its unusual design the cylindrical building is a "Hollywood landmark" and a tourist attraction. A Capitol Record source says, "It's overlooked by few visitors to the area, since most of them get a good view of it from the Freeway. As a result, Capitol does a brisk business in its twice-a-week tour of the building—for which tickets are given out free to all inquirers."

In California, the music business has at once declined and expanded fantastically in the past five years. The Hollywood screen musicals have been pretty much prostrate. Except for title songs and background music, there is very little action. For example, the recent Oscar winners in the best-song category were from nonmusical productions such as "Moon River" from *Breakfast at Tiffany's*.

Today, there are about two dozen record companies—major ones as well as the smaller specialized outfits—based in California. The major headquarters of Capitol, Dot, Liberty, Warner Brothers, Reprise Records are all on the West Coast. And all the top Eastern-based labels have offices here, including Columbia, Victor and Decca. And, adding to the excitement are the jazz firms such as Fantasy (jazz and Lenny Bruce) and World-Pacific.

A California informant says, "There is tremendous recording activity, day and night. There are about thirty-five recording studios, all making a good buck." Everybody records out there, Frank Sinatra, Ella Fitzgerald, Bobby Pickett, and Allan Sherman. One of the independent recording studios, Conway Records, points out that its "Studio B" is "especially applicable to rock and roll, small bands and combos, and getting 'the Nashville sound.'"

Irwin Zucker, Los Angeles record publicist, recently explained some of the reasons why there has been a recording explosion on the West Coast. "In this electronic age, records can now be pressed in L.A. just as fast as in New York—the entire country can get records at the same time. In years past the Coast was about two or three weeks late on records pressed in the East. The sunny clime has made California a home for more entertainers, who like to record near home. Las Vegas, a great entertainment capital, has also made it easier for artists to record in L.A. And the kids on the Coast, with their modern surf ideas, help advance recordings here. The kids are sharp in L.A., sparking ideas for recordings. Often the rest of the nation follows California."

To make the story complete, there is a modern, four-story building, 6515 Sunset Boulevard, which is "fast becoming the Brill Building of the West." It is currently the newest building on Sunset Boulevard. In it are housed such music business personalities and companies as Henry Mancini, Nevins-Kirschner (Music Publishing), Era Records, Monogram Records, and entertainment publicists.

Nor is this all. Scheduled to come up shortly is a show-business oriented twenty-two-story building at Sunset and Vine; and just completed is a thirteen-story RCA Building on Sunset near Cahuenga Boulevard, both in the heart of Hollywood. These new structures may challenge the "6515" as the West Coast Brill Building, as the new buildings are expected to house many in the record- and music-business complex.

Today's modern popular music scene is far from the familiar Hollywood image of songwriters in cubbyholes banging out songs to show to a publisher who resembles the late James Gleason. (The song then becomes a hit as sung by Alice Faye.)

It is a rough, multi-layered organism. Sleazy elements, middle-brow elements, old "pop"-music minds who go back to vaudeville and song slides; swing era devotees who really were alive in the days of Benny Goodman, Charlie Barnett, and "live" radio; college-educated young men and women who know about atonal music and *Wozzeck;* the theater-music groups who seldom mix with the "pop" music crowds; the jazz-composers, arrangers, musicians, and "explainers" (liner-note writers) all coexist.

Mostly Tin Pan Alley is modern. Even the cheap music galaxies, the rock 'n' roll vocalists, the vocal combos operate with personal managers, publicity writers, booking offices, and that electronic marvel, the 45 rpm and the 33⅓ long-playing record.

The modernistic glints can be gleaned in the milieu, the décor, the methods of work. Record companies employ costly quality control equipment in manufacturing records, handsomely designed LP packages in all art media—water color, oil, *gouache,* woodcut, photography—are tossed off with great rapidity. Some record distributors use electronic machines to keep abreast of inventories.

The modern popular music business is not necessarily an ethically improved field or better aesthetically or more fun to be in or friendlier. But it is different.

3 · THE STAR-MAKERS: TEENS AND SUBTEENS

> Why can't they be like we were
> Perfect in every way
> What's the matter with kids today?*
>
> —"Kids" from *Bye Bye Birdie*

Mad, a magazine which employs the comic-strip form to peel away the idiocies of our time, not long ago helped conceive an album titled, *Mad Twists Rock 'n' Roll.* Released by Big Top Records it had such typical favorites as:

> "When My Pimples Turn To Dimples"
> "She Got A Nose-Job"
> "Agnes, The Teen-Age Russian Spy"

In an accompanying album which parodied the Sing-Along craze, *Fink Along With Mad,* there was a tender item of total commitment called, "When The Braces On Our Teeth Lock."

These song satires have one thing in common: they deflate popular music's preoccupational disease—music and lyrics about teenage problems, teenage love, teenage insecurities. And in its own lampooning way *Mad* magazine bears witness to the power of the teenage market in popular music. There are 20 million teenagers in the United States, which is approximately one-ninth of the country's population of 180 million. And when you mention figures like that you cause Pavlovian reactions among the makers of jeans, cosmetics, junior-miss dresses—and record manufacturers. The adolescents are the influential shapers of much of Tin Pan Alley, and if you don't please them, as one record executive put it, "You might as well get out of the popular music business."

Having a power they did not ask for, America's teenagers, and increasingly the subteens, have unwittingly emerged as the counterrevolutionaries of today's popular music. Since the early 1950's they have pretty much turned their backs—or been manipulated into doing so—on the whole heritage of superior popular music and performance, toward

*Copyright © 1960 by Edwin H. Morris.

duck-coiffured singers and little-talented vocal groups who look like kids who flunked algebra in school.

Teenagers, not all of them but enough of them to count, have toppled the old icons, the old standards of craftsmanship, the "good music old-guardists," and staged a *Putsch*. Not before the Brill Building, Tin Pan Alley's presidential palace, but at the country's record shops they have accomplished a coup d' état. Not with plastic bombs or revolutionary dialectic, but by spending almost $2 million a week—and more— buying the "pop singles," the compact vehicle by which most new songs and new record personalities are heard and promoted.

As one music executive has asserted, "The kids with the ninety-eight cents, they are the dictators today." (Actually, at Goody's or Alexander's in New York, you can buy records for sixty-six cents, and at similar cut-rate prices in discount operations elsewhere.)

Interestingly enough, these trend-setting singles are being bought by a younger and younger element, indicating that perhaps the graybeards of fifteen, sixteen, and seventeen are rebelling at something—the prices, the contents, or the artists.

In *Time* magazine there was this portrait of the buyers of 45-rpm singles (March 15, 1963):

There she sits, desperate, unhappy, twelve years old. She is cursed with the catastrophe of parents, and her boy friends complete her misery by being too young to drive. She sulks behind a screen of bobby pins, slapping at her baby fat, mourning the birth of her acne. She is a worried sixth-grader, an aging child, a frightened girl—and the queen of the $100 million a year popular record industry.

When 41-year-old Bob Yorke became head of the Artists and Repertoire Department of RCA in 1960, he decided to discover how to please the teen record buyer at first hand. But he was somewhat at a disadvantage, for as a mature individual he didn't possess the outlook of a youngster; and besides he grew up with the big bands and such vocalists as Ray Eberle and Helen O'Connell, who represented a brand of fine musicianship. What could he do?

Like a fighter in a championship match, he went into training. "I forced myself to listen to the top hits, to analyze them. I went to the record shops. I regimented myself to find out what the ingredients were. I think I know what they are now. It's not something tangible. Many hits are released and have no real values. But they have a great *feeling*. Many records are totally void of musical values. They're just rhythm designs. Otherwise there is no explanation for what happens. I can't detect a hit now, but I can tell a failure."

RCA Victor may not produce hits all the time, but its popular single-outlet is definitely slanted toward what *Variety* calls "the juve market."

In buying these "pop" singles records, the girls are the big spenders. They yearn for romantic idols. They want singers that sound like a boy in their neighborhood; they want untrained voices. As one veteran record executive put it: "They don't want polish, a good sound. Vic Damone is a good straight baritone with a clean sound. They don't want Vic Damone. He's too good."

The girls get attached to singers. They must have the new Dion. Besides buying recordings for their private record collections, they employ them for parties, and to dance to by themselves or with their girl friends.

Why they buy what they buy was analyzed by sociologist David Riesman in his book, *Individualism Reconsidered.*

Most of the teenagers in the majority category have an indiscriminating taste in popular music; they seldom express articulate preferences. . . . The functions of music for this group are social—the music gives them something to talk or kid about with friends, an opportunity for competitiveness in judging which tunes will become hits, coupled with a lack of concern about how hits are actually made; an opportunity for identification with star singers or band leaders as "personalities". . . . It is not easy at this stage to state the precise way in which these indiscriminate listening habits serve to help the individual conform to the culturally provided image of himself. To discover this is one of the tasks of research.

Confirmed listeners to disc jockey programs, many teenagers are acutely aware of the "top ten" popularity charts. One New York City girl observed of her younger sister's record buying habits: "If she buys a record and it doesn't reach Number One, she gets very mad."

Why teenagers have become the power elite in the popular music recording field is the saga of a marketing revolution. Much of it reflects a changed America. During the height of the depression, more than twelve million Americans were unemployed. Teenagers had little or no money to spend. Popular music singles cost thirty-five cents and that was a lot of money in those days. Many young people left home, rode the freights, or joined the youth camps—the Civilian Conservation Corps (the CCC). In 1933 of the Great Depression decade, over-all record sales of all genres—classical, opera, popular, jazz, folk, country and western—skidded to $5.5 million (retail value).

Since then, of course, there has been a big change, though a handful are still not aware of it. Recently, for example, Louella Parsons quoted Gloria Swanson as saying that women aged forty to ninety have money to go to the movies, but that the movies do not make romantic films for that audience. She added that "unlike teenagers, they are the women who have the money to buy the tickets." Miss Swanson must be living in the equivalent of the molting *Sunset Boulevard* milieu.

Today, many teenagers walk around with more money in their jeans than heads of families did in the thirties. Collectively, twenty million teenagers have allowances and earnings of some $10.5 billion a year.

According to the U. S. Office of Education, grades 7–9 (junior high school) total some 11,700,000 pupils. It is these youngsters who support much of the 45-rpm "singles" business.

In 1960, *Seventeen,* whose publishing success almost parallels the growth of the teen market (the magazine began in September, 1944), conducted a survey of modern girl teenagers and their folkways.

From a sampling of more than 4,500 girls, the following portrait emerged:

"What is the teenage girl like in 1960? She has a weekly income of $9.53, gets up at 7:43 A.M. She listens to the radio two hours a day."

Equally noteworthy highlights:

Disc jockeys and radio: "76 per cent of the teens favor disc jockeys. Radio ownership is high with 53.5 per cent owning portable models."

Phonograph records: "During an average day the teen girls listen to records. Seventy-two per cent own record collections of which 19 per cent include classical records. Seventy-one per cent buy records with earnings and allowances."

Despite widespread teenage unemployment and school dropouts, the teenage market seems to be expanding by the weight of sheer numbers. In 1963, *Cash Box,* which keeps a watchful eye on trends that may affect popular music ran this story:

TEENAGE POPULATION BOOM
IS DISK INDUSTRY BOON

NEW YORK—The disk industry can continue to look forward to an expanding teenage market with great purchasing power.

As a result of the post-World War II birthrate explosion, the number of youngsters aged 15 to 19 will increase 40% during the 1960's, which compares with a 12% to 22% increase in the adult population.

Teeners now have allowances and earnings of some $10.5 billion a year and will have $14 billion to spend by 1965, according to Gilbert Youth Research, Inc. The figure was $9 billion five years ago.

Besides the strength of teenage purchases in other consumer product fields, teeners are major buyers of discs, phonos, and transistor radios. Retail outlets are reporting teen disc sales as up to 70% of total volume; phonos 40% of volume and transistor radios at up 60% of volume.

One retailer notes that there are more kids getting out of grade school into junior high school, where they "really begin spending money."

Nobody consciously blueprinted a master-plan to write and produce popular music to fit teenagers exclusively. But certain forces edged the music and record business into it. During the early thirties and forties most popular music was written, sung, and recorded to sell to popular music devotees of all ages. That went for the ten-inch "pop singles" as well as the bulky two-and-three-record sets. There was no thought to produce music and lyrics and recordings to fit a twelve to fourteen-year-old group, or a fifteen to sixteen-year-old group. But then certain forces edged into the picture and caused a conscious fragmentation.

Just preceding World War II, the Madison Avenue marketeers—and the record industry, too—started to be aware of the burgeoning teen market. This was the era of bobby-soxers, Benny Goodman, and the dancing in the aisles at the Paramount Theater in New York.

By 1944, statisticians noted that there were 8,039,000 girls between the ages of thirteen and nineteen. Following the war, singers replaced bands and the big draws, as more and more girls built up new romantic idols to replace Frank Sinatra, Dick Haymes, Andy Russell.

In 1949, there was a technological thrust that practically drove the adults out of the popular "singles" market: the long-playing, 12-inch, 33⅓ recording. Adults discovered that a three-dollar album containing twelve selections was a better buy than a 45-rpm single with two selections was at ninety-eight cents. Making the LP's still more attractive was the rise of the discount stores and the price wars between the discounters and the department stores. LP's got lower and lower in price.

While this was happening, a combination of forces, as noted earlier, intruded. Payola got stronger, as more and more independent record manufacturers entered the field, all of them fighting for air time. TV knocked out the movie musicals by reducing domestic movie grosses upon which U.S. film musicals depend. Veteran members of the American Society of Authors and Composers (ASCAP) insisted that its rival, Broadcast Music Inc. (BMI), was force-feeding its poor BMI songs upon the suspecting public through its connection with the broadcast interests. To which BMI replied, "Nonsense."

Meanwhile, a new wave of popular music, amateurishly written and amateurishly performed, hit the popular music scene and drove old Tin Pan Alley out to sea. As writing standards got worse—whatever adults left in the popular-singles market pretty much departed, exiting to the rocking afterbeats of rock 'n' roll and the teen beat. Teen lyrics, teenage themes, teenage performers, simplified musical patterns, even teenage A & R men took over. And, as far as "pop singles" are concerned, teen tastes are still in control.

The result? Late, late into the night, grown men labor—their children and wives strangers to them—over little pieces of brown magnetic tape. They painstakingly build a performance out of "takes" by basically untalented singers and vocal groups. They have one yardstick: "Will the kids buy it?"

How does the expanding teenage market affect popular music? It affects it in every conceivable way, from the concept of the songs, the lyrics, arrangements, the type of artists developed, the packaging, even the means of promotion and merchandising. Much of the subject matter, for example, in the vocal music, intellectually and emotionally is hooked to the teenager; his world, or his world as imagined by money-minded adults who want to cash in on that buying power.

Certainly there have been, and are now, popular songs and instrumentals that do not fit the rigidly adolescent mood. And the reason is sheer arithmetic, varying subjective tastes of record-makers, artists, and audiences. Seven thousand 45-rpm singles a year, equal 14,000 numbers. In this broad group, there has been a layer of "oldies" (such as Connie Francis' hit recording of a 1922 song, "Who's Sorry Now"), show songs, Latin-American materials, historical songs ("Ballad of Davy Crockett"), and country and western favorites. But the increasingly dominant note in new material has been on the teen tack. This is audible in hundreds of recordings released during 1950-1964, and evident in any study of the "top ten" lists published by the trade papers.

The teen themes are as visible as a *croissant* in a Paris café. There are the obvious references to graduation day, going to the prom, Saturday night dates, and to such ornaments as charm bracelets.

The Tin Pan Alley standby, the straightaway ballad, is frequently recast in teen terms, as in the recent hit "Venus In Blue Jeans."

> She's Venus in Blue Jeans
> Mona Lisa in a ponytail
> She's a walkin' talkin' work of art
> She's the girl who stole my heart
> My Venus in Blue Jeans*

Lyric writers are often inspired by teenage folkways, summer style. Here is the lyric to a song entitled "Vacation."

> V-A-C-A-T-I-O-N, in the summer sun
> Put away the books, we're out of school

* Words and music by Howard Greenfield and Jack Keller. Copyright © 1962 by Screen Gems-Columbia Music, Inc.

The weather's warm, but we'll play it cool
We're on vacation, havin' lots of fun

V-A-C-A-T-I-O-N, in the summer sun
Grab a bite at the pizza stand
Write love letters in the sand
We're on vacation, and the world is ours

V-A-C-A-T-I-O-N, under summer stars
We'll hop in your jalop to a drive-in movie
And never look at the show
Hug 'n' kiss, just like this
I can't wait to go
Mashed potato to a juke box tune
Park your car 'neath an August moon
We're on vacation till the start of Fall
V-A-C-A-T-I-O-N, we're goin' to have a ball
V-A-C-A-T-I-O-N, gonna have a ball.*

Turning to less happy affairs, there is the song that illustrates the quiet struggles between parent and poor abused teenager, "Party Lights." In this one, a girl complains to her mother that there is a jazzy party across the street, but mother "won't let her make the scene." The girl goes on to sing:

Oh, momma dear a look-a here, look here
I'm feeling oh so blue
They're doin' the twist, the fish,
The mashed potatoes, too
I'm here a lookin' at you.**

In "Lyrical Ballads" (1802) William Wordsworth observed that poetry was "the spontaneous overflow of powerful feelings." "Hard rock 'n' roll," which was predominating in the fifties, lashed on with honking sax and loud frantic singing and might fit this description, if you accept it as poetry. But here were the kinetic lyrics associated with early Elvis (an unorthodox name for a national love-idol):

"All Shook Up"
A-well, a-bless my soul
What's wrong with me?
I'm itching like a man on a fuzzy tree
My friends say I'm acting queer as a bug

I'm in love! I'm in love, I'm all shook-up!
Mm-mmm-oh-oh. Yeah! Yeah!*

Oscar Hammerstein once analyzed this song for me. He pointed out:
"Note that 'bug' and 'shook-up' don't rhyme. It's sloppy writing."

These days rock 'n' roll writers don't like to be called that. The description has been attached in the public retina with juvenile delinquents. The phrase, supposedly invented by Alan Freed, who used to accompany these screaming tunes by pounding a telephone book with his open palm, doesn't seem in favor. Those sympathetic to the genre prefer to call it "rhythm and blues." For the most part, today's rhythm and blues are rewrites of the rewrites of the earthier, poignant "race records" made famous by Bessie Smith or Lil Green. They are an uncreative travesty of those songs which concerned themselves with unhappy human relations, poverty, and a troublesome world. Musically, they are as individualistic as cell blocks.

Some are getting quieter. Here, three of the decade's most successful producers of rock 'n' roll records veer to a tender frame of mind with this 1962 hit, published by Elvis Presley Music, Inc. The trio of writers are Jerry Leiber, Mike Stoller, and Doc Pomus, and the song is "She's Not You."

> Her hair is soft and her eyes oh, so blue
> She's all the things a girl should be
>   but she's not you
> She knows just how to make me laugh
> When I feel blue
> She's everything a man could want
> But she's not you**

But the noisy, clamorous songs are still with us, as witness Jackie Wilson's (Brunswick) popular 1963 recording, "Baby Workout."

> Come out here on the floor
> Let's rock some more
> Come out a here on the floor
> Honey, let's rock some more, yeah.
> Now when you get here
> Don't cha have no fear
> Put your hands on your hip

> And let your backbone flip—and workout
> Mama, mama, move up
> Party move back
> Shuffle to the left
> Wobble to the right
> Now it's plain to see you're headin' for me
> But it's a natural fact
> Huh! I like it like that, so work out.
> Yeah, baby, work out.
>
> Work it, baby, work out, honey work out
> Work it, baby, work out baby, work out
> Work it, baby, work, shout until it's comin' out
> Work it, baby, work out.*

Dance tempos are as much in evidence in today's popular music as Saturday refund lines at department stores. Allen Stanton, a former musician, music publishing executive, and now A & R man with Kapp Records, said recently, "More and more it is important that teenagers have something to dance to. I ask myself, when considering new material, 'Is it good for dancing? Can it be a new dance craze—like the rock 'n' roll, the twist, the cha-cha, the bossa nova, the mashed potatoes?'" (Ironically, just after he said this, he got a number-one smash hit with a quiet ballad, "Our Day Will Come.")

The dance image runs deep in today's teen-oriented songs and recordings. One recent hit goes:

> Everybody's doing a brand new dance
> Now c'mon baby do the Locomotion
> I know you'll get to like it
> If you give it a chance.**

From "Hully-Gully Baby":

> I said, a-hey girl, I love you
> What ja wanna do
> An' she said a-hully gully, baby
> Hully gully, baby
> All I wanna do with you
> Is a-hully gully, baby
>
> We said goodbye to Mammy
> Hit ev'ry joint in Miami

> We danced all night
> Till dawn's early light
> I said, a-hey girl, I love you
> What ja wanna do
> An' she said a-hully gully, baby.*

The "Wah Wah-tusi":

> Wah Wah Wah-tusi
> C'mon and take a chance
> And get with this dance
> Wah Wah Wah-tusi
> Oh, Baby, it's the dance
> Made for romance**

The twist course is represented in such songs as "Shake Sherry."

> "Shake Sherry"
> Shake, Sherry, Shake
> Shake, Sherry
> Shake, Sherry, Shake
> Shake, Sherry
> Shake, Sherry, Shake
> Shake, Sherry, Shake
> Now listen, you can dance the dance
> You don't even see
> All the girls love it so
> No one loves you as much as me
> So dance by me, please, before you go
> And shake, go, go, go
> Well, dance to the east
> Now, dance to the west
> Now dance to the one girl
> That you love the best
> Is it me? No! Is it me? No!
> Is it me? No! Is it me? No!
> Me? No! Me? No!***

A professor of education at the University of Southern California, Dr. David Martin, who has completed a two-year study of rock 'n' roll, has observed that many of the teen songs are based on real problems. "A very real problem for today's youngsters," he says, "is the fear of loneliness and alienation."

He added that many songs "sing of school as a jail, of popularity with the opposite sex, of adult understanding, or of their longing for acceptance. There is very little blatant sexuality. On the contrary, with few exceptions, the love theme in finding one true love to marry."

One who sympathizes with the new "teen music" is a former radio actor ("Henry Aldrich" program), Dave Kapralik, head of Popular Artists and Repertoire for Columbia Records. A one-time company trainee, he has shot up to the dizzying heights of being in charge of popular music recording. Small-boned and highly articulate, the record executive sat in his office early one Saturday afternoon, and talked about the current brand of popular music.

"The popular music business is reflecting a situation without parallel in history: the thirteen- or fifteen-year-old girl who finds, for whatever the transcending social reasons, that she has an emotional attachment to a young man and a deeply felt one. I think the phrase 'puppy love' is now obsolete. And suddenly this deep attachment is imperiled because there's a tousled-haired blonde chick in her class who has wooed the boy away. I think that in other years this situation didn't have to be coped with until they were eighteen or nineteen years old. But more and more children in their early teens are coping with this situation. And perhaps, and now I may be speaking of a given socioeconomic group, but I don't think they're going and seeking the counsel of their parents or their teachers or their priests or rabbis, as children in other eras did. They are seeking the counsel of their peers, for better or for worse.

"I'm telling it as I feel it and I learn it from the young people who are writing to communicate to the adolescent. And their peers might be Bobby Vinton or Bobby Vee, Gene Pitney or the Shirelles, or Connie Francis.

"And in their songs they tell not only how to cope with the situation, but it also gives whatever comfort may be derived from it—the knowledge that the situation that this thirteen- or fifteen-year-old girl is in is not a unique one; that it's a universal experience for girls of that age.

"I never question the depth of emotion of adolescents and preadolescents. It's as strong as the emotions that you have and I have. Or perhaps stronger. Adolescents perhaps feel more alienated today than we adults."

Kapralik said that one of the most popular themes is epitomized in

Bobby Vee's "Take Good Care of My Baby." That's a prototype, he pointed out, and there are hundreds of songs like it.

"The song says," Kapralik went on, "I love this girl. But I know that she's fallen for you. And I'm going to continue to love her. But you'd better take care of her because if you don't, then you have me to account to."

The recording executive stated that another popular song specie is "Roses Are Red." He said, "It's a situation where a young man was in love with a young girl, and she went away to school, and he went away, and he still loves her, but she's married to somebody else and his heart continues to break.

"Years ago, they didn't reach the same kids who are being reached today. The twelve- and thirteen-year-olds didn't know about Sinatra in the heyday of the Paramount. Their sixteen- and seventeen-year-old sisters did. We're reaching further down—eleven and twelve. Kids of eight and ten who will buy a record will buy it for different reasons than the twelve- or thirteen-year-old. It's just as if you would take an eight-year-old or a sixteen-year-old to see *Lolita;* they'll see different things.

"The focus on teenagers happened because of factors having nothing to do with the musical world. It's happening with kindergarten girls wearing lipstick."

In appealing to the young teenagers, the most fervent buyers of the 45-rpm "singles" and of a good many popular albums, packaging is almost as important as the lyrics, if not more so. For in the 45's many of the record firms put two- and three-color photographs of the "idol" into the sleeve. Some merely have a company-identifying name, plus its individualistic logo.

More grandly ambitious are the graphics of the teen-focused long-playing albums. Recently, Brian Hyland (ABC-Paramount) had a popular hit "single" which was translated into LP form—"Sealed With A Kiss." On the LP there was a face shot of Hyland, with his blue eyes neatly highlighted along with a white shirt, blue tie, and blue suit, against a pale blue background. The photography was strictly from *Photoplay.* And around the album, the title of which was printed in lipstick red, there were four rosy-red lip prints. As if you didn't get the point, there was a gold, half-dollar-sized seal on the edge of the album, once more displaying the lip print, with the juvenile word "SWAK" ("Sealed with a Kiss").

A great many of the covers are sweater crazy. Like the high stool for TV singers, this is *de riguer* for many teen-oriented albums. Many of the Johnny Mathis Columbia albums are graced by the lean tenor in bulky-knit sweaters, or smoother textured sweaters—which give him a relaxed, "young" feeling.

Frequently, the record companies pick a simple face-shot approach with a marketing twist. You can detach the picture of your idol and "mount it in your room." Often, there is a portfolio of candid photographs of the star at home. In the case of a recent album of Annette, of Disney's juvenile TV programs, there were photographs of the brunette teenager from her earliest baby-fat days through her TV fame as a "mouseketeer."

Frequently, the "star" writes a letter to his or her fans, on the bottom of which there is a replica of the star's signature. In an album of Christmas songs (Chancellor) there was inscribed on the front cover this note by Frankie Avalon: "Wishing You All the Joys of the Christmas Season."

Important "How to" information is also tucked into the album—such as how to reach the star. In many Paul Anka albums (he recently married a European model, and there are meetings on how this is going to sit with his fans) you will discover the address of the star's fan club:

Paul Anka Fan Club
National Headquarters
Shyana P. O. Box 166
Times Square Station, N. Y.

A great deal of the popular music packaging has a "teen-feel" in the choice of inserted materials—singalong song sheets or layouts of dance steps.

The backliner notes verge on ripe love-magazine prose. Consider the RCA Victor album, "Neil Sedaka Sings His Greatest Hits." Pictured on the cover is a moony-faced teenaged girl in blouse and slacks, alongside a lamp and table on which sits a gold-framed picture of Sedaka. She seems in ecstasy over her idol, though she is probably thinking how nice it is to get an hour's work posing at the RCA Victor photography studio.

And then there comes the prose, composed allegedly by a girl named Carol. Excerpt follows:

My little brother loves to poke fun at me because I have your pictures plastered all over the walls of my room. He's just jealous [how did this lurking hint of unwholesome sexuality get there?]. . . . "The kids at school also think you're the greatest. Every transistor in the corridor seems to be turned to 'Next Door to an Angel.' "

Despite the lordly disclaimers that record albums provide much of the record company's revenues, the popular "singles" business is of crucial importance. As Bob Yorke put it recently: "We must have the single record. It's where you can develop the new talent, the new personalities for the sixties and seventies. If they can't perform credibly on records, they won't become major entertainment figures. And through the single, you can develop major album sellers. Andy Williams came out of the singles, so did many others. Then it's a simple matter of money. It costs us $50,000 to launch a major album artist. You need only 10 percent of that to launch a singles artist. Singles are also effective, efficient means to launch unknowns."

The 45-rpm single is a versatile bit of vinyl. Compact, it (1) provides disc jockeys and record librarians with easy-to-handle discs; (2) gets into juke boxes neatly; (3) can build up grosses for movies and Broadway; and (4) it taps the foreign market more easily, since the consumers there buy the less expensive 45's rather than the costly LP's which are often beyond their reach financially.

This is of critical creative significance. For most of the new music and lyrics are exposed on the 45 rpm. And the "pop singles" are bought—with rare exception—by teenagers. The logic suggests that the future Gershwins, Porters, and Berlins have to fabricate teen materials if they want to be heard. The superior vocalists—Sinatra, Ella Fitzgerald, Peggy Lee—do original material on singles, but each have about six releases a year and of these there is a goodly amount from shows or movies (title songs).

Of course, there are the heretics, the mavericks. There are teenagers who buy good folk music, the better singers, jazz, quality mood music, and show albums. And there are a few adults, too, or college students who must have a new Peggy Lee 45 or a Kingston Trio "single" which they have heard on the radio. But the largest body of single-record buyers, day in and day out, are the youngsters, and they buy predominantly a "teen product."

And even when the more mature, craft-conscious recording artists or groups select material for the "single market," there is a highly developed tendency to examine the lyrical content, the musical structure, the arrangement, with an eye to the question: "Will the kids like it?"

These days a fifty-year-old Frankie Laine, or a Burl Ives will go into a studio and record "singles." But the "singles" are designed to go through the teenage curtain, which isn't easy.

The teen influence in "singles" is as obvious as a triplet. But RCA Victor's Bob Yorke offered statistics to illustrate that the teenage approach cannot be bypassed in long-playing records either. He said that 1963 LP sales, percentage-wise, worked out this way:

Show music	16-20%
Mood music (Peter Nero type)	20%
Male vocalists	32-40%
Female vocalists	10%
Jazz	5%
Comedy, spoken-word, misc.	5%

Yorke observed: "The male vocalists are the single most important commodity even along LP sales. And it's the young ladies that buy the biggest single chunk of those."

When a teenager goes to a department store or dime store or record shop to buy a disc for his or her little portable record player, the youngster can propel into motion enormous communications media, involving radio, TV, styles of singing and songwriting. If a sizable group of teenagers buy the same 45-rpm recording, it will soon turn up on the "top 100" charts of *Billboard, Cash Box,* and *Variety.*

These charts appear weekly. There are other charts printed by newspaper syndicates and individuals; some are put out by radio stations, disc jockeys, or record retail shops. But the most important are the trade-paper charts.

The recordings which show up there are then programed with great monotony by the "top 40" commercial AM stations who merely program by the charts and have pretty much abdicated creative, individualistic programing.

Once they appear on the charts, most of the nation's AM radio stations, 5,000 of them, will start putting that recording on their turntables, and so will the operators of the nation's 500,000 juke boxes. Thus, via radio and the juke box, all America will be hearing the same recording—tune and artist—whether they are in New York, Philadelphia, or Iowa.

The funny part of it is that this national popularity is based on perhaps 500,000 teenagers buying the record. All America turns out to be a captive audience of a recording selected by 500,000 teenagers. A 250,000-record seller will be programed as often, and thus the country is treated to six weeks of an overdose of a recording chosen by a quarter of a million youngsters.

Nor does the influence stop there. The stars of the recording often get TV and Hollywood offers. Producers of records in all companies examine every line of the melody of the "best seller," the arrangement, the lyric, the singing style, or the instrumental approach to see how they can do something similar, but with a slight little twist.

Studying the record, much like archeologists pouring over ancient hieroglyphics, are the songwriters, music publishers, arrangers, record company executives. For they go by the pragmatic commercial standby: "If it sells, it's good."

As a result, these charts begun by *Billboard* in 1935 help push teen-age tastes upon the country to an inordinate degree, far beyond their numbers. The charts are considered useful to the record business. They are supposed to reflect patterns of consumer buyings.

As far as charts of top-selling LP albums are concerned, they are not harmful. They pretty much reflect national tastes, for here adults are computed into the picture by their purchases.

But the popular-single charts have been a deadly influence in American popular music. They weaken the idea of choosing the best material from the vast supply of recordings available to play on radio or put in juke boxes or sing on TV. They are in many ways a mindless capitulation to commercialism. Their popularity has resulted in a situation where the charts—and they are spread everywhere through the Associated Press and United Press International—solidify the impression that what a quarter of a million youngsters are fond of is the popular music of all America.

4 · THE POOR PROFESSIONAL SONGWRITER

> Every good song is a triumph; it raises the craft standards of
> songwriting. Every bad song is a defeat, and brings with it
> a horde of imitators.
>
> —Anonymous songwriter

Franz Kafka once wrote, "Writing is a form of prayer." Popular music
writers—composers and lyricists—pray, too. They pray for a million
recording sale, a smash Broadway musical cast recording, or the title
song of a movie whose popularity exceeds that of the picture.

In this age of specialization, popular music writing is no laggard.
It is composed of specialists, all of whom do writing that requires discipline and a special tack. There are roughly ten species of functioning
composers and lyricists in today's anxiety-ridden and highly fragmented
popular music scene. They range from Jerry Leiber and Mike Stoller,
the Rodgers and Hart of urban rhythm and blues, to Richard Rodgers,
from twenty-eight-year-old lyricist Howard Greenfield, whose hits include "Stupid Cupid" and "Venus in Blue Jeans" to Alan Jay Lerner
of *My Fair Lady* fame. They could be classified somewhat as follows:

1. The Tin Pan Alley writers (trained in the popular music tradition of
   commercial music)
2. The Broadway show writers
3. The rock 'n' roll writers
4. The "teen writers"
5. Rhythm and blues writers
6. Jazz writers
7. Film composers and lyricists
8. The folk music writers
9. Country and western writers
10. Foreign composers and lyricists

Writers do criss-cross and move from one orbit to another; for example, a teenage writer may be asked to write the score for a teenage
motion picture. But generally, the lines of demarcation are as rigid as
highway dividers. A teenage writer generally will not be asked to write
the score for a Broadway musical starring Ethel Merman.

43

Since the 1950's, a substantial portion of these popular music writers have been jubilant, prosperous, and even proud of their product. The rock 'n' roll writers, thirteen years old and up, have been hammering out best-sellers *a capella* and on the guitar; the creators of "country-pop" have discovered that there's more money in songs than farming. The writers of TV themes have discovered that scoring backgrounds for tales of mayhem and sadism can earn a pretty penny. They are quite pleased. The dance-craze creators of the twist and the hully-gully and the mashed potato have been far from disenchanted. The writers of modern "folk songs" too have had more than five years of commercial acclaim, and there is still no sign of the hootenannies' dying out.

And, for more than a decade, amateur writers have been tickled pink over the novel direction of the popular music and record business. Sigmund Romberg, the operetta composer of *Rose Marie* and *The Student Prince*, once wrote an article, "So You've a Song to Publish" (reprinted in 1955), in which he said, "hits are not written by amateurs." In 1955, the Kiplinger, *Changing Times*, similarly advised: "The successful songwriters are usually good musicians, able to play and sing their own songs.. They understand counterpoint and they understand singers, and they have a strong sense of human values and human desires."

Both the composer and the magazine couldn't have been more wrong. Since the 1940's, amateurs have invaded Tin Pan Alley with the relentlessness of hungry locusts. In the past decade, hundreds of vocal combos and singers, who make up their own words and music, have triumphed. Their songs and recordings have catapulted to win fame, fortune, and disc records selling in the millions. In fact, the "dumb sound," the amateur sound, has become the vogue in the 45-rpm singles field, the new yardstick, the standard.

Leonard Bernstein, Richard Rodgers, Rex Stout, Paddy Chayefsky, Stephen Sondheim, radio and TV critics, and columnists have all critized much of the popular music we hear. Composer Gene de Paul ("I'll Remember April"), creator of the score of the memorable musical film based on Stephen Vincent Benet's short story, *Seven Brides for Seven Brothers*, observed not long ago: "The music industry today is in a state of mystery and confusion. Too much of the new songwriting talent leans toward the rock 'n' roll style. This is understandable because it's easy to write. One simply forgets about rhyme, reason, and intelligent construction."

Recently, the Hollywood team, Jay Livingston and Ray Evans, told a meeting of the National Academy of Recording Arts and Sciences that they couldn't start in today's business because of the subterranean level of contemporary popular music. Evans, co-author of "Buttons and Bows," said: "If you can't write for the teenage group, you're in trouble as a songwriter." Conductor-arranger Paul Weston told the assemblage that there is overproduction of "bad music."

Harry Warren, winner of three Academy Awards for movie music, noted, "The general state of popular music is sad." Writer Bobby Scott, who is also a singer, jazz pianist, and A & R producer for Columbia Records, has asserted that the recording field wants only "one-sixteenth of your talent." He went on to quote roughly from Eugene O'Neill's play *The Ice Man Cometh* in which a character says: "You want to make pimps of us all. That's not the world I want."

The world of "pop" rock 'n' roll is awful, and much of the old rhythm and blues is now indistinguishable from it. But occasionally there is a song that has a raw type of realism. One such example is "Rat Race" (Leiber, Stoller, McCoy) which begins:

> You know it's true
> Out here in this rat race
> There's just one rule
> Out here in this rat race
> Out here in this jungle
> You got to fight from nine to five
> In the steel and concrete jungle
> You got to fight to stay alive

The lyric continues:

> If you don't want to starve
> You got to be like a hog
> There's no such thing as friendship
> Out here it's dog eat dog
> It's a rat race!*

It is set a lean, blues-colored percussive beat. Some argue that during the 1950's, country and western music got a chance to break out of a Brill Building, Shubert Alley–Vine Street prison which "controlled" the music industry. They argue that we now have a more representative popular music.

Some sophisticates insist that the best popular music has always been "show tunes" from Broadway, and that all the rest has been "hack

*Copyright © 1963 by Trio Music Co., Inc.-Cotillion Music, Inc. Written by Jerry Leiber, Mike Stoller, Van McCoy.

writing." But a study of recordings and sheet music does not bear this out. Here are a few outstanding single songs which did not originate in any movie or Broadway musical:

"STAR DUST"	"WHEN SUNNY GETS BLUE"
"TENDERLY"	"ST. LOUIS BLUES"
"BLUE SKIES"	"HONEYSUCKLE ROSE"
"THE SYNCOPATED CLOCK"	"AIN'T MISBEHAVIN'"
"MOOD INDIGO"	"BLOWIN' IN THE WIND"
"TUXEDO JUNCTION"	"MISTY"
"THE LAST TIME I SAW PARIS"	"DINAH"

Returning to the "realism" of rock 'n' roll, facts suggest that a few lyrics do hint of a real world, as in "Rat Race" cited above, but Americans have had to endure more than a decade of musical idiocy, poor structure, and amateurism.

Country and western music has enjoyed considerable popularity. But how good is it? It is really a true regional music? Much of it is sixth-rate musically and lyrically, and in many ways it resembles the worst of popular music.

"Most guys have no pride in their work. All it means is a dollar," says composer Philip Springer. "It's tough today. There is no fun. Everybody is walking around either looking gloomy or arrogant. There's no joy any more in writing.

"The joy of Gershwin and Arlen meeting and playing for each other, we don't have those things any more. The great joy of creation is not there.

"Oh, I suppose even in a rock and roll song, if it comes off well, there's a certain excitement. You feel good, but that's not real pride, because if the song doesn't make it, it becomes just another piece of trash. In the old days, if a song you were proud of didn't make it you always had the feeling that you could bring it back some day. Today you don't have that respect. You judge a song by how much fast action it gets."

Thirty-seven-year-old Philip Springer, his wife Judy, a delicate-looking former member of the Israeli army, and his small daughter live in an airy Central Park West apartment in the Nineties in New York City. A big-winged grand piano stands guard in the living room. A psychiatrist lives in the apartment below the Springers and Philip, who plays a driving piano, has had to learn to play softly because the music intrudes on the doctor's sessions.

Rangy and boyish-looking, Springer has turned out teenage song laments, rock 'n' roll, ballads, rhythm songs. He writes for Tin Pan Alley to survive. Though mainly interested in opera and musical theater, he has been co-author of several million-disc songs—"Santa Baby" (Eartha Kitt), "The Moonlight Gambler" (Frankie Laine), and "The Next Time" (Cliff Richard). Of a scholarly turn of mind, Springer holds a degree in musicology from New York University. He represents the trained Tin Pan Alley writer.

Springer was born in New York City, grew up in Cedarhurst, Long Island. He graduated from Lawrence High School, entered the Army, went to Columbia University and later to New York University.

When he was seven years old, he started taking piano lessons. He studied piano till he was about fifteen and then became interested in composition and began composing music. His lawyer father was very much against it. "He was always asking me to practice the classics, when I was trying to write my own music," says Springer.

He began selling songs without success in 1943. However, he wrote a good deal. He composed the music for an army show called, *Don't Touch That Dial,* a satiric revue, and a college "book musical," based on "The Streets of New York," a melodrama. He also was music director of and composer for a summertime musical stock company at New York's Lake George. "I was musical director of a grand orchestra of two pianos."

His first song, published in 1949, was written with Dick Adler, co-author of *The Pajama Game,* and *Damn Yankees.* It was called "Veloa" and concerned a little South Sea Island girl. It made $60 for each of them. Springer had studied piano with Adler's father, a noted piano teacher, and Springer himself has given lessons.

Springer says, "Psychologically, what the writer has to face is repetition. You're writing usually one message, 'I feel sorry for myself because you have left me, my darling.' Most songs are variations on that theme lyrically. And it's very difficult for a mature person to write down to this level. But you're writing to an age group of from ten to fifteen. That's what they understand. First love and all that stuff.

"Musically, it's very difficult for me as a composer because the new idiom musically is very different from the old idiom. The old idiom is approximately the same as show music is today. That is, it used free tempos, free chord changes, chromatic melodies, and so forth, but in the popular field the music has changed to a very simple folklike expression. It's a combination of rhythm and blues, which is the kind of music you used to hear only in places like Harlem. And country music.

"Both of them are very basic, primitive forms of musical expression so that harmonically, or chordally speaking, in the key of C you will only use the C, A minor, D minor, G seventh, occasionally D seventh chords. You almost never use, for instance, a diminished seventh chord, or a ninth chord, or God forbid, an eleventh chord. Whereas in the old days, you take a song like 'Tenderly,' it's got minor ninths, minor sevenths, elevenths, and so forth. In other words the harmonic expression was sophisticated. Now, melodically speaking, you must stick strictly to the C minor scale today, that goes without exception, if you're writing in the key of C."

Continuing his analysis, Springer went on: "Today's melodies are very diatonic. You never go between the keys. If you're in the key of C, you simply don't have a note land on B flat. In the old days this was perfectly possible. You changed keys freely. You still do in theater music.

"If you look at a piece of rock and roll sheet music you'll notice that the chord changes on the first beat of every bar, or every two bars. There are no irregular chord changes as in sophisticated musical writing. The harmonic patterns are very simple and regular.

"This rock and roll is simply ceremonial. What is the ceremony? It's simply that the teenagers are looking for mates. They're getting sexually excited by dancing to this type of music. It's a ritual. Look at a teenage dance, and you'll see it is a mating ceremony. And they want to dance essentially to ritual music. Primitive and exciting."

Contrasting this music with "freer" music, Springer spoke about a song he wrote with lyricist Carolyn Leigh eight years ago called "How Little We Know" which was sung by Frank Sinatra. "It used very Wagnerian changes. For instance, the first release had a chord change in F to A minor to A flat to C augmented, add a sharped ninth. Now such complex harmonic structures are unheard of in popular music, except in the show field. It used to be possible in the pop field. As long as your song had a message you could get away with it. It's still possible today for a Peggy Lee to record a sophisticated song. That is, musically speaking. However, the chance of its being a hit are small. So you simply have to learn to write rock 'n' roll music if you want to survive."

A young man, Springer feels like an octogenarian. "A guy who's had his thirty-third birthday is an old writer today. Not only because he's over thirty, but because today the average writer, the average A & R man, is a fellow in his early twenties. Psychologically, you feel like an old man because you can't write the way you'd like to, the way you used to, and in fact the way you would if you were writing for the theater. It isn't that you can't write good music, it's that you are forbidden today to write good music if you want to survive.

"So it's psychologically difficult. And a lot of the guys have quit. They've just stopped writing. They can't force themselves to submit their creative efforts to a teenager who is in the position of an Artist and Repertoire man at some very important music company, who is dressed in a sweater, who hasn't had a haircut in six months—you know you just can't do this. I can understand why a lot of fellows have quit.

"Those who have left, most of them live on their ASCAP ratings, which is another problem, because ASCAP is getting more and more stringent in its distribution. In the old days you could depend for the next fifteen years of your life on your ASCAP rating being pretty good. Today, unfortunately, all kinds of rules are being made which tend to make it even more difficult on a non-active writer. As well, in fact, as on the active writer. Don't ask me who is benefiting.

"Many writers survive on their ASCAP rating. Some of them just hang around the Brill Building two hours a day and go home and that's it, that's their life. I mean, they feel as if they're still in the business. But they're not with it."

The older writers—those who wrote yesteryear's "pop" music hits—are singing the blues, according to Springer. "When I look in their faces I see an attempt at bravado. Of course, several who were hit writers fifteen years ago are still hit writers."

In this category, he cited George Weiss, whose latest hit is "A Walkin' Miracle." Springer says: "It's as groovy a tune as you can write." He named lyricists Bob Hilliard, noted for his "Coffee Song," and Sylvia Dee, known mostly for "Too Young," as two more who are still making money in today's market. Springer also mentioned his partner, lyricist Buddy Kaye, who wrote the words to a million-disc global hit, "Speedy Gonzales," based upon a Warner Bros. cartoon character.

Ticking off more changes in today's music and record business, the composer also noted the extinction of "advances." He said: "There are so many songwriters around that there's no such thing as advances any more. In the old days you could get by for years without a hit on your advances. Today it's impossible. No one will give you an advance because they're not sure they'll get a nickel out of it. Every week two hundred or more songs are released. That was unheard of in the old days. There's no premium any more on a songwriter's talent. You used to get a $50 or $100 advance from a publisher on any good song you wrote. So if you wrote enough good songs, you could get by. Today, not a chance, no publisher will give you an advance. If you have a record that's a hit, yes, then he'll give you an advance on that hit song, because he knows it's making money. So instead of keeping you waiting for six months he'll give you your money now, but he will not give you money on speculation."

Despite the poor music vogue, the composer believes that there are rays of sunshine. "The fact that the large majority of the entertainment media still uses the old style of music, the sophisticated style of music with the sophisticated lyric idea, is encouraging. Television still uses great band arrangements. You listen to the background for a television singer, and you'll hear some great brass figures. Night clubs still use the old form. Although rock 'n' roll and the twist have made their dents even in the adult market, the vast majority of live entertainment still is based on sophisticated thinking musically and lyrically."

One of the most successful writers of the past few years has been a young lyricist, tall, soft-voiced Howard Greenfield. In the offices of his publisher, Nevins-Kirschner, now a wholly-owned division of Columbia Pictures, he spoke about his remarkable seven-year career which has resulted in approximately fourteen hits. Recordings of his songs have sold more than fourteen million 45-rpm "singles" and hundreds of thousands of long-playing recordings. His triumphant song successes include three No. 1 records—"The Heart Has a Mind of Its Own" (Connie Francis), "Everybody's Somebody's Fool," (Connie Francis), and "Breaking Up Is Hard to Do" (Neil Sedaka).

What's his technique? "I kind of write for myself, and then I try to take the thing and put it in a teenage situation," he says. "I had a hit called 'Venus in Blue Jeans.' This was taking a situation of, say, what the girl next door would be and what a fellow would think about his own girl, and I used the various art things, going from art to teenage, like she's 'Venus in Blue Jeans'/'Mona Lisa with a pony tail'/'she's a walking, talking work of art'/'she's the girl who stole my heart'/. And the bridge says: 'They say there's seven wonders in the world but what they say is out of date, there's more than seven wonders in the world, I just met number eight.' Then it follows straight through.

"You always start with the title. Take a song like 'Happy Birthday Sweet 16.' Now a birthday is always a good subject. I guess if you take the percentage of sixteen-year-old girls, and that is your market; so I came up with this title. I tried to write it as a teenaged 'Gigi,' where he suddenly discovers her. Like: Tonight's the night I've waited for, because you're not a baby any more, You've turned into the prettiest girl I've ever seen, Happy Birthday, Sweet Sixteen."

Greenfield's knack at picking out teen themes has been rewarded by fourteen "top ten" recordings. They really don't sell in the millions. "My first hit was in 1958 with 'Stupid Cupid.' That sold about 800,000 records. A 'top ten' record today is 500,000 records."

He asserted, without too much enthusiasm, that the teen-appeal songs can have "adult appeal." In "Happy Birthday, Sweet Sixteen," there are lines, he says, "that would appeal to anybody."

> Tonight's the night I've waited for
> Because you're not a baby any more
> You've turned into the prettiest girl I've ever seen
> Happy Birthday, Sweet 16
>
> What happened to that funny face
> My little tomboy now wears satin and lace
> I can't believe my eyes, you're just a teen-aged dream
> Happy Birthday, Sweet 16
>
> When you were only 6
> I was your big brother
> Then when you were 10
> We didn't like each other
> When you were 13 you were my funny valentine
> But since you've grown up
> Your future is sewn up
> From now on you're gonna be mine.
>
> So, if I should smile with sweet surprise
> It's just that you've grown up before my very eyes
> You've turned into the prettiest girl I've ever seen
> Happy Birthday Sweet 16.*

"I wouldn't say this was an adult song, but it does have adult appeal," says Greenfield, "because there are inter-rhymes at the end of my bridge. That, with the combination of the melody, makes it a very catchy thing. You take another 'pop' song like 'Crying in the Rain.' Now this could be an adult song, or a teenage thing. It's the story of a fellow or girl who has too much pride. And therefore: 'I'll cry in the rain so nobody can see my tear drops.'"

> I'll never let you see
> The way my broken heart is hurting me
> I've got my pride

And I know how to hide
All my sorrow and pain
I'll do my crying in the rain.*

"I'm twenty-eight years old, but I'll write situations about myself that will definitely be the same situations a teenager feels. All you have to do is keep it simple and to the point. If I were writing for adults I would write the same songs, only my choice of words would not be as simple. I could elaborate with my analogies. But, basically, people are people whether they're fourteen or forty. I feel that this is the right approach. I used to go to teenage parties, dances, etc., but I found that this was very unimportant. I used to feel that would be the right thing to do. I went to record hops to find out what the kids were thinking, but I found out that when you try to interview a youngster, a fourteen-year-old, and you play a record for him to get his opinion of it, he right away wants to show his intelligence, so he's apt to give a view that is not necessarily his own. If you play him a song, he's apt to find fault with it, just to show off. So I've found that it isn't a good idea to go directly to a teenager."

But Greenfield studies the "top ten" like a Wall Street security analyst pouring over a company's annual report. "Your top ten records are the ones that are going to set the trends. You can get an idea of how the business is going by the top ten. You can see if there are going to be pretty songs, or country songs, just because a song is in the top three and may be a country song. So you write a country song. You're not imitating the song, you're imitating the *trend*. You can elaborate on the trend."

Greenfield had a whopping "country-pop" success not long ago with "Everybody's Somebody's Fool," sung by Connie Francis. Here, the New York Tin Pan Alley writer shows that he can write like a Nashville expatriate.

He asserted that there are plenty of strictly rhythm-and-blues writers on the scene, including Otis Blackwell and Clyde Otis. But most of them, he claimed, branch out into all phases of popular music. He considers Berry Gordy, Jr. as a good rock 'n' roll writer, that is, a writer of rhythm and blues. Gordy has written for recording personalities under the Tamla-Motown label, and as a result the Marvellettes and Little Stevie Wonder have sung his songs. Greenfield says, "I hate the phrase rock 'n' roll because it has gotten such a bad connotation. I don't believe there's rock 'n' roll any more. There's 'pop' music, there's

*Words and music by Howard Greenfield and Carole King. Copyright © 1961 by Screen Gems-Columbia Music, Inc. Used by permission.

rhythm-and-blues music, country and western. I started out with rock 'n' roll but I don't consider myself a rock 'n' roll songwriter."

The tall, long-legged lyricist disputed the charge that popular music has declined over the past decade. "I can name songs that came out in the past two years that can match any of the 'standards.' How about 'I Left My Heart in San Francisco,' 'Moon River,' 'Never on Sunday,' 'All Alone Am I,' 'The Exodus Theme,' 'Theme from a Summer Place,' 'I Wanna Be Around,' 'Firefly,' 'Go Away Little Girl,' or 'Blame It on the Bossa Nova.'

"In years to come the proof will be in these songs, by how many times these songs are recorded over and over again. There was 'Because of You,' a few years ago, and 'Cry.'

"If you exclude show music, you would have to exclude 75 per cent of your standards from the good old days."

Who are today's good new writers to replace the giants of yesteryear? Greenfield pointed out that today's market has some good writers— Gerry Goffin, Helen Miller, Barry Mann, Cynthia Weil. Gerry and Carole King wrote "Go Away Little Girl" for Steve Lawrence. Barry Mann and Cynthia Weil have collaborated on that masterpiece, "Blame It on the Bossa Nova."

The daily milieu and working conditions of songwriters—composers and lyricists—vary with each writer's success, aesthetic approach, and type of writing. A handful are employed on a yearly basis as contract writers by such firms as Chappell or E. H. Morris or Frank Music. Most are free-lancers, self-employed. They are gamblers, gambling with their time, their marketing savvy, their present and future. If you don't sell songs that get recorded you don't make money and you don't eat. Neither does your family. Like the characters in *Waiting for Godot,* songwriters are always waiting. They wait to hear what the music publisher says about what they've written. They wait to hear what the A & R man says. They wait to hear what the recording artist says. Finally, if a musical composition is recorded, there is the problem of having it released.

Even when the record is released to the disc jockey the professional writer waits to see if it turns up on the charts, waits for his statements from ASCAP and BMI regarding performances of the song, and waits for his royalty check covering record sales from his music publisher. So the process of writing, marketing, and promotion is so packed with uncertainty that the writer is alternately enthusiastic or depressed. He is akin to the stock-market gambler psychologically; but unlike the stock marketeer, he has produced a product.

Most popular music writers cluster around three main points: New York, Nashville, and Los Angeles. If you draw an arc, covering an hour's traveling distance from these popular music and record and TV and Broadway centers, you will probably circle all the professional, functioning writers.

Out on the West Coast there is quite a writing colony, a geographical hangover from the days of the movie musicals. But there is also much TV production there, and an expanding group of recording firms. The old-time Tin Pan Alley expatriates, who wrote many of the big movie songs, live in comparative retirement, as befits makers of $30,000 to $50,000 a year, based upon previous hits. In the trade they're known as "those who sit on their 'ASCAP's.'" Actually these writers have become silent with the near-extinction of the Hollywood musicals. As for single songs, these men cannot descend to the teen market. So they swim, play golf, and complain. Sammy Cahn and composer Jimmy Van Heusen have ridden out the poor music decade by becoming ballad Boswells for Frank Sinatra. They have written many tunes for Frank Sinatra films (*The Tender Trap, High Hopes*) as well as the TV musical based on Thornton Wilder's touching play, *Our Town*. Wherever Sinatra goes, there you will find bantam Cahn and big-boned Van Heusen. Cahn also writes song parodies for night club performers.

Far from unhappy are the composers of the movie sound tracks and the TV writers. Such writers as Dmitri Tiomkin, Elmer Bernstein, Alex North, and Miklas Rozsa are overwhelmed with movie and television assignments. And interestingly enough, the themes from the sound tracks have done well in the form of 45-rpm "singles" and on long-playing records. It is the songwriter and the lyricist who are withering away in "lotusland."

Most of the working writers in New York stick pretty close to Manhattan. Rock 'n' roll writers ("Have guitar, will travel") pour out teenage anguish in Brooklyn's Bedford-Stuyvesant area or in Harlem. Composer Joe Meyer, who wrote many jubilant songs, including "California, Here I Come" is a Manhattanite who travels to Europe frequently. Most of the Broadway theater writers can be found not too far from Shubert Alley. Wracked with pain, Cole Porter lives despondently in a palatial Waldorf-Astoria suite; in summers he visits his Massachusetts estate, "Buxton Hill," in the Berkshires. In the Village, sophisticated "folkniks" fabricate new "folk songs." Lee Hays lives in Brooklyn Heights.

Lyricist Bob Hilliard ("Civilization," "The Coffee Song") is a Leonia, New Jersey suburbanite, a town where so many of the faculty of Columbia University reportedly make their homes. An eight-bar vamp from his home, Hilliard has a year-round, heated swimming pool, topped by a half-moon plastic bubble.

Kal Mann, who has knocked out many hits in the past decade, works in Philadelphia, near Cameo-Parkway Records. He is a sort of "company writer." Oscar Brown, Jr. makes his home in Chicago, Dave Brubeck resides in Connecticut, and the country and western writers congregate in and around Nashville.

Some men do much more than writing. Most of the jazz writers are also instrumentalists or bandleaders, such as Duke Ellington, Paul Desmond, Charlie Mingus. Tall, lean, composer-lyricist Tony Piano is a music executive with Joy Music. He also writes liner notes for albums produced by Joy Records, markets material to record companies, and in his spare time—midnight to 3 A.M.—he writes. Leonard Bernstein, of course, is a TV personality, conductor of the New York Philharmonic, as well as one of the brightest of the composers in musical theater. Jule Styne, a fire-ball of energy, is a Broadway producer as well as composer.

There are no figures on what professional songwriters earn. Most probably earn between $1,000 and $10,000 a year. Those who have some strong hits—"standards"—behind them may earn $15,000 to $30,000 a year. A fairly substantial segment, whose credits include the much-performed, much-recorded songs, earn $25,000 to $75,000 a year. Quite a few in this bracket are active in the stock market. One top songwriter began our interview with a long account of a stockbroker with whom he had long done business; he wondered whether he should switch brokers. He had been losing steadily for the past few months.

Sexually, some are hyperactive, and there are constant rumors of wild parties. But the business of music publishing and songwriting has become less and less exotic. However, "switch parties" are not unknown among bachelors, and local Christine Keeler's are contacted to take care of certain disc jockeys, record distributors, or record executives.

In the summer, the hungry proletarian songwriters, with little behind them, pound the offices of the music publishers or invest their scanty dollars to produce "demos." The more affluent take to the seashore—Fire Island, Southampton, and Hampton Bays. Richard Rodgers has a country place in Southport, Connecticut. E. Y. Harburg summers at Edgartown, Martha's Vineyard.

An ex-tanner, William Billings (1746-1800) was one of the earliest "professional" American songwriters. He wrote—and collected—a group of original hymns, *The New England Psalm Singer,* published in 1770. He made little, if any, money from his writing. In colonial times, of course, there was no vaudeville, no radio, no TV, no movies, no recording industry, no juke box industry. Today's modern writer of popular music and lyrics has a fabulous entertainment structure which pays him for his creations. However, in each area, the writer has had to battle to protect himself from economic and aesthetic exploitation.

In 1785, as Herman Finkelstein points out in his booklet, *These Things Are Mine*, the Commonwealth of Massachusetts pioneered in recognizing that "There is no property more peculiarly a man's own than that which is produced by the labor of his mind."

This was a happy theory, but not easily translated into protection for the creator. In the mid 1800's, there was a picturesque, highly active music publishing industry which put out patriotic songs, humorous songs, sentimental songs, topical songs, and dance music. Home entertainment thrived, interspersed with visits to minstrel shows, vaudeville houses, concerts, "opera houses," Chautauqua tents, taverns, burlesque shows, and the beginnings of more elaborate musical theater, such as *The Black Crook* in 1866.

Besides straightaway songs, songwriters prepared special material for vaudeville acts, song parodies, and musical sketches, for which they were generally paid flat sums. But in all of this, there was only phantom legal and economic protection.

In the United States the profession of songwriting slowly evolved with the growth of the music business. *Item:* In 1906, as Douglas Gilbert pointed out in *Lost Chords*, there were thirty-six successful or "hit" tunes. Two of these were phenomenal sheet-music sellers, "Meet Me Tonight in Dreamland" (1909) and "Let Me Call You Sweetheart" (1910). They sold nearly five million copies each at fifty cents each. Men could become rich, writing and publishing songs. That is, the songwriters could get rich, if they could get an accurate account of their royalties. William "Billy" Jerome, wit and music publisher himself (George M. Cohan's "Over There"), caught the ethical tone of turn-of-the-century Tin Pan Alley with such humorous cracks as "Loyalty and royalty are two things almost unknown in songland." "Simon Legree would have made a great publisher." "Did anyone ever see the right set of books?"

Muted by fancied paternalism, the bathos of early popular music, and the lack of any economic guidelines to follow, the songwriters were fleeced right and left. They often sold valuable copyrights for quick cash. Then, by an odd turn of events, the music publishers and popular music writers became allies. In 1914 Victor Herbert visited Shanley's restaurant, and heard an orchestra playing his melodies. But he wasn't being paid for the use of the music he had created. Neither was the music publisher compensated. From this irritation evolved an alliance between the music publishers and the writers—The American Society of Composers, Authors and Publishers (ASCAP).

Through a U. S. Supreme Court ruling, ASCAP won a historic decision. It said that any business enterprise that used copyrighted music (restaurant, tavern, hotel, bar) to attract patrons had to pay for the usage. Thus was established the concept of music for profit or "performing rights."

Radio entered the American scene in the 1920's, and there began a much underpublicized battle of broadcasters versus writers and music publishers. The broadcasters didn't want to pay for usage of popular music. They fought it in the newspapers, the courts, the state legislatures. They claimed that they were publicizing music. But the early legal Gideons of ASCAP finally got the radio broadcasters to pay for music it employed on the airwaves. Later on, silent movies, sound movies, television, followed suit.

During this time, the recording industry was beginning its ascent. In 1919, a young orchestra leader named Ben Selvin recorded his version of "Dardanella" for RCA Victor Records. It proved to be the first recording to sell a million, and gave a hint of the potentialities of the record business.

The entertainment structure of the United States was slowly expanding, and along with it, the songwriter's discontent. In 1931, a trio of songwriters, Edgar Leslie, George Meyer, and Billy Rose formed the Songwriters Protective Association (SPA). As the name implied, it was a songwriters' guild designed to protect the songwriter against rapacious music publishers. SPA has made spectacular progress. In a booklet, *What Every Songwriter Should Know,* it has ably outlined the improvements it has achieved:

ROYALTIES: Before SPA, songwriters got 15% to 25% of all recording royalties. Now they get 50%.

SHEET MUSIC: Before SPA, songwriters got 1 cent a copy royalty. After SPA a minimum of 3 cents per copy.

AUDIT: Before SPA, the songwriter had to trust the music publisher to give him a proper accounting. Now, the Uniform Songwriter's Contract provides for the right to audit the publisher's books.

STATEMENTS: Before SPA, the date for statements to be issued to the lyricist-composer were not fixed. Now, statements have to be issued twice a year, along with a check for all earned sums.

Within a half century the profession of popular music writer has become much more stable, and more businesslike. As a group, songwriters are guided by highly-rated counsel. In addition, the more successful composers and lyricists have their own agents, lawyers, corporations, press agents. In some cases, they have built their own profitable music publishing companies. If Stephen Foster had lived in modern times, and had composed songs as popular as "Jeannie with the Light Brown Hair," he would have died a millionaire, instead of penniless in Bellevue Hospital. His copyrights would be worth their weight in gold and would earn money year after year through new recordings of his work and usage of his material on radio and TV.

In 1940, a portly CBS lawyer, bespectacled Sidney Kaye, conceived of a new performing-rights organization backed by the broadcasters. He thought that such an organization might make ASCAP scale down its demands for more money from the radio stations and the networks. This developed into Broadcast Music Inc. (BMI) and the enmity between ASCAP and BMI continues to this day. The country's songwriters belong either to ASCAP or BMI; a few belong to SESAC, all of which are performing societies.

In this context, the popular music writer functions. He writes within a highly elaborate twentieth-century music and record business that has developed craft techniques and writer's organizations. He is padded around with fairly secure economic and legal safeguards. But he is troubled by payola, the dual performing rights societies, the difficult mazes involved in getting a commercial recording. The practicing professional has been nettled by the way the craft of songwriting has become diluted into teenage-level forms.

Financially the songwriter thinks he is still being shortchanged. Songwriters are chafing at the two-cent royalty rate for recordings set down in the 1909 U. S. Copyright Law. This means a songwriter gets one cent, and the publisher gets the other penny. He wants an area of maneuver in which he can ask for three cents or five cents, whatever he chooses to sell his product for. The record industry is repelled by the idea. They want to retain the two-cent-a-record royalty because they say it will prevent monopoly; the little record-makers won't be pushed out by the big recording firms who will outbid them for exclusives on new works.

The professional popular music writer also is behind bills to force juke-box operators to pay "performing fees," just as night clubs and radio-TV do. The professional songwriter would also like to see TV use more original music, and, of course, they would welcome an expansion of musical production on and off Broadway and in Hollywood.

"Art and mass distribution are simply incompatible," observed novelist Mark Harris, author of *Bang the Drum Slowly.* "The writer has no reason for trying to reach a mass audience." Unlike many other forms of writing, popular music by nature is a mass commodity, since it circulates through an awesome system of daily publicity and exposure—radio, TV, juke boxes, movies, and night clubs. It cannot be too "inside" or it loses the mass.

Yet, Gershwin, Kern, Youmans, Porter, Berlin, Rodgers, Lerner and Loewe have shown that popular music can be both mass-directed and superb musical art. In the past decade there have been some excellent and imaginative and witty popular songs composed. But more of them have been only fair, and most of popular music has seen a retrogression, a rejection of musical craftsmanship, word-values, the desire to probe for new insights and expression. Even those writers who have accomplished some good work have been distressed by the cynicism toward the product, the downgrading of writing skills.

Slick packaging methods, high-pressure distribution techniques, payola, catering to the backward teenage market, the dominance of the trade-paper "charts"—all these things have tended to de-emphasize the musical craft. These conditions have damaged all writers, for they brutalize and desensitize vast portions of the audience. They have also created confused goals for the music writer. Whom shall he write for? Teenagers, mature adults, or the musically "hip"? Will the audience accept musical originality, lyrical inventiveness? What do the charts indicate?

Composer-lyricist, Julie Mandel, has painted the commercialism that prevails for most popular music writers in this humorous song:

"IT'S COMMERCIAL"*

If it's love, love, love, love, love, love, love
You're writing about
It's commercial, commercial.
And if ev'ry line's the kind of line you used to throw out
It's commercial, commercial.

Don't find new words to rhyme
All originality is a crime
And imagination's not worth a dime

*Copyright © 1964 by Julie Mandel.

But you're bound to be admired
If you're truly uninspired

If it sounds like twenty other songs that you can recall
It's commercial, commercial
If it proves, without a doubt, you've got no talent at all
It's commercial, commercial

And for the best of results,
Write a song that's sure to drive away adults.
If it's sweeping the land
And it's being acclaimed
If when someone says, "He wrote it,"
You're a little ashamed,
—It's commercial, commercial, my friend.

5 · THE ERRAND BOYS: THE MUSIC PUBLISHERS

> Did you hear about the publisher who couldn't get any records? The songwriters no longer came around, his secretary quit, and his wife left him."
>
> —Overheard in Tin Pan Alley

Music publishers aren't music publishers. Talent managers are music publishers. And music publishers are in talent management. And recording companies are music publishers. And music publishers are recording companies. And A & R men, producers of recordings, are often *sub rosa* partners in certain musical copyrights. And college-educated folk singers and high-school dropouts are music publishers. It is that wild and complicated—music publishing in the '60's.

The words "music publisher" definitely bears redefinition. Few music publishers publish sheet music. In today's popular music business, few people will pay seventy-five cents to buy the sheet music of a top song, save perhaps for some show tunes or an occasional movie theme. The twin reasons for this are the quality of the "pop" music, and the growth in "spectatoritis," a reflex of automated entertainment in the form of television, films, the juke box, the phonograph.

If he is forced to publish music, a music publisher will call in a third party. He subcontracts the publishing of his tunes or themes, even those on the best-selling charts, to printers and distributors. Much of this subcontracting is done by a New York City firm, Hansen's. It acts as the music publisher for many firms and prints and distributes sheet music for a fee, plus 15 per cent commission on each copy sold. "A music publisher doesn't want to bother with sheet music any more," says one veteran of the Brill Building.

The decline of sheet music is but one fragmentary change in modern music publishing. Actually, cumulative changes have wrought a complete revolution in music publishing. The old methods of song-selling, promotion, the ingrained prestige of being a music publisher, a pride in craftsmanship, have given away increasingly to "deals," and an "anything goes" attitude, aesthetically and ethically. Ghostly music publishers have appeared on the horizon. They don't print sheet music

61

or maintain offices or employ promotion men. They do not aim particularly toward building a catalogue or having a long-range equity in important copyrights.

A veteran Tin Pan Alley music publisher put his white telephone back on the receiver, leaned back in his modern black contour chair, and lamented, "The music publishing business has deteriorated tremendously. The newcomers don't know what the word publisher is. They think you open up a firm or a company for $50 and you're a publisher. It costs $50 for a New York State license, I believe, to become a company.

"But that doesn't make you a publisher. Actually what they want to do is collect everything without really doing the job. The writer, the artist, the manager, the record company, the arranger, the delivery boy—everybody's a music publisher. There are set-ups where the artist, the manager, and the A & R man for the record company will set up a publishing company with the writer. They may have four or five different companies spread out. But that's not being a publisher.

"A music publisher, is somebody who has a 'feel' for things, who has a nose for a good song, or where a song should go. If he likes a song, he fights for it. If one artist doesn't do it, he goes on to the next . . ."

In the 1920's and 30's there were only a handful of Tin Pan Alley publishing firms. Since the 1940's there has been a vast proliferation of "music publishers," many of which are merely letterheads. *Billboard's* 1952 *Music Industry Directory* lists 402 firms, and even this is incomplete.

Today, everybody is a music publisher, because a music publisher shares in record royalties (one cent a copy) and in performance money received from radio and TV usage, here and abroad. It is a pleasure for these people to know that every time they hear one of their copyrights on radio, they are hearing the sound of money, their money.

Consequently, practically every teenage idol is a music publisher—either openly or *sub rosa* through a "cut in." The popularity charts are full of music publishing companies nobody ever heard of, and they are generally owned by the artist, in collaboration with the record company, the arranger, or his manager. Besides Tin Pan Alley's new wave, there are the veterans, too, who represent a kind of absentee ownership of music publishing entities. They aren't personally very active in these firms, but they hold sizable stock in them.

In this manner, Frank Sinatra, Elvis Presley, Nat Cole, folk singers, country and western artists, ethnic authorities, Hollywood composers and lyricists, Broadway theater writers (Jules Styne, Richard Rodgers, Cole Porter) are "music publishers." Harry Belafonte is a music publisher. David Susskind of Talent Associates, Ltd., is a music publisher. He has a firm to take in earnings from such TV themes and bridge music as is used on his TV shows, for example "East Side/West Side."

Practically every record company has a publishing wing. Paul Anka runs a vertical-type organization. He may conceive a song, publish it in Spanka Music (his), own the artist, produce the record under the auspices of Camy Productions (his), and lease the "master" to a record company for distribution.

None of this intramural corporate webbing is illegal, but it does stifle and eliminate from competition the pure music publisher, a man who has become a vanishing phenomenon. These days, the larger music publishing firms, mostly those with an ASCAP affiliation, have been living off their catalog of "standards." They try to compete, but the varying types of "cut-ins" make it difficult for them.

Because of the many "angles," it is tough for a straightaway music publisher to survive unless connected with a movie or TV production company. Those firms that are owned by the movie and TV companies, Music Publishers' Holding Corporation (Warners), The Big Three (Robbins, Feist and Miller), MGM, are still powerful. They have access to TV themes and movie sound tracks, which are getting more saleable. And of course, there is no stronger tie than the umbilical cord.

Those music publishing firms that are thinly disguised "fronts" for recording artists do not have to beg to have their songs recorded. They can pretty well call their shots, even though the record company may object to such nepotism. You will seldom, for example, hear Elvis Presley singing material not owned by Hill & Range Music or Elvis Presley Music, because he is financially involved in ownership of copyrights that go under both escutcheons.

In this completely changed era today's independent music publisher must go around and scrounge hard for recordings. There is a man attached to the envelope or attaché case containing "demos" (demonstration records of new material). He may be clever, highly paid, well-dressed, even ride in cabs to travel three or four blocks. But he is an errand boy.

"We may be beggars, but we're creative beggars," says Howard (Howie) Richmond, lanky former press agent, and today one of the most successful music publishers in Tin Pan Alley. His firms (Ludlow and Cromwell) and those allied with him have published scores of popular hits, folk songs, and the music from the two Broadway productions, *Oliver* and *Stop the World, I Want to Get Off*.

Richmond goes on. "The publisher is at the mercy of the user of music, the man who controls the record company, the man who controls the motion picture, the man who controls the Broadway stage, the man who controls the radio station, or the singer who controls the time on these areas. Or the A & R man at the record company whose decisions matter, so that the publisher is in a sense a salesman. And a salesman is always a beggar in the sense that he's dependent on the other person's whim.

"But we can be creative beggars. First of all, we can get the product these other people want. Then we won't have to beg long. We may have to say, 'Please look at my wares.'"

As to his subjective tastes in popular music, Richmond pointed out that he works on songs that he believes in, and that he can promote and exploit. The words "exploit" and "exploitation" recur in his conversation. "I have no feeling for rock 'n' roll. I wouldn't know a good one from a bad one. But I'm not prejudiced against it." Later he explained: "Those who make rock 'n' roll music recordings are comic-strip merchants. I'm probably selling slick magazines like *Collier's*. I hope I'm not actually selling *Collier's* because *Collier's* went out of business. Gershwin is probably fifteen cuts above us."

Born in 1918 in New York City, Richmond turned to music business press agentry in 1937, and for a long time worked publicizing Glenn Miller, Larry Clinton, Woody Herman, the Andrew Sisters, and Guy Lombardo. Sometime after, he joined the "Big Three"—Robbins, Feist and Miller—and prepared and wrote advertising copy. In 1949 he did record exploitation for Frank Sinatra and Dinah Shore, and at about the same time he started becoming an active music publisher. In that year he got lucky with some folk-flavored songs, including "Goodnight, Irene." His folk catalogs now list the work of top folk writers, including the late Leadbelly, Woody Guthrie, Lee Hays, and Pete Seeger. He owns both ASCAP and BMI music firms.

A great believer in exploitation, Richmond described his early days and technique this way: "My hours are not the same as they were before. I worked around the clock and never knew the difference between weekends and holidays. And when I was dating my wife, she'd come in and type labels (glued to record-mailer envelopes) to disc jockeys.

"Today, we send about 500 45's to disc jockeys. We used to send 1,000 or 2,000 but the record companies do that so we're down to 500 and even 300 is enough. We used to send little notes with them, but since the payola scandals we don't even do that.

"I don't exert any pressure. My feeling is, when I write them a letter, they'll do me one favor and listen to the record once. That's all I want.

After that, they're on their own. They may like me, and say, 'I'll give it a spin because he's a nice guy.' But frankly, I don't give a damn about that any more. Because if a record hasn't got it, don't play it. If it does, play it."

Married and the father of five children, Richmond enjoys foreign films, books, and golf. He describes music publishing in terms of an entertainment industry *Baedecker*. "When you're a publisher, you're a distillation of the places you've been—geographical places, locations, clubs, record companies. The more wings you have, the more you can do.

"Now when you're a young fellow, you do this by going around the clock, seven days a week. I never stopped. Everywhere I went, I worked. I went to California, Nashville, Europe; I listened to people, talked to people, heard things. You have to be a virus. You have to get around.

"You can't have prejudices. You have to try a little of everything. Now when you do that, you don't have a home life, and you don't have a family life. Now I use the tape machine to listen to new material. I spend only half the time I used to spend on it. I have people with me here—Happy Goday and Al Brackman—and they go places I don't go."

Today, the myriad firms owned by Richmond, and those connected with him, are fat with important copyrights in the folk field, the bossa nova, and recently with the theater music from the two British imports. However, he still asserts that there are no "musical standards," that too many amateurs have entered the field. He has many opinions, and he lines them out like a long-ball hitter at batting practice.

About television: "Television is concerned mostly with music that is already established." Night clubs: "A song may take ten years to come out of the night club circuit. But they do. The LP "potential": "The first record that was made of our song, 'In Other Words,' which is now 'Fly Me to the Moon' was in an LP. It's about eight to nine years old." On the music business: "I don't think it's comparable to the clergy." Ethics: "I find no difficulty in deciding when I want to give up on a song. That's my decision. But paying royalties is a matter of integrity. Like paying gambling debts or taxes. Some people don't pay all their gambling debts. The music business has immorality in it. And the rest of the world has immorality in it."

Lately, there has been a tidal wave of selling and reselling and buying up of music publishing firms. Small firms are being snapped up by larger firms. Quiet-voiced Paul Barry, a conservatively dressed, well-groomed man, used to have his own music business firm in partnership with Sam Weiss. But not long ago he and his associate sold their firm to cowboy magnate Gene Autry. The Weiss and Barry catalog has since been resold to Pickwick International, a producer of budget-priced long-playing albums sold in supermarkets and dime stores. Barry said that he sold out mainly on account of the tax structure. "People want to avail themselves of the capital gains. That was my main reason."

A former singer turned music publisher, Paul Barry now works as a hired hand for Southern Music, one of the world's largest houses of its kind. He is not lugubrious about the "good old days." He is happy, for example, over the changing nature of music exploitation.

"We used to devote a lot of our time at night contacting big-name orchestras to get the actual performance plugs. Now, our lives are much different. We are not required to spend as much time at night. Today, we do most of our business as other business people do, with regular hours."

Barry reported there has been intense competition in music publishing, some legitimate, some of it questionable. "A lot of record companies have their own publishing affiliates. And a lot of people working for the record companies have their own companies quietly, or possibly known to the owners of the recording companies. There's an awful lot of companies in existence."

The reason for a record company's flier into music publishing is more earthbound than aesthetic. "If recording companies owns the publishing rights, they can immediately give themselves a break by licensing the song for a cheaper rate. That's one of the reasons so many recording companies have bought into publishing companies. They use the material and they don't pay a [publisher's] royalty because it's their own property. They pay a royalty on the books, you know, but there are many ways that they can move around from a tax angle."

Barry asserted that you can make more money than ever before in the music and record business because of greater revenues earned from performances domestically and the world market. "We had a song that was fantastic, Chubby Checker's "Limbo Rock." We sold 1,800,000 the last report I had. Sheet music sales were below 30,000. But publishers make up for that loss on performances. ASCAP is paying so much more than they used to years ago. And BMI pays off on performances. And so whatever revenues might be lost in sheet-music sales, they more than make up from performance credits. Not only here in this country. There are performing rights societies all over the world logging these things. And the performances are credited, and even if it may take a year or two before the writer and publisher get paid in this country, it still comes through and it adds up."

Southern Music, he said, is one of the largest companies functioning overseas. "They do a fantastic business in recordings and performances all over the world," he said.

He does not "put down" rock 'n' roll. He claims that some of it is of quality. "Personally, 90 per cent of the songwriters I see are teenagers. It doesn't matter whether they're teenage writers or not, but if they have a teenage song that influences me at least 90 per cent of the time. Because I know it is easier to get the song recorded. I call it 'chart music' and that's what the current trend is. I make it a point to see teenage writers. Why shouldn't I?"

Of 45-rpm "singles," he says they have to be teen-oriented. "The 'singles' market is so insecure today they *have* to be leveled at those kids, because they're the only ones buying them. Everybody else is buying an album."

Leaning back slightly he added, thoughtfully, "Personally, I like the business of music publishing better today. It gives me more time to be at home with my family. I don't like to look back in the past, recalling the 'good old days,' because as far as I'm concerned, *these* are the good days."

It is perhaps symbolic that today's independent music publishers are pretty much forbidden to be present at recording sessions in which their own material is being, as the phrase goes "cut." Years ago, the music publisher was the power, the big-wheel. In cartoon and in Hollywood musical he was portrayed as the man who held in his manicured hands the future of songs, singers, and songwriters. Today, he is merely a hard-pressed errand boy delivering "demos" to recording companies.

Once upon a time, he would tell the record company producer who he wanted to record his "No. 1 plug." The record company man listened for the big-time music publisher possessed a superb exploitation apparatus with extensive contacts. He would say meekly: "Who do you see doing it?" And the music publisher would flick his big Havana-leaf cigar and tell him. But as the record companies developed their own proficient exploitation apparatus, and learned to cooperate with that new radio phenomenon, the disc jockey, they became increasingly independent of the music publisher. Before long, recordings replaced live air play and live performances as the crucial factors in making songs and musical themes popular. The shifting nature of song exploitation helped escalate the record company A & R men to power.

Equally crushing was the fact that little independent record companies, employing material from obscure sources, began to get hits. The "wise" old publisher wasn't that important, the argument ran.

· Less puissant than ever, today's independent music publisher picks at his deep-dish cheese cake at Al & Dick's, and contemplates his predicament. On the surface, things appear rosy. There are perhaps 7,000 "singles" or 14,000 songs, being recorded annually, and perhaps 1,000 LP's, each containing 10 or 12 popular songs or musical themes. With such a wealth of production, it should be much easier than in the 1930's, where there were only a scant two dozen firms of any consequence. Today, a music publisher can do business with perhaps 300 to 500 record firms who function fairly regularly. The arithmetic isn't too melancholy.

But there are many obstacles. There has been—and there is—payola. There are many music publishers who compete by offering record executives a piece of the song in return for a recording. Many music publishers have "bought" recordings with direct cash payments as well because they need performance credits on the air, to bolster their logging credits with ASCAP and BMI. Without recordings they are dead, and so they invest money to make money; and who knows, the recording may turn out to be a hit. Of course, such tactics make it tough for the legitimate music publisher who just fights with his personality and a sample recording.

Besides the clandestine corruption, there is the fantastic competition a music publisher faces. First, practically every regular recording artist has his own publishing firm or affiliation. This goes for every type of artist—straightaway "pop," jazz, country and western, Latin American, or folk music. In this, the pear-shaped tone, the "hip" slang, the country twang, the south of the border accent speak the same language.

Moreover, A & R men have their own secret, or even not-so-secret publishing concerns. Record companies, too, own their own lively music publishing firms. United Artists Records is corporately tied to Unart and United Artists Music Co., Inc. Columbia Pictures counts Screen Gems Music and Colgems among its subsidiaries. Jobete Music is associated with Tamla-Motown, the aggressive Detroit recording company. Decca has several music publishing affiliations, and so does Kapp Records. Capitol Records is "big brother" to Ardmore Music and Beechwood. MGM Records is legally married to the "Big Three"— Robbins, Feist and Miller. ABC-Paramount Records has two music publishing firms. Even the ethnic-slanted Folkways Records, under the guidance of volatile Moe Asch, is a music publisher of "folk songs."

Faced with such inbred competition, the area for maneuver for the truly independent music publisher is exceptionally cramped. Rival show-business power blocs (record artists, record companies, movie studios, TV packagers) have stolen much of the green pastures on which the independent music publisher has historically grazed. The grass for him is getting as parched as Egyptian papyrus.

Equally disturbing is the fact that though there are hundreds of recording firms, the ethics of these financially insecure firms leave much to be desired. The little record firms are reluctant to pay royalties, and getting money from them is as easy as finding burnooses styled by Balenciaga. Then there are the high costs of promoting a new piece of material. Years ago, the music publisher himself would demonstrate the song or bring a piano-player along. Today, music publishers have to prepare and pay for expensive "demos," which may cost from $100 to $750. Small publishers have to invest $5,000 to $15,000 in hard cash a year just making these song samples. Some are so elaborate they eventually are released as "masters."

Besides these problems, the popular music landscape is dotted with new power formations. Songwriter Jerry Leiber and Mike Stoller combine songwriting, talent management, record producing, record manufacturing, and music publishing. Singer Bobby Darin has TM Music (BMI), writes songs, acts as a record producer, guides talent, and is a music publisher. Lyricist Bob Hilliard has his own active music publishing firm. The competition is never-ending. Throughout the past decade there has also been the emergence of independent A & R men—"indie producers," as they're called—with no single company affiliation. These men—Bob Crewe, Don Costa—have their own music publishing entities. In many ways, music publishing has become one strand—a by-product of record-making and talent management and songwriting—rather than an end in itself.

In self-protection—or zest for profits—the common tendency in recent times has been for some music publishers to turn to talent management, even record manufacturing. A sign on one speckled-glass office door in the Brill Building states: TABB RECORDS, BARTON MUSIC, SANDS, JAMES VAN HEUSEN, DING DONG MUSIC, MIDWOOD." Joy Music puts out Joy Records. Occasionally, Mills Music, Redd Evans, and Howard Richmond, all primarily music publishers, produce and release recordings.

Some informal popular music historians state that publisher-connected record company ties were spawned in the country and western field. One of the biggest C & W recording firms, Hickory Records, began under the close aegis of Acuff-Rose, the prominent hillbilly music publisher. To round out a confusing picture, even record distributors have turned to record making and "music publishing."

Probably the most refined and successful new type of power bloc is the "Aberbach Group." It has under its wing the following music publishing companies: Elvis Presley Music, Tiger Music, Bennie Benjamin Music, Noma Music, Johnny Cash Music, Inc., Hill & Range Music Songs, Inc., Gladys Music, Inc., Valley Publishers, American Music, Alamo Music, Ernest Tubb Music, Inc. Johnny Cash, the popular country and western balladeer, of course finds Johnny Cash Music material irresistible. The Aberbach Group also has its record company, and quite active, too—Bigtop Records. Its corporate embrace of singers (Johnny Cash, Elvis Presley) songwriters (Bennie Benjamin) reveal the interconnectedness of the operation.

The Aberbach Group symbolizes a new Tin Pan Alley, where organization, built-in tax advantages, corporate thinking hold sway. Or as one Brill Building habitué expressed it: "The accountants have taken over."

Boxed in by this complex and agonizingly competitive climate the independent music publisher, the one-man or five-man music publisher has rough going. Even the wealthy old-guard is singing the blues. Mostly, they derived much of their revenue from properties spun off Hollywood and Broadway musicals. Today, these two sectors are having production problems. In addition, the larger companies—Famous Music, Chappell, E. H. Morris, Music Publishers Holding Corporation represent a certain tradition, a certain brand of popular music. Today popular music writing standards do not exist firmly. The aesthetic guidelines are gimmicky, primitive sounds with lyric content aimed at teenage folkways and these publishing executives in their fifties and sixties are not "jeans" types.

Though they are unhappy, they are perhaps making more money than ever, for their catalogues of the great popular songs are more valuable than ever. There is more recording being done than ever before in the history of the phonograph record. "Star Dust" has more than eight hundred recorded versions in every conceivable tempo and style. Somewhere at this very moment, the work of Jerome Kern, George and Ira Gershwin, Harold Arlen, Cole Porter, Irving Berlin, Warren and Dubin, Rodgers and Hart, or Rodgers and Hammerstein is being put on tape, to be made into a popular recording.

The enormous worth of "catalogue" points up another gap between the authentic music publisher's outlook and the recording company's. As one former music executive explained it: "The music publisher wants better songs to make it. They can become valuable properties. The record companies don't really care what makes it. They want quick noise-makers."

But in the struggle for survival which goes on daily among many small independent recording companies, the noise-maker theory out-tops the others. The only occasions for sunlight the music publisher sees are the LP's by such better popular singers as Barbra Streisand, Terri Thornton, Nancy Wilson, Tony Bennett, Peggy Lee, Frank Sinatra, and Mel Torme, all artists who aren't afraid to try new material. Here good songs can be introduced and "exposed."

The music publisher hopes, too, that the much-vaunted cultural explosion will do a little exploding in the 45-rpm field which can get a lot of quick exposure and your competition is only the other side, the "flip side." On an LP, you have to carry on a promotional war to get your "cut" or "band" played from the ten or eleven other songs.

But most of the independent music publishers (unrelated to singers, record companies, A & R men) are in trouble. And should the sky clear and one of their copyrights break through, there is still the agonizing anxiety over the problem of accurate accounting. Will he get a short "count"? There aren't too many recording companies whose "books" are considered free of manipulation.

Today, the music publishing field is a singularly declining and vanishing type of profession. Generally, the few who enter are those with a built-in tie-up with a singer, a motion picture producer, or a TV enterprise. Power blocs of allied music and record interests are taking over and are assuming greater and greater power in popular music.

The hardy breed, the old-line music publishers who go back to the days of vaudeville, of stereoptican slides of song lyrics flashed upon the screens of movie houses, and of exciting radio "remotes," sit at Al & Dick's, pick at their cheese cake, and contemplate the future with grave concern.

6 · THE TASTE-MAKERS

> A profession, after all, is ever consecrated and responsible. Responsible to itself, I mean. And not to itself as a power group, but to itself as the sole possible preserver of its knowledge and skills. A profession that is not intellectually autonomous is merely a trade and its product merely a consumer commodity. When music shall have become just another consumer commodity like chewing gum, its grand epoch will be over.
>
> —Virgil Thompson, *The State of Music*

"My job," balding, moon-faced Milt Gabler, vice-president of Decca Records and a veteran A & R man who has worked with the Billie Holiday, Bing Crosby, Louis Armstrong, and many current recording artists, once observed, "is trying not to kill myself and to make money for the company."

This doesn't sound like the view of a member of a power-hungry élite. But A & R men are the nervous decision-makers of popular music. There are approximately three hundred of these record producers functioning daily for such companies as Columbia, Decca, Capitol, MGM and Mercury, as well as for smaller labels such as Swan or Liberty. Records are king in the popular music business, and it is the A & R men who are the uneasy rulers of the vinylite monarchy that uses a record spindle for a scepter and a glass-enclosed booth for a throne room.

They are spectacular activists in a glamorous profession—on the surface. For with a cardboard coffee cup and an AFM rate card detailing costs of musicians on "dates," they are the workaday taste-makers of the brand of popular music America listens to—or profoundly dislikes. They sign the singers or other talent to recording contracts. They frequently suggest the tone of the arrangement, another key element in musical style. They choose the musical material for the recording artists to execute, which is, of course, crucial. For musical materials have a certain weight, texture, and quality. They cotton to certain artists and certain records and often support that type of musical approach with

72

evangelical fervor, and with the resourcefulness of many talents, from graphic artists to the disc jockey promotion specialists.

But with the poor-quality music of the past decade, they are looked upon with less than adoration. In one songwriter's fanciful but cynical image, A & R men are compared to the foremen of a big cattle ranch. They are cowpokes turned executives. They keep a tight rawhide rein on the ranch hands (the songwriters, the music publishers, the managers of talent). They see to it that the cattle (the recording artists) are protected and content and fattened up for market. They want a good price for them.

Even persons with the skimpiest knowledge of the show business scene have heard of Sam Goldwyn, Darryl Zanuck, Sam Goldwyn, Fellini, Vittorio de Sica, Carol Reed, Ingemar Bergman, Josh Logan, David Merrick, Elia Kazan, or Herman Shumlin. They are, of course, "brand names," people who produce and direct motion pictures and Broadway shows. But the producers of popular music recordings, either of Frank Sinatra, Doris Day, Elvis Presley, or the newest teenage rage, are as little known as the anonymous industrial chefs who supervise vast ovens and cooking vats. Unlike motion picture or Broadway directors, their creative contributions are murky. Of course, they can make superb contributions to a recording date. But their contributions are not that stylistically individualistic: changes of tempo, changes in arrangement, changing keys, electronic manipulation. If they simply get out of the way of real talent, give them good material, and choose good arrangers—they can assist in the creative process.

There simply are no David Griffiths, or Eisenteins or George Stevens, no Fellinis among the A & R men. And in the current popular music framework, if an A & R man would claim historic distinction it might be for such dubious feats as (1) the first to introduce the multi-track overdubbing (which allows Patti Page to sing with herself); (2) the first to produce a "gospel-pop" record; (3) the first to set Jerome Kern to rock 'n' roll; and (4) the first to go overboard on a California sport and produce the first "surfin' record."

One of history's first A & R men to get into the crazy mixed-up business of choosing musical material and repertoire was the partially deaf genius, Thomas Alva Edison. Some cynics exclaim that after listening to much of today's popular music, perhaps all the record producers are similarly handicapped. Edison got into the business accidentally in 1877 when he discovered that he could preserve sound with paraffin discs. In an effort to commercialize on his invention he started putting out recorded "sounds"—sounds of dogs barking, chickens unlimbering barnyard ballads. The shock of hearing sounds emanate from a machine was an evening's entertainment in the early days of the phonograph.

Later, Edison, along with other pioneering record producers, started putting out recordings of opera singers and orchestras. He often participated in preparing for record dates—choosing material—and suggesting that the pianos be suspended off the floor for better acoustics.

From Edison's low-fi days to today's stereo era, A & R men throughout the relatively young history of the phonograph record have been animated by a "Johnny-one-note" theme: to record what sells. Early record producers, operating with scratchy equipment, regardless of background or aesthetic sensitivity, have always been pretty much aware that recording is a business, as well as an artistic cultural responsibility capable of shaping the taste of millions. But it was for decades a truly small endeavor. In modern times the A & R man has a lion by the tail. He has at his disposal superb technology, a fantastic entertainment and merchandising structure by which his musical statements can be heard by millions in the United States and throughout the world within a week.

To Goddard Lieberson, President of Columbia Records, the A & R man is hydra-headed, a strange animal. "He is a combination of musician, creative man, businessman with a flair for all of these." Bob Yorke, who hires and fires A & R men as head of the A & R department at RCA Victor Records, has added: "They're five-figure men, expensive men. Their mistakes are costly mistakes. They can blow $4,000 just like that."

It is interesting to note that A & R men do not seem to rate themselves highly. In a recent seminar on Tin Pan Alley, A & R Men and Methods, Milt Gabler suggested that the crucial factors in the making of million-dollar hit recordings are these:

1. The song
2. The artist
3. The dressing, or "arrangement"
4. Promotion
5. Sales campaign

Note that nowhere was the A & R man's contribution underlined although he exercises his authority in all areas.

When A & R men have a string of hit recordings on the "charts," they are Tin Pan Alley *wunderkinds*. When recordings produced under their wing don't sell, they are blamed. They often change music and lyrics, sometimes without asking the composer's or lyricist's permission. They play Professor Higgins to countless young Elizas (or Elvises) and tutor them in the pronunciation of lyrics, interpretation of lyrics, dress, hair style, manners. Some are shrewd opportunists, others are as business-like as an IBM operator. Some can be gentle about suggestions. And some can be nasty, but even this nastiness can be commercially inspired. One of the most famous A & R men brusquely told an outstanding singer to quit trying to be artistic: "Who are you singing for—your 'hip' friends?"

With the growth of the popular music recording industry, there has been growth of A & R specialization. There are the general utility all-around A & R producers who will do anything from silky mood music to raucous rock 'n' roll. Some specialize in teenage music, some are jazz A & R men, and there is a growing band of folk music A & R producers. In and around Nashville the recording companies have country and western record producers. There are also specialists in Latin American-material and ethnic-folk. Goddard Lieberson is the administrative head of Columbia Records. Yet he turns A & R producer for Columbia's original-cast albums of Broadway musicals.

Every segment of the popular music industry has power and a certain area of maneuver. The music publisher, the singer, the vocal group, the record distributor, the radio station librarian, the song-plugger, the disc jockey can all propel or slow down the progress of a candidate for the exclusive community known as "Hitsville." But it all starts with the A & R men, the decision-makers, who alone have the authority to say: "Let's make this."

Who are some of the men who call the top tunes? Sid Feller (ABC Paramount) from Brooklyn has worked with Ray Charles and is a former musician. From the bandstand, too, has come Voyle Gilmore and Lee Gillette (Capitol), Andy Wiswell (RCA Victor), Jack Lewis (United Artists). Danny Davis (MGM Records) is often in the control booth at Connie Francis sessions. He has sung professionally and has played in bands. Steve Sholes (RCA Victor), who persuaded Victor to buy up the contract of a Tupelo, Mississippi, boy with the unlikely name of Elvis Presley from Sun Records, was a former messenger with a strong interest in the saxophone.

For color, there's Nesuhi Ertegun, the son of a former Turkish ambassador to the United States, who is part-owner and an A & R man for Atlantic Records. Some are former trade-paper reporters, such as Joe Carlton, A & R producer for Carlton Records. As a student, Milt Gabler spent a good deal of time tending his father's radio and record shop in midtown Manhattan. And Dave Kapp, one of the oldest A & R men in the business and founder of Kapp Records, was active in record retailing in Chicago. One of the few girls active as an A & R "pop" producer is Ethel Gabriel (RCA Victor).

The A & R man does much more than pick songs, musical material, and talent. That's only the bare bones of the job. A & R men also possess a working knowledge of sound engineering, including overdubbing, splicing, sound balance, and stereo recording. Often he does his own market research.

The A & R man also thinks up new album ideas and bargains with Tin Pan Alley publishers to reduce royalty rates. Frequently he has the unhappy task of dropping stars of yesteryear from the roster. If the A & R man is also an arranger, he may whip up arrangements for his artists. Often he turns ballyhoo man to publicize his stars.

The top A & R men get $20,000 to $40,000 a year. Some at smaller labels make $10,000—and have a bonus arrangement depending on what kind of a year they have. There are also independent A & R producers, about which more later.

What are the qualifications for an A & R man? Arnold Maxin, a former musician and a Temple University graduate, now President of MGM Records, says: "The obvious qualification seems to be that you need to be a musician. Actually this is of secondary consideration. You have to have definite musicality. But the most important ability is to have a common touch. The A & R man also has to be a merchandiser, a promoter, and an exploitation man."

Boyish-faced Don Costa, formerly A & R man with ABC-Paramount and United Artists and now an independent record producer disagrees: "The singers respect you, if you know music."

The A & R man has to put out a product that will compete with the product of a thousand other firms. Then there is the delicate matter of artist relations. The A & R man has to learn how to get along with an artist and yet not let the artist run him. Once, for example, Don Costa, then working for ABC Paramount, was visited by a top singer who brought over some new songs he wanted to do. Costa examined them and then said: "I don't like them."

"But I like them and think they can be hits," replied the star.

Costa said: "I don't think so."

"How do you know?" shot back the star. "Nobody's a genius."

This is the difficulty faced by the A & R men. They cheerfully admit they're not geniuses. But they are in charge and they feel that they have a better objective grasp of quality and selling power than the individual singer.

In choosing material, the A & R men keep one unwavering eye on the trade-paper charts. During a meeting concerning A & R men, George Avakian, a free-lance producer, asked the audience, "How many read *Billboard?*" Most did. He then added: "I was going to start off by explaining how to use *Billboard*, but I see that's not necessary."

In truth, the A & R man is largely a failure. Ninety-five per cent of his 45's and LP's do not succeed. He lives for the few big hits that will carry him. If he doesn't get those singular hits, chances are that he will be dropped. Therefore, the A & R man is boxed in, despite his own personality and sensitivity, by what he construes to be the demands of the marketplace. Yet, in the mystique of popular music, nobody knows what will succeed. Bad songs make it, bad singers make it, and even a few good compositions and singers make it, in the 45 rpm sector.

How do A & R men choose material? First, each A & R man receives batches of "demos," as many as 200 a week. From these, plus foreign material, movie scores, Broadway shows, hits of yesteryear, folk songs, and compositions brought in by singers and arrangers, they select material to record.

Music publishers who submit material often are brutally treated; some are lectured. An A & R man himself, who was once a music publisher, tells how one of the most noted record producers responded to material. We'll call the famous A & R man "Gerald":

"Gerald will not be content to say 'No.' He'll destroy a song. He'll make a long speech saying how badly written it is. He'll tell you how many songs were written on the same subject, and written better.

"Sometimes he'll search for a record and play it as an example of a song written on the same subject, a song that's better, a song that he turned down."

"Or: 'Where did you dig up that garbage?'

"If he's in a good mood, he'll say: 'Good idea. Didn't come off.'

"Or he'll say: 'I have nobody to do it.' Or: 'That's a show tune.'"

The A & R men may be taste-makers, but most of them are very much "organization men," even though they wear sports shirts and Italian custom-made shoes at work, and come in at noon. Every A & R man knows that his "P and L" (Profit and Loss statement) has to show visible black ink—or else. One man who sits in judgment on a covey of A & R men is Bob Yorke, youthful, fortyish head of the A & R department for popular and classical music at RCA Victor.

A former swing band buff, Yorke is "Little Nipper's Voice" so far as RCA victor's record producers are concerned. His staff of record producers are stationed in New York, Nashville, and the West Coast.

He himself does not produce records in the studio, but his concepts and views determine a great deal of what does come out. He is the boss.

"The creative guy here isn't given an iron corset to wear. There are some controls, but these are largely financial," he said recently in the East 24th Street, Manhattan headquarters of RCA Victor. "The A & R man is very important here, because there has to be a relationship of an artist with people. It's hard to believe in a colossus like RCA Victor. It's hard to believe in largeness. An artist must feel intimate with somebody.

"At RCA right before the beginning of the year, around November, we have product-planning sessions. We figure out what we will produce, how much we plan to move out. We sharpen our pencils and allocate money to each A & R producer.

"Evaluations are made of the sales history of each artist. If an artist is going downhill or is a comer, the A & R man knows it. If an artist is going downhill, management asks the A & R man 'Where are you going?'

"We try to figure out how many 'singles' to produce, how many LP's. We go into commitments for Broadway cast albums. We go into motion picture deals. We plan as much as we can, but some things you can't plan, such as what to do when an artist gets hot.

"During any calendar year, we may put out 140 to 150 albums. RCA Camden may produce 40 country and western, and then special items such as jazz releases or a few religious 'singles.' We're one of the smallest companies in 'singles.' It's hard to digest too many 'singles.' Years ago, we had as many as twenty 'singles' a month.

"You can't do business at all without the right product. I can't detect a hit. But I can tell a failure. As head of A & R that's one of my jobs. You've got to have somebody who says: 'This is not a good record.' A producer can always find something virtuous about a recording. He'll pick out the musicianship, or the performance. He loses his objectivity.

"In the beginning the producer may have hated a piece of material. After thirty-three takes, he changes his mind. They take it to me and it's just plain lousy. You've got to have somebody who says 'No.'

"Almost all 'pop' records have no real musical values. But they move the teen audience. First, there is great feeling in the records, and secondly, there's great meaning to that audience. Otherwise, there's no explanation for what happens."

Just as carefully as it plans 45-rpm releases for the teens, RCA Victor plans what LP's it will produce for the complete popular record-buying audience.

"General (David) Sarnoff seems interested in our activity in popular music," says Yorke. "But his favorite is classical music. However, he and his associates know what's on the 'charts.'"

A great believer in marketing strategy and charts, RCA Victor pretty much plans how many units it will produce, and how much profit it hopes to make. Yorke said: "If things go well, and there's lots of activity on the charts, for a day or two I breathe deeply. We've got to keep volume up, otherwise we're in big trouble.

"We like to sell records. We're not in business to lose money. We stick to the Ivy League philosophy. Lose with sportsmanship. But don't lose, otherwise you get a new coach." (Yorke has since been replaced as head of A & R at RCA Victor by Steve Sholes.)

Dave Kapralik works in a similar capacity to Yorke at Columbia Records. He is the Executive Director of Popular Artists and Repertoire. No musician, he is a former radio actor, a self-styled "vocational itinerant," who succeeded in executive training sessions run by his company, a monumental corporate division of Columbia Broadcasting System. He is a relative newcomer to the record business. He is partial to big words: "I feel that an A & R man has a dual responsibility. One is to create products which will sell. Products that either can be directly reflective of social situations or deeply creative. I don't think it is the responsibility of a commercial Hollywood producer or a commercial record executive to direct public education. We have public responsibilities. We have a responsibility not to be destructive. We should create a product which relates to the mores of our culture. But I don't feel that it is the role of the producer in any media to crusade. We can crusade creatively.

"As producers, it is incumbent on us to be as creative as we can— not a carbon copy of what other people do."

If there is any poor-quality popular music, Kapralik blames it on the "great amorphous public." He goes on: "The problems and criticism which may be directed at adolescent music or television goes far deeper. I think that throughout history there has been a broad public taste which has been at an elementary level, a basic level. We now have mass media of communications. I don't think adolescent music is to be condemned because it reflects this. It is to be lamented. But I think that if there is such a thing as decadence, it goes far deeper than the music business." (Kapralik has since been replaced by Bob Mersey.)

Power is what A & R men have plenty of, but they are hardly the kingfish they used to be. Sometimes they are mollusks. The birth of record stars and music publishing enterprises tied to the stars, the advent of the artist-composer, the power of the arranger and the manager of the record artist have through the years eroded a considerable portion of the A & R man's dominion, notably in the choice of material.

As Jack Rael, Patti Page's manager, once said: "Every big star has veto power over the type of material to be done. And if an artist and an A & R man fight, they may compromise. Do one side the A & R man wants, and one that the singer wants."

In the battle to get his material done, the music publisher often does the end-around the A & R producer. He goes to the manager of the artist, the arranger, anybody in the star's entourage who may be helpful at court.

The record company A & R men have been undercut also by that new species of shrewd *luftmensch* who are poaching on their territory— the independent A & R men. These men—songwriters, arrangers, entrepreneurs, musicians—are not employed exclusively by any single record company; they are free-lancers. Some of the most successful of them are Mike Stoller, Bob Crewe, and Jerry Leiber (songwriters), and Don Costa (an arranger).

Unlike staff A & R men, they get a producer's fee for producing the "master," and what's more important, they get record royalties.

The growth of independent A & R men is largely a reflection of the fragmentation of the "pop single" market after World War II. With all kinds of artists and all kinds of records and all kinds of songs making it, and with the discovery that a maverick label can somehow compete with multimillion-dollar phonographic colossi, somehow this group edged into business for themselves.

These "indie" artists and repertoire men have become the formidable suppliers of the 45-rpm single records. Jerry Wexler, vice-president of Atlantic Records, told *Variety:* "A label can't be in on all the local sound trends. To get different sounds you have to be able to be all over. Many independent producers travel light and move fast. Others work in an area that they know and are much better than a guy who is sent in with no equity in the place."

Cash Box has analyzed the role of the independent A & R producer thusly:

Only a few years ago everyone depended almost completely on house A & R men and kept an eye out for a breaking disc that might be picked up. When the price of breaking hits became prohibitive, companies began closing their eyes to charts and opening their ears to new and unreleased masters that could be acquired for considerably less. Companies could take a chance with many more unreleased masters because huge advances were unnecessary. Many of these masters featured new, unknown artists that the indie producer had nurtured along and written for over a long period of time. The material for these masters was frequently the property of the indie producer—a practice which is still very common.

But during the past year or two producers have expanded their activities by recording many leading artists for other labels on a royalty basis, frequently waxing material which is not their property. In doing so, they have upped their status greatly and have given the business a new dimension.

There are quite a few advantages to the independent A & R men so far as economics are concerned. First, they can't be told what to do. They can't be fired by the company. They can get a percentage of the record royalties. And equally important, they can build up music-publishing entities by promoting their own songs or the musical material they are financially interested in. Also, if an artist clicks under their aegis, this happenstance can lead to many juicy assignments (TV, movies, etc.), in which they can profitably share.

These independent free-lance A & R men have operated most successfully in the "pop singles" teen field. They fabricate broad-spectrum music enterprises which (1) produce the "date," (2) own the music and lyrics, (3) often own the writer, (4) own the artist, and (5) hire the arranger.

Aesthetically, they are no different from company A & R men. They are hypersensitive "chart followers," creators of "sounds" rather than a superior musical product. Frequently, through editing that has been compared to "diamond-polishing," they have taken performers or groups and given them a "gloss" of professionalism. But as Luigi Creatore of RCA Victor remarked of these "tape creations": "They're still not artists."

The A & R man's quest for "hits" is unceasing, neurasthenic, and semi-comical. He wakes up in the morning looking for a hit. He asks his progeny what records their friends are purchasing. He looks at a dinner plate and remembers a "demo." He tries to bring out the best in an artist, and he seeks to do so by a kind word, a bear hug for the girl singers, or a bottle of Jack Daniels with the more mature performers. For youngsters he may have popcorn or soda pop. He rides to work and wonders if the rhythm of the car can be woven into an arrangement (after all, kids are car-crazy). He tunes in to the early disc jockey programs to find out if the company promotion men are doing their jobs. He is wined and dined by the music publishers; often he and they are secret partners, with the A & R man getting 25 per cent of the publisher's record royalties.

Basically, what the record company is most concerned with is profits.

"A good A & R man," says Mitch Miller, probably the most publicized record producer of the generation, "is judged by how many records he sells. If he sells a lot he is OK."

Courage is an odd word to use in such a money-conscious world as Tin Pan Alley, yet some A & R men are sensitive to their over-all responsibility and fight hard to do better material. Some, perhaps most, are acquiescent; they are the button-down-shirt soldiers, who are below the battle.

In a highly competitive field the record companies, however, desperately search for the big payoff, even when they seemingly rebel against formula record-making.

Consider this "Help Wanted" ad which appeared recently in *Billboard:*

WE ARE A MAJOR INDEPENDENT RECORD COMPANY AND WE NEED A YOUNG MAN WHO CAN CREATE AND PRODUCE LP'S AND SOME SINGLES.

WE NEED SOMEONE WITH FRESH IDEAS. SOMEONE WHO CAN THINK FOR TODAY. SOMEONE WHO IS NOT A "RUBBER-STAMP."

WE DO NOT NEED "MORE THEMES FROM HOLLYWOOD" OR "THE ITALIAN HITS RIDE AGAIN." THE MAN WE NEED MUST BE ABLE TO SEARCH OUT NEW TALENT WHICH CAN SELL ON RECORDS. WE ARE NOT INTERESTED IN ARTISTIC TRIUMPHS WHICH DO NOT SELL.

7 · THE ARRANGERS: TECHNICIANS IN A TRAP

> Things are seldom what they seem
> Skimmed milk masquerades as cream
> —Gilbert and Sullivan, *HMS Pinafore*

He sits moping at a lead sheet. He turns on the radio and listens to the latest, best-selling records to hear what the current "sound" is. He may hear one of his own confections, now a "chart item," and sigh. For the recording artist made a fortune, while he made $150. If pinched for time, he may dictate the arrangement to a musical copyist on the telephone. Later, he may go to the studio with his newly prepared arrangement and conduct the date. During the rundown, he may suggest a leaner brass mixture, for it is clouding the singer. Frank Sinatra depends on him. So does Peggy Lee, Nat Cole, Johnny Mathis, Chubby Checker, Elvis Presley, Harry Belafonte, and the latest adolescent rage. He is the musical journeyman-for-hire—the popular music arranger.

Popular music arranging is one of the minor art forms. It is not as important as the initial creative impulse or creation itself, otherwise all arrangers would be Cole Porters, Richard Rodgerses, George Gershwins and Jerome Kerns. But they are—at their best—artists in their own right. They try to bring out the best of the musical materials given them and provide commercially attractive frames in which the popular music makers (singers or orchestra) can shine.

In this age of specialization, there are all types of arrangers: the all-purpose popular music arranger who will tackle any genre; the jazz-arranger (Gil Evans, Johnny Mandel), the show-music arranger (Robert Russell Bennett, Sid Ramin, Hershy Kay), the folk-type arranger (Robert De Cormier), the country and western arranger (Chet Atkins).

There are perhaps a quarter of a million arrangements of popular songs or musical themes prepared each year for recordings, night clubs, theater, and TV. It has become a big industry. Its ranks include talented arrangers, musical hacks, and a host of "musical strategists" who wouldn't know an Ab from a flat tire; arrangers are former press agents who are now record executives, songwriters, and managers of talent

who confess their artlessness but who claim they "know" how to manufacture the "hit sound."

Sitting in his rather luxurious office at Decca Records on Park Avenue
in Manhattan, arranger-conductor, A & R producer Dick Jacobs spoke
about the arranging craft.

"Let's take 'Lonely Teardrops' with Jackie Wilson, a million-disc
seller. I think it was one of the biggest rock 'n' roll hits ever recorded.
I think two things made this record, besides Jackie, of course, who is in
my mind, one of the greatest artists around today. The background
figure . . . the 'shoo-be-doo-wah-bop-bow.' Then the group answering
him with 'Say what you will, say what you will.'

"It's the kind of repetitious, monotonous figure that the kids like.

"When we did the record, the whole introduction with a group went
'shoo-be-doo-wah-bop-bow.' Now this type of syllable background is
tremendously popular today and tremendously important. It is non-
sensical, but this is what the kids like.

"The arranger's actual physical work is less difficult than it used to be
in the old days of the big bands. In those days, the arranger set the
whole style of the band. He was the king. Today he's a very important
part, but he's definitely not the king, because you can go into a record
date without arrangements. If you have a rhythm section, if you have
capable musicians, you can go in with lead sheets, with just melody
and chord lines, and let the boys run it down a few times. And you
get a record and a pretty good one, too."

Why does rock 'n' roll sound so much alike? Jacobs explained:
"If you start to analyze all the rock 'n' roll records and try to get it
down to where you want it there's only about five or six basic beats in
the rock 'n' roll field. I think this is one of the reasons it's been so
successful.

"First there's a triplet beat. This was the start of rock 'n' roll, the
basic element of rock 'n' roll—the straight triplet.

"Then the second basic beat is what we call Spanish triplets, which
are the triplets with a slight Latin American flavor. That's still a straight
triplet beat with variations. A triplet intermingled with sixteenth notes.

"The third basic beat is the cha-cha beat, which we call in rock 'n'
roll a 'chalypso,' which is half cha-cha and half calypso. Actually you
can do a cha-cha to it. You can do what they call a chalypso dance, but
if you're going to get down to it, it's almost a variation of an old Latin
rhumba.

"Then, of course, we go into the twist beat which is so tremendously
popular and which has many variations.

"The fifth basic beat is the straight two-beat, up-tempo rock 'n' roll thing.

"Going down the *Cash Box* list for this week, the rhythm on 'I Will Follow Him' is a chalypso. 'Puff the Magic Dragon' is not a rock 'n' roll record. It is a folk song with a normal, old-fashioned beat. How it got up there I'll never know. 'Can't Get Used to Losing You' is definitely a novelty type of beat but somewhere around a slow chalypso type of beat. 'If You Wanna Be Happy' is an old-time calypso beat. 'Pipeline' is a strictly rock 'n' roll bass-type figure, almost a variation of an old boogie-woogie type of figure which would have been my sixth figure as basic rock 'n' roll.

"Now here comes a new thing in rock 'n' roll—'Surfin' USA.' The surfin' tempo has become a new thing. This is, of course, what they do out on the West Coast with surfboards, but since they wrote this song the surfin' tempo is a new kind of tempo—a little faster than what we've been used to in the old rock and roll. But the bass is basically a one and three beat. This is the newest thing to come along in popular music today. The bass plays on the first and third beat, which is actually a throw back to the old days. But surfin' has become a new type of thing.

"Then we come to 'He's So Fine' and 'Foolish Little Girl' which are straight chalypsos. 'Reverend Mr. Black' is a folk song again; 'Two Faces Have I' is a chalypso; 'Losing You' is a ballad, country and western style.

"The straight triplets, while they were out of favor for a while, are starting to come in. Practically all of the Four Seasons stuff is chalypso, too.

"Most always the songwriter presents the song with a demonstration record made, and they really put it down in the tempo that they feel it. I will say that this has made the arranger's life a much easier task. As a general rule we pretty much adhere to the demonstration record. But sometimes we change the tempo. But in most cases we keep the feel of the 'demo.' We will enhance it possibly by a different type of figure, but the style and feel is kept. One of the big reasons for that is because the artist usually learns the song from the demonstration record, and if you change the feel on the arrangement you're liable to have a real panic, when they come in for the record date, because they've learned it with the feel from the demonstration record and find a completely different type of tempo.

"I usually have the whole arrangement planned in my head before I write it. I usually do this planning before I go to sleep at night. The writing is the least. I can sit in the office with the phones ringing and everything going and write the arrangement. Everybody says to me, 'How do you do it?' Sometimes I work at the piano, sometimes I don't. It takes me an hour and a half to two hours to do a rock 'n' roll arrangement. A ballad arrangement takes about three hours. I don't get much of a chance to do ballads any more."

For years now Jacobs, who is dark-haired, wears glasses, and exhibits a friendly manner, has been constructing arrangements for groups, singers such as Jackie Wilson, Vincent Edwards (TV's Ben Casey), and big bands. "The Brazen Brass" series of Decca LP's featured Henry Jerome and contained many of his orchestrations.

There's a "vocal-group" sound that is quite important, too. Jacobs says: "For example, you take a group like the Four Seasons. Now they're creating a sound in the vocal voices by overdubbing their own voices and using a falsetto voice. It almost sounds like girls on the record, but it is all boys. Bob Crewe produces their records and I imagine he would be the most integral part there.

"In certain cases the arranger for the song will do the vocal arrangements, in certain cases the group will have their own arranger. Basically, if it's a group record, the group will give their vocal arrangement to the arranger who does the background instrument parts. But I think in the Four Seasons records, the basic thing that's causing the great sound there, and the fact they're having hits, is in the group arrangement itself, in the vocal arrangement. I think most of these vocal arrangers are part of the group.

"You'll find that in the majority of cases none of the kids in the group read music. It's all stuff they make up out of their own heads. They hear these things in their own minds, they fake the harmonies; it's not difficult for them because in today's market most of the songs are written with very simple chord progressions. You'll find that most of the songs today are composed with three, four or five chords. They go through the I, IV, and V progression. Possibly the dominant key for the release, but very simple progressions. No intricate harmonies, for example such as the Hi-Lo's or the Four Freshmen would use.

"One of the other big things that is so vital today is what we call the 'echo sound' on records. It's of tremendous importance. There are two types of echo you can use, natural echo or what we call 'tape reverb,' which means a delayed echo. In other words, in natural echo the sound just goes through a mechanical echo chamber or through a room chamber. On tape reverb, the echo is fed into one tape machine with a delayed beat and it comes out of that tape machine and goes onto the tape machine you're actually recording on. Now, of course, the public doesn't know precisely what's being done, but they do recognize the sound when they hear it on a record. It's not delayed a musical beat, it's just a fraction of a second, but it gives the big sound, it gives the edge to the voice that's selling in today's market."

Occasionally, Dick Jacobs seems to face north and south at the same time, possessing mutually contradictory craft ideas: "The basic truth in producing a record date today is to actually make the record seem like it's not being produced. The record should almost have the feel that the artist is singing with a few musicians behind him at a party."

Later on he remarked: "Most of the top records are definitely professionally produced records and they sound professionally produced. I think if you go down the list right now—'I Will Follow Him,' 'Puff the Magic Dragon,' 'Can't Get Used to Losing You,' 'If You Wanna Be Happy,' 'Pipeline,' 'Surfin' USA'—I don't think any of those records sound amateurishly produced at all. I think the amateurish sound is definitely on the way out."

Sometimes accident plays a part in the art of arranging. "I had a very big hit on a record I did with Buddy Holly," recalled Jacobs, "with a song called 'It Doesn't Matter Any More,' which was written by Paul Anka. The record date was in the evening, and Buddy came in that afternoon and said he had found the song and we had to write a very, very quick arrangement to it. And he played the thing on his guitar and sang it to me. We didn't even have time to make a lead sheet and I wrote the arrangement as he sang it to me. We had violins on the date, and I had no time to harmonize the violins or write intricate parts. So we wrote the violins all pizzicato, and the record was such a big hit and the effect was so well accepted that Buddy Holly became a legend in England, and a whole crop of Buddy Holly imitators sprung up there, and everyone of the arrangers who wrote a Buddy Holly background used this type of thing with the pizzicato strings. And I can tell you right now, that was the most unplanned thing I have ever written in my life."

According to Dick Jacobs, there are actually rock 'n' roll "classics." He listed the following: "The Great Pretender," "Why Do Fools Fall in Love," "A Tear Fell," and "Heartbreak Hotel." He also mentioned "Bo Diddly," "I Almost Lost My Mind," and "I Will Follow Him," as potential "standards." Besides these, he noted that he thought highly of "I Left My Heart in San Francisco," "I Wanna Be Around," and "Spring in Manhattan." "Three great ones," he asserted.

Jacobs thinks that the first rock 'n' roll record was probably made by a church group, by some people who sang in a church choir or in a gospel choir. They went into a recording studio and put on tape the same feeling they had in a gospel church.

Jacobs assumes a semi-mystical state about the nature of rock 'n' roll arranging. "I think a lot of people attempt it but don't get it. You have got to hear the guitars, and you've got to hear the drums, and you've got to hear the beat coming through, and you've got to hear the sound of the voice.

"The record has a feel, or it doesn't have a feel. Everybody goes in and tries to get it, and sometimes you don't. Sometimes the feel can be missed in a tempo, it can be missed in an arrangement, and it can be missed by the musicians on a date."

"Soul music," so far as Jacobs is concerned, is "just ballad rock 'n' roll songs." He added: "The soul records are done very simply, very few instruments in the background, other than the rhythm section (piano, drums, bass, guitars)."

Philosophically, Jacobs doesn't feel that he is writing down when he does a lot of rock 'n' roll arranging: "I liked rock 'n' roll right from the beginning, I didn't have any problems. I know a lot of very, very fine arrangers who will have no part of rock 'n' roll whatsoever and they—well, I guess their business suffered badly. But frankly I really like rock 'n' roll. I'm making no bones about it. I really do like it. I think it is definitely a new form of American music. I don't put it down one bit. I think it's great. I love the beats, I love the songs, I love the way the kids do it. I think it's their own type of music. I think it's one of the freshest American type of things ever originated.

"Adults here don't understand it. It's kids' music. Everything in it is slanted toward the kids. Its almost like a kid would play marbles and and adult wouldn't. I think the kids grow out of rock 'n' roll, too. My boy is eighteen years old. He still loves it, but he listens to good music, too. The kids get past a point and they graduate to Frank Sinatra. And he appeals to them. I don't think it has any influence in shaping their taste whatsoever. I think they take it as it is; when they're through with it they drop it and go on to more sophisticated music. But there's good rock 'n' roll and bad rock 'n' roll just as there have always been good and bad ballads."

One of the least known arrangers is Bill Ramal, a heavy-set man with a touch of the dandy about him. He lives in New Jersey. A former Juilliard School of Music student, he has played in bands as a saxophonist and is heavily involved with rock 'n' roll.

"Generally," he says, "nothing you can do record-wise is stimulating musically. Like if you're doing a cha-cha album. It's just cut and dried. You can watch television and write it. But if you're doing a horrible rock 'n' roll tune, with a horrible singer, and all of a sudden you get a hit out of it, it's like a sense of accomplishment."

He paused for breath in one of the small offices of Don Costa Productions. "In school, I wrote symphonies. You know—the whole thing. But professionally now I do rock 'n' roll. It's what I prefer. I grew up in it; I played it as a musician.

"Seventy-five per cent of the time the tune and the singer are horrible. But there's no correlation as to what singer or what tune makes it. There's no way you can figure it out. I can give you stacks of great arrangements that were [the records] bombs. Sometimes the singer is the main thing that makes it, sometimes the song. But usually it's a combination. Mostly, it's the song.

"To my musical mind, 90 per cent of the popular music recorded is tripe. Roger Williams is tripe. Montovani is tripe. If you're talking about musical intellect, recording-wise, you can't do anything," he said. " 'Frank Sinatra Swings'—well it's not the same as studying Beethoven or Verdi or Wagner."

Ramal is equally abrasive about show music. "Show music is good in its way just as rock 'n' roll is. Show music may be more stimulating than rock 'n' roll, but it's still tripe compared with the masters."

The arrangers asserted that the basic change in popular music has been the beat. "There's the same harmonic changes. Technically, there are different chord patterns. There is more accent on gimmick sounds. Every time you do an arrangement you look for some kind of gimmick sound. If you're going to have an instrumental passage, or something behind the singer, you always try to find something unusual that will catch somebody's ear. Whereas before, arrangers would stay straight on the song.

"The song dictates what the arrangement will be like to a certain extent, but I also have to deal with the producer of this record, and many, many times I'll have a song and an artist and I'll want to do it with strings, and they'll say, 'No, horns are happening today, so do it with horns.'

"So the song influences you maybe 50 per cent. But the trend of today's market is the big influence. Like when I was playing, a song with a flute solo was a big hit. So every session I was playing flute. The same thing when the country music came; everything I was doing was country music. Whatever is there, that's what they do.

"Rock 'n' roll was not very popular with the Juilliard students when I was there in 1954," says Ramal without rancor. "When I first started I went through all the jazz things as a player. I studied with Lennie

Tristano and I wouldn't work professionally. Then I was married at nineteen and I happened to get a job playing a rock 'n' roll thing. Before that I was playing bandstands, weddings, things like that, with old men. I had nothing in common with them. Didn't know what they were talking about. Then I played a rock 'n' roll thing weekends because I needed money, and people were clapping for my playing. People were excited. And I said, 'Well, this is great.' You know? I said to myself I'd rather do that and have people clap for me, like patting you on the back, than just sitting with a bunch of old men.

"That was just about the beginning of the rock 'n' roll era. So I was with it from the very beginning, and in the meantime I was in Juilliard. I finished Juilliard in three years and I went to Columbia for four. The last year and a half at Juilliard I started working, so when I was going to Columbia I was working with a rock 'n' roll group and during intermissions I'd go downstairs and do exercises in sixteenth-century counterpoint.

"But I found it very stimulating because I found that while I was working with the group I'd lose all my inhibitions and just think about having fun. It was like having mental relaxation. That was the difference. I'd sit with the old men—they'd never laugh and things like that—but with the rock 'n' roll they were more my age, and the people in the clubs were my age, so it became fun. I can just go by my feelings. I liked it. And I think it's because of the element in it. Like the people, and actually my own age group. Because for years, like when I was sixteen playing with the old men, it was very good to show my caliber as a musician, but it was a drag. And when I got with the young people, I had laughs and it was a ball."

In naming some hit recordings which may be traceable to his arranging skills, he pointed to "Run Away," sung by Del Shannon. Ramal said it was backed by a small group of about seven pieces. "There was an unusual rhythmical figure running through the tune. Then there was a solo passage with an organ-type instrument which we worked out and built ourselves."

He also singled out recordings made by Johnny and the Hurricanes. "I did them for years with different sounds, and they made it with just using old folk songs like 'Red River Valley.'"

Continuing on the theme of recordings helped considerably by arrangements, he pointed to "Save the Last Dance for Me" arranged by Stan Applebaum for the Drifters. Applebaum, according to Ramal, "used a two-part contrapuntal string thing, which at the time was unusual but since then has been done to death."

In preparing an arrangement much thought and maneuvering goes into pleasing the client, whether it be a vocalist or vocal group, according to Ramal. "You've got to consider the client, the things he likes, and his past performance, or the group's past things. What he's done before, his last record, and whether his things have been hits or not. You just listen to him and try to get his feeling into the song.

"In some cases, I've torn up arrangements after I've done them because they're too good. If a thing is supposed to be 'dumb' and 'horrible' they hire me to write it that way. And I get hired a lot because I *can* write that way. I can produce sounds at a session that sound like they were recorded in a cellar. That's where the market is. The cellar sound is a bad recording sound. Instead of doing things that sound real clear, you add things on to sort of fuzz it up."

Once, Ramal recalled, he did an arrangement with strings and chorus. "Everybody in the studio was flipping. 'Great!' they said. And the record came out, and it was a big hit. But the only thing you could hear was the singer and the drums. They lowered it down so when you heard the record, you had to listen hard to hear the strings."

Ramal's brows knitted up. "To be a successful arranger in popular records, you have to keep up with the times. It means buying all the records that come out, knowing what's in them, and being able to duplicate them."

Today even cowboys get social security. And as skyscrapers and motels and industrial plants reach deeper into the rural hinterlands, country music, now centered around Nashville, Tennessee, is being affected. For years now, the pure "country sound" has been seeded with the "beat" of rhythm and blues, as illustrated by the early Elvis Presley recordings. But this, too, has given way to an increasing Tin Pan Alley sound.

One of the most noted figures in country and western music and its trends is Chet Atkins, guitarist, and Manager of RCA Victor's Nashville Division. Says Atkins: " 'Country pop' is in vogue now. I make few records that are strictly C & W. Ninety-nine per cent are 'country pop.' "

On instrumentation for country and western record sessions, Atkins revealed he uses a rhythm section, vocal group, Hawaiian steel guitar, and fiddle. "For 'country pop' sound we would use rhythm section, vocal group, and violins," he says.

There is a certain amount of "purist" country and western repertoire being performed and recorded. And a lot of "standard" repertoire (the compositions of Hank Williams). But there is urbanization going on in every aspect of the field—the style of the music, the pronunciation of the lyrics—the arrangements (which often include flutes, strings, and trombones), and the choice of music. In fact, one of Chet Atkins' recent albums, released in the summer of 1963, was titled "Teen Scene" and included such "country songs" as "Bye Bye Birdie," title song of the Broadway musical hit.

Russ Garcia is a talented arranger of more than one hundred "singles" and 186 LP's, including the fine backing for the *Porgy And Bess* album with Louis Armstrong and Ella Fitzgerald on Verve. He is author of *The Professional Arranger-Composer,* published by Criterion Music. And recently he answered these questions in an airmail letter from Munich, Germany.

Q. Have good arrangers been pulled down by the advent of so many cheap songs?

A. No. A good arranger always tries to do something fresh and different even if he has to stay in a dumb framework.

Q. Can you give examples of songs "made" by superior and inventive arranging?

A. Ninety per cent of the records out!

Q. What can—and what can't—a bright arranger do with basically shallow materials?

A. Just what coiffure, make-up, gadgets, and beautiful clothes can do for a plain girl.

Added Garcia: "I live in Germany composing for TV, radio, publishers, etc., because there is more chance for artistic expression for me here now, and at the same time I have more time to enjoy life."

Possibly the luckiest of the working arrangers are those who have been connected with and attached to certain artists and recording projects that are not the quickie noisemakers. There is a sizeable market for the superior popular music LP, and operating in this area are such figures as Paul Weston, Henry Mancini, Hugo Montenegro, Billy May, Percy Faith, Ray Conniff, and Sid Ramin, artists whose efforts aren't uniformly imaginative but are often started with better music and unfettered by teenage performing talents.

One of these artists, Nelson Riddle, is an ex-trombonist from Oradell, New Jersey. Riddle and his counterparts in show music and jazz need not be inhibited by the teen market; their LP records are largely aimed at the adult market, and with this as a starting tack they are comparatively "free men," musically speaking.

"Arranging," says Riddle, "is largely an imaginative thing. When you put in the right sounds, you feel it. The only analogy I can think

of is that of a clown making up his face with white grease paint and
red putty nose. Suddenly the make-up transforms the man—it rings
true. He *is* a clown!"

Riddle is fortunate in being able to let his imagination loose. If he
were to arrange for inexperienced, musically and emotionally limited
singers, he, too, would be limited.

"With Sinatra," he has observed, "you can be more complex in your
backgrounds than in some instrumentals. With Frank you have more
latitude for you already have acceptance. But you still have to be on
guard against over-complication; it's not a sign of artistry."

Until rather recently few arrangers were known outside their own
twelve-stave orbits. But now more and more of them are acquiring
more prestige, publicity, and a "piece of the action." They are becoming
"stars" themselves. Their names are printed prominently on album covers with appropriate credit lines. Speaking rather purplishly of some of
these musical journeymen, the liner notes of one album describes them
as "a magic circle of men who turn out hit albums that are a joy to their
listeners and a credit to their own creative talents."

Another noticeable trend is that more arrangers are becoming recording artists themselves. Quite a few—Henry Mancini and Nelson
Riddle and Elmer Bernstein—have edged into the composition of film
scores, TV shows, themes, or background scores.

Some arrangers even assert that their creative contributions are such
that they' should get record royalties similar to the composer or lyricist.
But if the arranger gets a share, why not the musicians, the A & R man,
the designer of the album jacket? And what about the disc jockey promotion man who stirred up the public consciousness? The list of col-
laborative craftsmen that goes into the making of a recording are
lengthy, and once the logic is accepted it is endless.

An equally formidable objection to the arrangers' cutting themselves
in on record royalties, performance fees, and sheet music is the simple
matter of gambling with one's own time and talent. The composer or
lyricist of any musical material gambles on his own talent, supports
himself while he does the writing, and markets it. Often he cannot sell
what he writes. He may work two years on a Broadway musical and
not be certain of a production. The arranger is a technician-artist. He
comes in and gets paid as soon as he is committed to an assignment. He
doesn't gamble. He is paid for his job, which often takes but a few
hours of his day.

Though the arranger's star has gone up, he is mainly an earthbound
musical functionary. He is very much in trouble in today's "pop tune"

sector because of the level of writing and performance. The basic material rubs off. It is frequently imposssible to transcend shoddy material and inept execution, despite what some arrangers believe. Those in show music and jazz and folk music are freer, less constricted.

When the arranger can employ his imagination and craft around interesting musical raw material, he can turn out very inventive and provocative work. The arranger's aesthetic dilemma mirrors the contemporary state of popular music. When that dips low, then he descends with it, even though he sometimes puts a gloss on thirty-two bars of krypton. Very often, the arranger becomes cynical and merely grafts a few basic types of arrangements onto each type of tune. If a particular record is a hit, he will copy the "sound" and superimpose that "sound" on a new piece of material. In other words, copying is prevalent, or more accurately it is rampant and frequently mandatory.

The modern arranger has grown considerably in craft and in acknowledgement of his craftsmanship. But he also has been cut to Lilliputian size. As Harold Arlen once put it, most arrangers "puff up squeaky little tunes."

8 · TEENAGE GODS AND GODDESSES

> The recording industry, a fledgling during the heyday of vaudeville, has shown a steady remarkable growth until today it stands a major factor in the world's economy. Much of this growth is attributed to the fact that the industry has afforded this chance to new talent, as well as continually enhancing the names of established stars.
>
> —Press Release, Decca Records

Not long ago, Decca recording star, Ricky Nelson, a blue-eyed by-product of a TV situation comedy, sang this aorta-straining lament, a sort of Tin Pan Alley work song.

> *"Teen Age Idol"*
> Some people call me a teen age idol
> Some people say they envy me
> I guess they got no way of knowing
> How lonesome I can be
> I need somebody to be my baby
> Someone to tell my troubles to
> I got no time to ever find her
> 'Cause I'm just passing through
> I travel around from town to lonely town
> I guess I'll always be just a rolling stone
> If I find fortune and fame
> And lots of people know my name
> That won't mean a thing
> If I'm all alone
> I get no rest when I'm feeling weary
> I got to pack my bags and go
> I got to be somewhere tomorrow
> To smile and do my show*

More and more healthy youngsters are trying to acquire the anxiety voiced by Ricky Nelson. They are thrusting themselves into dimly-lit

*Copyright © 1962 by Nelson Music Publishing Company.

anterooms of recording companies and windowless recording studios, trying to become wealthy, famous, and "lonely"; in short, a teenage idol.

Not long ago, an interior designer put the finishing touches on the modernistic décor of an independent record firm, Atlantic Records. The executive at Atlantic was rather pleased with the execution of the furnishings, the color scheme, the choice of fabric and furniture. Then he spotted a long, expensive couch in the reception area, placed against a newly painted wall.

"Oh, one thing," he said, "put some washable stuff behind the couch. The kids hang around all day and their heads leave grease smudges on the wall." The designer dutifully put some washable vinyl on the wall behind the couch before the craniums took up oleomargarineous positions.

These days there are more than a few parents who read *Billboard,* *Variety,* and *Cash Box* instead of Dr. Spock. For next to baby-sitting and cutting the grass, teens and subteens have been taking up the popular music gambit. They rehearse in basement recording studios, in New York subways, in the streets just walking along. Not since the 1930's, since Deanna Durbin, Bobby Breen, and Shirley Temple have youngsters infiltrated popular music so successfully as entertainers.

While most youngsters are quietly cracking books late into the night to get good marks to get into college, these show-business youngsters are making the juke boxes jingle, jangle, jingle. They produce bestselling records, guest on top TV shows (variety and drama), sing teen-angled commercials, and perform, of all places, in Las Vegas. They appear in films, important feature-length productions as well as hurriedly cranked-out items such as that salute to a dance craze entitled *Hey, Let's Twist.* Some of these boys and girls—at their peak—earn $10,000 to $500,000 a year. A few—Paul Anka and Connie Francis, to name but two—have emerged as millionaires.

Except for the highly publicized record personalities, you have probably never heard of some of these teen idols unless you are under nineteen years of age. As Harry Reasoner put it on CBS-TV's "Calendar" not long ago, "Sinatra and Como are still among music's royalty, but to the kids they don't mean a thing. The popular singers are the Cascades, the Chiffons, Cookie and His Cup Cakes, the Vibrations, the Four Seasons."

Recently, Columbia Pictures purchased Nevins and Kirschner, a music publishing and talent management firm religiously devoted to the teenage stars, for $2 million. To trumpet the news the motion picture company called a press conference to which it invited the music-trade papers, *Billboard, Variety,* and *Cash Box,* as well as the daily press, including financial writers for the *Herald Tribune* and the *Wall Street Journal.*

After making the proud annnouncement of its million-dollar purchase, the film executive was asked by the *Wall Street Journal,* "What did Columbia buy?"

The film executive turned to Don Kirschner, and said, "Why don't you take this, Don?"

Kirschner began his answer with, "Well, we have Little Eva and the Cookies."

Even if Kirschner had mentioned Dinah Shore, the *Wall Street Journal* might have been a little bemused. But, as one eyewitness put it, "Little Eva and the Cookies?"

But that's the present-day music business, or a good portion of it. By the time this reaches print, Little Eva, a teenage girl singer, or the Cookies, a girls' trio from Brooklyn, or the previously mentioned recording artists, may no longer be stars; or they may be considered burntout, crumbly meteorites. But it is in the nature of today's music business that other youthful stars will flash up into Tin Pan Alley's inexhaustible planetarium. They will replace the old galaxies which have exited, not with a bang but with a monophonic whimper.

The phonograph record executives, the music publishers, the TV variety show producers, lavish as much care on these adolescents as they do on Stravinsky and Casals.

"Unlike the old days when diskeries put on juve performers into the groove as a 'freak' attraction for adult listening, the artist and repertoire men of the various companies are treating the youngsters as serious performers for the ever-growing juve market," Mike Gross, of *Billboard,* observed recently.

There are no reliable statistics on the number of popular singers; it is an amorphous field that embraces Sophie Tucker, Frank Sinatra, and the pre-shave, pre-menstruation variety. The U. S. Government's *Occupational Outlook Handbook* on the performing arts has reported that "probably fewer people than 75,000 earn the major part of their incomes from singing engagements or vocal teaching in mid-1960."

These figures cover opera singers, members of the Metropolitan Opera choral group, church groups, and those who sing along with Mitch Miller. The government handbook cautiously added: "The typical popular song does not demand that the voice be developed to cover as wide a range on the musical scale as is required for classical music, and the lack of a powerful voice may be overcome by using a microphone. Although the voice training is an asset for singers of popular music, many with untrained voices have tremendous careers."

Youngsters of all social backgrounds and social strata have dived into the popular music swim. Perhaps this is because it sounds so easy; you open your larnyx and out pours honey and money. Not long ago, the son of Bennett Cerf, the book publisher and TV personality, recorded rock 'n' roll tunes for MGM Records. Senator Stuart Symington's son has tried a singing career. An ex-medical laboratory technician, Adam Wade, has become a singer with Columbia Records. Sinatra's daughter, Nancy, now records for Dad's firm, Warner Bros.-Reprise. The brunette daughter of a furniture maker, Bernadette Castro, who began her career in show business by demonstrating on TV that even a child with a sturdy pinky could open one of her father's sofas into a bed, has tried the vocalist's ploy. And recently, the daughter of a wealthy swim-wear manufacturer, Lesley Gore, joined the pop singer ranks with a best-selling recording, "It's My Party," a triangular soap opera of how her girl friend, Judy, stole her boy friend, Johnny.

To keep the grooves packed with the maximum teenage sounds, the record companies engage in highly publicized "talent hunts." They listen to mounds of new "demos." They beat the corridors of hinterland high schools for talent who not only can sing, but can also write their own material. Youngsters know this, and they live in hopes.

Not long ago, a young girl penciled this comment on a scratched-off patch of white plaster in a Broadway music business building:

"Marge, who will be a recording star soon, was here. 2/27/62."

The young boy or girl has always been a staple in music, even in classical music. Mozart was a child prodigy who toured Europe. So were Yehudi Menuhin and Anna Maria Alberghetti. In the old canvas-topped Chautauqua Circuit, and in vaudeville, there were youngsters who were soloists or part of family acts. Judy Garland and Eddie Cantor learned their craft that way. But today, most youngsters are instant "smashes" on the basis of one 45-rpm disc. The youngster is not a performer whose cuteness has intoxicated the adults. The youngster is a star because of teenage consumers, who apparently want idols in their own adolescent, gawky image.

There are formidable economic and legal differences, too. Years ago, many youngsters were exploited by shady managers and agents and buyers of talent. Nowadays there are show business unions which protect the teen performer. They are also protected by Coogan's Law, named after movie actor Jackie Coogan, who was mercilessly taken advantage of. Under this law, the court appoints a guardian for a teen idol's money until he reaches the age of twenty-one. Usually an attorney gives the performer an allowance and banks the rest. Bobby Rydell, before he came of age, used to get $6.25 a week spending money.

The youngster, if he begins to "hit it big," finds himself surrounded by shrewd financial advisors. Before long, he or she is a corporation, owning music publishing firms, real estate, stock portfolios, and motels.

Old-time performers view the newcomers astringently. Eddie Cantor told West Coast reporter, Hal Humphrey: "I am disturbed by the younger generation in show business. They seem to think first of capital gains and bank accounts in Switzerland. You know something? When Fannie Brice, Will Rogers, Bert Williams, and I were in Ziegfeld's *Follies,* our first consideration was how to be a hit in the show."

Of course, not everybody idolizes the teenage idol.

"And what of the Great Pop Singer," critic Marya Mannes cried in the *Saturday Evening Post.*

He never took singing lessons or learned to read music. But after a few years of canny press agentry he is worth thousands of dollars a night. Reports have it that he has neglected his family, become a woman chaser, and pushed aside old friends and engaged in highly dubious business deals that in no way impede his progress, or reduce his prominence. By no standards of any kind was he ever an artist. Without his microphone, his build-up, and his servile cronies he would be nothing more than a jerk with a pleasant way of delivering a song. [In this, Miss Mannes seems to take on all popular singers as well as the teenage variety and confuses morality with talent.]

Taking deadly aim at teen singers in particular, Fred and Grace Hechinger in their book, *The Teen Age Tyranny,* assert:

The most important common denominator of most teenage idols is that they are mass-produced. They are really not people with individual characteristics; they appear to have been made in a mold. They are managed. They are "handled" commercially. They did not *grow;* they were manufactured by press agents, publicity departments, and the vast efficient machinery of public relations. Their success story is told almost entirely by dollar signs, Cadillacs, and swimming pools. They share with teenagers a semi-illiterate jargon and total absence of original ideas. Yet, in an obscenely labored way, they strive to be "wholesome." They love "Mom" and "Dad" and moon over childhood sweethearts.

With minor variations, this is the portrait many people paint of the teenage singer. Some even feel this way about the more chronologically mature vocal artists, including Paul Anka and forty-five-year-old Frank Sinatra. The world of the popular entertainer is shaped considerably by the pressures of the popular music business itself, whose rhythm is fast, frantic, and replete with spurious values and ideals.

The young singer, of course, doesn't know what he is getting into. Few have had any orientation such as is possible with New York's unique High School of the Performing Arts, which offers a solid academic curriculum as well as grounding in the basics of show business. They learn as they go along, in a high-octane world of fierce and frightening ambition.

Today's manufactured limelight falls on those temporal stars of the juke-box hierarchy—The Beach Boys, Dion, Elvis Presley. But there are lesser-known personalities who are quite popular, such as Lou Christie, who records for Roulette. Christie is a good-looking, Italian boy with several hit recordings to his credit.

"It's more difficult than I thought it would be," Christie said recently in the Manhattan offices of his press representative. "You think you make a hit record, and you have all kinds of gold rings, and you're driving around in a Cadillac. This is all false. It's hard work. And it's not all glamorous. The glamour is, I guess, when you're on stage.

"You can't live the business twenty-four hours a day or you will crack up.

"I'm on the road traveling a lot—so much that I get very little time off. I'm on a lot of teenage tours. I've been on Dick Clark tours, which last about thirty-five days, and some other tours that really kept me busy.

"The tours can be murder. Sometimes you have to pick up and go five hundred miles. Usually you go right from the bus to the stage. A tour may start in Florida, go up to Montreal, and then swing southwest sharply to Texas, all in one thirty-day period. A lot depends on who you're on tour with. You can have a lot of fun with the kids. But it gets to be a drag.

"And then when I get a week off I usually work at a club, or I'm doing promotion or publicity or something. I love it. It was really lonely at first, because I missed my brothers and sisters. But I'm getting used to it now."

These teen tours are mobile pressure-cookers and the caged-in atmosphere frequently erupts into scenes. One rock 'n' roll star tells of a well-known singer who "put me down. I knocked him down three times, and they threatened to put me off the tour."

Few popular music personalities are sit-at-home personalities who merely walk in and out of a recording studio and go home until the next recording date. They make appearances, visit disc jockey shows, fulfill TV, theater, country fair, and college dates. Speed is the occupa-

tional characteristic of their lives. A few years ago, three young pop
singers, Buddy Holly, Ritchie Valens, and J. P. ("Big Bopper") Rich-
ardson were on a charter flight between Mason City, Iowa, and Fargo,
North Dakota. They had been on a bone-wearying bus tour. They decided to take a plane to the next stop, so they could secure clean laundry and rest up a bit. Just outside of Mason City (the locale of Meredith Willson's *The Music Man*) the plane crashed in a corn-tasseled
field, killing all three.

Nor are the teen stars the only ones affected by the grueling pace.
On his way home to Shreveport, Louisiana, after an engagement, cowboy singer Johnny Horton's car collided with one driven by a Texas
A & M student. Horton died instantly. Horton had reached fame with
his hit recording, "The Battle of New Orleans." The obituary pages
also have listed the names of Jesse Belvin and Eddie Cochran, who
died in car accidents. And in March, 1963, a planeload of country and
western artists, including Patsy Cline, met flaming death while en route
to play a benefit for the widow of a Kansas City disc jockey they had
all known. The pace is fast and often deadly.

On the road or on promotion tours, young teen stars often discover
the delights of room service. But sometimes they request more than
food. According to the New York *Daily News*, one fourteen-year-old
told a recording executive brusquely that he wanted "a woman sent to
his room." The eyewitness said: "I wanted to spank him but you don't
slap a million dollars in the mouth."

Save for the confusion in the area of where to spank, there is a great
deal of moral confusion as these teenagers sing songs of love, sad love,
happy love, tonight is our night to love, and then are supposed to act
pristine. From this passion-tinctured milieu there has arisen incidents
and paternity suits, some of which have erupted into the newspapers.

Not long ago, a Hollywood girl named Edith Morgan alleged that
Frankie Avalon was the father of her daughter, born December 7, 1961.
Avalon's attorney revealed that for two years they paid the girl $14,000
to keep quiet. Eventually the girl broke the story on the eve of Avalon's
marriage to another girl. One lively footnote was the fact that the
girl named the baby Ginger, after Frankie's recording, "Gingerbread."
The case is being fought in the courts.

A close observer of the teen scene says: "They're not bad kids on the
whole. They have a sound and somebody grabs them and says, 'I'm
going to make you a big star.' Of course it goes to their heads. They
can't help it. Then they think they're stars. They think they're great
talents and really they're not. Too bad even their parents aren't realistic
about it. If I were a parent of one of these rock 'n' roll artists and he

had a number-one record, I would make sure that every penny possible would go into the bank, because it's gonna be a long, cold winter."

Favorably impressed by the teen idols is Joan Egan, a girl publicist who works for Connie De Nave, press agent for many young recording artists.

"I have been working for them for about a year and a half. I expected to find them a bunch of hoods. Instead I find they are intelligent young people, ambitious and hard-working. They are, on the whole, very happy, 'having a ball,' though they are on the road almost all the time and work very hard. They are different from adults in that they have more ideals, more dreams of success." She also finds them not as competitive as adults.

Another veteran of the record business disputes this rather candied portrait. "These kids have tremendous egos, tremendous drive. [If you've noticed they are small and slight.] But they are bad lovers, and most of them are bad earners," he says. "If I had a son, and he showed any interest in going into the music business, I would whip him."

An editor of a music trade newspaper is pretty glum about these youngsters, too. "One of the very earliest of the teenage stars, I could spank. He was very cocky, arrogant. But I understand he's mellowed a bit; but most of them are dumb little kids. They don't know anything but the song they sing, and the sound they make. It's all lollipops and sodas. The folk-music group has boosted the IQ level. But now it's getting a little synthetic, and its practitioners are a little above 'pop' rock 'n' roll.

"A lot of them have become very wealthy. They buy homes for their parents in New Jersey with 40-inch TV sets.

"They play shy. 'Sir, this' and 'Sir, that.' They're all going onward. They're going to be actors and serious singers. The 'pop' rock 'n' roll writers are all going to write a Broadway show. I think that's what they're told to say to the adult press. Some, I hear, are great sex athletes, particularly backstage between rock 'n' roll shows.

"I can't take them seriously. They're untrained. They have to do a little vocal trick, which is generally souped up in a recording studio. Actually, adults shouldn't be reviewing the records they make. They should be reviewed by a twelve-year-old."

Vocal groups are as evident in present-day Tin Pan Alley as lead sheets. The names they bear deserve recognition. There are the straightaway names of no particular significance, such as the Shirelles, the Chantels, the Crests, the Teen Queens, the Browns, the Falcons. Then there are the tricky-titled combinations: the Trans-sistors, the

Righteous Brothers, the Rocky Fellers. One group is called the Ohio Untouchables. On the scene, too, have been vocal groups inspired by automobiles: the Impalas, the Imperials, and the Fleetwoods and Cadillacs. No Volkswagens yet, but give them time.

The young singers and groups often appear ridiculous for two reasons. First, if they choose teen materials, they isolate themselves from the adult market. And secondly, if they try a more mature song with deeper meanings and more musical involvement—or very sophisticated lyrics—they appear to be way out of their depth. In either case, the singers and groups within the puberty and post-puberty age group are frequently impaled on these twin dilemmas.

In the musical theater and Hollywood films, young people haven't been that estranged and that torn apart by the demands of two "markets." As a pigtailed youngster in *The Wizard of Oz,* Judy Garland's singing was a vocal triumph to young and old alike; her MGM original cast recording from the sound track is still one of the classics of popular music recording. So are many of the individual songs she sang in motion pictures as a youngster, because they were written to fit a character and a story line.

Similarly, young performers in *West Side Story* had material that developed character and story. Young artists *can* make contributions, but this can be done best in musical theater or musical films, rather than in single songs in which lyrics, music, performance, and arrangement are grooved for different "markets."

The young performer's role in the record business is a daily concern of Columbia's popular A & R chief, Dave Kapralik. "One of the artists I'm most proud of is Dion," he stated. "Dee is twenty-two now, and I'm most proud because I think that—not exploring the area of whether what he is saying is good or bad societally—he is a prime and effective *communicator.* That he is perhaps the best communicator, and by that I also mean reflector of the disoriented, querulous, frequently frightened, lonely, questioning adolescent—and, I might add, a good segment of the adult population.

"Another artist is Barbra Streisand, who I will parallel with Dee, though vocally they are not related. She is a prime communicator. I call them *'truth persons.'* They talk truth and they talk directly without the imposition of archness or slickness or stage craftiness or self-consciousness. They feel something and they communicate it."

Applying his "communicator theory" to today's songwriters, Kapralik observed: "I would define 'good' as that which works. Something pragmatic. I'm not qualified to interpret 'good' [writers] for you, beyond saying just if they communicate effectively . . . it's good."

Kapralik's "truth" theory seems to be this: anybody who writes or sings songs that sell, regardless of talent, communicates and is therefore a "truth person." Miss Streisand happens to be a fine talent. But if many who reach the charts, including Dion, are "truth persons," then the whole history of musical art may be expunged, the North Pole is interchangeable with the blistering sands of Arabia, and balsa wood is mahogany.

If anybody wants to listen to a covey of "truth persons" who successfully communicated to the adolescent market during the 1950's, here's a compact discography: Alan Freed's "Memory Lane" (End LP 314); Alan Freed's "Golden Pics" (End LP 313); Elvis Presley's "Golden Records," Volume I (RCA Victor LPM 1717). For a more recent collection of modern communicators, there's Murray K's "Golden Gassers for a Dance Party" (Roulette); the "Dimension Dolls" (Volume 1); and Chubby Checker's "Your Twist Party" (Cameo-Parkway P. 7007).

Years ago, singers were brought up gradually through apprenticeship with bands, and they acquired musicianship through osmosis, or at least a respect for musicianship. The bands were the little red schoolhouses for Frank Sinatra, Ella Fitzgerald, Peggy Lee, Lee Wiley, June Christy, Chris Connor, Jo Stafford. Without ever having heard of Professor John Dewey's activist philosophy they were learning by doing—in a milieu of craftsmanship, of respect for musical value. Gifted arrangers tried new things. Bands were the popular articles, and so a musical approach was elevated.

But as the song says: ". . . but that was long ago." However, despite the corrosive and bleak influences at work in the past decade, popular music's good music tradition is still an influence. Building on the best of the past, there have emerged fresh and captivating talents over the last few years. Most are not "originals," but they do have talent, taste, musicality. There is Jack Jones, Ray Charles, Tony Bennett, Barbra Streisand, Nina Simone, Oscar Brown Jr., Johnny Mathis, Eydie Gorme, Steve Lawrence, and Andy Williams.

Among the arranger-conductors to come along have been Henry Mancini, Ray Conniff, and Nelson Riddle. In jazz there is a plethora of raw talent. In folk music, several major talents have come along songwriter-singer Bob Dylan and singer Joan Baez, also Harry Belafonte and Odetta. In the popular folk idiom, there are the granddaddies of campus balladeers, the Kingston Trio.

Still popular are the more mature artists and groups—Frank Sinatra, Nat Cole, Perry Como, Mary Martin, Ethel Merman, Peggy Lee, Jo Stafford, Mel Torme, Ella Fitzgerald, Pete Seeger, Erroll Garner, Count

Basie, Duke Ellington, Stan Kenton, Benny Goodman, Bing Crosby, the Weavers, Percy Faith, Paul Weston, Louis Armstrong, Dinah Shore, Margaret Whiting, and Judy Garland.

Most of the above talents represent the Golden Age of Popular Music—mid-thirties and forties. The "sing along" poobah, Mitch Miller, the Grandpa Moses of choral singing, is really not an artistic force, one way or the other, except as a curator of musical Americana. He knows better, but he is content to work his gold mine.

The outlets for more mature artists are the long-playing record, TV variety shows, Broadway, dramatic movies, world tours; night clubs, and "concerts," which are not really concerts at all, but old-fashioned "stage shows," with singing groups, jazz groups, and the solo artist. These more mature artists represent the highest standards of American popular music in terms of performance. Their work is the musical standard by which all new young popular performers are judged. This group makes a living because they are true performers, even though they may or may not sell vast quantities of records. They are true "pros" of their craft.

There is an immense chasm between the teen popular artist and the more mature singers, instrumentalists, arranger-conductors, and band-leaders, and that is largely craftsmanship. The teenager has simply not yet learned his trade. He is an impermanent idol, often dependent on microphone amplification, gimmicky "sounds" and tape editing.

However, the "pros" can be faulted, too. Too many of them have been treading comfortable grounds where they can walk with their eyes shut. They do not try enough new material. They are content to run down a list of "standards." Sinatra has yet to appear in an original Hollywood musical of quality which will challenge his musical and acting abilities. Judy Garland sticks largely to reprises of her past achievements. They have not been able to employ their talents in exciting, provocative new ways—and with new content.

"I feel sorry," Nat "King" Cole once said, "for the newcomers rushed into the limelight with their fake 'million sales' announcements and then quickly dropped." What has happened to some of the teenage "veterans," the recording stars of the 1950's? A few have stuck to it, and are clinging on desperately, and many have fallen along the way.

Murray Kaufman, who calls himself, Murray the "K," a popular New York City disc jockey, recalled recently, "I see one of the boys to this day who had the number-one New York record, 'Tonight, Tonight.' That is one of the rock 'n' roll 'Goldies' ('classics'), the favorite of all the 'Goldies' in New York, in every contest or poll. He just got promoted. He was a bus boy, now he's a captain at the Copacabana."

To sustain himself, a member of a top-ranking vocal group of the decade, the Harp-Tones, has worked as a delivery boy on a truck. Some of the girl members of vocal groups are now married with little rock 'n' rollers of their own. Some of the male groups have been splintered up by the Army. Frankie Lymon, who at the age of fourteen wrote and recorded a smash hit, "Why Do Fools Fall in Love?" is now married, but he rarely records. However, his agent, Bob Redcross, reports that "Frankie still works. And he makes $400 to $500 a week when he works clubs."

The Bobettes, a high-school singing group, are now out of high school, but they have never reached their previous status when they had a hit recording concerning their school principal. "The mortality rate is fantastic," says Murray "K."

"The big stars are still around and still working. Pat Boone, Frankie Avalon, Fabian, Bobby Darin, Elvis Presley, Connie Francis, Brenda Lee. Lloyd Price is around, but he's not popular any more. The Platters are around. Bill Haley's still around, but he has lost his popularity. By the kids, Patti Page, Rosemary Clooney, Georgia Gibbs, they're passé now."

Of the young juke-box stars, Kaufman noted: "What's the old saying, 'It's better to have loved and lost than never to have loved at all?' Then, too, how much have they prepared? Have they put five or six years into it? Then I feel sorry for them. Have they just gone and made a record and had a good break and they're out? Then I don't feel sorry for them."

A Tin Pan Alley observer says: "There are hundreds of them maybe, who had a little flicker of success and then the flame just disappears. It's blown out, and nothing remains, nothing. It's a shame because most of these kids are spoiled for life.

"You see them around every day. Just go to the Brill Building. You see kids who had hits four and five years ago. And they're still coming around. They're starving but, 'Oh, my next record's going to be a hit'— if they can get a record. They go to all the publishers, they keep going around looking for managers, and they become vulnerable.

"So they get into the hands of managers who sign them up to ridiculous contracts. The manager figures, 'Well, the kid had a hit. Maybe I can get him a record deal and if he clicks maybe I can make a lot of money with him.' They don't really do anything with him. They don't try to be constructive. They don't try to build them."

Nineteen-year-old Marcy Jo once had two hit discs. A recording artist who is a friend of hers says that she is now quite dispirited. "She's had about five releases lately, and nothing has made it. But she's living with her parents, and she's going to try to get a job now. But she still wants to continue. She's going to be a secretary or something. But deep down in her heart, she'll always try the business again. She is a great talent, but it seems like they're just cutting the wrong things with her. And she can't tell them what to do, because they don't listen."

Show business is notoriously packed with sudden, violent shifts. Irving Berlin once philosophized in that sunny, show business anthem, "There's No Business Like Show Business," that "Yesterday they told you you would not go far, tonight you open and there you are, next day on your dressing room they've hung a star."

The reverse is also poignantly true. Yesterday they made you a star, and tomorrow it is the line at the unemployment insurance. The predicament has been stated by two young songwriters, Cynthia Weil and Barry Mann, in this journalistic ditty:

> *Teen-Age Has-Been*
> Oh, oh, oh, they call me a teen-age has been
> The kids all pity me
> Oh, oh, oh, my first record sold a million
> My second one just sold three.
>
> My mother bought one
> My father bought one
> And I bought one.*

9 · WHAT PRICE PAYOLA?

> Terrible teen-singer: Do you really think you're going to get
> disc jockeys to play my song?
> Record Executive: It's getting tougher. But I'm on my way
> to see one . . . right after I stop off at the bank.
> —Stan Freberg's "The Old Payola Roll Blues" (Capitol)

In 1957, a low-budget Paramount Pictures film appeared called *Mister Rock And Roll*. It starred "the king of the big beat," a lean, highly excitable, popular New York disc jockey named Alan Freed, a man who accompanied lashing rock 'n' roll records on the air by whacking his hands on a fat telephone book. Ads for the motion picture rhapsodized: "*New Music Not Just for the Young . . . it's for everyone. A new kind of American Folk Music is sweeping the world just as jazz and swing did before.*"

As the picture progressed, Alan Freed, playing "himself," took to the microphone, according to the *New York Times* "to prove to a news editor that rock 'n' roll isn't really a bad influence on youngsters."

Five years later, a debt-ridden, saddened, dispirited forty-year-old Alan Freed stood before Justice John Murtagh in New York's Criminal Court and pleaded guilty to accepting bribes from record companies to play their recordings on radio and on TV. The disc jockey had been accused of accepting $30,650 from seven record firms.

Corruption didn't originate with Alan Freed. Nor was he alone among his contemporaries, nor was he the biggest offender. The biggest taker of them all, according to government probers, was the disc jockey with the face of a shiny Eagle Scout who had just walked a little old lady across the street—Dick Clark of TV fame. As Representative John Bennett of Michigan put it: "I think it is pretty convincing that Clark was involved with payola as all the other disc jockeys, but on a much larger scale."

The congressional disclosures about Clark's lucrative interlocking interests in popular music didn't bury payola. And neither did Alan Freed's conviction or the destruction of his radio and TV career. Payola still goes on under the turntable.

Despite the Oren Harris Committee investigations (1959-60), despite the cease and desist orders by the Federal Trade Commission, despite a more watchful station management and the convictions of a handful of disc jockeys, payola continues. With one striking change, however. Since the Oren Harris Committee exposed corruption evidence in the form of canceled checks, today's givers and takers are far more circumspect. It is all on a cash basis.

The contemporary consensus of record officials, music publishers, and record distributors over the extent of payola is divided. Some say that it is "on the decline," that it "hardly exists." Some say it is back "as big as ever." One music executive says that you can't stop payola because there are all kinds of clandestine ways to dispense it. He put it mysteriously, "There's ways, there's ways."

Some of the workings of payola have the flavor of a rollicking Keystone Cops comedy. *Billboard* (February 16, 1963) sketched these scenes which occurred at a West Side Air Terminal in New York City:

[The setting: people are buying tickets and magazines and waiting for the airport limousine.]

Scene 1: Suddenly a car pulls up. A man gets out. He is lugging two cartons of 45-rpm records. He enters the terminal, stops in front of the 25-cent lockers. He opens the locker door, puts the 200 records inside, puts in a coin, locks the door, and leaves.

A few minutes later, a man enters—a different man. He stops in front of the same locker. He opens the door with his key. He takes out the two cartons of records. He carries them out to his car. He speeds up and over the West Side Highway with his records, stops in front of a discount record shop. He sells the records to the proprietor, pockets the cash, walks out.

SLOW DISSOLVE TO:

Scene 2 (same terminal): Two more men enter the West Side Airlines Terminal. They pay no attention to the people downstairs, but go upstairs to the gent's room. After they are inside, one man hands the other some money—in small bills. The second man pockets the cash. They exit.

SLOW DISSOLVE TO:

Scene 3 (same terminal): A man walks in. He buys a ticket for a plane to Washington. He pays cash. A few hours later a different man walks in. He goes up to the same airline counter. He tells the young lady that he had to cancel his trip. He redeems the ticket and pockets the cash.

FADE OUT.

When this story appeared under the headline, "And Now They're Calling It Flyola," a prominent New York disc jockey scoffed at the article's authenticity. "Who needs to go into such jazz? You can just send the guy a batch of money in a plain envelope through the mail."

Regardless of the skepticism as to the methodology, few in the music and record business believe that payola has stopped. In the wake of his conviction, Alan Freed observed: "Payola is just as prevalent in the business today."

For those who are uninitiated in Tin Pan Alley slanguage, it might be worth defining payola, for it has obvious and *sub rosa* meanings. Here is a good working definition employed by the Federal Trade Commission (FTC) in its complaints regarding unethical practices of record companies and record distributors: *Payola:* "money or other valuable considerations given to disc jockeys to expose records in which record companies have a financial interest."

The government definition continues: " 'Exposure' means playing a record, day after day, sometimes as much as six to ten times daily and substantially increasing its sales. The disc jockeys conceal the fact that they are paid for broadcasting the songs and misrepresent to listeners that they select these records independently and without bias either on each record's merits, or public popularity.

"This deception has the tendency to mislead the public into buying the 'exposed' which they otherwise might not have purchased, and also to advance these recordings in popularity polls, which in turn tends to increase their sales substantially. The payment of 'payola' has the capacity to suppress competition."

The largesse need not go to disc jockeys alone. In the LP version of the late Huey Long's "Share the Wealth" program, valuable considerations also went to record station librarians and program directors who had the power to suggest recordings to broadcast, or even insert them on programs.

As ever, corruption in the popular music field has more angles than the famed geodesic domes of Buckminster Fuller. Some experts say that payola is still active, particularly among rhythm and blues disc jockeys who play an inordinate amount of rock 'n' roll, bastardized "gospel pop," and rhythm and blues on the Negro-oriented stations. Those who pay out the money in return for exposure and air play are

(1) record manufacturers, (2) distributors, (3) record promotion men, (4) managers of record talent, and (5) owners of the music and lyrics, the music publishers. More about the rhythm and blues disc jockeys later.

Then there is the borderline kind of payola, the expense account variety. This is hardly a modern invention. Here record and music business interests pay for out-of-town disc jockeys to come to New York, and take in the big city, all expenses paid. They pick up the tab for the hotel, theater tickets, good food and entertainment.

The disc-jockey-run record hop is still a formidable aspect of corruption. Disc jockeys insist that acts come down to their dance promotions for which they charge teenagers admission. Or else they won't play the artists' records, or won't play them frequently, which is equally vindictive.

Though the disc jockey has been singled out, there exists, and always has existed, vertical payola. The grand design is as follows. Payola begins with the creation itself. Sharp-shooting music publishers pay A & R men a percentage of their record royalties (25 to 50 per cent) for having the record producer use his product.

Unethical A & R men often exact this from the music publisher. Sometimes the record producer is paid to liberate a previously recorded disc that is imprisoned "in the can." This is trade jargon for the hundreds of songs recorded that are on tape, but that are not yet released and on the market.

Songwriters, too, are asked to contribute. Composer Philip Springer, co-author of three million-disc single records and such popular 45 rpm's as the slinky Yuletide invitation to Saint Nick, "Santa Baby," sung by Eartha Kitt, says: "I have been asked to contribute toward illegal payolas. I've been asked to give 'insurance,' to give a part of my song away.

"This has happened many times. In fact, it's not the exception to sign away one-third of my song in order to get a top artist to sing it. That one-third would go to the top artist. I don't know who took it, but that was the price I had to pay to get my song recorded."

Besides the artist or his personal manager demanding one-third or one-half of the record royalties—otherwise the artist won't tarnish his golden larynx—there is another problem: the music publishing houses owned by record stars. There is nothing illegal in this tactic. But it puts the legitimate music publisher in a squeeze, and forces the songwriters to gravitate toward the star's own corporate entities. One music executive says: "This does not mean the star will sing junk just to make a few extra dollars. They won't endanger their career singing cheap stuff. But they could put it on the 'B' side." Some 'artists' are so greedy, they'll sing anything if it's going to profit them."

And with the low standards of music and lyrics in today's popular music business, the gulf between varying popular music materials are seldom audible. In most cases, the record artists are choosing between swatches of *Kitsch*, the highbrow terminology employed to denote "aesthetic junk."

There is TV payola, too. Behind the scenes there is a fabulous and complex subterranean war going on in connection with the music you hear on variety programs, "game shows," situation comedies, dramas, and westerns. TV themes, "bridges," cues, because of their widespread usage, are important money-makers to the owners. So music publishers, songwriters, TV program packagers, and TV musical directors are all involved in involved deals, as sinuous as the multi-colored twisted wires inside a thick cable for a piece of the video music action.

Jack O'Brian, New York *Journal-American* columnist, once reported: "One big TV name owns several music publishing projects with one old Tin Pan Alley trio, and another in partnership with several other TV stars via still another veteran tune tycoon. Probers [Oren Harris Committee sleuths] so far estimate that he fills about 80 per cent of his TV opportunities from his own unpublicized opportunities . . . A quiz show firm got $40,000 advance (plus other profits) from one of Tin Pan Alley's big firms for an 'exclusive pact' to play only said firm's music but got scared a few months ago when the quiz fix got too hot. The 'Feds' know all about this, too. They split what ASCAP calls [and frowns on] 'secret performing credits.'"

Short, fragmentary pieces of TV music—"bridges," cues, themes "can earn upward of $20,000 over a period of years," says Ivan Mogull, music publisher and an East Coast representative of Four Star Tele-vision, in which Charles Boyer and David Niven, among others, are partnered. With the syndication of many programs, the performance credits for these video shows are lucrative and of lengthy duration, in the U. S. and in foreign markets. Foreign performing rights societies pay a pretty penny to those owners of the music heard on TV screens.

"Some big-name writers won't take on the writing of a theme for a TV series unless they own the music publishing rights," he asserted. "They say, 'Look, I'd like to do it, but you have to give me the publish-ing rights.'"

When Jack Paar exited the NBC-TV "Tonight" program, Johnny Carson came on in his place and brought with him a light quizzical manner and a spanking new theme song titled "Johnny's Theme." Behind the theme lurked an interesting story uncovered by William Carr and Gene Grove in the New York *Post:*

[Johnny's theme] is played perhaps a dozen times during each evening show, and it earns handsome royalties every time it is played. The royalties go from BMI [Broadcast Music Inc.], a performing rights organization, to the song's publisher, Spanka Music, owned by Singer Paul Anka, and to the theme song's writers, Anka—and Johnny Carson.

The two reporters observed, "How much Carson contributed to the writing of the song [actually a musical theme], only he and Anka can say, but there's no question but that he had the power to decide that the song would be used, and thus earn thousands of dollars in royalties."

Record retailers, too, have been rooting in the thickets of payola. Today very classy record shops in important, heavily trafficked shopping areas in the U. S., and some not so elegant or dignified, demand costly "free albums" in exchange for putting one in their shop windows. This often goes for Broadway musical cast albums, as well as less noteworthy products.

Of this device, *Variety* recently stated: "A quick tour around the Broadway area shops points up the situation with products spotlighted in certain store windows by company and some individual platters on display that seem remote picks in terms of customer interest."

Payola is color-blind. Years ago, Abel Green of *Variety* noted: "All the major labels recognize that in the R & B [rhythm and blues] field, they can't compete with the independents who thrive strictly on the 'pay-off system.'" Today, it is still going on. There are approximately eight hundred Negro disc jockeys on about two hundred stations comprising what might be called Negro radio. A lot of these stations are owned by whites. For example, a pioneer German-language announcer from the crystal set days, Egmont Sonderling, now owns a chain of seven coast-to-coast stations from WWRL (New York) to KDIA (Oakland, Cal.).

Historically, Negroes have been barred from getting jobs in American "white radio." Consequently, Negro-oriented stations arose. These days they are profitable, going concerns; and they are beamed toward a rich market. Not long ago, *Sponsor* (October 11, 1962) put out a special directory of Negro-appeal radio stations, and editorially observed: "1963's Opportunity: $27 billion spending force of Negro consumers is uncommitted; high market is waiting to be tapped."

These stations have their own approach toward showmanship; some battle hard to expose slumlords and exploitation, and they cover the integration fight in great detail. Negro radio even has its own news service supplementing the AP and UPI, called ACNS.

The disc jockeys on these stations aren't paid as much as their white brethren, and many are not members of the radio and TV union—AFTRA. They play a lot of rhythm and blues and rock 'n' roll, rock-a-billy, certain kinds of teen music by those impossible vocal groups, and also gospel music (pure and denatured), as well as jazz. Not all of these disc jockeys have the outstretched palm and are taking; only certain choice individuals, who can command fervent listener loyalty in key markets.

These Negro rhythm and blues disc jockeys are important in the broader mass of the popular music for they pride themselves in "breaking"—the trade term for initiating and exposing and playing new hits. A recent trade paper headline put it this way:

R & B JOCKEYS PACK LOTS OF WEIGHT
IN GETTING NEW ENTRIES OFF AND RUNNING

WIELD SUBSTANTIAL INFLUENCE ON KINDS OF
SINGLES COMPANIES MAKE

The influence of these rhythm and blues jockeys in popular music cannot be downgraded. Some have estimated that as many as 20 to 30 per cent of current kits are "kicked off" by R & B disc jockeys.

The less rectangular jazz field, which prides itself on being "unsquare," has not been immune from the standardized patterns of payola. Many jazz disc jockeys may read *Downbeat,* but they take their real politik from Dun and Bradstreet. So far as taking is concerned, "jazz disc jockeys are no exception," jazz columnist Ralph J. Gleason has observed in an article, "Is Payola Here to Stay?" He noted: "We hear about deejays that hit the courts. We don't hear about the others. The more money at stake the greater the degree of corruption." He painted a corrupt picture of the underside of jazz that perhaps only George Grosz could sketch. Gleason reported:

Racket money is legitimized by funneling it through night clubs, promotion enterprises, song companies, and/or record manufacturers. Complex tie-ins with night clubs, record companies, publishing companies force the artist to record albums of songs published by a certain company in order to get a two- or four-week booking in certain clubs. A disc jockey says "play my club" or "play my concert" and I'll plug your records.

Follow the course of song promotion and publicity and you follow the course of payola in popular music. In the earliest days, perhaps the most important media of song exploitation was vaudeville. Consequently, music publishers paid acts—singers, vocal groups—$25 to $100 a week to perform their material on the Albee and Keith circuits. If a big-name sang a certain song night after night, in theaters across the country, that song had a chance of becoming popular. It was a mixture of Pavlovian—conditioned reflex and "the two-a-day."

All during the 20's, 30's, and 40's, the most popular musical performers were approached, and many didn't run from temptation. In his book, *My Time Is Your Time*, Rudy Vallee candidly says: "Throughout the years Jolson, Cantor, Harry Richman, Sophie Tucker, Gene Austin (and Vallee) have been 'cut in' on songs they made into hits."

The one-time Ivy League idol of millions went further, and argued that taking payola is perfectly all right. "Nuts, I've said it and I'm glad. After all, without an entertainer working on a song, a song very often languishes on the shelf."

When radio entered the music scene in a big way, there began an era in which singers and bands could reach hundreds of thousands in one fell swoop. This "plug" beat vaudeville handily. Song pluggers, pleased by such centralization, converged upon bandleaders and singers on radio. Soon payola began to be the style. The big band era of swing and eagerly listened-to hotel broadcasts brought payola to a high gloss of development. "Some of the biggest and most revered names in swing were takers," said one music authority recently. "They were great guys, but notorious takers."

Up until the 1940's millions listened to big swing bands and such up-and-coming vocalists as Frank Sinatra, Nat Cole, Dinah Shore. If you didn't like any of them you could turn the dial and hear a "house band," or studio orchestra. Hundreds of stations had their own bands with their own styles. But the man behind the turntable, the cheap and economical mechanical music man—the disc jockey—was slowly gaining power and prominence. These music men didn't have seventy-six trombones, but they had 50,000 watts.

By 1944, there were more than 3,000 disc jockeys on more than 900 stations. These platter-spinners included Martin Block, Lois January, Arthur Godfrey, and Al Jarvis. With daily programs, bits of patter, and "live" interviews, the disc jockeys became increasingly popular.

With the rise of TV and the subsequent decline in radio revenue, the disc jockeys replaced the more costly "live remotes," the studio house bands. Since the 1950's the disc jockeys have become the undisputed princes of popular music promotion and exploitation.

As they reached thousands of popular music devotees daily, it was perhaps inevitable that they were approached by men in wing collars bearing gifts. They were asked to favor certain records for a fee. Favoring is the genteel, almost Victorian expression for it. Actually piquant expressions blossomed to describe the process: "giving it a ride," "laying it on," "the hype." The "hype," of course, came from the word, "hypo," short for "hypodermic."

There followed a wild, wooly, and incredible decade, which to many observers affected the very musical tastes of the nation. For years this was sort of hinted at, guessed, whispered about, and only the bribers and takers knew. But in 1959, a committee with the unlikely name of the House Committee on Legislative Oversight, headed by a be-spectacled, subdued Congressman from Arkansas, Oren Harris, started probing. Its findings—and the implications of the findings—are still only dimly understood. But the cute angle and stratagems were beau-tifully set forth in the beige-covered official report of the Oren Harris Committee titled: *Payola and Other Deceptive Practices in the Broad-casting Field.*

The hearings produced front-page headlines all over the country:

DEEJAY GOT 15G PAYOLA FOR 'LISTENING'

FTC POURING IT ON PAYOLA
ISSUES 10 MORE COMPLAINTS

PROBERS CALL CLARK TOP PAYOLA MAN

By the time the gavel was sounded ending the hearings, the in-vestigating unit announced that it had turned up $263,245 in payola—payment by record companies to 207 disc jockeys and other broadcast personnel in 42 cities to plug particular records. The figure would have to be multiplied several times because these figures came merely from a "mail survey." Had a fine-tooth-comb investigation been conducted, the figure would probably be several million dollars.

The hearings also disclosed the fabulous interlocking interests of Richard (Dick) Clark, then the most powerful single promotional force in the music and record business because of his daily two-hour ABC-TV program, "American Bandstand." His interests were detailed in charts that resembled a table of a business organization. Here are a few of the companies in which he was financially involved:

1. Swan Records (50%)
2. Jamie Records (25%)
3. Chips Record Distributing Corp. (33⅓%)

4. Hunt Records (100%)
5. Ownership of musical copyrights to 160 compositions
6. Mallard Pressing Corp. (50%)
7. Globe Record Manufacturing (100%)

Clark also owned 100% of the following music publishing enterprises: Arch Music Corp., January Music Co., Sea-Lark Enterprises.

The "Bandstand" program, with its video dance party format—couples danced as a record star "lip-synced" to his new recording—started in August 1957. As it boomed to popularity, Clark became connected with all sorts of enterprises as well as those noted above. He got involved in the manufacture of record carrying cases, teenage jewelry, the inception of a teen publication (which interestingly enough never got off the ground). To those suspicious minds who inferred that he used his post as a popular TV broadcaster to further his own businesses, Clark replied that he had done nothing wrong. And there was nothing wrong or particularly unusual in his multi-faceted activities. He said: "You will find gentlemen who are disc jockeys who are record manufacturers, who are managers of artists." As to payola, there was this priceless dialogue:

Q.: Do you know of your own knowledge that other companies have engaged in payola to pay someone to play their records?
Dick Clark: Of direct firsthand knowledge?
Q.: Yes, sir.
Clark: I've only read about it in the paper.

Clark was really a big banana-fish. He earned approximately $576,-000 from 1957-59 from varied off-the-screen sources. Leonard Goldenson, President of the American Broadcasting Company, reported that the "Bandstand" program, then a top-rated daily show, had brought in $6 million in revenue.

Since the hearings, Clark no longer has his daily program, but still can be seen on ABC-TV once a week. He also has a successful syndicated radio disc jockey program. In June, 1963, he published a book which counsels on etiquette for teenagers. A trade-paper ad for the book stated: "National promotion and publicity by Dick Clark." The volume had a fascinating title: *To Goof Or Not to Goof.*

Clark's technique was indirection: he didn't seem to be paid directly on a weekly basis. Mostly he was involved in music and record interests which benefited from his association with television. However, many disc jockeys were on a weekly or monthly retainer; sometimes they got paid on a per-recording basis.

Frequently the disc jockey would take payola to play records that he would have put on the spindle anyway. Here is the dialogue between a committee investigator and Norm Prescott, a prominent Boston disc jockey, who admitted taking payola on this apparent electronic oddity.

> *Mr. Bennett:* It is hard to believe that they would pay you for playing something you would play anyway.
> *Prescott:* They were guaranteed a certain exposure on their labels. They did not care what became a hit, as long as it was their record that you played, and not somebody else's.

Some disc jockeys got paid in any number of imaginative ways. One, an ex-advertising man and ex-legitimate actor turned disc jockey, thirty-two-year-old Joe Finan, a $40,000-a-year Cleveland radio and televison personality, disclosed more twists and sharp angles than a good auto-test run. Finan was a key voice in Cleveland, a big Midwest record market over KWY. Wherever he turned people offered him money, and like Ado Annie in *Oklahoma,* he couldn't say "No."

Finan said he got money as an expert "consultant." He got paid thousands of dollars as a "listener." As an example, for two years he was paid $50 a week to listen to each and every 'pop' record Mercury Records put out. Of course, if he found them of broadcast quality he would play them. But he had scruples, he asserted: "I have absolutely refused to play a Mercury Record that was bad," he told Congressional probers.

In a satirical recording, "The Old Payola Roll Blues," quoted earlier, Stan Freberg created a funny documentary of a young vinegar-voiced kid pulled in off the streets to be groomed as a rock 'n' roll star. During the text, Freberg implies that the big firms didn't engage in payola, only the "little rock 'n' roll labels" run by characters such as "Barney Schlock." Freberg's Barney Schlock says: "Us little rock 'n' roll labels got a good thing going. We pay off a few guys in key cities here, rig a few charts there, and BINGO! a new hit parade."

Independent distributors and "swingin'" record companies may have begun payola—modern style—in a fierce, competitive situation. But before long, practically all the big, respectable companies joined in. Those who opened their billfolds to Finan consisted of executives and individuals connected with the marketing of RCA Victor, Decca, Epic, United Artist, and Mercury. These companies aren't small operations.

In one case, Finan worked out a deal where he got a "commission." He and Joe Carlton of Carlton Records worked out an arrangement whereby Finan got "2½ cents per thousand sold in the Cleveland area, and 3 cents if the record went over 20,000."

In Finan's testimony, and that of Norman Prescott and other disc jockeys, a point is underlined that is often missed in understanding the role of payola. When a record manufacturer paid off disc jockeys, they were in a sense, buying air time or "spots," like an advertiser, except that the station didn't get its share of the revenue. The manufacturer knew that a $50 or $100-a-week payment could not conceivably guarantee the popularity of a record among fickle teenagedom. But he knew that without exposure the record might just as well have stayed inside the metal "stamper" and never been thrust into the cold, cruel world.

As Joe Finan put it: "It was a physical impossibility to listen to 200 [records] a week."

Payola was a device by which the record interests at least knew that their records were listened to, and that they received exposure.

Equally Byzantine dodges developed in Tin Pan Alley's own "Teapot Dome" hearings: making disc jockeys co-owners of songs; having disc jockeys report to trade papers or local listings certain new recordings as "smashes"; having record distributors use radio station letterheads to send in reports ostensibly by disc jockeys, on which were the most popular records then on the air, or "breaking out"; paying off record station librarians, particularly those whose word carried weight with certain key disc jockeys.

All these dodges had one purpose: to build unknown recordings into national significance. Does aesthetics enter into these clandestine merchandising operations?

Certainly, according to Norman Prescott:

Mr. Bennett: Well, do you think without payola that a lot of this so-called junk music, rock and roll stuff, which appeals to the teenagers would be played anyway, regardless of the payola?

Mr. Prescott: Never get on the air.

Mr. Bennett: Do you think payola is responsible for it?

Mr. Prescott: Yes, it keeps it on the air, because it fills pockets.

It started innocently enough at Miami's airport. Voices of welcome rang out, "Welcome DJ's." A fleet of limousines stood at attention as record executives and record publicists, and the chauffeurs hired by them, sang out greetings to the first flush of disc jockeys arriving. They were converging for the "Second Annual Radio Programing Seminar and Disc Jockey Convention of 1959."

Some of the disc jockeys even brought their wives and children along. But it turned out to be far from an event for wives and kids. For the next three days turned out to be three days Miami will never forget. For three days, the winged gods of the music business turned the city inside out, and even made the help at the famed Americana Hotel, convention headquarters, gasp. There were free all-night parties, free barbecues, free poolside bar service. Pretty call girls, the $100-a-day variety, were there for the taking—free.

To the swinging beat of Count Basie and the sultry songs of Peggy Lee, who entertained, the hi-fi hi-jinks took place on Memorial Day weekend, May 29, 30, 31. Of course, Miami isn't a prudish town, and plays host to lots of conventions, from nurses to college frats, where fun and frivolity are not exactly banned. But even the natives never heard of such goings-on. So much so that one Miami newspaper characterized the gathering of record industry high society as "Booze, Broads, and Brawls."

The three-day jamboree was so wild it figured in the Oren Harris Congressional Committee investigation. But the full extent of the "on the house" orgiastic activity at the "convention" has been suppressed so far, even in Congressional testimony.

One record executive who has since departed from the record field ("after ten years I've got nothing to show for it") described the goings-on: "It was a swinging affair with about sixty to eighty call girls around. They ran out of Miami girls and had to import girls from New York, Puerto Rico, and Chicago.

"One record firm had a big suite at poolside. It had five girls in one room, seven in another. Disc jockeys were lined up waiting their turn. At night, the call girls would show up and approach the tables with the disc jockeys sitting there with their wives. The embarrassed disc jockeys would jump into the pool.

"One night, there was a poolside party with pizza and beer. People were sitting singing folk songs. And the call girls joined in."

Some hootenanny.

There were but fractional attendances at the "seminars" on radio programing. Most of the disc jockeys were getting crocked or engaging in sensual pleasures in convention headquarters or in nearby hotels. For three days they were cocks of the palm-lined walk. Two disc jockeys busily used their time spending real money to buy Confederate paper money. Reason? RCA Victor had announced that disc jockeys who visited its suite would be given "paper money," which later could be used to "buy" valuable prizes, including a trip to Europe and a new car. This team of platter spinners went around Miami scrounging up paper money, often going on their knees to fish some of it out of corners. When auction time came, they outbid everybody. They came in with cardboard cartons of paper money and won practically all of the valuable prizes

The 1959 Florida convention—which gave the music and recording business a black eye—revealed that the disc jockeys weren't Puritans. Of course, the private sex habits of disc jockeys are nobody's business but their own. But the sex in Miami wasn't private sex, but a commodity, a business investment, aimed at influencing the disc jockey's choice of popular music, which is a public matter.

Some of the disc jockeys revealed themselves to be cheap chiselers as well. For example, some disc jockeys took advantage of record company largesse from the start. They mooched air travel and hotel expenses from the companies and record distributors to their own convention by the plea of poverty: "How am I going to get there?"

And they further exploited their benefactors by taking their vacations after the close of the conventions. Some "deejays" didn't leave their hotel suites; yet they stayed a week and ten days after the convention. And the record companies and the distributors had to pick up the tabs. These disc jockeys bought expensive shirts and sportswear in the hotel shops and charged it to their rooms. This, too, the recording companies and distributors had to pay for.

Payola is now under sharp scrutiny. After the 1959 payola scandals, an Amendment to the Federal Communication Act of 1934 was passed with stricter provision against corruption in radio and television. Anybody convicted of payola could receive a $10,000 fine and a year in jail. Also, commercial bribery laws in some states—laws which are on the books—are occasionally enforced. Making it rougher for the disc jockey, anxious for fringe benefits, is the fact that radio-station management has created a committee system which develops a "play-list" from which the disc jockey may choose records to play. The disc jockey knows that if he programs certain recordings over and over again he may be suspect. "Bread," the synonym for payola in the music business, is getting harder to come by. And disc jockeys resist the starch diet for fear of jeopardizing their jobs.

However, payola still continues, but more furtively than ever. And along with its continuance there are some who find that payola isn't so abhorrent. Former bandleader Jerry Blaine is a handsome, natty, ex-musician who led his own band from 1931 to 1941. He now runs one of the country's largest record distributorships, Cosnat, named after two extinct record companies that only old record collectors may remember, Cosmo and National. He also puts out popular music and comedy albums on 45-rpm and on long-playing records under assorted labels, including Jubilee and Josie.

"I wish," he said recently in Manhattan, "they had left it the way it was [with payola]. Well, at least we knew what records were being played. We didn't waste any money. If we paid, at that time, to get a record played, at least the guy or disc jockey was obligated to us, and we know we got the record played. Today, if the fellow says, 'I'll play it for you,' we don't know whether he'll play it or not. I think it's a lot cheaper, a lot cheaper to have payola than it is today. Because we spent X amount of dollars on a record and we got it played. And if the record didn't have it, we got off the record. Today we don't know how long the record's going to take or who's playing it. It was better with payola."

Such ambivalent honesty deserves a considered reply. Payola may be a compact, economical way of exploiting songs for record manufacturers, record distributors, and record promotion men, but it also is too costly. It plays havoc with a precious aspect of man, his sensitivity, his taste, and the democratic process. Taste is a dynamic, moving process. It can change for the better or for the worse. The theory underlying democratic concepts and enlightened humanistic psychology is that everybody has within him the potentialities of acquiring a heightened sensitivity, greater breadth and vision. Tin Pan Alley's apology for much of its inferior product is that there is something in the genetic make-up of man, and of teenagers—particularly teenage girls—that makes them bewitched by the tawdry and the tinsel. It may be the reverse: that certain business folkways, corrupt practices, our ways of marketing music are more at fault than the buyers of pap.

Some music reporters used to scoff at payola, asserting that payola cannot "make a hit." This is quite true. Payola cannot guarantee hit recordings or even good-selling items. It cannot catapult any kid-off-the-street and make him a national idol. And what makes it equally confusing, there are discs that are "sleepers" that rise to the top without too much synthetic disc jockey flagellation.

But that is the narrow truth.

The broader sociological truth is that with the payola approach, fantastically heavy during the fifties, there was the most fabulous exposure of a cheap genre of music that ordinarily might have been wastepaper basketed; discs that depend on dull repetition, gimmicks, and electronic manipulation.

Perhaps one hundred to two hundred disc jockeys in key markets whipped up a storm concerning certain records. As some of these crashed through, these recordings became the models for rivals to copy;

and soon a genre, a style, a sound, a lyric content was born. And a certain kind of pawky, no-voiced adolescent was heard throughout the land, with the adults quizzically wondering why.

Political campaigns, public relations, the mass media, entertainment publicity have demonstrated that anything can be sold, if it is marketed astutely enough, if enough pressure is applied. There is such a thing as cultural brainwashing, and acquired taste. Modern advertising has shown that if you pour enough money into a product it *can* be sold; cheaper products, promoted more carefully, can outsell superior products, ineffectually merchandised.

In *Sociology*, William Ogburn and Meyer Nimkoff state . . . the propagandist, like the puppeteer, generally works out of sight, so we are influenced without knowing it. . . . Publics are often scattered, loosely organized, and confused. On the other hand, there are in modern society various organized groups of individuals who know what they want and are out to get it. They have products, or services, or ideas they wish to sell and are in search of as large a market as possible.

Rock 'n' roll, "dumb pop" balladry, and country and western "pop" developed in an era of unparalleled payola, during a decade when Hollywood movie musicals were pretty inert, and Broadway was holding out for quality practically alone. It surfaced in an era of tremendous struggle between the American Society for Composers, Authors and Publishers representing the big-city sophisticated music, and Broadcast Music, Inc., which represented more than 95 per cent of the rock 'n' roll writers, the country and western writers, the rhythm and blues writers, and the amateur writers. Within this context, the "dumb music" got appreciable exposure and made its way.

It may be that teenagers would have chosen the "big beat music," the "dumb music," without being propagandized through undercover payola paid by what *Variety* once termed "avaricious disc jockeys and sharp-shooting record manufacturers and local distributors." It is possible that people would freely choose cheap products, movies, TV programs, and inferior books and magazines without advertising or promotion whoopla. It is possible that Adolf Hitler would have ascended to power without his mesmerizing voice at highly-staged, open-air meetings and on radio, and without his astute use of propaganda, just on the virtues of National Socialism. However, modern society doesn't exist without powerful forces vying for attention, to sell *something*—products, political ideas, or popular music.

When an important regional disc jockey reaches 100,000 teenagers daily, the choice of his recordings—and what he plays over and over again—is bound to have an impact. By his manner, his tone of voice, he can suggest that this certain artist is a "comer," that a certain recording is a "driving version," and he can whip up a lot of enthusiasm, particularly among youngsters. An audience of millions watching Dick Clark at his candy-coated zenith over ABC-TV was bound to be affected by the choice of artists he put on, and what they played or "lip-synced." To argue otherwise is really "blowin' in the wind."

Disc jockey payola must be eyed clinically as a form of special pleading, musical propaganda. As the Celler committee pointed out, "The greatest song in the world cannot gain popularity unless the public is given a chance to hear it." Pincered by overproduction of records, recording companies, record publicists, distributors paid off key platter-spinners. These disc jockeys did proselytize rock 'n' roll and "dumb" music, as well as other types of music. Sometimes the deal would be for a disc jockey to "lay it on" for all the lines that a certain record distributor carried. But eventually the disc jockeys did sell the rock 'n' roll "sound" and artists—and the teen "pop" songs. The payola merchandising did pay off.

The "swinging" record interests—who didn't compete on terms of quality, didn't have the "name singers" or the access to the best new material by the most expert writers—got off a few hits. Religiously addicted to trend-watching, the record business saw rock 'n' roll as the coming commercial thing. They jumped on the pelvic bandwagon, and produced copies and imitations of the hits. Before long, practically all the record companies were rocking and rolling. Thus a new genre—singing style, lyrical approach, instrumentation—was helped along.

What started as a trickle became a mighty torrent that inundated areas other than the music and record business. Because of the interrelatedness of much of modern show business, cheap music fricasseed millions on TV, and even spread to Hollywood movies. And magazine publishing was also affected. Soon the pages of important U. S. magazines were graced—or disgraced—by picture stories and articles about the new teenage idols. And though these articles and stories were often less than idolatrous, the fact remains that in the minds of many, they represented popular music. This still goes on.

Payola continues, although whether it continues at the feverish pitch that existed in the late 50's is open to dispute among students of corruption. However, the types of music it helped put across, the styles, the "sounds," and the lyric-content are not in dispute. The records and "top ten" charts are audio-visual evidence.

Speaking of taste manipulation, the New York *Herald Tribune* ran a penetrating editorial in the days that followed the 1959 Congressional disclosures of payola in the music business that is worthy of reprinting at length. It went:

It may be tempting to dismiss the whole business with the thought that most of the music played by disk jockeys is so bad that it's almost a relief to learn that they had to be paid to play it. But "payola" is only one aspect of a disturbing situation, and not even the most important one. For the entire atmosphere engendered by the "pushing" of songs toward the teenage market, with its accompanying debasement of taste, is degrading and unhealthy. The race for best-sellerdom in "pops" records, like the race for top ratings by quiz shows, inevitably is a race toward the lowest common denominator. Musically, the end result of the race is rock 'n' roll. And when the teenage balladeers and the "deejays" themselves become national idols of sorts, more than musical standards are being abandoned.

To punish the fakers and takers is a relatively simple operation. But to restore lost standards and repair shoddy goods, to try to elevate low tastes rather than pandering to them—these are tasks that are as difficult as they are important. But they are the price of "payola."

10 · CORRUPTION UNLIMITED

Oh, the shark has pretty teeth, dear.
—Berthold Brecht, *The Threepenny Opera*

W. ("Walter") N. Currier is a Tin Pan Alley private eye. Since 1958 he has specialized in investigative work in the music and record field. Unlike the fictional detective, his job isn't the pursuit of the murderer who kills with rare curare poison or the one-eyed fiend who seeks to terrorize the world with a blinding, magenta super-ray. Currier's job is to discover the hard-to-find invoices resting in record manufacturers' files. Or to observe the wear of metal stampers and try to estimate how many records have been pressed by them.

Not long ago, an unhappy popular music publisher called Currier. He had had a smash hit on the "charts." Upon receipt of the record company's statement of royalty earnings, he was stunned to find a rather dehydrated figure. He suspected cheating. Would Currier investigate?

Currier took the case. He found out who pressed the record for the independent record company (the record company supplies the "master"; the pressing plant makes finished copies—a common practice). But the pressing plant didn't want to give Currier any information, for fear of losing the account.

One night, Currier penetrated the record pressing plant, disguised as a plant guard. Stealthily, he headed toward the office. He finally reached his destination—the files. After much riffling through the papers and file folders he spotted the pressing orders given by the record company. He took the papers to a corner of the room. There, underneath a blanket, he photographed the invoices with a flash-camera.

The Tin Pan Alley music publisher was delighted. Armed with the photographic copies of the record pressing plant bills, he confronted the record company. The facts were pretty much self-evident. Many more records were pressed—and presumably sold—for the record was a truly, big-selling item. Without going to court, the record company made a cash settlement with Currier's client.

A man of about forty-five, Currier is assisted, depending on the flow of cases, by approximately twenty agents, male and female. His offices are at 5 Beekman Place, New York City. Elsewhere he has a fantastic work-file of deception and illicit activities in the music field. From time to time, he is active in the marital affairs of music personalities; but mostly, his case-load covers the business aspects of the music business.

Several leitmotifs recur in Currier's work: (1) music publishers who suspect that they are not getting an accurate audit; (2) records artists who suspect they, too, are being given a short count by record companies; (3) "moonlighting" by sales promotion men who handle several freelance accounts while in the employ of one record company; and (4) artists and repertoire (A & R) men who take payola.

Crime, popular-music style, is a serious multimillion-dollar business. There are a raffish band of wheelers and dealers, including some very respectable men from very respectable firms who engage in cheating and dubious illicit practices. This is white-collar crime, but there is also a bloodier side—beatings and terrorism in the juke-box industry practiced by *Cosa Nostra* ("Our Thing") and unaffiliated hoods. The payola scandal shocked the American public. But it hardly touched the music industry's clandestine activities, some of which resemble Laurel and Hardy, as revised by the poet-dramatist of corruption, Jean Genet.

One type of popular music operator is the "disc pirate," who operates with a sample disc and a record label, instead of a black eye-patch and a cutlass. In the known annals of the record counterfeiters, there are few to equal the brass of the man who came into a major record company not long ago. He wanted thousands of copies made of his sample disc. Every large record company manufactures "singles" or LP's for anybody who will pay the freight; in fact, RCA Victor, Columbia, and Decca compete for their "custom-pressing" business. The record company produced the recording asked for by the man—in quantity.

Later it was discovered the "new" recording was a copy, note for note, of one of the parent company's own discs. The record was unwittingly pressed, labels were put on, and the disc was retailed before the imitative nature of it was discovered.

Tin Pan Alley music publisher, Redd Evans, once observed that "You'll find more enlightened people in darkest Africa than you will in Tin Pan Alley." It is not easy to quarrel with his rather dyspeptic evaluation. There are recording companies that do not pay record artists earned royalties, or at least do not pay them the accurate amount. The cheating record companies practice understatement with music publishers as well. And continuing this daisy chain of interrelated rookery, many music publishers do not give composers and lyricists the right "count" so far as record and sheet music royalties are concerned.

Equally important in the shadowy "flip" side of the popular music business is the multimillion-dollar counterfeiting racket. A continuing scandal is the dominance of the racketeers in the lucrative juke-box industry. There is also the fascinating undercover form of music publishing known as "the fake books." And there are the equally devilish marketing inventions that are the product of intense jugular-competition—the "freebies" and the "return privilege."

Nor is this litany of subterfuge exhausted. In a field, where everybody sings of love, love, love, there are hateful little promotional gambits that injure the American consumer, directly in his pocketbook and aural awareness. An expanding and perfectly legitimate part of the record business are the co-called "budget lines," long-playing records of show tunes, country and western, polkas, Latin American materials, twist records, dance records, which sell at supermarkets and dime stores for less than one dollar.

Many budget discs are of excellent quality, and are well worth the money. But one of the favorite tactics of the low-budget producers of inexpensive discs is to produce albums starring a popular music "name." That personality's photograph—and his name—are emblazoned in large type on the record cover. Yet an examination of the LP, and even of the cover, reveals that the popular artist can be heard on only two or three musical selections. The remainder of the LP is filled up with unknown artists. Because of the impulse nature of the sale, the consumer does not discover this until he puts the LP on his spindle.

Kewpie-faced Connie Francis has practically kept MGM Records in business over the past decade with a fantastic string of 45-rpm "pop single" hits and LP best-sellers. Yet she has had acrimonious rows with that firm over royalties. Singer Brook Benton recently sued Mercury Records claiming $750,000 in alleged unpaid royalties. Lesser-known recording personalities have taken to the courts when they have discovered the record company had deducted large sums for photographs, radio and TV exploitation expenses, and extremely costly record session expenses.

Some record companies shrug off accusing fingers with the piquant statement, "We're as honest as the next guy." Or: "We use IBM machines." Meanwhile, the battle of artist versus record company over disc royalties continues.

In self-protection, the established record artist—or his personal representative—will call in his own accountants to check the record company's books. The artist is sometimes given the contractual right to fine-tooth comb all the pressing orders, shipping invoices, and the distributor payments concerning the artist's recordings. Sometimes these accountants get a percentage of what they find as a sort of "finder's fee."

One accountancy firm was hired to go on a "treasure hunt" through the books of a record manufacturer. It found enormous sums due the artist. But the artist didn't, apparently, want to pay a hefty percentage to the accountancy firm. The artist turned around and signed a new contract with the record company containing greatly improved guarantees of yearly earnings and other worthwhile provisions. The rejected accountants were left holding the ledger entries. So they sued the artist.

Why these things happen can be traced to multiple reasons: the company's cash position, or a poor financial year; the management's free-and-easy usage of the artists and music publishers' royalty money to promote new "product"; in some cases of small independent labels, naked self-enrichment.

Besides record firms who cheat their artists, there are actual unresolved differences of interpretation over two marketing processes. These focus on three terrible words: "freebies" and "return privilege."

Hundreds of thousands of "pop singles" and LP's are given away as free merchandise. It has been customary for a record distributor to buy 1,000 "singles," and receive 300 free. He may buy albums on a two-for-five deal, and receive seven LP's; two "freebies" for the five purchased. According to the record company accountants, neither the singer, vocal group, or orchestra conductor, nor the music publisher, nor the composer-lyricist need be paid royalties on merchandise given away by the record companies in a special "deal."

In this era of discounting, the record company VIP's assert that "freebies" are promotional giveaways; that they stimulate the buying and marketing of recordings. The record-artist-publisher-writer, whose economic good health is tied to the royalties on each disc, asserts that he should be paid the normal royalty rate on every record.

Practically every record company favors this no-royalty-on-"freebies" philosophy. It is not easy to fight this battle, for the record company can fight back with all sorts of dodges, such as cutting down the promotion of those artists who fight too hard. One music publisher says: "It is not easy to enforce the royalty structure. Music publishers do not have the bargaining power to force the record companies to pay." Unstated is the potential danger that if one music publisher pushes the record company too aggressively to pay royalties on "freebie" merchandise, the record company A & R executives, who reflect management, may retaliate by not recording that publisher's material, or at least by diminishing the number of musical copyrights used from his catalogue. Clearly some sort of legal ruling is needed; thousands of dollars are being lost as a result of a questionable marketing strategy.

The record companies do not feel that they are being unethical. Their argument runs this way: "We're [the record company] not getting paid. So you [the music publishers] don't get paid." But one music business attorney asserted, "It's a rationalization. The contracts in connection with royalties read on *'records manufactured and sold.'*"

The artists (and music publishers and songwriters) also complain along another sensitive zone—the "return privilege." The return privilege, briefly, means that the record dealer or record distributor is allowed to return, or exchange, a certain percentage of his purchase. Some record manufacturers hold back sizable royalties claiming that they don't know if the records are coming back.

The recording artist gets bruised in such a bind; a good portion of his earnings can be lying around in the record company's account. This can be a considerable sum, and the records could already be on some collector's shelf. But as far as the record manufacturer is concerned, he feels that they might come back—from the record distributor, from the dealer. There is no official reporting back to the record company by the record dealer on what he has actually sold. So the return privilege results in a present-day situation whereby moneys are retained by record companies on the basis of a futuristic pessimism. "Who knows when the returns start coming in?"

One music business attorney says: "There has to be a time limit on this return privilege. Otherwise record companies hold onto your royalties for years. After a few years, if you plague them, they'll pay it in dribbles, a little dribble at a time."

Another angle that hurts record artists is the matter of the artist paying for the cost of a recording session. Some record companies will take a serious look at their books, right before royalty time. They may see they owe a certain artist $6,000. So, quick as an automatic record-changer, they'll schedule a series of 45-rpm "pop single" record sessions, or an LP date. By the time the sessions are over and the tapes in spools, the royalty account of the artist is canceled by the cost of the record sessions. In fact, the artist may owe the company money.

You may ask: doesn't the record company have to pay for the session? Yes, but except for payments to the musicians, they can frequently stall the recording studio where the session was conducted, the free-lance A & R man sometimes employed. Meanwhile they can retain a portion of the $6,000 to keep wheeling and dealing.

Its cable address is "Songrite." It is a 35-mm.-frame away from the 55th Street Playhouse, a Manhattan motion picture theater, and its entrance is through a jet black door which modulates into the offices of the American Guild of Authors and Composers, formerly called the Songwriters Protective Association. A grizzled veteran, devoted to protecting the professional composer and lyricist, AGAC has long been concerned with "short count" writer's royalties.

In the late 1950's, AGAC came up with the "collection of royalties plan." Simply put, the plan puts crack accountants onto auditing the music publishers' books. For this service, the songwriter pays 5 per cent of his publishing royalties. Some music publishers objected, but they saw the light when AGAC waved authorizations from the healthy segments of important songwriters. Today, most composers and lyricists receive a more accurate count—and a check for what they have earned.

This is one of AGAC's happiest achievements, and the one most personally fulfilling to big-boned, tall Burton Lane . . . president. Composer Burton Lane is as concerned with the minutiae of Washington tax laws, juke-box exemptions, dodges of music publishers and record companies, and world politics as he is with notes on a staff. A talented music writer, he has written the music for "Everything I Have Is Yours," and "There's A Great Day Comin', Manana," but he is most noted for his lovely score for the socially-conscious, humor-flecked fantasy, *Finian's Rainbow*.

He told the songwriters in his 1962 report:

And now we come to my favorite subject, the collection plan. This is my favorite subject because it is a meat and potatoes subject; it deals with something tangible. The results we get from our efforts are immediate. You can put it in your pocket, or you can deposit it in a bank.

Since we started the Collection and Auditing Program, I am convinced that this is the most significant service our Guild has ever performed for our members. Throughout the thirty-one years the biggest single complaint we had was that writers were not being paid their royalties on time, or that they weren't being paid all the royalties they were entitled to, or they weren't being paid any royalties at all.

Let us see to what extent this plan has corrected the situation. During the first two years we recovered for our members, $250,000. Last year we recovered $91,019.65. Now listen to this, so far through our auditing program we have uncovered for our members $106,744.17. Imagine, these were monies, your royalties, which for one reason or another were never paid to you, and which our auditors discovered. And we haven't scratched the surface yet.

Lane once recalled that when a music publisher was confronted with his neglect to send one songwriter a considerable sum of money, he replied: "I don't know where to get in touch with him."

Lane added that AGAC had just retained the firm of Price, Water-house Company which has world-wide connections and offices. "We believe," said Lane, "that it is in the foreign field where we sustain our greatest losses."

AGAC, the songwriters' watchdog, is on its way to cracking much of the writer-royalty problem, a historic economic headache. For since the birth of commercial music-publishing, songwriters have been denied a portion of their earnings. As songs became more important commercial commodities with increasing usage by the recording industry, radio, movies, TV, and foreign licensing, there has been increasing temptation to dishonesty. Many of the better Tin Pan Alley music publishers did keep to a reputable position, but there is no doubt that most of them needed careful auditing.

Today, the songwriter is protected in terms of radio usage by the two licensing agencies, ASCAP and BMI. But he still receives a huge chunk of money from the multiple recordings by thousands and thousands of recording firms, both fledgling and vintage. But the songwriter does not receive from the record companies directly—whether it be Columbia, RCA Victor, or Decca, or Swan, Scepter, Vee-Jay, Cameo-Parkway, Hickory, or any one of others—a statement of who used what, and how many of each recording were sold. Nor does he receive such a statement from foreign record manufacturers. These are sent to the music publisher. The music publisher has the responsibility of preparing a statement of earnings, accompanied by a check.

No individual songwriter could possibly keep track of the many labels which may have pressed his song, in the U.S. or abroad, even if he wanted to. For many years, the songwriters have groaned about the situation, but couldn't think of any way to check up on the music publisher. Needless to say, in the beginning many major music publishers stood like middle-aged Horatios at the gates guarding the "books" against AGAC's accountants. If many a writer of popular music can buy a new pair of shoes, a new car, a house, or a college education for his son or daughter, they can thank AGAC's digit-detectives, and the men who dreamed up the plan and sold it to the songwriters.

The Tin Pan Alley music publisher—a crusty breed that has managed to survive the lunatic, unstable enterprise built on thirty-two bars and some record star's erotic as well as musical appeal—has got his troubles, too. He has to get paid by the thousands of record companies that have sprouted up in the past decade, and that have employed his copyrights in recordings.

Walter Douglas, tall, silver-haired president of the Music Publishers

Protective Association, claims that getting paid isn't easy. "There are those who completely scorn the responsibility of reporting on the records they have pressed. Some partially tell. They say they've pressed 25,000 when they have pressed 50,000. Added to this are the bootleggers who merely press recordings illegally.

"Some record companies have hundreds of excuses not to pay. First they claim they had unusually heavy returns. Another excuse is the lack of immediate cash. The record retailers aren't paying them. And then they'll argue that a protected work is PD (Public Domain). They stall and kick. They have 3,000 excuses."

To make record companies toe the line, the Music Publishers Protective Association doesn't resort to shooting tactics. Instead they rely on Harry Fox, the publisher's financial watchdog. In his sixties, Fox heads up a giant auditing service and licensing agency for several hundred music publishers, including Mills, Chappell, the Warner Brothers group (MPHC), Frank Music, and Famous Music. Fox operates out of plush Park Avenue offices in the Olin Mathieson Building. But he is rarely there. According to an associate he is "frequently out of town reviewing audits." Harry Fox, Agent and Trustee—his official title—sees to it that record companies, film and TV producers, at home and abroad, take out licenses for recordings, or taping, or TV, or motion picture synchronization. Through these licenses he can check up on whether those who were supposed to pay, did pay. He charges 5 per cent for this financial bird-dogging. He reportedly finds thousands in unpaid royalties due music publishers, and indirectly due writers, too. He operates—as does the AGAC—through accountancy firms who specialize in the music business. One music business attorney says: "He apparently is a fine financial prober. The music publishers are happy with his work."

In an out-of-the-way record manufacturing plant at this very moment, some scholars are locked in thought. No high-school teacher preparing for the principal's exam ever studied any harder, or with more devotion. Their text? *Billboard's* and *Cash Box's* best-selling charts.

The question is: which of the 'hot singles' of best-selling long-playing popular music albums should they produce? The "scholars" include the record manufacturer, a small printer of record labels, a cardboard album manufacturer, and a distributor or record salesman. They are the record pirates, sometimes known as disc pirates or record counterfeiters, and they siphon off approximately $20 million a year from the record industry.

Counterfeiters take a regular commercial pressing, which they have bought in a retail store, and they reproduce it—the recording, the album cover, the record label, the liner notes, everything including the three-color jacket, and, of course, the logo of the original record company.

Some of the counterfeiters aren't too aesthetic. If they can't duplicate a brown label or a blue label, they'll use an orange label. The cardinal thing is to get the product out quickly, while it's hot.

The record manufacturers aren't the only ones hurt financially. "In addition," says Henry Brief, executive secretary of the Record Industry Association of America (RIAA), "the artists and composers have been deprived of their royalties and the federal government of its taxes. Perhaps most important of all, an awful lot of records of questionable quality have been foisted upon an unsuspecting public."

Continued Brief: "Because he does not withstand the costs of the legitimate manufacturer—the costs of recording, paying the musicians, paying for the promotion, publicity and exploitation, paying royalties to the music copyright owners and the artists, paying the various taxes involved, and maintaining costly equipment—the counterfeiter can undersell the legitimate manufacturer and yet come up with an extremely handsome profit."

Until rather recently the laws against record bootlegging were as thin as the polyethelene record bags. But through the prodding of the record and music industry, Congress passed a law with a little more bite. On October 9, 1962, President John Kennedy signed legislation which makes it a federal crime to counterfeit records and tapes. The FBI, it is hoped, will help run down these brigands of balladry energetically.

Besides counterfeiting, there are a host of other under-the-turntable activities. They include unauthorized duplication of recordings. Here, recordings are dubbed, in whole or in part, without authorization, and are then sold under other labels. There is also a minor Muzak-type industry in which certain companies sell a background music service without getting legal permission from the copyright owners of the music. These are programed from a wide variety of popular recordings and fed to office buildings, lobbies, restaurants, and other public places. This is a service for profit. Yet the background service merchandiser fails to pay a license fee for usage of the music, all of which works to cheat the music publishers, the composer-lyricists, and record manufacturers, who merely brought the whole thing into being.

Then there are radio syndicators who are "electronic pirates." They tape programs based upon material from phonograph records and sell the shows to radio stations, without paying a fee. The Record Industry Association of America has sponsored legislation to stop the flagrant and unauthorized duplication of recordings for profit.

Not long ago, a man who called himself "Mel Allen" put more than a thousand copies of a newly printed book into the trunk of a sparkling white Cadillac bearing Chicago license plates. He called on music stores and music-instrument stores. To the retailer, his approach would be simple.

"Would you like to have a terrific bargain?" he would ask.

The retailers frequently nodded, skeptically. "Allen" proceeded to flourish an extraordinary anthology of popular song hits, containing more than a thousand songs. The price of the book would vary; sometimes it would be $10, sometimes $12 or $15.

The retailer quickly saw the advantage of the anthology. A consumer could have a thousand "standards"—anything from "White Christmas" to "Dancing in the Dark"—for a nominal sum. If bought separately, the songs would cost approximately $650. This was a "buy."

He had few turn-downs, did "Allen." But eventually he was caught, for he was violating the copyright law. He was typical of the men who function in the subculture of the music business. He and his kind print, bind, and sell "fake books"—a multimillion-dollar headache to America's music publishers.

Alan Siegel, of Wattenberg and Wattenberg, New York music business attorneys, has analyzed some of the background of the "fake-book racket."

"Originally, 'fake books' were limited in number and in scope and were printed in the form of black loose-leaf books. At one time a version of the 'fake book,' which was well printed and professionally bound, was entering the country from Japan."

In 1961, the Music Publishers Protective Association became aware of the alarming proportions that the racket had assumed. They were convinced that the undercover publishing had, to a great extent, altered the character and volume of the sheet-music sales.

"There are approximately ten different 'fake books' in circulation," says Siegel. "These vary in content, format, and cover. The simple black loose-leaf book has given away to decoratively embossed and plastic-bound books. The books are being constantly updated when sufficiently new show and popular music has been published to justify a new book. The average book contains approximately 1,000 copyrighted musical compositions. We have, however, encountered books containing 3,000 musical compositions, and some with considerably less than 1,000."

The traffic in "fake books" has assumed such large proportions that its producers have deemed it economically sound to make books aimed at specific instruments. Thus, there is an "Organ Fake Book" and "Guitar Fake Book." One "fake book" distributor has estimated that the books have become a $7-million-a-year industry.

Characterizing such men who engage in the manufacture, distribution, and sale of these fakes as "immoral and unsavory," Siegel reports that the music publishing industry is bent on cracking this racket. Their private investigators go into retail stores and buy the fakes. Later, the publishers institute civil actions against such establishments for copyright infringements. Ultimately, they work backward, to catch the supplier and printer.

They shine, they glitter, they pour out music ceaselessly—happy sounds, unhappy sounds, country and western sounds, even waltzes and polkas. But they are all happy sounds to *Cosa Nostra* ("Our Thing"). The syndicate and regional subsyndicates run a considerable portion of the juke-box business, notably in the lush territories.

In the explosive inside story of Sidney Slater, one-time intimate of the Gallo group of Brooklyn hoodlums, which appeared in the *Saturday Evening Post*, Quentin Reynolds quotes Slater about the rivalry between the Gallo mobsters and the *Cosa Nostra* of New York led by Joe Profaci. Intra-mob rivalry, shootings, beatings had begun. Slater said:

"By now things had dried up around town. I mean numbers, brokers, bookies, *even operators of juke boxes* [my emphasis] were afraid of getting caught in the middle of the fight between two mobs, and a lot of them were going to Vegas or Hot Springs."

Many juke-box operators are legitimate, hard-working independent small businessmen—harassed and complaining about taxes and "help." But informed opinion indicates that the gangsters who are up to their pointy shoes in night clubs, restaurants, laundries, hotels, and trucking are profoundly involved in the juke-box industry.

Their influence upon the nature and quality of popular music is not decisive. But their juke-box holdings are extremely important. The blinking, multicolored hi-fi and stereo mechanical disc jockeys provide a steady source of funds for "buys" in the international drug market, prostitution, gambling, the takeover of legitimate enterprises; and they provide money for the concomitant of all illegal activity, political corruption, and police corruption.

Juke boxes started out as coin-operated entertainment devices in "penny parlors" around the turn of the century. Along with the title of the selection, the consumer was told the name of the composer and lyricist. Today, juke boxes do not mention the writers and cost ten cents a selection in the United States. They are everywhere—bars, restaurants, even recreation centers. The nation's juke boxes are the record industry's largest single customer. In 1962 they reportedly bought forty-nine million single records and LP's. Occasionally, a juke-box operator with syndicate ties has tried to push a certain singer, a certain tune, or a certain record company. But as one observer puts it, "This may get them into the juke boxes. But they can't make the people play the records. The 'hoods' want to make money. So it is to their economic interest to stock up on the most popular artist and re-cordings, and in this area they cannot dominate."

Juke boxes, this argument runs, basically reflect what is already popu-lar. Unknown tunes, unknown singers or vocal groups or orchestras won't do the syndicate any good.

The takeover of the juke-box field in key markets is annotated in the famous hearings on improper activities in the labor or management field of the 85th Congress, whose chairman was Senator John L. McClel-lan of Arkansas. Its chief counsel was Robert Kennedy. The report cov-ering inquiries in 1958 and 1959 does not make pretty reading. It recalls the not so gentle tactics of the Capone era.

Here, one small juke-box operator testifies how a group of hoods ap-proached him with a business proposition in the back of the Wagon Wheel restaurant in New York City. The proposition is that he should make them partners. He does not see the beauty of their logic. The hoods, notably one called "Kip," start punching him around the face and head:

Harry Saul (the witness): They kept saying to each other, "This fellow is an actor," because I was pleading with them to stop beating me. He kept pounding away at my head and face and it got to the point where I was just barely able to keep my head up. Every time I started to plead, Panarella [another hood] would lift a napkin holder, a commercial type napkin-holder, used in luncheonettes, with the open face on both sides, about ten inches high—he lifted it in his hand and said he would bash my skull in if I said anything else.

After a while there was a "breather," and then Kip started again.

Saul: Before I had a chance to look up, Kip was back at me, and this time it was really heavy, much heavier than before. I didn't know what to say, and I didn't cry, and I just went along and pleaded with them and kept pleading with them to stop beating me. This time I was bleeding from both nostrils and my mouth, and I felt myself going into a subconscious mind. Just as my head was slumping over, I could hear everything that was going on, and this Panarella said to Kip to stop but Kip didn't stop. He was like a wild man, and finally he jumped up from the table and he yelled something to him, *"Lascialo,"* which I later found out meant to stop in Italian, and with that Kip took his jacket and walked out.

In the drive to entrench themselves into the juke-box field, the government reports clearly disclosed that (1) the hoods terrorized independent juke-box owners, and drove many of them out of business; (2) they spawned fake labor unions and employed these "unions" as a shield by which they set up picketing of tavern owners or restaurant-owners who took their juke boxes from rival operators. The McClellan report noted: "Every area of committee inquiry showed collusive ventures by racketeers in operator associations and union locals to repress competition."

Because of their advanced infiltration in the multimillion-dollar juke-box industry, the hoods have a firm beachhead in the growing $3 billion-dollar-a-year vending machine business. American consumers are now buying soft drinks, ice cream, cigarettes, peanuts, chocolate, crackers, paper tissues, lipstick, and perfume from these glossy self-service units.

This "Incompleat Baedeker" to unethical folkways in the popular music business continues with the gambit practiced by some record companies against music publishers. They "request" music publishers to help pay, or pay completely, for costly trade-paper ads. If the music publisher rebels, his tunes will be badly received by that firm on the principle that he doesn't "cooperate." Record manufacturers are plagued by pilferage by employees. There's also the publishing of many "tip sheets," which are ostensibly sort of sneak previews of what recordings seem to be heading for a "hit." Frequently, such tip sheets are vulnerable to being "hyped," that is, artificially designating certain recordings as "comers" when in reality little has happened with them in terms of retail sales.

There are other deceptive practices, but in balance it must be noted that there are honest men in Tin Pan Alley. There are honorable, responsible men on every level of the popuar music business—in recording, sales, record promotion, trade-paper reporting, distribution, writing, and music publishing.

But the situation is still less than normal. Perhaps Tin Pan Alley is no more corrupt than any other aspect of American life. Congressmen put relatives on the payroll, General Electric's executives have been indicted for price-fixing in the electrical field, there has been conniving in connection with government contracts, there is the Billie Sol Estes case, and David Brinkley's NBC-TV exposé of the highway leading to no-where.

Perhaps Tin Pan Alley is not more corrupt. But it is not a happy, Currier and Ives situation. In the *Harvard Business Review* the Rev. Raymond C. Baumhart, S. J. recalled that a Greek historian, Polybius, once characterized a nation's decline in one remark: "At Carthage, nothing which results in profit is regarded as disgraceful."

11 · THE HARASSED DISC JOCKEYS

> Thanks, DJ's, for all those spins.
> —Tony Bennett (Columbia Records)

> Thanks, broadcasters, for getting me there.
> —Joe Harnell (Kapp Records)

> Our thanks to the nation's disc jockeys for all the spins, particularly on our new single, "The Reverend Mr. Black."
> —Kingston Trio (Capitol)

> Thanks, DJ's. I'm grateful for your wonderful support.
> —Lawrence Welk (Dot)

> Dear DJ's. Thanks-thanks-thanks.
> —Duane Eddy (RCA Victor)

These are just a few of the messages taken at random from music trade-paper advertisements paid for by artists and record companies to acknowledge their debt to their electronic helpers.

There are an estimated eight to ten thousand larynxes, attached to bodies of varying sizes, weights, and attractiveness, who sit before a microphone, either with an engineer or acting as their own engineers, and play popular music recordings on radio, AM and FM. They are, of course, the disc jockeys, sometimes known as "platter spinners," "deejays," "DJ's," or by the more picturesque Arthurian term, "knights of the round table." The music and record business all kneel before these semi-automated human juke boxes.

The romance between the music and record business and disc jockeys is more fervent than the love affairs of Héloise and Abelard or Romeo and Juliet. Trade-paper ads; gifts (golden cigarette lighters) from record stars and budding neophytes, record companies, both those that exist largely on paper and such greats as Capitol Records; record distributors; personal managers; all persistently express their love for those who play recordings. But the power élite of popular music, the disc jockeys who reach millions daily, are singularly unloved by masses of the adult population. There is a satirical routine concerning an airliner that is in trouble. It needs to lighten its payload or crash. A check is made on those who are the most socially useless among the passengers. Two are chosen to be thrown overboard: a used-car salesman and a disc jockey.

Everybody is a disc jockey these days: college sociology students on campus FM, teenage girls, blind persons, former vaudevillians, salesmen, record collectors, speech instructors, arrangers, even religious figures. Father Norman O'Conner is famous for his jazz broadcasts, and there is a Reverend John De Brine of Boston's Ruggles Street Baptist Church who plays "sacred" music recordings. His program, he says, is syndicated to over two hundred stations, and he calls himself "America's First Religious Disc Jockey Show."

It is an odd profession, or avocation, that attracts more varied types than can be found in a good linotype house. But it is a field that is rapidly becoming quite specialized. There are the majority—the strictly "pop" music disc jockeys who stick pretty much to the discs listed on the best-selling trade paper charts; there are country and western disc jockeys who adhere to what is known professionally as "C & W." The Country Music Association reports that it has a mailing list of 2,500 C & W disc jockeys who keep the spindles spinning with Chet Atkins, Tennessee Ernie Ford, Johnny Cash, and Brenda Lee on almost 1,500 stations.

Nor is jazz neglected, as some of its deluded partisans believe. There are approximately 350 to 400 jazz disc jockeys on AM and FM, and their tribe seems increasingly fecund. Less specialized are the "good-music" middle-of-the-road players of recordings. They will program anything they consider of quality—pretty show tunes, jazz, the best of movie music, old standards, even folk music. Such an approach reflects the listeners no longer prisoners of prepackaged labels, and one example of such a disc jockey would be William B. Williams of New York's WNEW.

That doesn't end the list of platter-spinner types. There are approximately 800 rhythm and blues disc jockeys who broadcast over Negro-slanted stations. The race-angled disc jockeys play jazz, rock 'n' roll, rhythm and blues, and gospel music.

There is also a growing minority who hug the microphone and proclaim the virtues of folk music, from such originals as Woody Guthrie and ex-murderer and balladeer, Huddie ("Leadbelly") Letbetter, to the more sophisticated urban groups such as the Kingston Trio and Peter, Paul, and Mary.

A handful of syndicated disc jockeys also jog the public's consciousness of popular music; khaki counterparts do a similar job over Armed

Forces Radio; and some record stars market their own taped programs.

There are also disc jockeys who cannot speak a word, or utter such crowning pronouncements as, "And now, coming up." They are the electronic disc jockeys. Many stations are turning to automated programing, which makes disc jockeys candidates for unemployment insurance. One of the leading U. S. producers of a prepackaged combination of popular music and playback equipment is Programmatic Service, an affiliate of the Wrather Corporation, with headquarters in New York City. Its general manager, John Esau, recently disclosed that "more than 125 stations have used and are using our service."

Broken down into time segments for easy handling, Programmatic Service's "O-Vation Music" features "eight-hour tapes of new and exciting instrumental and vocal arrangements, programed to today's adult audiences, performed by top talent and reproduced in true tonal quality. Programmatic start-stop automation provides for preselected news breaks, commercials, local broadcasts, allows creative broadcasters to build their own format."

In other words, all a station broadcaster has to do is to intersperse this service with news, time signals, and call-letter identification, and he is in business. Naturally, the charm of this mechanization is economy. One station executive revealed: "Programmatic very definitely saves at least three salaries: we save payroll costs of a music-librarian-programer and two engineers in our FM operations." Also, the station doesn't have to "bog itself down" in buying of new recordings or broadcast material. And the disc jockey is, of course, technologically unnecessary.

This particular service sticks to "middle-of-the-road" music—"standards," show tunes, movie music. "None of our music," says Esau, "is oriented to rock 'n' roll or to the more serious music."

In October, 1963, the FCC revealed that the following radio stations were licensed for broadcast:

AM stations	4,021
FM stations	1,205
Non-commercial and educational FM	243
	5,469

From these varied outlets pour out uncountable hours of vocals and instrumentals—sweet, touching, torrid, twitchy, and terrible—that bathe Americans in a mist of popular music. The movies, TV, and classical music have nowhere the publicity exposure granted popular music by the disc jockeys.

You can see disc jockeys as well as hear them on TV. Some video stations have personalities who host popular music shows similar to Dick Clark's, in which couples dance to records while the camera follows them around. These programs, or TV dance parties, do not play recordings alone, but often have an artist "lip-sync" his recordings.

The TV disc jockey program is still an elusive format, unless you get a vicarious thrill in watching teenagers lock arms, or in observing budding breasts and a variety of teenage hairdos. Of approximately 550 U. S. TV stations on the air, perhaps a hundred of these "pop" music peepshows are of any importance regionally.

The assorted pied pipers of popular music operate atop hotels, inside campus buildings, in broken-down commercial buildings, in modest one-story brick buildings, in the corn belt, the Bible belt, and the urban sectors. Their accents may vary. But to the popular music industry they represent the most formidable force yet unveiled to expose new songs, new recordings, new singers, new LP's, incoming Broadway cast albums, and Hollywood sound tracks.

In approach and format, there is enormous diversity among the nation's disc jockeys. A few talk very little, and rationally, and play a lot of music. Some talk a lot, and play very little music. Some spice up their shows with weird noises and girls' giggling, with wolf-calls or electronic sounds. They wail about the "Silver Dollar Survey," or "The Top Ten." Their names range from the straightaway Paul Brenner, Jack Lacy, and Lee Jordan to "Hot Rod" (WWRL) and "Hattie Chattie" of Charlotte's WGIV.

In today's radio structure, the disc jockey is as crucial as a transmitter. As one observer put it: "The deejay sells the goods that brings the station its profits."

Though economically vital to the broadcasters, the disc jockey social status pendulums between an ogre and an ill-informed, chattering idiot. He has also been a "baby sitter," and a panderer to the lowest musical tastes, a glib opportunist. Mitch Miller once told a convention of disc jockeys they had abdicated their roles to the peanut-butter set. In 1960, a report on disc jockeys prepared by the Listener's Lobby of Detroit, a nonprofit citizens group, said the disc jockey programs were not designed to cultivate musical taste, set examples of vocabulary or diction, or in any way to educate their audience.

"As an institution, the disc jockey tends to relegate the whole teenage group to an inferior position in the social class structure—and then to keep them there," said the report published in the *New York Times.*

In his WCBS office on West 52nd Street, Manhattan, tall, bespectacled Bill Randle was suffering from a heavy cold. But as long as he was "ambulatory," as he put it, he continued to work on his two shows, one a daily program over WCBS, following Arthur Godfrey, and another on Saturday mornings. He has been a disc jockey for more than twenty-one years, even before they called those who played records "disc jockeys." He originally began playing rhythm and blues records late at night on a Detroit station, WJLB. It was called, "The Interracial Goodwill Hour."

He worked for a man who bought the airtime. "I did the announcing," Randle recalled. "We played 'race records,' today we call it rhythm and blues. I played early Nat Cole things. Things like 'The Drifting Blues.'" Later he had a program called "Strictly Jazz," and after his Detroit days he switched to Cleveland's WERE and there established himself as a "hit-breaker" and one of the nation's top disc jockeys. He is a student of etymology, the science of words, and of political science and the music business, and today he broadcasts from New York City. He frequently reviews books on music for *Variety*, and he has acted as an A & R man.

"The disc jockey isn't an artist," he said. "He is a vicarious exploiter of other people's talents. He's a selective exploiter. He's not creative in his own right. Basically he does the commercials in-between. He makes it hang together.

"I don't think there are many disc jockeys. I'm using the word as a professional classification. There are very few qualified people in this business who have been successful at it, who determine their own destiny and/or environment and who have made any money out of it. The field has been full of people who knew nothing about the business, who today can recreate a group of numbers and have a certain amount of glib ad-lib facility. But they're not disc jockeys in the sense that I would use the word. They are professional announcers who fit into a format of radio and they make a fair dollar out of it. I don't think any of these people make really good money. I think that the few performers who made big money are, (and I include myself among those) and were, people who came into it with more than just a casual interest in the music. There were jazz collectors, jazz fans, people who were very well acquainted with Negroes in the society. These are the people who are successful.

"Martin Block doesn't reflect this, admittedly. Neither does Al Jarvis in California. But I'm talking about the people who came on from 1940 to the last few years. Alan Freed, regardless of his own personal background, was one of the greatest performers in this business. An incredibly involved performer who lived every beat of every note of the music that he played until he got corrupted by the kind of environment that ultimately destroyed him."

There are some Grand Guignol types in disc jockeyland, according to the tall WCBS disc jockey. Describing one of them, a midwestern radio personality, Randle said: "He's a screamer. I call him one of the psychopathic personalities in the business without the legal connotations of psychopathology. He performs in a pathological way. He's the nuttiest, the wildest. He will do anything, will say anything. It doesn't have to make sense. He will do it. He's what I call a supra-performer."

An eastern disc jockey operates in the same manner as the midwestern specie, Randle added. "The two are a pair. They scream. They shout. They giggle, like a bunch of psychotics. You listen to this, and say, 'How can anybody do this, and then go home and face their wives or family or friends?' You'd think they would at least use another name. Yet people look at them with some awe because they're on radio."

When he first started in Cleveland, Randle worked pretty much on the basis of a word-of-mouth, oral agreement. As he blossomed into an important radio personality, the oral contract gave way to a twenty-page legal document, with clauses involving tax savings.

To many, the disc jockey is a glamorous idol, rolling in luxury, but Randle asserted that most resemble pin-striped proletarians in button-down shirts. "None of the disc jockeys have any security whatsoever except a minimal contract.

"A contract becomes important when a lot of money is involved. Most do not work on this kind of contract. They work on thirteen-week contracts that are renewable by the employer, and are cancellable by the performer. At the end of any thirteen-week period the disc jockey can be out with four-week's notice. That's standard at NBC, CBS, any big outfit. There isn't a radio contract that holds up under scrutiny.

"The average disc jockey can be fired any time, give or take union restrictions. There is severance pay based on the number of weeks or years chalked up by the disc jockey."

Most disc jockeys are factory-tooled, off the assembly line, Randle stated. "These people don't even have an identity. They're faceless and brainless, almost. In some cases, the station owns the name, and when they throw him out they put somebody else in. It's a rough business. These people [disc jockeys] come and go from one station to another."

Randle estimated that the really "important" people in the business of playing popular records don't number over a hundred.

"Most of the disc jockeys don't really care about picking the music. In his heyday, Martin Block never really picked the music. A man named Morris, who worked for him, picked it. They don't feel that the music is that important, give or take the image that they have. They want to play 'nice' music so they call it that or 'good' music if they call it that, or 'top 40,' or 'middle-of-the-road,' or whatever it is. From the viewpoint of getting ratings it's better that a station reflect the same things over and over.

"The newer kids [disc jockeys] feel that they dominate the business. They're the ones with the 'Number 23 is coming.' They have this jargon they rattle off, 'The time is 6:18, and this is Johnny . . .' They do have a lot of these weird patterns going for them. Some are more glib than others. They feel that they're the young swingers, the newer kids between nineteen and twenty-six, and maybe a few guys of twenty-seven or so who have been in it five or six years now."

These young "Turks of the turntable" would like nothing better than to dislodge the veteran disc jockeys. "A guy like myself," he said, "would be a has-been to them. 'That's old style,' they'd say, 'old style.' It doesn't happen to be true. But it happens to be true that very few performers working today were big names five years ago.

"These young disc jockeys are not worried about the artistic level," Randle stated. "They're only worried about their own involvement in it. They're worried about getting to be well known enough to go to Chicago or New York or Cleveland to make more money."

Randle, credited with ballyhooing many new recordings into best-selling status when in Cleveland ("The Yellow Rose of Texas"), doesn't believe in "overnight hits." The audience doesn't recognize a hit the first time they hear it, he says. "I don't think the business recognizes a hit. It has to be hammered home, it has to be sold to people.

"Music is a commodity, like a piece of bread. In 1925, for example, John McCormack sang 'All Alone,' a great song by Irving Berlin, on the first Victor radio program. The song the next day was a hit because that's all that anybody listened to that first night, so he had the whole audience available to him. John McCormack, he was a great star at the time. And a tremendous machine of Irving Berlin's went into action the very next day on that song. That's what made the hit. If Irving Berlin hadn't had offices all around the country, music jobbers, sheet-music salesmen, players, bands being promoted to play it, if this hadn't been done, then 'All Alone,' regardless of the interest of the public, would never have been a hit. The exposure—constant exposure—is what does it. It's like cigarettes, like Lucky Strike commercials, you stop advertising and you stop selling."

Articulate, well-informed, and speaking quickly—an occupational disease—the veteran disc jockey who calls himself a performer crisply volleyed a lot of opinions on the world of popular music.

Personal taste: "There are certain things I obviously won't play. I won't play records that are chauvinistic. I won't play a diluted version of a song, if I can find a better version to play. I won't play a record that's insulting to people's intelligence."

Selling: "I'm a salesman, too, when I work as a performer."

Image-building: "I have to cop a certain plea during the day that people will know they're listening to Bill Randle, smart, Bill Randle, thirty-nine, Bill Randle, white Anglo-Saxon Protestant, all of these things. I mean nobody says these things overtly, but you drop enough clues along the way as a performer. Example: 'I like teenagers, but I don't like hoods.' 'I like Puerto Rican music,' which means, by the very nature of the audience reaction, 'If he likes Tito Puente, he can't dislike the average Puerto Rican guy walking down the street.' In a way, that's a demagogic manipulation of the audience. But with me it's fair, because I do believe these things. I don't use them unethically."

Wearing a bright orange sweater, an Indian madras shirt, tight Italian-tailored gray slacks, and bootlike shoes that curl up in the back like Robin Hood's footgear, disc jockey Murray ("The K") Kaufman was having an involved telephone conversation with a manufacturer over the delivery of some Murray "The K" T-shirts which youngsters would get free with every purchase of an album of his.

No musician or singer, Kaufman emcees or "hosts" albums. His albums, collections of teenage favorites, bear such titles as "Murray The K Golden Gassers," "Murray and Jackie The K's Golden Gassers for a Dance Party," "Golden Gassers for Hand Holders," and "Murray The K's Sing Along with the Original Golden Gassers." A recently popular LP had an "on location" ring to it—"Live from the Brooklyn Fox in His Record Breaking Show Murray The K."

Occasionally his voice rose in anguish: "If I don't have those shirts ready, my name will be mud all over town."

An inexpensive Woolworth print, framed in unfinished raw wood, hung on a slightly discolored wall of his office. Kaufman spoke easily in a soft, southern accent. He is a native of Richmond, Virginia. Heard over WINS, New York's Westinghouse station, he is one of the most important "pop music" disc jockeys in the country.

After completing complex logistics concerning the delivery of the T-shirts to two department stores, one in Brooklyn, and another in Long Island, he said that getting to the top of the disc jockey pyramid isn't too difficult. "I mean if you've got something on the ball. The main thing is to sustain."

Murray "The K" is on the air every day from 7 to 11 P.M. A disc

jockey since the end of 1952, he prepares his program in collaboration
with the station. There is a "station play list." From this list, based
largely on trade-paper charts and approved new recordings, he chooses
what he wants to play. Within this broad spectrum, there is personal
latitude concerning which artists and which materials to broadcast.

This procedure differs from the pre-payola scandal days. Years ago,
the disc jockeys, as the phrase went, "pulled their own shows." That is,
they picked the recordings they wanted to play, and they didn't have to
pay homage to any officially certified and homogenized list.

Kaufman pays very close attention to what he plays, and the order
in which recordings are programed. As Murray "K" puts it: "I select
the records myself because I believe the pace is the personality. But
I do have one of the librarians assigned to my show to help me do
research. Then I have a gal and of course, Jane, [his wife] who is my
assistant. We have a meeting every week and make up a list that we
play. But everyday there are *my contests*. As to new releases, we listen
to them and we pick five that we consider to be the best, and they go
on that night."

From time to time Murray "K" consults with his fellow disc jockeys,
Jack Lacy and Pete Meyers, on the best of the records they've heard,
the ones that seem worthy of air play. Concerning his "contests," Murray Kaufman described one such joust as a popularity poll in which
he chose four singers, Fabian, Frankie Avalon, Bobby Rydell, and Gene
Pitney, and asked his listeners who they would go to see if they had a
chance to see any of this quartet.

There is a class structure among disc jockeys: the proletarians and
the VIP personality types. Kaufman tilted his straw hat back and
explained: "There are two types of contracts in New York which the
American Federation of Television and Radio Artists have with the
station. Number one is staff man. You get a minimum guarantee and
so much per commercial in a quarter-hour period. You do so much,
and you get so much. Then there are people like Jack Lacy and myself.
We're what you call 'talent men.' We have individual contracts where
we get just a straight salary."

Queried about the criticism in the *Saturday Evening Post* by critic
Marya Mannes that current young rock 'n' roll singers are no-talented
"jerks," he stormed like a newly erupted volcano. "She must look at
the people she says are fine, now. Benny Goodman, Artie Shaw, Tommy
Dorsey, Ella Fitzgerald. They were all called jerks, contributors to
delinquency in young people, during the days of swing. Then it wasn't
called music. It was called noise."

He added: "Rodgers and Hart wrote a song, 'I'd like to recognize the
tune. I'd like to savvy what the band is playing. Must you bury the

tune?' Because the band would play a quick sixteen bars of the melody and go off on some tangent. And now this is an art form.

"Did you ever hear those swing bands today? You can't listen to them. They're dull. It's old music. It's like listening to ragtime. Musicianship be damned! They do more things now than they did in those days. You got to progress. We're not going backward, we're progressing. American music has cycles. You people only remember the good. What about the bums we had in the 30's and 40's? People don't talk about that.

"People have no right to criticize rock 'n' roll that way. Why should they, if an era has passed them by, or if they can't keep up with a certain era? Outside of sex, music is the most personal thing in the world and I think it should be enjoyed and not discussed. It's up to the individual. What do you want to do? Burn the books? Burn the music? Burn the records? Ban it?"

Besides his disc jockey activity, Kaufman has been active behind the scenes in the music and record business. He helped publicize the famous Johnny Mathis. Now Mathis reciprocates by showing up from time to time to play in Kaufman-produced rock 'n' roll shows though he is hardly a rock 'n' roll "jamboree" type. Bobby Darin once lived in Kaufman's home for a year and together they wrote one smash hit, "Splish Splash." Kaufman himself produced the hit recording. In his bachelor days, Kaufman also roomed with Broadway composer-lyricist, Bob Merrill, who wrote *Carnival.* He has also been involved in music publishing. But his primary fame and force has come through being a disc jockey.

The payola scandals of 1959 have hurt him economically, he says, because broadcasters have become very stringent. "I feel restricted these days. Years ago, Martin Block had the fruits of the business. If I make an album, I can't play it. If my wife makes an album—and she's been in show business, too—I can't play it. 'Cause it could be a conflict of interests. Even if the albums are on the play lists, I can't play them. As Westinghouse [the chain for which he works] says, 'It isn't evil, it's the appearance of evil.' They don't want anybody to point a finger."

Perhaps the country's first disc jockey was a Westinghouse engineer named Frank Conrad. Of course, he didn't call himself that. But right after World War I he had established an experimental station, 8XK, in his garage in his home town, Wilkinsburg, Pennsylvania. From there he made regular talks. Later he began to play recordings. The amateur "hams" loved the idea. When Conrad had completely finished playing all of his record collection, a nearby Hamilton Music Store in Wilkinsburg, with fine entrepreneur's vision, offered him as many recordings as he could use on the air, providing he would say that he had purchased them at the Hamilton Music Store. Dr. Conrad, stuck for new material, said "Yes."

That started the whole profession, if it can be termed that. Most of the pioneering radio stations played records until the shellac wore out, and that was it. As a result, as early as 1912, Secretary of Commerce Herbert Hoover put a temporary ban on records on radio. Later, government regulations developed the credo that the airwaves belonged to the people, and somehow this meant a cultural responsibility to present something more than inanimate discs.

As time went by, more and more broadcasters turned to "live music": studio concerts, studio orchestras, and later, "remote" broadcasts from night clubs where bands would be picked up. Some samples of programs and artists: John McCormack, Guy Lombardo and the "sweetest music this side of heaven," the famed Atwater Kent variety programs, and the singing voice of Joseph Lewis, "The Silver Masked Tenor."

Increasingly, as the networks formed in the mid-twenties (NBC was the first, November 15, 1926), fans out there in radioland could hear the best and most popular singers, bands, and vocal groups. Backed by national sponsors and big-money advertising revenues, radio could afford to buy the biggest names, even though many top entertainers couldn't stand the raised "tomato can," the name given to the microphone.

But small independent radio stations, strapped for money and talent, never stopped playing records. In 1927, the newly formed Federal Radio Commission again deplored "unnecessary" use of records. For a while records took a back seat, but by 1932 recordings "took up a major share of air time," according to a study prepared by the American Federation of Musicians *The Struggle to Keep Music Alive.* Despite the opposition by the large networks, who wanted "live entertainment," records continued to consume blocs of air time. There then arrived a new twist: transcribed shows, which were actually recordings of programs put on extra-large discs and syndicated. Of these transcribed shows quite a few concerned themselves with popular music.

Beneath all this bustling activity of the early '20's was much controversy surrounding broadcasting over the question: Who shall support radio? In many ways the resolution of this crucial debate shaped the merchandising and even the aesthetics of popular music, though only a few saw it at that time.

Secretary of Commerce Hoover, for example, thought broadcasting should be subsidized by industry. Some believed that the selling of air time was the answer. A few voices thought that broadcasting ought to be supported by licensing radio set users, or by voluntary donations. A fourth road was plotted by some, among them David Sarnoff of the Radio Corporation of America. He believed that radio should be endowed, similar to museums, libraries, and educational institutions, since it was such a potent cultural force.

As everybody knows, the advertising concept won out, perhaps because few really saw the potentialities of this mass media, built by pioneers, and the kinetic enthusiasm of amateur crystal-set kit builders. Perhaps if radio was attached to the cultural institutions, a culturally enriched FM concept may have developed as far back as the twenties. The cultural horizons of millions of Americans would have been immeasurably broadened, including their musical horizons.

As the advertising concept developed, and rate cards made their appearance, there was much maneuvering and discontent spawned by popular music recordings on the new flourishing entertainment medium. The musicians' union sensed that discs meant the eventual extinction of live music. Also, some of the record companies took the position that the playing of recordings would somehow kill the sale of their 78's. They refused to send the early disc jockeys and program directors sample records. If an audience could hear them free, why pay good money for them? Decca Records even instituted lawsuits in many states against the playing of records on radio. So did other record manufacturers.

In the late 30's and into the early 40's the disc jockey made deeper and deeper inroads, particularly on small independent stations that could not compete with the big networks and network affiliates for talent and stars. By 1947, even before the rise of television, the disc jockey was becoming a personality of importance himself, and an important publicity medium for the popular music business. However, the big variety programs, the Jack Benny Show, the big remote pick-ups of the big bands from hotels and night clubs, were still the best "plugs."

However, the shift was undeniably made to discs. By 1942, 76 per cent of broadcast time was music, and 55 per cent of that was recorded or transcribed. Out of Chicago, James ("Jimmy") Petrillo fought bitterly against the dwindling of live music—house bands and symphony orchestras. But the bespectacled, short, picturesque leader of the American Federation of Musicians couldn't stop the move toward automation—and disc jockeys. Thousands of musicians employed by the broadcasters were "pink-slipped," victims of phonograph records.

To compensate in part for this, the union conceived the Recording Industries Music Industry Fund. Royalties are paid to this fund by record manufacturers on every record manufactured. These funds go to pay musicians who play classical concerts, band concerts in the park, dances, musical programs in community centers, schools, old-age homes, veterans hospitals, "Y's," and churches.

The gradual silencing of live music on U. S. radio brought forth many changes. Radio stations used to have a neatly-indexed library of brightly colored sheet music and hand-crafted musical arrangements. These were supplanted by rows and rows of records. Once, practically every station of some stature possessed a "house" musical unit of its own with its own distinctive style. Now each station had access to the same sounds and was inferior to no competitor, as far as popular music was concerned.

In 1949 and 1950 a "low comic" with a big cigar, floppy clothes, comedy sketches, and the unlikely name of "Uncle Miltie"—Milton Berle—put television on the map. His comedy thrust millions aboard the video bandwagon. As television got bigger and bigger and drained off many an advertising dollar from radio, the few remaining "live" programs on radio got scarcer and scarcer. But there were some bright notes. Television itself brought a weekly paycheck back to many musicians who labored on variety programs such as the "Ed Sullivan Show" and the "Perry Como Show." It also provided a new medium for the exploitation of popular music and recording artists. But the video tube has never replaced the radio disc jockeys—still the front-line promoters of the popular music. Save for the Dick Clark TV program, television relied mostly on the famous songs of yesteryear and already established new music and lyrics.

Today, of course, the disc jockey is as much a part of the American scene as the transistor radio: you hear him everywhere. However, the disc jockey's profession is bedeviled by status and the caste system. If the disc jockey broadcasts in key and medium-sized markets (New York, Philadelphia, Dallas, Houston, Atlanta, San Francisco, St. Louis, Cleveland), he is romanced and sent new recordings by the truckload—free. But those disc jockeys in the hinterlands, the recesses of Mississippi, Missouri, the plains of South Dakota, the rocky ranges of Wyoming, far from discount chains and record shops, are not so fortunate. They have to beg for records, the new releases, like puppies asking to be fed. Recently, this poignant letter appeared in the *Music Reporter,* a trade publication:

. . . Sonny Du Bose, PD at WDKD, Kingstree, S.C., says "the record service most of us get is sick." He adds, "I know the 'big' boys get their share of the records, but I feel that we in the smaller towns play almost as big a role in record sales as they do. We cover 26 counties but our record sampling service from most of the manufacturers smells and smells. . . . all except Liberty and Capitol. Their service is wonderful. . . .

The record companies do not flatly ignore the stations that do not rate: they offer them "radio subscriptions" or a "radio service." Each record firm has a plan by which radio stations can buy new releases and catalogue items, 45's and LP's at minimum rates; from 45 cents to $1. Some record companies realize upward of $50,000 a year on these services.

Supplementing the free record promotion and the subscription plans, there are private popular music radio services. For example, there is RSI (Record Service Incorporated), which is owned by the trade paper, *Billboard*. The plan's main virtue is that it offers a radio station or program director new albums ("pop," country and western, jazz, mood music) put out by a variety of record firms, not the product of a single firm. It recently reported that more than two hundred radio stations take its "pop album service."

Today's disc jockey is very much like any middle-class gray-flannel-suit organization man. Since payola and the furious war of ratings, radio broadcasters now devise "station policy" which virtually tells the player of recordings when and where to breathe. "Station policy," according to Bill Gavin, a *Billboard* columnist, "is simply another way of saying 'what management wants.'

"Station policy controls the kinds of music to be played; the range of disc jockey discretion in programing his own shows; the amount of humor he may—or must—use; the handling of time; temperature, and weather announcements; the use of production gimmicks; the frequency of call letter and personal-name mention; and so on. These requirements vary considerably from one station to another."

Such manipulative control in part, is traceable to the 1959 payola scandals, and in part to the broadcaster's own attitude of how best to make his station develop a stance, or money-making personality. Whatever the reasons, the harassed disc jockey is in electronic peonage.

Discontented, disc jockeys are a fast-moving group of silver-voiced vagabonds. They're constantly hopping radio from station to station as if they had hot electrodes on their backs. Though they cultivate the aura of being "hip," or slick, or involved in the glamour of show business, they are merely technicians for hire. They resemble factory workers, and practically all of them have to punch a timeclock.

One student of disc jockey folkways has observed: "There are about 150 changes a month. Some fellas get out of the business. Some deejays change jobs. They go from station to station. Certain personalities are not happy with station management. Some disc jockeys do not fit into a certain type of programing. In the past year, I'd say there were about 2,000 changes."

Insecure and never knowing when the pink slip may fall, the disc jockey puts on record hops, promotes concerts, owns record shops, and participates anywhere he can make "a buck."

As to disc jockey earnings, the contrasts are sharp. A handful of "big names," broadcasting in the large cities (New York, Chicago, Los Angeles), receive $50,000 to $100,000 a year. In the medium-sized cities, there are a few who make $35,000 to $50,000 a year. A reported two hundred or so count on $15,000 a year. However, the majority, who reach millions hourly, earn less than $7,500 a year.

There are even a number of nonunion radio stations, operating in Anytown, U.S.A., where the disc jockeys perform multiple chores. They announce the news, sweep the floors, sell advertising. They often labor four hours on the turntable and four hours on the "board"—the multidialed cockpit of radio stations. For this their pay is a grandiose $1.25 an hour.

Many disc jockeys belong to AFTRA (American Federation of Television and Radio Artists Association), the show business union which embraces such television personalities as Lucille Ball, Ed Sullivan, and Dick Chamberlin. (Interestingly enough, Dick Clark was once treasurer of a Philadelphia AFTRA unit.)

And, in fighting for better pay and working conditions, some disc jockeys display remarkable picketline wizardry. In 1963, disc jockeys at Philadelphia's WGIB staged a sit-down and lie-down strike in front of the station's entrance. The human wall was designed to keep away record promotion men coming in with new discs for the station. The strike was called to raise disc jockey pay from $150 to $300 a week, in line with nearby communities.

Today's modern disc jockey does more than show up at airtime in his jazzy new sportscar, stroll over to the turntable, and spin a few records. He has to engage in all sorts of tangential activities—promotions, staff meetings, and the preparation of features for forthcoming programs.

Negro disc jockeys are discriminated against in two ways. For years, they have been unable to win jobs in "white stations," and, they are paid much less by the owners of Negro radio. And additionally, their approach and language is often plagiarized. One Negro disc jockey, Del Shields of Philadelphia's WDAS, complained in *Open Mike* that:

In general, radio has adopted most of the slang, the "hip" phrases, programing policies of the smaller Negro stations. In fact the general stations owe their slam-bang-approach success to Negro radio. It is a pity to listen to a jock on a 50,000-watter trying to ape the phrases of the "hippy" on the 250-watter. It is a disgrace to learn afterward that the differences in salary may range from $4,500 to $50,000 though they are using the same material.

Many disc jockeys feel alienated from their own shows, for they cannot put on what they like, but only those recordings that turn up on the trade-paper charts, the "play-list," or listener requests. Those employed by the "top 40" stations are supremely wedged in. For they have to program largely from the "top 40" of the popularity charts.

Consequently, more and more disc jockeys spend more time preparing promotions with department stores, contests, and special events to keep the audience and station management in a state of synthetic excitement, than they do in preparing programs. They fabricate "sleepless marathons" where they go on the air *ad infinitum* for a charity. Some originated "walkathons" to tie in with the late President Kennedy's physical fitness drive.

Of course, there are a discernible minority who happily work for the "good music stations." They are sensitive to music, to the history of popular music, and they take pride in picking what they shall play and whom they shall devote their air time to. They want to pack into their segments a certain level of musical performance. They are not oracles of musical depth, but they do possess taste and do not assault your ears with tasteless mediocrity and inane chatter. From time to time some "wild men" get on the air, and though they are disc jockeys their main appeal is in satiric commentary, or bits of "business"; sometimes they will toss cheap popular recordings out the window. But they are in a minority. There have always been mavericks in radio. Funnyman Jackie Gleason once employed as a disc jockey, used to run dances in the studio while on the air. A station representative walked in while his friends were dancing to records and fired him.

Owning nothing but his voice, his appearance, his little supply of copyable mannerisms and sayings, the disc jockey feels none too secure. He is a replaceable cog. Just as easily as an engineer can put in a new tube, the broadcaster can thrust in a new "voice." The disc jockey's distinctive qualities—voice, intelligence, sensitivity to music—are not that distinctive.

Since he does not have exclusive recordings to broadcast, save on a temporary basis, his programing cannot be truly original. And the jargon of one disc jockey is indistinguishable from another disc jockey 1,500 miles away. He is kowtowed to, but not respected. He is the middle-man of popular music, the thirty-two-bar transmission belt. The disc jockey is an odd soul; he does not sing or play an instrument. He is a descendant of all the theatrical introducers—the narrator reciting the prologue in Greek plays, the ringmaster in the circus, the night club "emcee," the TV "host." He may be a great Mahatma in the popular music structure. But few adults look up to him, except to envy his earnings, which are usually less than they are imagined to be.

The peculiar craft and profession of the disc jockey is inextricably tied up with the fortunes of American radio. So far, AM seems to be carrying its economic weight. And it is on AM radio that the disc jockey thrives. Somehow, adequate numbers of radio listeners can listen to continuous streams of the "pop hits" and commercial jingles to justify the advertisers spending their money on record shows. And it is the advertisers who pay the disc jockeys' salaries.

But there is a listeners' rebellion. Many adults no longer can listen to AM radio and its endless commercials. They are turning more and more toward FM, with its more cultural orientation (plays, the spoken word, foreign language broadcasts). On FM, the mongoose cry of the disc jockey is scarcely heard, save on certain college-connected stations. On FM, there is a minimum of commercials and a maximum of resistance to juke-box culture. And if FM continues to expand, the disc jockey power may weaken, and this may trigger a complete rethinking of popular music merchandising, exploitation, and product.

A study by the Harvard Business School recently prophesied that FM radio, now taking in $13.7 million a year, would pass AM's revenue (currently about $700 million a year) by 1975.

Should FM gain dominance, a musically diverse format will probably emerge. Stations will put on all kinds of music—classical music, folk music, jazz, opera, the best in show music, and contemporary popular music in any twenty-four hour period. These stations, catering to more culturally aware listeners, will not be bound by the "top 40" juke-box concepts. Cheap "pop" music will probably find it tougher going under such a demanding orientation.

This seems to be the trend, as more and more FM sets, car FM radios, and FM portables are being bought. These purchases represent a rebellion against the strident "pop" music and dehydrated news ticker format that is the staple of much of AM radio.

Should FM's more imaginative and more open type of programing prevail, the AM commercial "disckery" might be marked for lingering death. Though there is much cultural backwardness in the country, notably among the teenagers, the death of the commercial "pop hit" philosophy isn't a hallucinatory dream.

The contemporary disc jockey is, in some ways, a man to be pitied. He is playing a role structured for him by the radio broadcasters. He has only a small area in which to maneuver, depending on station management, to display his own personality and influence. In some ways he can carry on guerrilla warfare against cheapness by trying to play the best he can of today's music. But there is a controlling hand, derived from the deadly rating wars, the monotonous stuffing of commercials within fifteen-minute time-segments, and "station policy."

Much depends on the power structure, the owners of the radio stations. If they don't care how they make their money—and many can't even listen to their own stations—then, of course, commercial AM programing will stick to its rut of tasteless chatter and cheapness, spiced with the station's own noisy logos.

The issues can be drawn and looked at, and they go to the heart of AM radio broadcasting, which is only a little more than forty years old. As the former Commissioner of the Federal Communications Commission, Newton Minow, put it: "In too many communities, to twist the radio dial today is to be shoved through a bazaar, a clamorous Casbah of pitchmen and commercials which plead, bleat, pressure, whistle, groan, and shout. Too many stations have turned themselves into publicity-franchised juke boxes."

12 · WILD AND WACKY WORLD OF DISC PROMOTION

All CDRC people, from desk clerks to branch managers, will drop everything for three hours Monday to telephone every radio station in their territories. We're going to make sure that every disc jockey and librarian knows "Wings of a Dove" is a "pop" as well as country and western hit, and that Ferlin's is the original.

—Capitol Records press release proclaiming
"Wings of a Dove" day

Eddie Miller is presented with new Wham-O-Limbo game at Woolworth store in New York City by Herman Boetine of Betta Rewelo Distributors. Game is tied to new teenage dance craze.

—Picture caption in *Billboard*

In conjunction with [new Ricky Nelson LP on Decca] a special format has been written into "The Adventures of Ozzie and Harriet" on which he appears that night. In the show he will sing five or six songs from the album and his single, "String Along."

—News Story

Bunch these three items together and you form a picture of modern record promotion and publicity that is slick, gimmicky, funny, even "Brave New World-ish." All are aimed to sell recordings, known in the trade as "product." Developed to a fine art over the years, popular music promotion and publicity works at four basic areas simultaneously: (1) the consumers, (2) the disc jockeys, (3) the record distributors, and (4) the record dealers. No tack in the publicity workbook is left unturned in this effort: news stories, trade-paper stories, stunts, radio and TV contests, giveaways, cocktail parties, press conferences, and personal appearances by recording artists.

Record companies have a publicity tapeworm, they never reach the state of satiety. Columbia, RCA Victor, Capitol have large staffs, and they are divided into radio-TV contacting, newspaper and magazine publicity, and exploitation. Sales promotion specialists back them up with window streamers, displays, counter cards.

The smaller record companies have one or two multiheaded people who do a bit of everything. They write stories for usage in the trade papers (*Billboard, Cash Box, Variety*). They contact syndicated newspaper columnists on popular music—Dick Kleiner of NEA, William Laffler of United Press International, or Hugh Mulligan of Associated Press. When they have a moment to breathe they are on the telephone trying to arrange radio and TV guest appearances, writing liner notes, securing photographs for album covers, or contacting distributors to urge them on. If a disc jockey is coming to town, they are busy entertaining him. They are the workhorses of the platter industry. They have no economic security and no unions to negotiate for them or protect them.

Every record distributor of consequence has a promotion man, and there are an estimated three to five hundred free-lance record promotion specialists who focus their energies largely on getting disc jockey air play. They don't do too much in the way of newspaper or magazine publicity.

Active, too, are the music business "contact men," once known as "song pluggers." The music publisher has a stake in the outcome of a recording on which his music is heard. The job of the song plugger is to see that the publisher's side is played. This often results in a clandestine civil war. The record company has picked one side for the "push," known as the "A" side; the poor publisher has the other side, the "flip" or "B" side. Apart from this, the song plugger for a music publisher may also be engaged in contacting recording company A & R men to secure recordings for new and old copyrights. The song pluggers belong to the Music Publishers' Contact Employees Union.

This is the solid phalanx of record promotion. In back of them are concentric circles of publicity men—the artist's own private press agent; the TV program publicists for whom a recording artist may appear; Broadway press agents who use a cast album or a single song from the show's score to sell tickets to the show, rather than for any economic interest in the sale of the recording itself; or movie company publicists, who beat the drums for a movie sound track so the film's title can be hammered home.

Sol Handwerger is a hard-working record publicist. A gray-eyed, big-boned man, he handles publicity and promotion for MGM Records, Verve, Lion, Cub, Metro Jazz, as well as for firms whose recordings are distributed by MGM, such as Ava (Fred Astaire's company) and Deutsche Grammaphon.

He started out as an office boy in the Loew's Theater advertising department. He rose to become a movie theater press agent, as which he covered the neighborhood film palaces all the way from Coney Island to Mount Vernon, N.Y., in one day doing assorted stunts and promotion. His present post is Advertising and Promotion Director, a post he has held since MGM Records was organized by Metro-Goldwyn-Mayer in 1947.

"Confusion is the backbone of this business," Handwerger said one early afternoon. "It can't operate without confusion. Nothing can be thought out because of the fierce competition. Nobody can help themselves. At the last count there's 1,800 record companies, 1,800 labels on the market vying for radio play, for newspaper and magazine space, for distributor attention, for dealer window space. Can you imagine the confusion with trade papers getting 200 records a week to review?

"People don't know what promotion means and how to use it. The only thing promotion means to a distributor or a promotion man is delivery of a record to a radio station. That is basically wrong. Promotion covers advertising, publicity, exploitation, stunts, contests, gimmicks—anything to make the public, the distributor, the dealer aware of your product.

"If it's a new artist we want to introduce, we make up a special sleeve for the 45's. This we feel is an attractive way to bring our product to the attention of the distributor. This, I feel, has excitement. It may be black and white, it may be in color, and we try to get the record picked by the trade papers, by the reviewers. When you get 'picks' or 'spotlights' (in *Billboard, Cash Box,* or *Variety*) it creates trade excitement. There's something better about this record than the other records. We reprint these and make a direct mailing to the disc jockeys and the one-stop operators, to the dealers and the chain store operators, and to the discount houses, showing them that this has now trade acceptance.

"We try to work up gimmicks in various territories. We go to many disc jockeys throughout the country and we run contests. A contest we did was on a Mark Dinning record about a dog. We gave away real live puppies as prizes. We gave about twelve puppies in twelve markets to winners.

"Sometimes we give away records as prizes. We arrange for the artist to call certain disc jockeys to key markets. And through 'beep-a-phone' we have telephone interviews with these people on the air. So when the disc jockey plays it back, he has a 'live' or 'simulated live' artist on his station.

"We may get a spark in a certain city. If we get a spark—if the record begins to hit in a certain city—we fan that spark, we continue until it spreads. Once we get the hit going we go on to something else."

Handwerger knits his activities together with about half-a-dozen field men who are sales-minded. Their job is to get the distributor excited enough to buy more MGM and Verve product, and to inform him what the home office is doing to help him sell more merchandise. The field man sees the dealers, troubleshoots, and hovers over developments.

Having been in film publicity and promotion, Handwerger is a great believer in "showmanship," which he feels recording companies scarcely know about. "I have tried to institute this feeling for showmanship, this flare, this excitement that the motion picture people create.

"In the situation where we have a sound-track album or music from motion pictures, we are the only company that works closely with motion picture theater managers who are known as exhibitors. We have contests, which give the exhibitor as well as the record dealer an opportunity to win money. And they share equally in cash prizes. They expose the record in the theater lobby via lobby displays; they expose it in auditoriums via recessionals, before the picture goes on and after the picture goes off. In many cases we have announcements on the record itself, that you are listening to the title of the record and mention the title of the album, and then if it's a picture tie-in the voice says 'Coming next week to this theater.' We also run contests with theaters where we give albums as prizes. We use records as prizes for bathing beauty contests, musical instrument contests. This is the kind of excitement that I try to bring to the industry."

To Handwerger, the record business is unique from a product viewpoint. He explained, "We sell a new product practically every day. There's a new record almost every day." To keep up with the vortex of work this dedicated publicist employs three secretaries—a senior secretary and two typists. He dictates stories, memos, bulletins, and biographies, and these are rushed out daily to newspapers, trade papers, news magazines, and photo editors.

Handwerger observed grimly in his work-cluttered MGM Records office, "It's a rat race. A pressure business. You can stay here all day and all night and never finish your job. There is no such thing as a finished job. It keeps going on and on and on. New records, new artists, new ideas all the time.

"I'm here at 8 a.m. That's because you can get a lot of work done between eight o'clock and nine o'clock, before the telephone rings, before the people start coming in—the publishers, the artists, and the managers, and before all the problems start. Then the telephone starts to ring and you can't do any creative work. So I try to handle all of the emergency things during the day, and then most of the creative stuff—writing, layouts, copy—I do at home at night in the peace and quiet of my home because it's physically impossible to work in an office in this business and be creative. I put in from ten to fourteen hours a day sometimes, and I take a package home. Something that has to be ready the very next day.

"And I write it at home, or lay it out, or design it, and bring it back in the morning and we're ready to go. It's murder. When I finish the day here, I go home, unless we have an artist opening in a club. Then I go out and see the artist or I got a stunt going at night, then I gotta be downtown. Or we got an opening of a film which we have a sound track of—that's the way it goes.

"I live in Levittown, Long Island, and I have two children, a daughter, nineteen, and a son who is graduating from high school, sixteen-and-a-half. My daughter does folk-dancing and my son plays the guitar. They like records. I like records, too."

When RCA Victor signed the Limeliters in 1960—as *their* Kingston Trio—the publicity moguls started plotting a "campaign." Most of the campaigns are pretty much the same, like Hollywood press books. But they do offer an insight into the way record companies reach out for the consumer. In a four-page booklet devoted to the comedy-flavored folk music group, Herb Helman, Director of RCA Victor Press Information, blueprinted the attack:

Photographs, biographies, trade stories, reviewer letters, and the LP's themselves will be used for maximum impact on all critics and reviewers. Columnists and feature writers will be invited to hear the Limeliters in person . . . to listen to their first RCA Victor album, "Tonight, in Person" . . . and to interview the group. Whenever the Limeliters are booked for television or personal appearances, the entertainment press will hear about it first. We will try to keep you informed as to the Limeliters' potent commercial appeal through our "What the Critics Are Saying" enclosure in the *Mailbag*. And to add the icing to this excitement and interest the group always sparks, every national magazine in the country will be alerted to the possibilities of the Limeliters as a feature story of unique interest.

RCA Victor's advertising department got into the act, too. A memo reported:

RCA Victor Advertising gets into the Limeliters' act with a campaign we trust will make everybody happy. Disc jockeys will be bombarded with special mailings (this brochure's the first!), copies of the album, kits with original programing aids. There'll be striking displays for stores and special displays for cities where the trio's booked on tour. Novel, interestingly devised ads will break in national trade publications and consumer magazines. The Limeliters have promised (wherever possible) to be available for network radio interviews and local TV appearances. In other words, we're convinced the Limeliters rate the full VIP treatment. One critic said of the Limeliters simply, "They sing great!" We've keyed our advertising along those lines!

The Limeliters' planning apparently paid off, although the same plan used with some other recording group or artist may not. That's the mystique of modern publicity and promotion. At thirty-six, Herb Helman has been with Victor for approximately eight years, beginning as a field representative for several independent record companies. He called on record retailers, distributors, newspapermen, and disc jockeys. He met some Victor executives, and they offered him a publicity job with the company. He is now head of RCA's publicity department, embracing both classical and popular music.

"The job at Victor in the publicity department, as I see it," said Helman, "is a service. We are first of all a service internally to the artist and repertoire department, to the sales department, and to the merchandising department. We take our lead as to what is to be publicized or attempted to be publicized from these three areas. When it comes to a new artist, they—these three divisions of the company—make the decision as to which artist of the company we are to publicize. We then attempt a campaign in conjunction with the advertising and promotion department, to launch a new artist.

"The publicity department is made up of (including myself) seven people. We have two other contact people besides myself who call on the press and work with the classical and popular artists. We divide our artists up into stables. I take certain artists and the other two people take the other artists. We have a writer who turns out information which we think is helpful to the press. We never talk about it being the greatest recording ever made, but we try to give them information which would not be found on the liner notes. Things about the recording, why we did a certain recording.

"As to the total number of people in the advertising and promotion departments, a rough guess on my part would be somewhere around fifteen people who work out of this office. There is another area which is called Radio and TV Relations. They have a staff of about eight people who call on disc jockeys throughout the country, under Mr. Allan Clark's direction."

Sometimes you can whip up a lot of publicity, but nothing happens with the artist in terms of consumer popularity where it counts—at the record counter. Helman noted:

"I can do a composite on a boy artist and a girl artist who had much the same story. We launched a campaign on both artists. The girl was more of a 'pop-jazz' flavored singer, and the boy was a teenage idol type, and in both cases we were very fortunate in having the press respond to them as personalities. We had layouts in major publications, in *Life,* in *Time,* in *Newsweek,* in both instances. In the case of the boy, his first record sold maybe 250,000 which is pretty good. The girl made an LP for us which didn't sell hardly at all and she's still around.

"I see her on television occasionally. I think she's a fine singer, but she just didn't appeal to the public. In the case of the boy, I read recently where he went with a company, but he hasn't had a record hit since. I think they were both fine artists. They just didn't have whatever *it* is. Or at least they haven't gotten it across to the public to date."

Publicity, according to Helman, is a skilled craft, and cannot be robotized. The personal touch is crucial. "The formula part of it is to prepare a press and promotion kit which contains a 'bio,' interesting stories about the young artist and his newest record, and some photographs. But if we ended it there I don't think we'd get any publicity.

"More important is personal contact and going up to the magazines and talking about an angle that might appeal to them, knowing the publication well enough to realize what might appeal to an individual type of publication. Just as important is knowing when not to go up, because many times you will have an artist that you believe in, but if you're honest with yourself you'll know that this type of a publication just won't be interested in that artist. It gets into personalities. There are editors of certain publications that you know are not going to buy a certain type of singer, a raucous rock 'n' roll singer, say, but perhaps would be attracted to a ballad singer. So you just don't bring up the rock 'n' roll singer to that particular publication. And the reverse is just as true at other magazines."

An important blood-flecked arrow in the publicity man's quiver is the punishing "tour." Helman says, "These tours are vital. There are so many records coming out every day, every week. To get one started above another is a job.

"In traveling around the country with a new artist, it's rough. It's from eight o'clock in the morning until two or three A.M. the next morning. Like the last time I can remember we went out. We get into a city and there's a person from the promotion department as well as one from the publicity department. And we're met in the town by the local radio-TV relations man who covers that territory. And he has already arranged, before we get there, to have interviews on radio stations, and he takes the artist away.

"I go to the hotel room and if I haven't done my job from the office of making long-distance calls to the city and setting up interviews, I get on the telephone, talk to my contacts in the local press, and arrange interviews. They could be anything from 'Let's have breakfast together,' to 'Let's have cocktails,' to 'Let's meet at a night club at twelve o'clock when I'm through covering a new act that's appearing in town.' That's the press man talking. We're always on the go. It could be at any time because we're trying to service the newspapers, and they're really doing us the favor. So we accommodate their schedule. We hold interviews wherever it's convenient for the press person. We go anywhere. Generally it is either at the hotel or at the newspaper itself.

"I would say mostly it's tiring to the artist because in the main he's repeating himself. I think it's the sign of an intelligent person that he is able to vary his stories slightly, or at least enough so that he doesn't get bored with it. And I think most of the successful artists have that capability. I think you can almost predict which artist is going to be successful by the way he handles an interview—making things a little bit more colorful, saving things that he considers gems, knowing intuitively he shouldn't give the same story to two men. We try to tell them that in front. But the brighter boys, I would say, know that without our telling them. It's quite amazing to see that. And most of them have never had an interview before.

"What we do is try to send them to smaller cities, break them in out-of-town, you might say. I consider a small city anything up to about 100,000 population, as compared to your Philadelphia and your Baltimore, Washington, Boston, and New York areas. A tour can last anywhere from four days to three or four weeks. We've gone that long and longer. Across the country.

"I've seen the artists dog-tired and anxious to get to bed, but I've never seen them break down over it because I think most of them—almost everyone of them—are in this business because they believe in themselves, and to believe in yourself that much that you're going to get up in front of an audience, then you must be somewhat of an extrovert. And therefore they really relish this. I think the repetition is what gets them down. I have found it becomes harder to get an artist to make a second or third tour once they have established themselves. It's difficult to get through to them that though they have a big audience and in many areas they may be mobbed by the kids, there are still thousands and thousands of people who have never heard of them, and it's our job to see that these thousands do hear of them. I would say the reluctance, as time goes by, to go out on more tours makes our job a little more difficult."

Not long ago, a short, rather harassed, ex-road manager during the big band era walked into a block-and-a-half discount complex in Wantagh, Long Island. There was nothing particular on his mind. It was Saturday, a thriving day at the stores, which carry everything from auto accessories to food. They also sell records. He saw a bin marked "George Shearing," and he flipped through the polyethylene-wrapped Shearing LP's. When he found Shearing's latest, he put that one in front of the old ones. It was an automatic, unthinking reaction. Though the sale of any Shearing recording would have pleased him, he wanted the latest one exposed.

This was Paul Brown, one of the myriad free-lance record promotion specialists. He lives in Wantagh, but he operates five days a week out of an office on Fifth Avenue. Forty-six years old, he has been in some phase of the music business since he started out as a musician, a drummer. Later he swapped his percussion instruments for a job as road manager for Charlie Spivack. After World War II, he started out on his own as a record promotion man. Through the years he has promoted the discs of George Shearing, Ramsey Lewis, Nina Simone, and various rock 'n' roll groups.

"The most important thing is to get an artist's record played," said Brown one afternoon. "The idea of free-lance promotion, and one of the selling points that we try to stress to an artist beforehand is this: You see they record for certain companies and each company has their own promotion staff, but having forty or sixty artists in their roster they just can't give each artist individual attention. So the artist comes to my office and hires us to exploit their records with the disc jockeys around the country.

"I cannot make hits. If I could I'd be worth a million dollars, but what we try to do is to get those extra plays to try to get the public to go out and buy the *single record* or album or whatever we're working on.

"I have developed through the years a very close friendship with a lot of disc jockeys around. Through my mailings, my phone calls, and everything that I do for the fellas."

Brown is pretty much a one-man shop, although he has the aid of a part-time secretary. The first stage of any promotion campaign, according to him, is to get at least a hundred recordings, whether it be of a single record or of an album. He proceeds to mail the recordings to a selected list of disc jockeys; he matches the recording to the taste of the disc jockey. "I don't rely on the company to send them out," he says.

Brown takes pride in his modern equipment—addressograph machine, high-powered mimeograph machine, and a folding machine which can make mass mailings to disc jockeys a simple matter instead of a bone-wearying chore.

The mailing may be merely a news squib that a record artist has been signed for a TV program. Or it may take the form of announcing that the recording is "taking off." Sample phrases from a typical Paul Brown disc jockey mailing piece:

"COUNTRY MEETS THE BLUES"   RAMSEY LEWIS
Moving up on the charts.

GEORGE SHEARING'S "CONCERTO FOR MY LOVE"
This LP is getting loads of play.

SHIRLEY HORN "WILD IS LOVE"
The immediate reaction on Shirley's single is good.

AHMAD JAMAL "AT THE BLACKHAWK"
All the trades gave the LP a "PICK." Ahmad coming to the Embers, N.Y., Nov. 26th.

He keeps an up-to-date master file of disc jockeys on three-by-five cards; this information is also set forth on addressograph plates. "I spend thousands of dollars on postage alone. I'm always trying to figure out new ways to improve my service," he says.

"Across my desk I get anywhere from one to two hundred letters a week from disc jockeys around the country. From what they mention in the letters we know just what we have in certain sections. Then I call certain fellas around the country and I know what's going on. They tell me what they're playing. I've found out that when you strike up a pretty close friendship with a lot of the disc jockeys they are very honest. They'll say to me, 'Paul, nothing's happening with it.' Or 'Paul, we're getting so and so, what shall we do?' and I'll say, 'Well, can you increase the plays?' and according to the merit of the thing they'll do it. As a whole, the fellas have been very honest about the thing. This way I have pretty much of a cross-section, and within a couple of weeks I have a pretty good idea if they're going for the record or they're not going for it.

"The type that I handle is a very specialized type of a business. I came up in the era of good music and always liked good music. I've handled a lot of rock 'n' roll music and I've been pretty lucky with a lot of rock 'n' roll records, but as a whole I just don't get the feel. You see, some of the stuff, you just don't believe in it that much. A lot of material that's out in rock 'n' roll is good material. But there's a lot of stuff that's junk."

He also has an expensive Roberts tape-recording machine, and explained its usefulness this way:

"I do a lot of taping for the disc jockeys here in the office. Disc jockeys, college stations, AM and FM stations send in scripts where they want the artist to say something like, 'Hi, I'm George Shearing' and then add 'listen to station so and so.' I bring the artist into the office. I keep 'em here two or four hours and we do all the taping. I edit the tape on a three-inch reel, and we send it out. This has been very very effective. I started it about ten to twelve years ago, and it's been very successful.

"An artist comes to you and says, 'We want you to work on the record or album eight weeks.' They figure the normal run of a record is about eight weeks. And you say OK and you set up a fee and you go to work. And maybe you get a little lucky with it and they say 'Well, stay on it,' and before you know it you've been on it a year or so handling all their work. But with the majority of people you handle it's an eight-to-twelve-week deal. But I have about four or five people that I handle on a yearly retainer, which is very good.

"I get close to $1,000 on an eight-week job. Most of the time it's an oral contract. Once in a while it's written. But it doesn't mean that much. They can't cancel a contract, but if I've worked on a certain record—not with a name artist, but with a semi-name—if I've worked on a record about six weeks and we don't get any action on it at all, you know, we get some plays but there's nothing doing; and I've developed a kind of friendship with them, so I'll finally say—after six weeks—'Well, let's forget about the other two weeks,' and a lot of them appreciate my not holding them to the full price."

Expenses are included in his $1,000 fee for eight weeks' work. "I get one of the highest prices in the business, because what I do no other promotion man does. Some promotion men work for a half or a quarter of what I get. But some of them just do local jobs. Some say they do 'national,' but they do not do 'national.' I have equipment here in the office that costs me thousands and thousands of dollars, where I can put out a mailing within hours. I cover over 1,500 disc jockeys.

"I don't have anything to do with payola. The type of people I handle I don't have to pay for. The disc jockeys I work with have never asked me for it. Another thing, I couldn't afford to start paying off disc jockeys. Because if I started this thing I'd be in the clutch of certain disc jockeys and never be able to get out of it. So I've never had anything to do with it. I don't want to have anything to do with it. They picked the music business, but there is payola in every business."

One of his proudest record promotion coups concerns Tony Bennett. In this he worked with his friend, publicist Sid Ascher. "In 1951," he said, "we were put on Tony Bennett. Sid was doing the publicity work, and I was doing the record promotion. And we decided that this was a very, very important record for Tony, because it meant that if nothing happened now he would never have a Columbia contract. The record was 'Because of You.'

"Well, Sid and I sat down and we started figuring out different kinds of campaigns and stuff like this, and Sid started with his newspaper campaign on Tony and I started hitting the disc jockeys around the country. At that time there were two other records out, one by Jan Peerce and one by Johnny Desmond. And in the trade magazine, *Billboard*, Tony had the lowest rating of any of the other records. Sid and I decided we weren't going to let this stand in our way, and we started a real campaign around the country, with all the disc jockeys.

"So we started to hit disc jockeys around the country. I started making phone calls, made a couple of trips out to the disc jockeys, talked to them and so on. And then, by the good grace of God the record started to creep out. And before you know it, this was the record that hit for Tony. The Peerce and Desmond records were at first the ones that were being played. But I went around to a lot of the stations and they'd say, 'We heard it, we listened to the record.' And I'd say, 'Well, listen to it again, this has a sound.' And a lot of them would listen to it and say 'This sounds pretty good,' and start playing it. Then it hit the buying public. That's what we rely on, the buying public; when they start buying the record, then you have a hit. It sold over a million records. He got the gold record award, and I also received a gold record from Columbia on it. I actually worked on Tony for two and a half years. Then there was the 'Hit Parade' on radio and TV. 'Because Of You' was on their charts among the top seven songs for nineteen consecutive weeks. I think it was a run for any kind of a record."

Brown believes in gimmicks. "Polly Bergen had a record, 'Do It Yourself' and I came up with an idea about everybody being crazy about do-it-yourself things and I came up with an idea first about sending out some kind of a tool—a screwdriver thing. I have a book on different kinds of gimmicks. A friend of mine has this company—novelties and all these kinds of promotion gimmicks—so he brought me this book and I finally saw this little box with a thread and a thimble—a sewing kit. And on the cover we put 'Polly Bergen, *Do It Yourself*, Columbia Records,' and we put the music publisher's name, and we sent it out to disc jockeys and it was very effective.

"Even on myself I sent out a promotion gimmick. I have a friend, Bill Davidson, and he came in one day and said, 'I have something.' He brought it to me and it was a stand with a little black disc on it that looked like a record. And I had my name put on it, and it said 'Paul Brown, Record Promotion.' It had my address on it, too, and I had about two or three hundred of these made up and sent to clients or prospective clients.

"And the funny part of it is I never received any business out of this. But they're on a lot of people's desks around the United States. A year ago, Tom Morgan, who's one of the A & R men of Capitol Records, came in to record Nancy Wilson. And I went down to the date over at the 46th Street Capitol Studios. I walked into the studio, and Tom saw me and said, 'Paul, I think of you every morning.' I said, 'Gee, Tom, that's wonderful.' And he said every morning he sends his secretary for coffee, and when it comes he has my little black record set up like a coaster. He puts his coffee right on it and sees my name in front of him."

13 · THE DISTRIBUTION JUNGLE

SMART MONEY GOES TO ALEXANDER'S
SPECTACULAR RECORD EVENT

TOP MALE VOCAL LP ALBUMS
MONO AND STEREO RECORDS

$1.56 $2.16 $2.56

ALL TONY BENNETT, ALL ROBERT GOULET,
ALL ANDY WILLIAMS, ALL JOHNNY MATHIS,
ALL NAT COLE AND ALL FRANK SINATRA

—*Newspaper ad*

On most cartons packed with finished 45's and LP's there is printed in the bold type associated with the top line of optometrists' charts the legend: PHONOGRAPH RECORDS—KEEP AWAY FROM THE HEAT. But the fact is that the way records reach the American consumer resembles the heavily-strafed, heavily-bombed Burma Road during World War II.

The American record buyer goes to Sam Goody's or the Record Hunter in New York, E. J. Korvette in Hartford, H. Royer Smith in Philadelphia, Kroch's & Brentano's in Chicago, a branch of Music City in Los Angeles, or his neighborhood record shop. There he carries on in Hamlet-like indecision whether "to buy or not to buy." Finally he selects a recording from the bins or pegboard displays and brings it home to play and enjoy. He is unmindful of the fabulous, intricate record war that goes on daily with the neatly packaged "singles" or the glossy, laminated, cardboard-boxed, long-playing recordings.

He is innocent of the way commercial interests have jockeyed, competed, vied for window-display or shelf space in his favorite record shop or record department. Nor does he fully recognize how skillful, aggressive merchandising affects the output or "sound" of future kinds of popular music, for if one cycle or fad succeeds, it breeds swarms of imitative product.

But sometimes the record buyer can't help but be puzzled at the crazy-quilt price patterns in which he can buy the same Frank Sinatra 45 rpm for 64 cents, 69 cents, 88 cents, and 98 cents at varying retail outlets.

171

Record prices for a decade have had an Alice-in-Wonderland quality. Here is a bit of delicious dialogue from the 1963 hearings of the Federal Trade Commission into certain aspects of the record business. This colloquy concerned prices of Columbia LP's "listed" at $3.98.

Q. What price is Korvette's charging for similar records?
A. (by a Philadelphia record retailer): They vary in price from $1.77 to $2.79 or $2.98. I don't know what happened yesterday.

This situation has led *High Fidelity* to observe: "In the Age of Discount, records are a prime commodity; and the dealer who does not shave some percentage off "list"—the reduction can vary from as little as 5 per cent to as much as 50 or even 60 per cent—is faced with extinction."

The ordinary record buyer is bewitched, bothered, and bewildered by such (highly advertised) price manipulation. If he is in his thirties or forties, he has been chagrined at the loss of the cozy listening booths (once a pleasant way to spend a Saturday afternoon) and the emergence of the impersonal rows and rows of fluorescent-lit white pegboard record racks and bins. He is both pleased and slightly confused by the tremendous output of records—popular and classical—from hundreds of record companies. And he notes that whenever he shops for a tube of toothpaste, or for groceries, he encounters record racks. Without knowing it he has been witnessing a marketing and record-retailing revolution in the U.S. phonograph record business, which has grown from zero in 1877 to a multimillion-dollar industry today.

With exceptions, record retailing and merchandising was in a fairly primitive state in many parts of the country for decades. One veteran New England record executive reminisced recently:

"About seven or eight years ago, it was rather difficult to buy a record in Boston. Particularly if the customer found the only time he had to shop for a record was after 5 or 6 o'clock. Because in those days your record shops closed about then. There was, perhaps, one store in the city of Boston that remained open after that, and that would be a store catering more to the college student or jazz fan. But the person who wanted to buy a classical record or a 'pop' record, he had to buy it either during his working day or on his lunch hour."

Today, he observed, buying a record in all urban areas is relatively easy. Department stores increasingly keep late hours, and they stock recordings. So do discount chains in decentralized shopping centers. There has also been the multiplication of clean, well-run, attractive record shops in California, Florida, the southwest, as well as San Francisco and Los Angeles. College bookshops are also an important new record retail outlet. The Doubleday Bookshops sell a lot of records. Some of the bookshop-record shops are ambitious and enterprising. Besides selling an enormous amount of records, Washington's Discount Record, Book and Print Shop, in the nation's capital, visited by Congressional people and the foreign embassy colony, has sponsored concerts featuring the Philadelphia Orchestra, the singing satirist, Tom Lehrer, and folk-singer Tom Glazer.

But there still remain unkempt, sleazy shops that do no credit to the record business. Recently, one store in midtown Manhattan had this chaotic array of signs in the window:

Black-and-white photo finishing—Color
Photostats
Records
Free film
Record sale

Of course, this is not a true record store, but an obscure outlet for unsold merchandise, known as "distressed merchandise" by record company executives and distributors. Here, the records are not neatly arrayed. Nor are catalogues available, or copies of *Schwann's,* or are retail clerks knowledgeable about recordings and recording artists.

You can buy recordings by not walking out of your house, as millions do by belonging to any one of a number of record clubs: the Columbia Record Club, the Capitol Record Club, the RCA Victor Records and *Readers' Digest* Club, the Shakespeare Recording Society. And you can also belong to such record clubs as Citadel and Universal, where you pay a nominal fee and buy recordings of most record companies at a discount.

Some record executives have estimated that there are approximately 100,000 outlets for the sale of records. A Mercury Records official has asserted that there are 175,000 outlets. These record sales outlets—the middle-men of the vast popular music business—can be broken down as follows:

RECORD DISTRIBUTORS.
   "One stops." They sell all record labels, to juke-box operators mainly, and also to small record retailers.
   Juke-box operators.
   "Rack-jobbers." These are the new frontiersmen of record retailing. They sell to supermarkets, drug stores, dime stores. They'll even sell to underground garages and maternity wards, if it will pay off. They also run

record departments on a profit-sharing, or lease basis within heavily trafficked retail operations.

Record retailers.

Record clubs. A mammoth new development in record-retailing.

Record pirates. Counterfeiters of best-selling recordings.

Another important buyer of recordings, practically exclusively of LP's, is the armed forces exchange, here and overseas. For example, the U. S. Army maintains one of the biggest record-buying offices in the world for overseas PX's in New York City. Military posts in the U. S. buy from local record distributors. The military market has tremendous buying power. Profits made from the sales go to subsidize the recreational and welfare activities of the U. S. military posts, and save the taxpayers quite a bit of money.

In the record distribution picture there are approximately 125 "key accounts," according to one record executive. Some of the key accounts on the retail side are the Korvette's chain, Sam Goody's miniature network of seven stores, and such regional record chains as G. C. Murphy of Pittsburgh with approximately two hundred stores in Pennsylvania.

Very formidable in the record distribution scene, too, are the "rack jobbers." They stock the merchandise in the powerful department-store chains like W. T. Grant's, Woolworth's, and Whelan's. The chains receive approximately 15 to 20 per cent of the profits.

In terms of who buys how much, here are some interesting 1962 figures, which show the directions of modern record retailing. The figures were mostly compiled by *Billboard* which carries on the most intensive market research in the recording field. In 1962 the traditional record dealers accounted for $319 million. The record racks, largely a postwar innovation, racked up approximately 30 per cent of the industry's volume, or approximately a spectacular $197 million. The record clubs, which debuted in 1955, cut an increasing share of the pie, an estimated $100 million. The estimated 435,000 juke boxes spent about $35 million, and foreign exports totaled some $7.5 million at factory value.

Collectively, *Billboard* has estimated that the total record sales for 1962 was $651 million. That's quite a record for an industry whose death-knell has been predicted because of rival developments such as radio, television, and the taping of music from radio programs.

However, the digestive tracts of many responsible people have been twisted into cubist art deciphered only by gastrointestinal specialists because of the business tactics that have accompanied this growth. Attorney Earl Kintner of ARMADA, which is not a flotilla but the Association of Record Manufacturers and Distributors of America, told the 1963 ARMADA convention with very unlawyer-like bluntness:

"The record industry is full of illegalities, probably more than any other. . . . It is one of the unhealthiest industries in this economy." He spelled out two of the principal illegalities: transshipping and price-juggling.

Transshipping is a practice resorted to by record distributors. Here is the way it works. A Chicago distributor will sell a New York discount chain, which he is not supposed to do. This is the sales territory of the New York distributor. The New York distributor may sell to Detroit, and so it goes. Record manufacturers are unhappy about this jumbled state of marketing, but they often inspire this activity when over-zealous sales directors force product upon the poor distributor. Unable to rid himself of all that product, and unable to return anything but a small percentage, he makes a few hurried phone calls and frequently sells at cost. He doesn't want his much-needed cash tied up in inventory.

This results in picaresque bursts of sales activity. A Florida distributor suddenly starts reordering a popular music album, as if it were black Beluga caviar being sold at ten cents a can. But you cannot find the album anywhere in Florida. He is selling it to some midwest rack merchandiser.

Kintner also complained about the pricing structure. Frequently, big-volume buyers of records are given extra discounts, special "deals" on restocking programs, and extra "promotional" allowances. But a small buyer, perhaps one store, won't be given the same terms. This pricing favoritism tends to force the small record retailer out of business.

Equally candid has been the evaluation by Ira Moss, of Pickwick, a producer of low-priced recordings. Speaking of the "general climate of the record industry," he said: "A retail dealer cannot safely put a retail price on his merchandise. The consumer has lost the ability to understand record values and has lost faith in his local retailer as a responsible source for his record wants. Following a peak record-selling season, rack merchandisers are unable to pay their bills and manufacturers have bankrupted themselves."

This is no pretty picture. Dave Kapp, president of Kapp Records, whose artists include Roger Williams and Jack Jones, has long assailed the record industry for its hollow affluence, which he calls "profitless prosperity." In other words, the recording industry has been indulging in the selling of records to record distributors and sales outlets by offering them more and more discounts so they will buy more and more recordings. This is what is know in marketing language as "price-selling" rather than "product-selling." The by-product is that sales managers sell recordings at a price so low that the record company cannot make any profit. And you must have profit to continue in business.

Somewhere in your city or near where you live, there is an unimpressive one-story red-brick building, in the center of town or perhaps on the low-rent outskirts. In Chicago, the building may be a store with big-glass windows on "Record Row," South Michigan Avenue. In New York it may be a rabbit warren of offices in a dirt-streaked commercial building on gloomy Ninth Avenue, an area that could be marked for urban renewal and is quite a contrast to the beautifully designed product warehoused there.

Inside there are few glamorous offices—just girls working on bills at files and desks. In the back are the records—shelves and shelves of steel or wood. In the back or the front of the building, there is generally parking space. Throughout the day, Railway Express or private trucks park, bringing records to this structure or store. From it shoot out little trucks, Railway Express ones or snub-nosed Volkswagens, carrying cartons of Ray Charles, Chubby Checker, Connie Francis, Bent Fabric (there *is* such a recording artist)—"singles," LP's, good music, bad music, jazz, children's recordings, and no-music (spoken-word recordings).

These are the record distributors who supply the department stores, the record stores, the discount chains with "product." There are two main types of record distributors. One is the company-owned branch, such as those owned and operated by Columbia Records, Decca, or Capitol in key markets. Then there are the independent record distributors who market platoons of record lines—often, the more the merrier.

The "majors"—Columbia, Decca, Capitol—run and own their own sales organizations in the crucial markets where there is most consumer demand for recordings. They supplement their own apparatus with independent distributors in regions that are less critical sales areas. They function differently, for they can focus on a few key 45's or LP's to promote and publicize. They have no rival firms to handle, which could disperse their energies. The independent distributors, by handling ten, twenty, or as many as sixty record companies, find it hard to concentrate on a few records. They practice shotgun promotion and marketing.

A U. S. government report on the popular music business notes:

Besides selling the records to retail shops from which the public purchases them, distributors engage in various advertising and promotion ventures, such as contacts with broadcasters, and participation in sponsorship of "record hops" at which the labels handled by the distributor are featured. The distributor usually receives promotional allowances from his manufacturer-supplier [e.g., discounts] which he can pass on down the chain of distribution. In many instances, "freebies," at the rate of 300 [45's] free for every 1,000 purchased are provided to the distributor.

Everybody who has gained some maturity in the record business is concerned with the record distributors. Some promotion men will get their stars to phone key distributors and tell them about their new "release," which looks like a "hit." A record distributor's enthusiasm can incite enthusiasm among the local disc jockeys, and the local disc jockey is the pipeline to the teenage girl for "singles" and the adults for LP's.

There is a natural alliance between distributors and manufacturers—they need each other. Yet there is a permanent rivalry. It is a continuing tugging between the two. If a record sells, the manufacturer claims that it's what's in the grooves that counts. If it doesn't sell, the manufacturer blames its own sales branches or the independent distributor's poor handling, lack of window displays, ineffectual promotion.

In the record business, there is nothing more constant, more predictable than the announcements that "X" Company has changed distributorships in four cities. A year later "X" may take away his product from those four and allocate his recordings elsewhere.

Not long ago, a dusty traveler from the north, Buddy Basch, walked into one southern record distributor. A gregarious veteran of the music business, Basch goes back to the swing era. A promotion specialist, he collects record rarities: unreleased "dubs" and "air checks" of radio broadcasts. He has worked for Tommy Dorsey, Glenn Miller, Tony Martin, Connie Boswell, Andy Russell, Dinah Shore, Margaret Whiting, and, oddly enough, for Lady Iris Mountbatten.

This particular day, Basch was on a mission in behalf of a record company. "I was down in Charlotte," he said. "I walk into this distributor's office and say 'How are our records doing?'

"He says, 'Gee, they're not getting much play.'

"And I say, 'How come?'

" 'I don't know, the jockeys just didn't pick up on it.'

"Well, this is possible. So then the phone rings and he's going to take a call from New York or someplace. I motioned that I'm going to look around the back. So I got to his back room and I look and see the record I'm interested in sitting there in unopened cartons, and I know we shipped him like 200 promotional copies and 200 stock copies and there are my 400 records sitting there.

"Now I don't say anything to him, yet. I go back in and motion that I'll be back later. I get in my car and drive to the nine radio stations in Charlotte. I could be wrong. I'm willing to give him a break. So I go to the nine stations, which takes me half a day, and ask them if they got that particular record.

"And everyone of them says, 'No, I didn't get that one, yet.'

"Now I'm positive. So I go back and I say to him again, 'How's this record doing?'

" 'I don't know, we're not getting much play on it.'

"So I said to him, 'You chowder-head! You know why you're not getting any play on it?'

" 'No, I don't understand it.'

"So I said, 'Come with me a minute.' And I took him to his own stockroom. 'Now come here. I know how much we sent you on this 'cause we shipped every distributor the same 200 and 200.'

"Well, he looked at me and turned red, white, and blue alternately and said, 'There must be some mistake.'

"I said, 'Yeah, you're damn right there's some mistake. You didn't give out one of these records.'

" 'Oh, no, I must have given some of them out.'

"I said, 'Before I accused you or made any comment, not only did I look in your back room, but I went to every station in Charlotte—all nine—and not one said they got the record. In fact, one or two said they hadn't seen you in a month. And I've got another station who says if they want any of your records they have to come over here and get them. You won't even deliver them. Would it hurt to have one of your salesmen drop it off? Even if he doesn't want to spend much time?'

"Needless to say, we changed distributors in Charlotte."

The record manufacturers assert that they could fill up a two-volume book of distributor failures. Some accuse them of tricky trade practices. One record official was so allergic to distributors that he displayed a placard in his office which proclaimed: "All distributors are thieves."

However, the poor distributors assert that there is another side to the story, which shall be gone into shortly. Suffice it to say at this point that there are weak, forgetful, sloppy, untrained, greedy record distributors who do not lift a finger to help market product under its aegis, until it breaks out by itself through disc jockey play, or reviews, or word of mouth. But there are also good, functioning, and effective distributors.

One record executive who believes in distributors is a former record distributor himself. Chunky, fifty-one-year-old Sam Clark is president of ABC-Paramount Records, the parent company of Command, Westminster, Grand Award, and Impulse! After serving with the U. S. Navy he became a radio salesman, then a record salesman, and, following that, he took the plunge and became a New England distributor. He did such a good job that eventually he was called in to form ABC Paramount from scratch in 1955. It became a quick success in the popular music business, with early hits by teenager Paul Anka, who has since gone to RCA Victor.

"You must depend on your distributors," Clark said in his New York City headquarters recently. "You must have the effort that the distributor can give you. If you have a good relationship with a distributor, if he has been satisfied with the product you give him, the terms you give him, I think you get a greater effort from him. My experience as a distributor has taught me to respect a distributor's thinking, a distributor's idea of merchandising. *They're on the firing line.*"

His early days as a New England distributor, operating out of Boston, have, he says, sensitized him to record-distributor problems. Recalling those days, he told how he began with a bunch of miniscule record companies—Savoy, National, Deluxe. "I opened up a little store; I went out selling merchandise during the day, coming back after six o'clock, and then began packing the orders.

"My wife would come in during the days to wait for Railway Express, to deliver records or pick up records, after she'd sent the children off to school."

It was difficult for Clark to sell the popular music and jazz recordings put out by the companies he represented. The record dealers didn't accept the independent distributors and the independent record companies in those days. "In the eyes of the dealers of those days there were two or three record companies: RCA Victor, Columbia, and maybe Decca. Any other label was classified as a mongrel label.

"As a matter of fact, thinking back when I used to walk into a store with a Billy Eckstine record on National, the dealer would say to me, 'I'd love to have it, but can't you have it on RCA Victor?' It wasn't prejudice. I don't think they were aware of what independent records were or what a National Record was."

A few years later, the record retailers were less wary of the independent lines. For, from these unheard-of sources came hit records from unknown artists. The independents became increasingly powerful in record-making and record distribution. Clark developed into one of the most powerful distributors in New England. During this period, he took in a partner, Harry Carter, and together they ran Music Suppliers, Inc. until Clark left to form ABC-Paramount Records in 1955. In 1959–60 the firm figured prominently in the payola investigations as a source of payola to disc jockeys in and around Boston.

Clark sees two basic problems: transshipping and "allocations." Allocations is a procedure by which record manufacturers decide, often arbitrarily and unilaterally, how much a record distributor should buy of a certain "45" or LP. The distributor can complain. But if the record distributor keeps rebelling at allocations, the company may withdraw its "line." The withdrawal of the line, which represents a loss of income, is held menacingly over the distributor's head. Of course, if a record distributor loses his key lines, he eases himself out of business.

Clark reportedly is trying to spike the transshipping by threatening the distributor who does it with cancellation of his franchise. Other companies are allegedly trying this, too. As to allocations, Clark said that his company is a maverick in this respect. "We do not allocate merchandise. We announce a record. We send a sample of the record to our distributors. We suggest they take a certain number of records. It is only a suggested order and I'd say that in many instances this suggested order has been increased by the distributor. In other areas, it has been decreased.

"But we do not guarantee merchandise. We absolutely do not."

If you overload a distributor, you are encouraging transshipping, according to Clark. "If you don't overload him, he can't ever use the excuse, 'Well you sent me so much merchandise that I can't sell it in my territory. So you've forced me to go outside my territory.'"

The sales managers of independent record companies live on the telephone. They are constantly whooping it up for the newest release, mostly by long distance to their record distributors. The release is never less than "great," although in many cases they have never heard it. It is merely a code number on a neat order form. Lots of photographs in trade papers portray national sales managers phoning the distributors, who spend a good deal of their time, not working, but answering the telephone.

The telephone call can often "hypo" a record, but if the record potentialities are boomed out of proportion the sales manager for the label will find that the distributor will manage to send them back, guarantee or no guarantee.

Harold Drayson, who started as a sales clerk in a Broadway record shop at the age of fourteen, has been vice-president of LP Sales, the distributing company for Riverside Records, Battle, Wonderland, Jazzland, Prestige, and a handful of others. He has worked for MGM and

Caedmon Records. He once conjured up a checklist of how *not* to handle your distributors.

1. Call them up every day and ask them how they're doing.
2. Remind them of past-due bills.
3. Tell them they're doing a terrible job.
4. Tell them you are shipping them, no questions asked, the following allocation.
5. Ask them, "Where's the order you promised?"
6. Say, "Stop servicing accounts not in your territory."
7. Ask, "What happened to all your dealers?"
8. Remind them, "You haven't made your quota this month."
9. Say, "Why don't you change your salesmen?"
10. Suggest, "Try using your own stationery, instead of replying on ours."
11. Say, "Yes, but we have the best version of it!"
12. Or, "National reaction to the last release was great; what happened to you?"
13. Or, "I'm coming to visit you next month to collect our past-due money."
14. Or, "Do you, or *don't you*, want the *line?*"

The independent distributors take a lot of abuse, some of it justified, some of it not. They are often picked as "fall guys" for poor recordings, excessive-number releases, and inadequate record company publicity and promotion. From their point of view it is difficult to maintain enthusiasm over every single record, and every single LP. Besides, most distributors handle ten to fifteen record companies. In many regions of the country, considered less lucrative record markets, there are distributors who handle from thirty to sixty record "lines." They say the only way they can make a living is by servicing a great number of companies, that this pays "the rent."

It is naïve to think that anybody can handle sixty "indie" labels and do a conscientious job for them in terms of promotion, publicity, window display, and other aspects of record selling. Some of these distributors do not even listen to the new releases put out by the companies they are associated with. But many do the best they can with whatever forces they can afford.

Today's record-distributing scene is in turmoil. Quite a few distributors are going out of business; some are retrenching, some are sliding into bankruptcy. The problems are diverse. Primarily, perhaps it is because their economic stand-by, the independent record dealer, is being squeezed by the discount chains and the big department stores who can out-advertise the small retailer and who can offer "loss leaders" because they are anxious to bring people into the stores. The record retailer lives on the profit of recording sales and cannot compete that way. The distributor also asserts that the record retailers are being hurt by the record clubs.

Some record distributors have seen the retailing revolution explode, and they have moved to go beyond the distributor-retailer orbit. Very often, today's record distributor is also the owner of a rack-merchandising operation. Often he owns a "one-stop," which sells to the juke boxes, and the real penny-poor retailers. One of the veterans of record distributing in the United States is Amos Heilicher, considered one of the wealthiest men in Minneapolis. He owns a record-distributing company which handles the output of more than a hundred record companies from Abbott to Zen, including Atco, Chess, and 20th Century Fox. He also owns a large rack-merchandising operation. Heilicher is also an official of ARMADA, the policy-making body for the distributors.

The former vice-president of London Records, Leon J. Hartstone, is perhaps a forerunner of the future type of record distributor. He owns record retail shops; he owns a distributing company; and he runs leased-record departments and a rack-merchandising agency. He also manufactures records under the aegis of IPG (Independent Producers Group). His multifaceted enterprises cover New England, the Midwest, and California.

How does the average record distributor work? In a reply to a questionnaire, Southern Distributors of Nashville asserted that they have been in business four years, and represent sixty record companies. They disclosed that they had four promotion men and one girl. Their territory? Parts of Arkansas, Alabama, Mississippi, Tennessee, Kentucky, and Louisiana. For their part, they would like to see a changed distribution picture in which all the retail outlets would be equal, and there would be "no discounting."

Some of Southern's record salesmen, they assert, earn approximately $12,000 annually. And what about the charge by record companies that distributors are nothing but "order takers"? An official replied: "Then let them distribute and promote their own records."

The Jather Distributing Company of Minneapolis has been in business fifteen years, and handles recordings put out by approximately twenty companies. They reported four salesmen and two promotion men, and a territory that embraces Minnesota, North Dakota, South Dakota, Iowa, Nebraska, western Wisconsin. Jather has subregional offices in Omaha and Des Moines. They report that the average wage for record salesmen is $500 a month. To the charge that they are only "order takers," an executive replied: "Bunk."

The David Sales Company of Denver, Colorado, which has been

around for sixteen years, handles thirty record companies. They have five salesmen and one promotion man. David would like to see a "realistic approach to prices." As to the charge that some distributors are nothing but clerks who answer the phone, they say: "Some are and some are not, naturally."

In the Southwest, Buck Stapleton of Phoenix Record Sales has been in the record business fifteen years, and he markets the output of approximately twenty-five record companies. He employs three salesmen and one promotion man. His territory, Phoenix-El Paso, is considered a "one-percent market," in terms of national record sales. His chief hope is to rid the industry of the slogan: "Do unto Others Before They Do You." As to the complaint of record companies that they are "order takers," Stapleton said: "A performance by a distributor will never be satisfactory to a record company. The manufacturer only remembers the record you didn't promote. You are as good as what you can sell and promote tomorrow."

The rack business keeps going up. In 1962, the National Association of Record Merchandisers (NARM) reported that it serviced approximately 25,000 retail outlets. It is an interesting aside that many of the big chain rack-jobbers originally sold pharmaceuticals wholesale—brand name medicines and drug chemicals. As they got into records, they still retained the drug affiliation. Thus you have record-rack merchandisers with such names: Quality Drug Service Company, Des Moines, Iowa.

According to a trade-paper profile, the rack-jobber—the prophet of self-service—handles an average of three hundred locations. Dave Handleman of Detroit is the Gulliver of the racks, with approximately five thousand outlets which do an estimated business of $18 million annually. Approximately 70 per cent of the sales of rack merchandisers consists of long playing records.

The poor independent neighborhood and record dealer—what Sol Handwerger, MGM Records' publicist, calls the "Momma and Poppa store," is slowly being ravaged by intense competition and discounting. In the 1950's there were approximately 12,000 record retailers, dealing mostly in recordings, and they did about 90 per cent of the total volume. Came the discounting revolution, led on the East Coast by Sam Goody, and the picture changed radically. In 1962, the record retailers did about 49 per cent of the total record volume.

V. Anderson, of the Society of Organized Record Dealers (SORD), recently pointed out that approximately 9,000 record dealers were pursuing the old ways of record retailing in 1961. His definition of a record dealer is a merchant who makes 51 per cent or more of his money from records. In 1962, his estimate was that there were only about 6,000. He called the situation "a chaotic mess."

The independent dealer is fighting back as best he can. He is getting more merchandise-conscious, more exploitation-conscious. It would be a shame to see these dealers destroyed by impersonal forces. However, the future for them doesn't look too promising. Arnold Farber, editor of *Home Entertainment Retailing*, cannot see "the re-emergence of the independent record retailer," as in previous eras. He asserted that the big record companies are making their own sales. Increasingly, record manufacturers are promoting more heavily than ever in the big consumer magazines. They may even start to use direct selling on television. With these campaigns, the personalized service provided by a record retailer becomes less than vital. The consumer is being presold; all he needs to do is go to his local department or discount store, or any other kind of retail sales outlet.

There are some types of retailers who will survive—the "specialty" record shops and college bookshop-record shops—which stock the unusual, the offbeat, and in which sophisticated clientele want informed personal service or an aura of pleasant shopping.

But the bread-and-butter independent record dealer is finding it tougher and tougher to survive. This, of course, is not a unique characteristic of the record-retailing field; this is happening everywhere— the A & P, Grand Union, and Food Fair drive out the little grocery store or butcher shop. For the retailing revolution is toward money-consciousness, not service. As Kenneth S. Myers of Mercury Records expressed it in a meeting of his company: "The 'good old days' of the 50's are gone; the personality of retailing has changed. The illusion of value (call it discounting, if you will) is now the prime consumer motivator. Consumers are being accustomed to self-service shopping in exchange for this illusion of value."

Not an illusion is the fact that the record retailers are feeling the pinch, cash-wise, to use a Madison Avenue-ism. Many record retailers do not—or cannot—pay their bills. One Midwest distributor exited the record distributing field by remarking, "Record distributing has become largely a business of banking. Distributors are expected to act as bankers for their dealers or else they don't get the business.

"Today's dealers do only a small portion of the record business. The bulk of the retail volume is now being turned over by the chains, discount houses, and rack-jobbers in supermarkets. And practically all of them are cutting out the distributor by buying direct. What has

The world of popular music is a very large pie. These are the segments, not in proportion to their importance.

The Brill Building, the undistinguished-looking "capitol" of the music world.

Through the portals of the Brill Building have walked the famous, the infamous and the not-so famous of the pop-music world.

The pop-music world is not entirely centered in New York. Nashville and Los Angeles are a large portion of the business. This is Capitol's center in California.

Decca's veteran A & R man, Milt Gabler with Caterina Valente.

Don Kirschner, head of Colpix Records, has based his success on countless hits slanted toward teenagers.

Mitch Miller, formerly head of popular A & R at Columbia Records, is perhaps the most publicized record producer of all times.

Dick Clark with Brian Hyland and Gene Pitney. Clark is no longer on daily television, but he is a syndicated disc jockey and organizes touring rock'n'roll shows.

The Beatles became international stars in 1963-64 and generated a craze known as "Beatlemania."

Stevie Wonder, a *
sensation, records
Tamla Records of .
troit.

Teen-age vocal gr
are a recent and pop
innovation. One of
more successful has F
The Shirelles.

Brenda Lee is one of the few teen-age idols who is married.

Bobby Rydell is ambushed by fans at the stage door.

The Beach Boys are a male teen group who have capitalized on the West Coast sport of surfing.

Paul Anka, the phenomenally successful recording star, in a garden variety publicity still.

Popular Murray "The K," teen-slanted disc jockey on WINS in New York City also produces rock'n'roll stage shows.

Sam Goody was one of the pioneers of record discounting. This chain of stores reflects the new retailing trends: discounted prices, self-service, and a huge inventory.

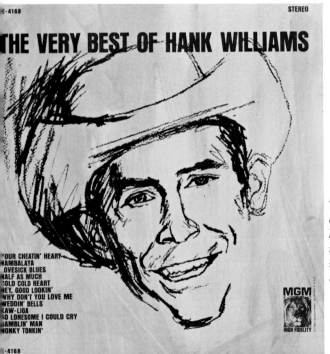

The late Hank Williams, a country and western music legend, whose records continue to sell at a fast pace. This album is a re-packaging of a number of his more popular songs.

Woody Guthrie is a "folk-original" who is one of the older leaders of the folk music vanguard.

Bob Dylan, a talented new folk personality, is a composer and singer who blends comtemporary social thought with the folk idiom.

Alan Lomax has organized many albums of ethnic folk music and edited a number of books. He is a prime mover in the ethnic folk music world.

Odetta is one of the top folk singers. Here she is recording a blues album, Sometimes I Feel Like Cryin'.

Stumpy Brown, Dean Martin, Bob Hope and Butch Stone in a spoof of folk singers on a Bob Hope Special.

Miles Davis at Carnegie Hall. Many recordings are now made of live performances.

The big hit on Broadway, abroad, and on records, How to Succeed in Business Without Really Trying, *is the work of theatre "pros" Frank Loesser and Abe Burrows. Bobby Morse (with razor) was a sensation in the lead.*

The arrival of sound gave rise to a new popular act, the screen musical. Here is Adolphe Menjou with a bevy of girls in Gold-Diggers of 1935.

Hollywood musicals once provided opportunities for some of the best writers to compose scores. Here is a scene from Rita Hayworth's Cover Girl by Jerome Kern and Ira Gershwin.

Fred Astaire starred in many Hollywood musicals. Here he is in Easter Parade with a score by Irving Berlin.

A new kind of musical, West Side Story, was a great international hit.

Elvis Presley, one of the early teen idols, now makes movies as well as records that are aimed at the teen market.

the distributor got left? Odds and ends. And we can't make a business out of odds and ends."

The business side of record distributing and record retailing may seem remote from Nat Cole, Peggy Lee, the Orlons, or Ray Charles. And remote from what you hear on the radio, the juke boxes, records, and TV. Yet it has a profound connection. Musical content and style and "sounds" in popular music follow sales to a large extent. The three most used, and most popular, words in popular music are: "It's not commercial."

A profound study could be amassed to show the relationship between the writing of popular music and record selling, and how one subtly influences the other. Needless to say, much fine product that is not ordinary, not usual, a little wayward, gets pushed aside by the hit-recordings that reach the trade-paper charts. The record salesmen, the distributors, the rack merchandisers concentrate on, feature, and display the "hot merchandise," the best-sellers. Similarly, whenever a "sound" is popular (surfing songs, hot-rod songs, bossa nova sounds) the record industry turns these sounds out in assembly-line fashion.

Here is one simple example. Increasingly, record consumers are pre-sold. But many still do browse in record shops and discount chains and buy what they see. But do they see everything that is available? Hardly. According to one sales manager for a small label, "Our problem isn't in getting good distributors. We have them. Our problem is getting our share of the retail business due to the influx of so many record companies who are fighting for representation of their record in the same shop; due to the limitation on the part of the retailer, both inventory-wise and financially."

The interplay between the business side of record selling and creativity goes on. Meanwhile, the record industry itself is taking a long, painful look at the distribution and retailing jungle. Responsible elements are trying to introduce some sanity and wholesome business practices into a lunatic world.

The lunatic economics have been sapping the energies of a multi-million-dollar industry. Some of these problems are worth summarizing—transshipping, unwise allocations, credit and collection problems, and the crazy-quilt pricing structure. Besides these problems there are adjacent problems—the lack of skilled record promotion men on the distributor level, and of informed retail personnel. Of course, the record shops can't really get too many first-rate people, because they pay them so poorly.

One of the most crucial problems is the price structure. In this area Columbia Records has lighted a candle in the darkness. In 1963 it announced what it called "The Age of Reason." The phrase was borrowed from Thomas Paine, who emphasized rationalism. The concept is an attempt toward price-stabilization. Columbia declared that it would adhere to a strict, unchanging, year-round price schedule on its "singles" and LP's.

For example, a $3.98 record would sell to the record retailer for $2.25. There would be no discounts, no "deals." There would be no special restocking plans at any time during the year, which benefit the big-moneyed buyers like discount chains and department stores and rack merchandisers. One retailer told *Billboard:* "It's a step in the right direction. I wish everyone would do it."

Similarly, Capitol Records has announced a new provocative "Stand for Stability." It has stated that it will put a brake on all special discount programs, and will sell recordings at one price the year round. Its new schedule, for example, is $2.02 for $3.98 LP recordings to all the middle-men, record shops, one-stops, and rack merchandisers, discount chains, department stores. The rack merchandisers and one-stops, seeing their 10 per cent functional discount being taken away, are as wild as untamed mustangs over the idea.

The record industry as a whole has not yet followed Columbia's or Capitol's lead. But it is a sound move. Also, the government, through the Federal Trade Commission in association with record manufacturers and ARMADA, representing record distributors, is exploring ways to curb unfair price practices and other illegalities.

Some record companies are also trying to engage in more conservative, realistic selling. Stuffing record distributors with excessive product, when they in turn must do the same to their retailers, doesn't do anybody any good. It merely leads to ballooning credit problems, the inability to collect, and transshipping; eventually it leads to huge returns of unsold merchandise. In some cases, record companies have by-passed ordinary policy on returns and have allowed distributors and retailers to buy on a "100 per cent guarantee." And sometimes they get back 97 per cent.

The record industry is like the patient who has been undergoing psychoanalytic therapy for five years. He may not be cured, or even improved, but he certainly is profoundly aware of the problems.

14 · THE ECONOMICS OF RECORDING

The scene would be worthy of an urban Winslow Homer. The place: outside an East Coast radio station whose transmitter and studio facilities are at the edge of sandy marshes. A disc jockey and another station employee are playing a game. They are tossing objects into the marsh grass to see who can throw farthest. The airborne objects are white-labeled, red-labeled, blue-labeled, black-labeled, 45-rpm "pop singles."

If the many persons—record executives, arrangers, composers, lyricists—who lavished their time, money, and energy could see one of their discs treated so cavalierly, they would probably have a heart attack. But unloved, unplayed, or little-played records—"singles" and LP's—are treated shabbily, largely because there is overproduction and also because making phonograph records isn't too costly.

As *Life* has put it: "Anyone—*anyone* can record and press 5,000 records for $1,200. So there are more than 1,500 little 'pop' record companies who press almost any song or sound that comes along and hope that lightning will strike."

What exactly are the economics of popular music recording? What does an Andy Williams "pop single" cost to produce? A typical "teen date"? Is a Joan Baez folk-music record session expensive? How astronomical are those best-selling albums of show music to make?

As to recording costs, each date differs with the type of songs (slow or fast), number of musicians, arrangement, and the "recording situation." One of the nation's top single hits was reportedly cut in Texas at the cost of a Neiman-Marcus back-scratcher, $185. Youngsters have even cut 45-rpm demonstration discs in the basement of homes on inferior equipment—and these have been released as "masters." The costs of these homemade recordings were just the price of the tape and the few cents worth of electricity to operate a little tape recorder.

But the average recording by a reputable record company ranges in cost from $1,200 to $3,000. An average 45-rpm record may cost $1,500. A Frank Sinatra "single," in which he is backed by a big band, may reach $3,000. The recent hit by Andy Williams, "I Can't Get Used to Losing You," cost in excess of $3,000, according to a Columbia Records official. And about the same time, a number-one hit was made by a top independent company—under union regulations—for one-third of the Andy Williams' date.

In 1963, bright, conscientious, thirty-six-year-old Al Stanton, producer for Kapp Records (its crest is a sort of glossy red and blue parade-grounds military hat) produced "Our Day Will Come," a record which reached the crow's nest of the trade-paper charts. It was done with an unknown group, four boys and one girl named Ruby and the Romantics. The recording was a fairly inexpensive date with six musicians. "It had a forty-dollar arrangement," recalled Stanton, "and the whole date cost about $1,000. The recording sold about 800,000 copies."

He added, "I have pretty much of a free hand in matters of budget. An elaborate session may cost $2,000 to $3,000. That's a lot of money for a 'pop single.' What brings up the costs considerably are the vocal groups for background and strings."

Sometimes a single record is taken from an LP and it will cost somewhat less. Not long ago, for example, Ray Charles took a country and western favorite, gave it a blues-flavored treatment, and it sold more than 2,000,000 copies here and abroad for ABC-Paramount Records. Initially it wasn't to be released as a 45-rpm "single," but a rival firm put out a recording imitative of it, and ABC, enraged, just released the track from the LP.

In one of the Ray Charles LP sessions, more than six songs were recorded. Here are the figures for one-sixth of that session:

Musicians	$ 535.00
Musicians Union pension fund	62.00
Cartage of instruments	3.00
Arrangement	250.00
Copyist	73.00
Eight vocalists (choral background)	159.00
AFTRA pension fund	8.00
Studio	102.00
Total	$1,192.00

Chubby, low-pressure Sid Feller, veteran A & R man for ABC Paramount who worked with Ray Charles on that "date," said that single sessions can go much higher. "With overtime and thirty to forty musicians, it's possible to run recording costs to $4,000 and $5,000."

He noted that there are fixed costs, and variable costs. Some of the fixed costs:

Musicians	$56 per man for a three-hour session, plus 8% AFM Pension Fund on the $56
Leader	$112
Contractor	$112
Studios	$65 per hour
Tape	$8-10 for a ¼ inch tape; ½ inch tape runs $20 per reel. Approximately two to four reels of tape per "single session."
Engineers	(part of studio costs) In some studios, overtime begins at 7 P.M., some get overtime after 12 P.M.

Musicians, he adds, get overtime after three hours in half-hour segments. Vocal groups, he pointed out, are expensive.

"They get paid a minimum of $18 per side. If you use six to twelve voices it adds up. If they do four sides, of course, it runs very high. The vocal contractor gets what they get and half of that more."

Unprofessionalism balloons costs, according to Feller. "Normally it takes three hours for four sides, if you have professional people. It depends on who is producing it, who the artist is, and how much preparation has been done. I know people who go into the studio with no preparation in front and work everything out in the studio. If they come up with a hit nobody quarrels with them. But it's very expensive making the original record. If you pay $56 per person for three hours, and you start experimenting in those three hours, and it runs over three hours, you are adding overtime. Wouldn't it be better if you knew what you were doing in front and could walk out of the studio after three hours?"

As to average cost, Feller believes that a normal four-sided session with a moderate orchestra and a first-class arranger has got to cost $2,500 to $3,000. This includes the arranger's flat fee of between $150 and $250 per arrangement. Collectively this adds up to $600 or $1,000 for arrangements. Copying costs are roughly $100 to $200 for four tunes, according to length, density, and how many parts they have to copy.

(Recently, the American Federation of Musicians successfully negotiated an increase in recording fees for the musicians, from $56 to $61 per three-hour session. The musicians also won mandatory rest periods, a "late" penalty-payment charged to record companies who did not pay on time, and time and a half for recording on Sundays, holidays, and after-midnight sessions.)

On the West Coast, recording rates are the same as they are for the eastern record companies. Sun-blessed or smog-kissed, all the reputable companies and recording studios are guided by the many show business and technical unions. Vocalists have to be paid minimum rates established by AFTRA (American Federation of Television and Radio Artists). For solo vocalists this is $65 per side or hour. And the audio engineers, who operate the array of dials in record studios, are paid according to scales set by the National Association of Broadcast Employees and Technicians and the International Brotherhood of Electrical Workers.

Though Capitol Records is reluctant to give out specific figures for specific sessions, it has disclosed the following: "A recent 'pop' session which was considered typical cost a total of $1,625. That was a three-hour session in which four sides were produced. The fourteen musicians cost $952 of that, and the tape used cost $58."

Can a smaller, independent producer, without a huge bureaucracy, if he is watchful of costs and time, produce more cheaply? Undoubtedly, but those in the big cities who are active producers of recordings still have to pay the going union rates. Consider one of the most successful music operations in the past five years, the Kirschner-Nevins combine, which chalked up upward of thirty hit recordings, many of which were "million sellers." It typified popular music's new look. It embraced music publishing, independent record producing, talent management, and record manufacturing. Recently purchased by Columbia Pictures for $2 million, this combine will produce for the film company's record division, Colpix, and accumulate copyrights for two music publishing firms owned by Columbia Pictures, one ASCAP and one BMI.

Art Kaplan, of this teen-oriented musical empire now ensconced with Columbia, analyzed the costs of making one of the Kirschner-Nevins hits, "Don't Say Nothin' Bad about My Baby." It was sung by a group with the aroma of fresh-baked goods, the Cookies.

"DON'T SAY NOTHIN' BAD ABOUT MY BABY"
(Production Costs)

Musicians—4 sax, 3 guitars, 3 drummers, piano, bass—$56 per musician for the 3-hour session	$672
Conductor (double the cost of a musician)	$112
Musical contractor (choosing and arranging for the musicians, Art Kaplan)	$100
Studio (recording session, time to remix, sometimes known as "mastering")	$500
Two reference dubs, $3 each	$ 6

The Cookies (a trio)—$22.50 a side each, or cost of an hour's
  recording, whichever is greater—AFTRA scale

Arranger ($150 per song) did three	$450
Copying, approximately $50 per song	$150

The $500 studio costs seemed high, as studio costs run around $65
an hour on the average. Kaplan explained, "Well, figure three hours
recording time, so $65 times three is $195. Then there is an extra-
mixing session. Gerry Goffin, the producer, is a perfectionist and he
wanted to get the exact Cookies' *sound.* So with the re-recording time,
synchronizing time, or editing time, and with extra dubs and references the costs go up."

It might be noted that the Cookies got the AFTRA recording scale
as do all recording artists (the vocal group rate)—independent of
record royalties. Added to the cost but not set forth was the producer's
fee for Gerry Goffin, one of the top songwriters and producers of recordings with the "teen feeling." He is on a royalty basis much like an
artist, and takes his earnings out of record sales.

The "reference dubs" are taken off the tape as soon as the session
is completed. These are recordings, and they are studied. The recording itself is produced on three-track tape. Later on, Goffin may listen
to the dubs and decide that he wants to change the blends of the instruments, bring one up and another down, or highlight the voice in
some way. This he can do by "remixing," playing with the three
channels.

All in all, the naked recording costs, excluding coffee, candy, or
cookies, totaled $2,123. This is exclusive of pressing copies of the
records, the printing of labels, the cost of cartons, the shipment to
distributors, and many other kindred costs.

Of recording costs, Dave Kapralik of Columbia Records says: "It
depends on the artist and what kind of session you do. It depends on
whether the session is done in Nashville or New York, whether it's
head arrangements or arranged by a handful of the most successful
'pop' arrangers, whether it's a rhythm section date, or a full-string-
complement date.

"A normal 'singles' session, which requires a complement of strings
and a primary arranger who charges $200 to $250 an arrangement,
would cost about $2,400. An album session might cost anywhere from
$8,500 to $11,000.

"Promotion and advertising expenses must be considered, too. So it's
illusory to say 'Well, a session cost you $2,100 and you sell 86,000
records to break even.'

"The cost for a major record company to record are disproportionate to the costs that small independent companies pay for a number of reasons. Major record companies, particularly RCA and Columbia, are affiliated with radio and TV networks. The engineering unions are the same, and there are certain union regulations that we have to relate to.

"The musicians' union perhaps looks more closely into the activities of the major record companies because they make more records than the small independents and there are practices among small independents which we would not and could not consider. These include making a session at 'demo' rates and then after it turns out all right you go back and pay union scale in releasing it. When we make a session it is a master session. There is no such thing as 'demo' rates for us. In a way it is unfair because the swinging 'indie' is our competitor just as much as our confrères at the other major record companies."

A rhythm tune record date is cheaper than a ballad, cost producers of records state. Sam Gordon of Udell-Geld Productions, which combines talent management, song publishing, and producing records says: "We've found that rhythm dates are always cheaper than ballads, because it's strictly a guitar and drum record with voice. We can do a total record, sides A and B, for $1,500—a rhythm thing."

He added: "We have found that if we want to go in, we can go in and do a single side for $750."

Udell-Geld Productions is one of a covey of independent record-producers. They are not tied to any single record company. This particular young show business enterprise often does "sneak previews" of record sessions, for self-analysis.

Sam Gordon revealed: "We do something I've never heard of anyone else doing. Before we go into a date we take the singer and we do a preliminary record with a few people, so it doesn't cost much money and it means we're much better prepared. We don't go in and pray. That costs a couple of hundred dollars to do. We don't do that on all, but on virtually all dates.

"It makes a tremendous difference because we are not going in there and reaching for something and we don't know what it is. We try to plan out the whole date so it will come out the way we want—start to finish. And I would say we have never torn up a tape or anything like that. Or had to go in and do it again. Which is, I think, very unusual. And it's a result of a good deal of planning."

The costs of making an LP, which generally consist of ten to twelve selections, can vary from about $3,500 all the way up to $70,000, the reported cost of Enoch Light's re-recording of the hit Broadway musical, *Carousel* on Command.

A vocal trio similar to the RCA Victor's Limeliters can execute certain albums for $3,600 to $4,400. Little jazz trios aren't too expensive, nor are studio-made recordings of some solo folk artists. But the big band outings of Duke Ellington or Count Basie or Melachrino or Percy Faith can mount up.

"We have done albums," said Sid Feller in his modest offices at ABC Paramount Records, "with thirty-six men, and if you run overtime this can run into a great deal of money. We have made albums that run $15,000 to $16,000 for twelve sides. That's the equivalent of three sessions which ran approximately $5,000 a session. Now if the album doesn't sell at least 30,000—the possible break-even point—everybody concerned loses a lot of money."

Folk music has now penetrated popular music—at two levels—that of the "pop single" field and the long-playing record best-selling charts. In terms of producing a folk session, it can be inexpensive, for often they combine the artist-musician-arranger in one. And without an arranger's fee, or a copyist's fee, or a musical contractor, or vocal chorus for accompaniment, the "date" could be fairly economical.

But there are exceptions. Though Joan Baez sings by herself, and accompanies herself, album productions with her are certainly not calico-cheap. Maynard Solomon of Vanguard Records, the company for which she records, explained it thusly: "You would think that folk music is less expensive, but there are many variables. Take Joan Baez's album, 'Joan Baez in Concert.' It was taped over a period of six months at over twenty concerts. We had two engineers following her around. I prefer not divulging the specific costs, but the album cost beyond $10,000."

What brings up the costs, too, revealed Mr. Solomon, is the artist's contractual right to reject material already taped. And though the artist is charged for recording expenses, the fact is that the important record artist receives guarantees "far beyond the costs of the sessions."

He said, "You have to figure out the guarantees paid to the artist plus the number of sessions and costs to get an accurate figure on how much the album really cost."

Harry Belafonte is one artist who is particular about what he will allow to be released. He goes over material again and again, and the costs mount up. But this may not be excessively burdensome, for he is a "staple," a big-selling artist.

What about the Broadway original-cast albums for which record companies fight and scheme and use all sorts of complicated royalty arrangements to acquire? The original-cast album is one of the desired properties in popular music recording. Aaron Copeland or Elliot Carter may write a new symphony or sonata and have it put on LP, but there is no Machiavellian maneuvering to get the rights. The reasons are these: (1) there is a highly developed group of musical theater devotees all over the country, many far from Broadway, who if they can't see the show, want to hear it; (2) musicals have tremendous prestige; (3) the publicity show albums are a great inducement.

Where did the idea of making cast albums originate, and precisely how much do they cost? In the 1930's two young enterprising record makers, the late Jack Kapp and his brother Dave, of Decca Records, heard of an intriguing European concept. Over there they were doing albums of popular operettas. "These were single twelve-inch LP's and they were called 'Gems' of this, and 'Gems' of that," recalled Dave Kapp recently.

In 1937, the two brothers decided to produce an album titled *Porgy and Bess*, with the original cast, including Todd Duncan as the legless Porgy, and conducted by Alexander Smallens. The maverick project cost less than $5,000 and formed three twelve-inch records in a set for $4.25. For some reason, the original-cast album idea lay fallow thereafter. In 1943—six years later—the then thirty-six-year-old Dave Kapp and his brother decided to produce the monumental hit, *Oklahoma!*

"I myself produced the *Oklahoma* album. It cost us about $10,000 or $12,000. The album consisted of six ten-inch 78's, and it sold for $5. It was released October, 1943. We used to figure then about seventy-five cents a record with fifty cents for the album container. Alfred Drake made more money out of the cast album than he did by playing in the show. In a year and a half it sold about 500,000 units. It has sold around 1,000,000 units in all."

In 1943, *Oklahoma* cost around $12,000. In 1961, Dave Kapp produced the original cast album of *Donnybrook*, based on the film, *The Quiet Man*. It cost $27,000.

Brown Meggs of Capitol Records has asserted that albums of *The Music Man* and *The Unsinkable Molly Brown* cost between $25,000 and $30,000. Where does all the money go? In an article in *Playbill*, Ren Grevatt noted the following financial facts concerning theater music LP's:

It costs up to $30,000 to record the [cast] album. That's just the cost of the studio, union rates for musicians, and a full week's regular salary for every member of the cast. Other costs—promotion, advertising, and exploitation—

can run the initial investment as high as $100,000. If the show doesn't co-operate by becoming a hit the record man can kiss his money goodbye. He has sustained close to 100 per cent loss on the project."

There are numerous "deals"—and variations—concerning the acquisition of original-cast albums. Grevatt observed: "The 'going' royalty in recent years has been 10 per cent (of each album sold) to the producer. Of this 10 per cent, 60 per cent usually goes to the writers of the book, music, and lyrics. Name players in the cast may also receive a specific share of the producer's royalty. Actually, this means a double pay-off for the writers. For each copy of the LP sold, the publisher of the music is paid a royalty of two cents per song per record sold, or twenty-four cents for the average album. One half of this the publisher pays out to the writers."

It might be noted that the producer gets a 4 per cent royalty free and clear. This doesn't go into the producer's pocket. It is considered income for the production.

The in-fighting between record companies for cast album rights is reflected in the escalating royalty rates "in front." Years ago, in the case of the *Oklahoma* album, for example, the only royalties went to the composer and lyricist and music publisher, apart from specific royalties to some in the cast. Later, Columbia paid 5 per cent extra to the producers for the rights to *Finian's Rainbow*. Now it is supposed to be 10 per cent, but that has been breached, too. Capitol Records went to 17 per cent to tie-up Richard Rodgers' *No Strings*, and recently it paid a reported royalty of 20 per cent for the musical *Tovarich*. As in all recording, the cost of the sessions are deducted from the royalties.

Except for the original cast-recording of *The Threepenny Opera*, by MGM Records, few cast albums of off-Broadway shows and revues sell. And since theater productions cost lots of money to tape, record firms are reluctant to do them, save for prestige reasons.

As a result, not long ago, an off-Broadway hit musical paid for its own recording of its cast album. This fantastic situation occurred with *The Fantasticks*. Despite rave reviews when it debuted in 1960, no company wanted to invest the several thousand dollars necessary to make an album of this charming work by Harvey Schmidt and Tom Jones which has a cast of nine and intimate orchestrations by Julian Stein. MGM displayed some interest but claimed it would be too risky financially. Producer Lore Noto thought it would do the show a lot of good, get the score around and played on radio, if there was a cast album. He struck up an arrangement with MGM Records whereby the *The Fantasticks* company paid for the recording date, slightly over $3,200.

In 1963 Noto reported that he has recouped the money from record royalties (more than 17,000 copies old), and the show has acquired valuable publicity by being heard on AM and FM radio.

An album concept can add immeasurably to an LP cost, particularly when that concept embraces the serving of an attractive buffet, a flowing "free bar," and several hundred guests. Not long ago, for example, RCA Victor and Peter Nero decided to produce an LP titled, *Peter Nero in Concert*. The "concert idea" is a staple in record company merchandising, as much so as discounting. However, rather than tape an actual in-person appearance, the powers-that-be chose to simulate a "live concert." So they invited trade-press people, disc jockeys, record dealers, sales persons from Goody's and Doubleday's, record buyers for department stores, and several hundred high-school youngsters to Webster Hall on a balmy Spring evening, March 25, 1963.

Clustered around the entrance to Webster Hall were a group of teenagers. Atop a simulated movie marquée glowed the legend: PETER NERO—RECORDING SESSION. Inside the long, ballroom-type hall, noted for its marvelous acoustics, there was a long, long buffet table. Piled high were mounds of crusty French bread, sweet and pickled gherkins, giant black olives, red peppers, delicious white cocktail onions. Behind the food was a sign: "HAVE A HERO ON NERO."

It was only 8 P.M., but already most of the meats were gone, consumed by those who had arrived early. The bread was there, the tasty cocktail appetizers, but no meat, and many hadn't eaten dinner because they were promised "food." A nervous RCA Victor VIP hurriedly dispatched a minion to buy more sliced meats, mostly Italian ham, cut paper thin but delicious.

At a bar, a long, almost quarter-block long bar, drinks were flowing like lemonade at a Sunday-school picnic, or Dr. Brown's celery tonic at a Jewish delicatessen. Down on the dance floor of the Webster Hall people were milling about, some of them taking photographs. Bald-headed Martin Block, the dean of America's disc jockeys, sat quietly.

On the walls of Webster Hall were painted balloons, and upstairs in a tiered balcony the youngsters sat, quietly and anxiously. Finally more food came, and there was a cry of welcome. The latecomers, who hadn't had dinner, surged forward. A little after 9 P.M. a man appeared on stage and told the audience that it was to be a "concert," and that the long-playing recording of it would be out in a few months.

To check the equipment he said, "Let's have a little applause." There was dutiful applause, and even some teenage whistling. Finally, Peter Nero, a bright, handsome young man of twenty-nine, appeared with a trio.

He proceeded to play and prefaced each selection with humorous commentary. "My first number is a collaboration between Buddy de Sylva and Mozart," he said. Later he remarked, "Somebody has suggested I do an album of spirituals, and the title might be 'Nero, my God, to Thee.'"

The trio couldn't have cost too much, and Nero himself—a prized Victor artist on royalty—didn't have to be paid. The food and the drinks probably cost more than the record session. But if you have an album concept of "in concert," producers feel that you must simulate that appreciative, excited feeling of a popular concert.

Cost of the food and drink? Perhaps $1,000. The cost of the raw recording, according to RCA Victor? "About $2,000," said Herb Helman, RCA Victor press information services director.

Newcomers to the record business, or even the small established recording companies, find that rental rates for recording studios are enormously variable. For example, you can rent the excellent Studio A of Columbia Records in New York City for one hour for $75. In Nashville, you can get Studio A of Columbia for $37. Columbia's Chicago recording studios will charge you $30 an hour. The rate card of Columbia Record Studio in Hollywood—on Sunset Boulevard—is higher—$85 an hour.

Record studios as a reflex of the phonograph record boom have proliferated in the oddest places. There is one in a former Hearst penthouse in Manhattan. Some are in basements, some in walk-in stores; the closet is the recording "studio." In Ashland, Ohio, you can rent studios for $15 an hour for "mono" recording, and $25 an hour for stereo recording. Rehearsal fees are $5 an hour. These are apparently the studios of Hilltop Records. This firm can press 1,000 records for $275 and have them released and distributed on the Hilltop or Big Country label.

The economy approach often leads some record producers to go abroad, particularly with projects with large, lush orchestrations involving many musicians or choral groups. Costs in England, Germany, Italy are one-third to one-half less than in the U. S. RCA Victor makes many of its low-cost Camden series of "Living Strings" LP's in London. They are not alone. Budget-priced reproductions of show scores are cut there, and sometimes you have interesting linguistic touches such as an English cast singing colloquially flavored American show songs.

Lest this lead to anti-European animosity—a charge that their musicians are taking bread out of the mouths of American musicians—it might be pointed out that American recordings made here are lavishly supported by European record buyers, indeed, by collectors of popular music everywhere outside the United States.

Once the recording is actually put on tape, what is the actual cost of pressing records—"singles" and LP's—and having them put in marketable shape for the U. S. consumer?

Here is a cost sheet that offers an idea of taking the "master" and making it into a salable item on your record dealer's shelves. These are figures from the Custom Record Division of one of the largest record companies. Many small record producers and independent companies have their records cut by the majors—Victor, Columbia, Capitol—all of whom compete aggressively for the extra business.

1000 Records (7")	*1000 LP'S (12")*
1. Pressings, $110 (11 cents each)	$400 (40 cents each) (Pressings include labels and inner sleeves)
2. Design Labels $100	
3. Plain Sleeves N/C (No charge)	$220 (22 cents each, Finished jackets)

Record-pressing prices vary. Many record-pressing firms can press 5,000 single 7-inch records for a cost of a little more than $300. That's slightly more than six cents apiece, including a one-color label. Some of the larger firms (as noted above) charge eleven cents each, plus $100 for label design and printing. However, the bigger record-pressing plants generally practice strict factory control over imperfections, and they use better raw materials.

Most of the major record producers make recordings, according to expert testimony, from approximately 85 per cent "pure vinyl," plus additional components. Vinyl is a word employed to describe a general family of chemicals and plastics. Vinyl materials include films, some plastics, and some liquids.

"It is accurate to say that all records are made of vinyl resins. However, there are countless variations in chemical make-up. Some chemical formulas, for instance, include an anti-static element," maintains a representative of Union Carbide, the company that owns the trademark "vinylite."

Those firms that produce "budget" records for less than one dollar—

collections of show tunes, dance music, instrumental music—frequently mix vinyl with a greater percentage of filler or "extenders." These are tossed into the chemical pot for "competitive advantage." In other words, more records at less cost.

Incorporated within these phonograph records, too, might be anti-statics, as well as virgin dry-blended resin powders. Heated and processed into recordings, the vinyl is the basic raw material by which you eventually enjoy everything from Rodgers and Hart to Bach.

Most recordings you buy are black—the most preferred "color." But records can also be red, blue, yellow, green, a tropical orange, and that shiny shade of gold. The West Coast seems to have an affinity for multi-hued colors. But eastern manufacturers say "it's just an added sales gimmick." "The trouble is that those multi-hued discs show up im-perfections glaringly. The records are all right for playback, but any imperfection is a reject, and that becomes a costly thing," reports one production executive.

Naturally, the more you press, the less expensive the LP's. Decca recently offered this estimate for anybody who wanted to press 100,000 to 1,000,000 monaural LP's on vinyl with groove guard.

Records 28 cents
Polyethylene bag 2½ cents
Plain white sleeve 1½ cents
Correlation (putting record in bag or sleeve) ½ cent
Total cost: A little more than 32 cents, from plant locations at Gloversville, New York, or Pinckneyville, Illinois

If the designer of the jacket is on staff of a record firm that's one thing, but if the designer is free-lance he may receive $100 to $150 for the artwork. If there is to be "outside" photography, an outstanding free-lance photographer like Ben Rose will charge approximately $150.

The sleeves of the small 45 rpm's sometimes carry multicolored pic-tures of the artists, which cost approximately a penny each. A "simple" sleeve may cost only half that amount.

But there are hidden costs which must be borne by these inanimate discs. There is the company overhead (salaries for executives, A & R men, secretaries, promotion people, free records to disc jockeys, postage, phone bills, wires, pencils, paper, erasers, mimeograph supplies). Since most of the recordings do not earn their basic pressing costs back, a lot depends on the big hits and on the "staple sellers," known in the trade as catalogue items, or recordings whose basic worth remain through the years.

In any event, a 45-rpm or an LP has a basic cost, and also a super-structure cost that is hard to perceive, since these costs are in loose relation to the number of recordings issued, artists' guarantees, and the record company's overhead.

15 · THE GOLDEN PIE—AND HOW IT IS CUT UP

> They say that the romance has gone out of the music business.
> But when you're making money, there's plenty of romance.
> —Mack Wolfson, Songwriter, co-author of "C'est La Vie"

Frank Sinatra snaps his fingers—the materialist world in his hands—and sings a haunting version of aloneness, "Lonesome Road." The song is put on rust-brown magnetic tape. Later it is mass-produced on vinyl at a factory, and before long it is packed in cardboard cartons and finds its way to a record distributor and then into a snub-nosed green truck. The truck carries the legend, in golden letters, KING CAROL . . . MAXIMUM DISCOUNTS . . . WHOLESALE AND RETAIL. The driver stops the truck at a Times Square store; he takes out a handtruck and rolls the Sinatra albums into the shop. Unpacked, they are put on the shelves, and shortly thereafter a consumer will walk in and buy a Sinatra LP. The cash register rings up the sale merrily.

The name of the store may be different, the singer or the song may be something else. But that is the road which recordings travel. Economically, exactly who gets what? What does the singer receive, the record distributor, the record dealer, the music publisher?

Of course, there would be no industry without something to put in the grooves, somebody to perform the material, whether it be Frank Sinatra or the ten-member New Christy Minstrels. Practically all recording artists receive royalties, a pattern of payment that evolved slowly. Years ago, when Thomas Alva Edison started to record, he would pay vocalists, opera singers, or vaudevillians a flat sum—a day's wages, maybe $30 or $50 or $100.

"But around 1912 when the industry became more of an industry, with rules and regulations, record companies started to pay royalties. In the days of Caruso there were royalties. Later, of course, came the matter of guarantees, but record royalties go back half a century," says one of the pioneers of the phonograph record industry, Frank Walker.

While this was the pattern, there were deviations. Many record artists received flat sums. Some artists preferred it that way, because they needed the money and didn't know if a fly-by-night record company would ever pay royalties. Some artists lost tremendous sums by such contracts. It is reported that the Andrews Sisters didn't receive royalties on their early hits on Decca, just a flat payment.

Today the royalty pattern is largely followed. However, there is no rule which insists that a record company pay record royalties. They are just bound by union minimums. If an artist wants to accept a royalty-free offer he can do so. Many competent singers still do; their "names" aren't sufficiently large for consumers to break down the record counters.

So far as "singles" go—the 45-rpm, seven-inch recordings—the artist can get a royalty of 2 per cent, 3 per cent or 5 per cent. More accurately, it is a percentage in those varying amounts of 90 per cent of the estimated retail price. The retail selling price is a figure as elusive as the symbols in Joyce's *Finnegan's Wake*, but today the percentage is pinned to what the manufacturer *says* is the retail price, even though he knows that it often isn't. It is a convenient mirage.

In practice, at 3 per cent royalty, the record artist will receive 2.7 cents per 45-rpm record. At 5 per cent royalty, which most of the name artists receive, the sum is 4½ cents. Recently, for example, Steve Lawrence, a very good singer with good taste, scored a commercial but unaesthetic hit with a ditty about a teenage triangle, "Go Away Little Girl." It sold more than 1,000,000 copies for Columbia Records. He earned, on that single record alone, approximately $45,000.

Few recordings reach the 1,000,000 mark. In the "top ten" there are highly popular "singles" which sell 500,000 (artist's share, $22,500) and 250,000 (artist's share, $11,250). From these sums, record companies deduct the cost of the record date, a practice which needs probing by a special commission of inquiry; nobody seems to know the reason for it. Broadway stars or Hollywood actors do not pay for production costs of plays or motion pictures. But somehow in the prehistoric past someone inserted a clause that the artists should pay for record sessions, and it has since become standard practice.

So far as long-playing records are concerned, most recording artists receive about 17½ cents per LP. This is computed by a method not quite as complex as Einstein's Theory of Relativity, but equally confusing. If you are statistically-minded, here's how it works (other readers can skip a bit): Artists receive 5 per cent of 90 per cent of the estimated retail price; in other words, 5 per cent of 90 per cent of a $3.98 record.

If diminutive Brenda Lee of Decca Records sells 250,000 LP's she receives, on a 5 per cent basis, the towering figure of $43,750. A million-selling LP would bring her $175,000.

Generally, record companies wholesale LP's from roughly $1.65 to $2.47 to distributors. Some artists receive 10 per cent of the wholesale price, which becomes a pretty swinging mathematical affair, because the wholesale price of $3.98 LP's is a figure of profound murkiness. ABC Paramount Records employs this method and its artists, like Ray Charles, the blind singer, get 10 per cent of this fluctuating figure. Ray Charles could get anywhere from approximately 17 cents to 24 cents per LP on this basis. The wholesale price of the LP can vary depending on (1) the artist, (2) the "deal," and (3) the sales department's desire to make a good showing by slashing the wholesale price.

Frequently, the recording artist makes more by owning a "piece of the song" through a music publishing company in which he is a partner. Most of the top artists now are allied to companies in which they participate. Here is just a random sampling: Connie Francis (Francon), Elvis Presley (Elvis Presley Music), Steve Lawrence and Eydie Gorme (Maxana, named after Steve Lawrence's parents).

If he owns a piece of the song or instrumental, the artist would share in the publishers' record royalties (one cent per song) and in the lucrative performance moneys received from air play through membership in ASCAP or BMI. This can add up. In 1962, after a long dearth of money-making records, Nat Cole had a million-selling hit with a mediocre country and western ditty, "Ramblin' Rose," written by two urban hillbillies and published by Sweco, in which Cole is a financial participant. In this situation, everything came up roses for Cole.

Most recording personalities receive the standard record royalty rates. But some "big names" are given "fat guarantees," upward of $100,000 annually. Such guarantees are often over and beyond the cost of the record session dates which are deducted from the artists' royalty statements. These guarantees have to be paid, regardless of whether the artist's records sell or not. And "flop records," commercially speaking, even by name artists are not unknown.

Speaking of records that do not sell, there are 45's and also LP's that actually do not sell one single copy. "It's hard to believe, but its true," veteran A & R producer Sid Feller of ABC-Paramount Records says.

The industry lives for the "big ones"—the artists who sell 1,000,000 "singles" or a $1,000,000 worth of long-playing records. For such a commercial achievement, Tin Pan Alley awards its biggest prize, which outweighs even the Pulitzer or Nobel Peace Prize—the "golden record." Golden records are juke-box society's highest accolade—the "Oscars" of the popular music business.

Years ago, it was not uncommon for a record company to announce a golden-record winner for discs that sold far less than 1,000,000 copies. In this way a manufacturer hoped to whip up a bandwagon psychology in the trade and to give the record more prestige and more air play.

More than once this dialogue would ensue:

Promotion Man: "Well, 'Unhappy Little Teenager' is in the first ten. How much has it sold?"

Record Executive: "About 400,000."

Promotion Man: "Should we announce a golden record?"

Record Executive: "Wait till it hits 450,000."

Since 1960 the Record Industry Association of America (RIAA) has attempted to inject some legitimacy into this marketing award. For a fee of $150 it will certify the sales figures by an independent audit. Those who wish to earn a golden record (handsomely encased in a lucite block) have to sell 1,000,000 45's or a $1,000,000 worth of LP's computed on the basis of the manufacturer's wholesale price.

Equally fixed is the fact that record royalties are generally paid twice a year. When a record artist gets hot, the tax experts go to work so the artist can retain some of it. Record artists invest in all sorts of ventures. Recently, Ken Greengrass, personal manager of Steve Lawrence and Eydie Gorme, revealed that the husband-and-wife team have money invested in a motel in the Caribbean, in other real estate, and in "cattle."

One of the most sticky points in record company economics is the phrase "break-even point." Few, if any, know what a break-even point is for a recording, and at what stage the record company starts earning a profit. There are diverse reasons for this vagueness. Each date doesn't cost the same amount of money; the overhead varies with each firm; personnel costs, publicity costs, executive salaries, pension plans, advertising costs are known, but how does one figure out these items in relation to the Profit and Loss statement of a particular single or long-playing record?

And the fantastic pattern of discounting, deals, "freebies" makes the price structure a wild affair. But a rough idea of what a record company makes on a record can be gleaned from the following price pattern:

POPULAR SINGLES

Record Manufacturer	*Distributor*	*Record Dealer*
98 cents (estimated retail price of 45-rpm singles)	37-45 cents	48-60 cents

LONG-PLAYING 33⅓

$3.98 "list"	$1.61-$2.01	$1.80-$2.47

These are some of the rule-of-thumb figures. The neighborhood record dealer or discount store then adds on its profit. This is the theoretical side. But there are so many "deals," so many variations, that you enter a cloud-cuckoo land of price manipulation.

What makes the record-maker's "unit-cost" figures complex, too, is the popular repackaging gambit. For example, Johnny Mathis may break through with one major hit. Columbia will then package a group of eleven other "singles" into a new LP, without having to re-record. (Mathis has since signed with Mercury Records. However, Columbia will still be releasing Mathis product based on repackaging and unused tapes.) Here, some editing costs and a packaging cost is involved. Decca is a past-master of repackaging. From its rich catalogue and archives it is constantly repackaging Bing Crosby, Ella Fitzgerald, and Peggy Lee, none of whom have been with the label exclusively for years.

Most record companies reach the U. S. consumers through the record distributors who sell the record dealers. The major firms operate their own company-run distributors, which handle their product exclusively in the top record markets. However, in some leaner markets even they seem to have independent distributors who also market the product of scores of other record companies.

The house-distributor economics can be somewhat obscure. But an independent record distributor makes approximately 15 cents paper profit on each 45-rpm single record. This is a classroom example, but if he buys the record for 45 cents, he sells it for 60 cents. But he can buy records at varying prices, sometimes for much less than 45 cents, depending on the "deal," the discounts, and competitive situations.

What about the paper profits on a long-playing record? William Shockett, treasurer of Malverne Distributors of New York City, told the FTC recently that Malverne bought Liberty monaural records for $1.61 (the $3.98 LP's) and sold them to the record dealers, department stores, rack jobbers, one-stops for $2.23. Profit? 62 cents.

Shockett said he bought Cameo-Parkways recordings (Chubby Checker, Dee Dee Sharp) for $1.63, and sold them for $2.16. Profit? 53 cents. He bought Verve ($4.98 "list" albums) for $2.06 and sold them to his customers for $2.60. Profit? 54 cents.

To boost profit margins, some record distributors buy heavily during "deals" in which record firms offer "buy 2 LP's, get 1 free" or "buy 10 LP's, get 4 free." On these deals, a portion of which he may pass on to his record dealers, the distributor may make extra profit. Or he may get good and stuck. In the latter case, he may transship out of his territory and sell the records at cost. (This is illegal contractually, but it's done.)

There are various "angles." Some record distributors will buy during an attractive buying deal just to get the 10 per cent return privilege. In other words, they may buy "singles," 25,000 of a top artist, and sell them to their dealers at cost, just to get rid of them. Consequently, they build up a return privilege of 10 per cent. This 10 per cent is money in the bank. They can return unsold, "dead" stock for fresh, selling merchandise. As Katzel of Roulette Records says, "The price structure is pure chaos."

Jackson Pollack's expressionistic art is clearer than record retail prices. Idyllically, a record retailer buys a 45-rpm single for 60 cents and sells it for 98 cents, making a neat 38-cent profit. He buys a popular music album of the Kingston Trio for $2.47 and sells it for $3.98, a paper profit of $1.51.

This is the controlled picture, but right now the price structure of recordings is footloose and fancy free. Prices for records were fairly stable in the 1930's and 1940's. Today, depending on competitive circumstances, the American consumer can buy a 45-rpm for 66 cents, 79 cents, or 89 cents. Few pay "list"—98 cents. Years ago, record albums cost from $2 to $3, depending on how many ten-inch recordings were inside. Today, prices of a Johnny Mathis or Frank Sinatra LP border on the occult.

To return to popular "singles," the average record retailer buys

45's for approximately 60 cents. Some sell them, as noted before, at varying prices up to 98 cents. A Queens record retailer, one of the oldest and most heavily stocked in New York City, said: "We have to charge 98 cents, especially on 'pops.' We've got to keep the price up. We're in a high rental area, we've got to have help. Records are our business. If we can't make a profit, we might as well put a lock on the door."

Some record retail shops do slash prices, but they are hovering toward the red-ink spectrum. But the opposition—department stores, discount chains—employ recordings as "loss leaders." These mass-merchandising retail units will sell singles for 66 cents.

As far as LP's go, the average record retailer—a nebulous but necessary phantom—will sell LP's purchased at $2.47 for from $2.79 to $2.98.

However, the neighborhood record dealer, or even the big-city record dealer finds that his profit-margins are dwindling. It is difficult to tell whether the large discount-type operations and department stores make money on recordings. Perhaps they do because of two facts: they buy on fabulous deals or are transshipped merchandise (often "free merchandise") accumulated by distributors via deals from 1,000 miles away. In actual fact, the larger accounts are sold at record distributor prices rather than as record retailers, which they are. Often the big department stores and discount-houses sell popular records (show music, jazz, top selling popular albums with name artists) for less than the record retailer can buy them.

What about the songwriter and lyricist who started the whole ball of grooved vinyl resins going? The composer and lyricist are paid one penny per record for music and lyrics. Two writers, if there are two, share the penny equally. Thus, on a golden record, that is, on a 1,000,000-selling "pop single," the team will receive $10,000 in mechanicals, known as "record royalties."

If this song is placed on an LP, the team still get one-half cent each. If there are two writers on a 1,000,000-selling 45, the big pay-off will be $5,000 each on record royalties, which isn't extraordinary, considering that a million-seller is a rare commodity.

The songwriter also gets substantial "performance moneys" from the U. S. and abroad, which will be touched on shortly. A 1,000,000-selling hit, though, in broad figures, is worth a minimum of $12,000 to $14,000.

A music publisher receiving the same one cent will earn $10,000 in record royalties on a 1,000,000-selling recording. Beyond the record and sheet-music sales (negligible amounts) there are performance moneys here, too—an increasingly important segment of the music business economics.

The music business is desperately aware of performance moneys. Performers, vocalists—from "pop" singers to the more socially aware folk groups—all want to get a slice of these moneys. Folk "writers," or collectors of folk songs, and folk groups often change the musical line or change a part of the lyric of a folk tune so that they can become "writers" or "publishers" and have access to performance moneys paid by the two major-licensing groups, ASCAP and BMI.

Here's how it works. A 1,000,000-selling record, or better still a record that climbs into the "top ten" on the trade-paper charts, will get an enormous amount of air play, notably on the "top 40 radio stations," so called because they program from the trade-paper listings of the top forty most popular recordings. This will go on for approximately eight weeks, before the record is edged out by up-and-coming hits.

The lucky songwriters and music publisher of that hit song will share heavily in the performance moneys paid by ASCAP and BMI. There is another licensing agency, SESAC, but it is rather small. In ASCAP, the performance moneys are not computed on air play alone. Its officials note (1) the performances; (2) the years that the author of the music and lyrics and publisher have been in ASCAP; and (3) the basic worth of the material (a show song is more valuable to an ASCAP committee, broadly speaking, than an evanescent "pop" song which will most likely fade quickly). There are other complex considerations—performances on TV, network-plays, and the song's use as a TV theme. From these computations, ASCAP officials arrive at the performance moneys, and these add up to earnings for more than one year. The hit song tends to boost your over-all rating and classification, which determines your annual ASCAP income.

BMI is based solely on air play. A BMI music publisher reports that a music publisher receives 2 to 3 cents per "play" on local radio; the songwriters get 2 cents for each "play" locally. A recording that catapults into the "top ten" is worth from $7,000 to $10,000 in performance moneys. This is upward of 250,000 logged performances, including more valuable network "plays," on CBS, NBC radio or television. In other words, a BMI songwriter or music publisher may receive approximately $17,000 from record royalties and performance fees.

The economic orientation of ASCAP aims toward building a yearly annuity that grows, something that endures. BMI is slanted toward the quick pay-off. In a tax sense, the BMI writer is more vulnerable.

In the golden pie you can't leave out a thick, juicy slice—the honking 500,000 juke boxes. According to *Billboard*, the average juke-box operator netted $11,059 in 1961. The "average juke-box operator" was described as follows by the trade paper:

He has 56 juke boxes on location, 44 of them monaural and 12 stereo; and of the stereo machines six are capable of playing records at either 33⅓- or 45-rpm speeds. The average operation takes in $840 a week with about half of the total going to the operator as gross income, and the other half going to the location as commission. The average location takes in $15 a week.

The nation's juke boxes buy about 50,000,000 discs a year, and account for about half of the single-record business. The music men—composers, lyricists, licensing agencies—are happy about the record sales. But they look upon the juke-box interests as "free riders" who make money on music but do not pay a royalty for its commercial use, such as that paid by a radio or TV station.

There are several bills now pending in Congress for revising the copyright law, and these revisions would force the juke-box operators to pay a licensing fee or royalty for the musical works. The juke-box interests claim that by buying the recordings they indirectly pay about $2 million in royalty to music publishers and songwriters. Also, they assert that they expose material, they push it along; besides that, they don't make that much money on the boxes, which now cost the American consumer 10 cents "a play."

Record clubs are a recent innovation. An expanding phase of U. S. record merchandising, they reportedly account for 20 per cent of records sold. They cut out the record distributor and record retailer, and zero in on the consumer. Club officials say they nourish a record-buying habit through costly, attractive advertising and direct-mail promotion. Record dealers claim that clubs are injuring them. The raging conflict has provoked hearings by the Federal Trade Commission.

Record clubs use LP's exclusively. A record club pays approximately 50 per cent of the normal royalty rate to artists. They pay approximately 75 per cent of normal royalty rates to music publishers and songwriters; instead of 2 cents per song, they pay 1½ cents. An extra royalty goes to the record company that created the album initially. Actually there is only one record club that takes in outside records at this writing, and that is the largest, the Columbia Record Club. The Capitol Record Club and the RCA Victor Record Club so far have picked recordings from their own catalogues.

Regardless of the complexity of the battle of the record clubs versus the record distributors and the record retailers, there are several uncontested facts: clubs provide a subsidiary source of revenue and resemble a "reprint" house. If his LP is chosen, the record artist makes extra money; so do the songwriter and the music publishers represented on it, and the firm that produced it originally.

Years ago, special tourist trains stopped at Thomas Edison's laboratory to "hear a machine that talks"—Edison's phonograph. The railroads were probably among the first economic units to earn money from the invention devised by Edison in 1877.

Since then, the record industry, the kingpin of today's music business, has grown from a novelty into a mass cultural structure, embracing radio, home entertainment, disc jockeys, teenage idols made by turntables, juke boxes, and record clubs. There has been a golden flood. Frank Sinatra, son of a Democratic party precinct worker, has become a millionaire with interests in radio, TV, music publishing, night clubs, motion pictures, and a record company of his own, Reprise. The phonograph record made him famous and helped him in all media. Elvis Presley and the Kingston Trio have waxed wealthy through recordings; so have Johnny Mathis and Harry Belafonte. In the high-income brackets, too, are a handful of songwriters (Richard Rodgers, Irving Berlin, Cole Porter), music publishers, record executives, talent agents, record distributors, and rack-jobbers who sell millions of popular music recordings to dime stores and supermarkets.

Though there has been a golden flood, not everybody has been anointed. There are many who earn less than $100 a week as factory workers in phonograph record pressing plants, retail record salesmen, employees in record-distributor warehouses, record company bookkeepers and secretaries. The discount chains merchandise an enormous number of records. But often, the "girls"—often grandmas—who keep the records neatly stacked and insert new products in the pegboard racks receive no more than the $1.25-an-hour minimum set by the federal government.

Yet there has been an explosive rate of growth in the popular music-recording complex and with it the surfacing of many tensions rooted in that old devil, money. Today's record singers, from the mature artists to the curly-haired teenage idols, ask for substantial yearly guarantees. Ricky Nelson recently signed a $1,000,000 Decca Records contract in which he is to be paid that sum over a twenty-year period.

The songwriters are discontent with the record royalty rate, asserting that the two-cent statute passed in 1909 does not represent current marketing conditions or allow a fair return for the song's creator. And they want the chrome-edged juke-boxes to pay royalties, too.

The record distributors do not like the way big record companies deal with big accounts directly, cutting them out. The record companies can't explain this jurisdictional intrusion, but are content to charge that too many record distributors are backward and "sit on their butts."

All this abrasiveness conceals the fact that each one is dependent on the other. Each bloc is mutually interconnected. Nothing can be sold without (1) the product, created by the writers and (2) performed by the singer or vocal group, or orchestra and (3) manufactured by the record company and (4) marketed by regional distributors and (5) sold by record-retail outlets. While the factions clash in this war of the cash-register and hope to moderate their differences in discussion and conference, the record industry keeps whirling on.

In this combative, highly commercial atmosphere, aesthetic judgments are shaped. Recently, at a meeting of the National Academy of Recording Arts and Sciences—the record industry's equivalent of Hollywood's Motion Picture Academy of Arts and Sciences—two producers for RCA Victor Records defined what is "good" in popular music.

They were tall, slim Hugo Peretti and chunky Luigi Creatore, whose father, "The Great Creatore," was the bandsman referred to in Meredith Willson's song, "Seventy-Six Trombones."

Hugo: "You know you got a bad record when the returns start coming in."

Luigi: "A good record is one that sells."

16 · SHOW BUSINESS' THIRTY-YEARS' SONG WAR

> Popular music and the taste of the public began to go to hell
> just about the time of the formation of BMI when the coun-
> try's radio stations and networks were flooded with junk music
> that could not get played before. The junk is still very much
> with us.
>
> —John Crosby, *New York Herald Tribune*

There is something irascibly admirable about show business' civil war
—its fabulous staying power.

It started in 1940, during World War II. Since then, Hitler has been
vanquished, Japan's dream of world conquest has been put to rest, and
the atomic bomb has been perfected. Roosevelt has died, and there
followed in presidential succession Harry Truman, Dwight Eisenhower,
John Kennedy, and Lyndon Johnson. The American Federation of
Labor and the Congress of Industrial Organization have teamed up,
and television has crossed the rooftops of the land. Atomic submarines
pierced the underlayers of ice to reach the North Pole. James Petrillo
retired as defender of the American work-a-day musician. During all
this time, the enmity between ASCAP and BMI has continued. The
Great Song War is now entering its third decade.

Less than a dozen city blocks separate the two antagonists. There
is the American Society of Composers, Authors and Publishers
(ASCAP) at 575 Madison Avenue, and there is its arch-foe, Broadcast
Music, Inc. (BMI), headquartered in posh surroundings in the Research Institute of America Building, 589 Fifth Avenue.

The best popular music writers America has ever developed—George
Gershwin, Jerome Kern, Cole Porter, Irving Berlin, Larry Hart, Richard Rodgers, Oscar Hammerstein, Frank Loesser, Duke Ellington, Harold Arlen—belong or have belonged to ASCAP, a half-century-old institution. Younger, twenty-four-year-old BMI has not yet developed any
writer to equal those giants of popular music. Both firms are million-
dollar operations—sleek, well-organized, well-financed, and aggressive.

The public, though concerned about the brand of popular music it
hears, has been singularly detached over the struggle between these two

musical giants. Few have realized profoundly that the popular music they have heard over the past quarter of a century has been subtly shaped by this legislative, legal, and economic war.

Few have realized that the quality of the music they hear on radio, over TV, on recordings, in juke boxes, has partial but formidable roots in the struggle that has been fought in walnut-paneled courtrooms in the U. S. Department of Justice and in the United States Congress.

The battle between ASCAP and BMI these days often assumes a humorous cast. Both fight to put their best foot forward. One year ASCAP puts on a show for the National Press Club in Washington, D.C., a show with the biggest names. The next year (the equal time principle is followed by the journalistic fraternity) BMI tries to outdo them with its own headliners. ASCAP is entrenched in Broadway. So BMI erects a musical theater workshop to build up its creative elements in theater music. BMI gets strong with its country and western music, so ASCAP sets up a Nashville headquarters.

This intramural competition hurts no one. The arguments against BMI concern democracy, aesthetics, and economics; and the processes that it set in motion. To understand this, a look at music business history is vital. This bores music veterans, but it is basic study toward an understanding of the popular music picture in the 1950's and the present day.

For decades now, popular recording artists and musical personalities have referred to BMI as the archetype of evil, something concocted by Rasputin. Bing Crosby has charged that the poor quality of today's music "is the result of pressures exerted by BMI. . . . It just galls me to see so much trash on our air lanes and TV screens." Frank Sinatra, Richard Rodgers, Burton Lane, and others have also assailed the licensing agency, as a manipulator of public taste. When still a senator, the late President Kennedy inserted a column which appeared in *Newsday* into the *Congressional Record* (Aug. 15, 1957) the gist of which was: "BMI needs probing." Oscar Hammerstein stated that "BMI songs have been rammed down the public's ears."

The new head of BMI is a stocky, crewcut-topped lawyer, Robert Burton. But during its infancy and growth its president was Carl Haverlin, a friendly Civil War buff and a former vice-president of the Mutual Broadcasting System. For years, Haverlin has denied, in Congressional hearings and out of them, any wrongdoing or conspiracy. He had frequently pointed out that BMI has helped break the tight, small monopoly of Tin Pan Alley and has helped "democratize" popular music by allowing country and western writers and Latin American writers to share in the popular music bounty. He and BMI have claimed that they have allowed young songwriters to make a living, whereas ASCAP kept writers out of the aristocratic "club" for selfish, greedy reasons.

The public has heard some of these crossfire arguments for years. Having worked in the mid-50's as a script writer for Broadcast Music, Inc., preparing programs for radio stations for approximately two years, I have had a close look at the implications of the struggle between these two seemingly overpowering abstract forces that are in a business the public hardly gets exercised about, "music licensing."

There are some unarguable facts, and some sticky, controversial premises. One unarguable fact is that the BMI is tremendously powerful in popular music. You cannot discuss physics without referring to Newton, the evolution of snap-crackle breakfast foods without mentioning Kellogg's, or the popular music situation over the past quarter of a century without referring to Broadcast Music, Inc. Regardless of the varying interpretations of its role, battler for the musically oppressed or clever manipulator of the mass media, BMI's influence has not been minor.

A folder put out by BMI and directed toward those who buy music, (radio stations, restaurants, sound-music systems) says:

BMI is a vital force in American music. According to all nationally accepted polls:

68% of the song hits listed in the combined polls reflecting public preference in *Billboard*, *Variety* and *Cash Box* during the eight years since 1955 are licensed by BMI;

58 of the 101 perennial single-record hits recommended by *Billboard* for year-round programing are licensed by BMI;

70% of the song hits listed in the combined popularity polls of *Billboard*, *Variety*, and *Cash Box* during the past twelve months are licensed by BMI;

Even in foreign countries, where locally originated compositions play a leading role, 32.3% of the favorite song hits are, according to a *Billboard* tabulation, licensed by BMI.

Such self-praise is not unwarranted. America's best-selling songs and the recordings on which they were heard throughout the United States during the week of October 5, 1963, according to *Cash Box*, were the following:

1. Blue Velvet—Boby Vinton, Epic
2. Be My Baby—Ronettes, Philles
3. Sally Go 'Round the Roses—Jaynettes, Tuff
4. My Boyfriend's Back—Angels, Smash
5. Surfer Girl—Beach Boys, Capitol

  6. Then He Kissed Me—Crystals, Philles
  7. Heat Wave—Martha/Vandellas, Gordy
  8. Cry Baby—Garnett Mimms/Enchanters, UA
  9. Busted—Ray Charles, ABC
  10. Sugar Shack—Jimmy Gilmer/Fireballs, Dot

If you looked at the record labels of these top ten 45-rpm "singles" you would discover three tiny letters alongside every one of the "sides": BMI. Show-business people know these letters stand for Broadcast Music, Inc., a firm that its detractors call "Bad Music, Inc." Sometimes you'll find that BMI is not associated with all top ten songs and recordings, but frequently you will find that works connected with the music licensing agency are "way up there" in quantity, if not in quality. This, of course, displeases its arch rival, ASCAP.

If much of the popular music heard over the past quarter of a century is quality-poor is it the fault of (a) uncritical, emotionally confused teenagers; (b) the nuclear age; (c) loss of creativity on the part of America's popular music-makers; (d) a natural reflex of mass-media standardization; or (e) does it have anything to do with the licensing war?

Composer Hoagy Carmichael cannot go around the country to radio stations, restaurants, and nightclubs and say, "Listen, you just played my song, 'Star Dust.' You have to pay me." Physically, he could not go to enough places or have enough ears to listen to the thousands of radio stations to determine who is playing what. So Carmichael and his fellow composers and lyricists belong to a music-licensing agency. The music-licensing agency represents the compositions owned by music publishers and writers. It prepares a contract with the radio station or TV station, the Copacabana, Gerde's Folk Centre, the Playboy Club, or the hungry i. The user of the music pays the licensing agency, and the licensing agency pays the writers and publishers.

There are French, English, Italian, German, Japanese—countless—music-licensing agencies throughout the world. Should "Star Dust" be played over Italian radio, the Italian licensing agency credits Carmichael with a performance and pays money to him and the song's lyricist, Mitchell Parish, and its publisher, Mills Music. Similarly, should an Italian hit like "Volare," be played in the U. S., American dollars are credited to the writers and publishers in Italy. Some music-licensing agencies are run by the government; some are private coalitions of music interests. Each agency pays writers and publishers according to varying plans, which relate to performances mainly.

In this country, there are two principal agencies. The oldest is ASCAP. A recent check discloses that there are 7,032 writers and 2,276 publishers belonging to it. BMI is the second largest, with 6,500 affiliated writers and a little over 5,000 music publishers. The third agency, SESAC, plays a much less consequential role.

ASCAP's history goes back to 1914, to a table at Luchow's on West 14th Street, where nine men sat at a long table. Among them were composers, lawyers, lyricists, and Victor Herbert, the portly gourmet. There, amidst the odors of red cabbage, sauerbraten, and the serving of frosted steins of dark beer, they decided to do something about the fact that musical works were being performed in restaurants, beer gardens, and vaudeville houses without payment to authors or publishers. From that meeting came the novel organization of ASCAP, which is not a union, not a craft-guild of workmen, but a voluntary association of composers, lyricists, and music publishers to protect their economic property rights.

The top songs of the ASCAP catalogues, which have no peer in this country, include "Alexander's Ragtime Band," "April Showers," "Begin the Beguine," "Night and Day," "April in Paris," "Star Dust," "White Christmas," "Tea for Two," "Birth of the Blues," "Over the Rainbow," "Lover," "You Made Me Love You," "Embraceable You," and "Summertime." Besides popular music, ASCAP licenses the classical works of Aaron Copland, Virgil Thompson, Leonard Bernstein, Gian-Carlo Menotti, Ned Rorem, Paul Creston, and Morton Gould, and the jazz of Duke Ellington, Fats Waller, and Dizzy Gillespie.

In 1962, ASCAP grossed $35,279,000. How does ASCAP make money? According to a recent story in the *New York Times*,

[ASCAP] obtains its revenues from about 40,000 licensees, who pay for the right to present the music of ASCAP members. The cost of the license depends on a number of factors.

The small Peoria cabaret might pay $60 annually, which gives it the right to play all the nearly one million songs in the society's repertory. A New York supper club might pay $3,000 a year, based on a percentage of its gross. The organizations that pipe music into office buildings also pay a percentage of the gross. But the society's biggest customers are the radio and television stations.

It was the radio money—and rates—that provoked all the fuss with the broadcasters. Writers and publishers of popular music are paid on the basis of many factors, including worth of the material, number of years the writer-publisher has been an ASCAP member, and performances on radio and television.

Describing the checking of performances, the *New York Times'* Milton Esterow noted:

Logs of performances, provided by the networks, are the principal check. In addition, society branches throughout the country send to New York headquarters tapes of music broadcast on independent radio and television stations.

Since it would be impossible to count the number of performances, projections are made on the basis of the tapes. The society has established that if every performance on every radio station were processed, it would cost the society $182 million a year.

Forty persons sitting in an office on Madison Avenue listen to the tapes— 60,000 hours of radio music and 15,000 hours of television music—each year. All the monitors have a musical background so that they can spot a tune if it has not been identified on the air. There are specialists in all types of music—Latin American, rhythm and blues, rock 'n' roll, classical, and religious.

A bespectacled corporation lawyer for CBS, Sydney M. Kaye, thought up BMI in 1939-40. He still functions as chairman of the BMI board. He makes very good "homey" speeches; he was always a featured speaker at company picnics and parties when I worked there.

In 1940, ASCAP asked for more money from the broadcasters, notably from the networks, NBC, CBS, and ABC. The radio interests, which somehow never really got acclimatized to the idea of paying money to the writers and publishers gave a shriek louder than those heard on the old "Witch's Tale" radio programs. So Kaye conceived the idea of a rival music licensing agency; he got the broadcasters to put up about $400,000 to start it. From a few battered desks and rafts of music paper for arrangers to prepare arrangements, BMI started its controversy-speckled career. There is nothing controversial about the fact, however, that BMI today is a prosperous music-licensing agency, second only to ASCAP, and in recent years it has whipped ASCAP in the unspoken competition between the two in the number of best-selling tunes each presents in the trade-paper polls.

During the early years of BMI's existence, there ranged a wild and tumultuous propaganda war. ASCAP pulled out all the stops to embarrass and mock BMI, its arrangements, and its freshly composed product. Not all the criticism came from ASCAP.

In a handsome portfolio prepared by Herbert Brean and the editors of *Life*, The Music of Life, which accompanied an anthology of popular music recordings, there is a bit of verse concerning the quality of BMI popular music in the 1940's:

> Little Jack Horner
> Sat in a corner
> With his radio turned up high.
> He listened, aghast,
> And turned it off fast,
> And said, "What a bad BMI."

BMI counterattacked. Here is a sample dossier, which consists of advertisements, memos, and newsletters BMI circulated to the radio stations under the title, *BMI is Your Music*. The Anti-Trust Committee of the Committee on the Judiciary investigating the song war told of Murray Arnold, program director of radio station WIP, Philadelphia. Mr. Arnold said:

For the next three months, let each station start programing 70 per cent ASCAP and 30 per cent BMI in the popular field. For the following six months, change the percentage to 60 ASCAP and 40 BMI; after that 50 ASCAP and 50 BMI. By this means, the acceptance of the song hits America sings will veer over from ASCAP to BMI more equitably. Don't forget one important angle. People can't like a song if they don't hear it.

From a BMI newsletter dated January 1, 1950: ". . . a reminder that pin-up tunes [printed lists of BMI tunes] should be played every day and the newcomers really ought to be heard twice a day. Perhaps not very subtle, but you get the idea."

One of the nation's most important disc jockeys, Martin Block, conductor of the "Make-Believe Ballroom," program received "substantial subsidies from BMI," says the congressional report. He got the money ostensibly for his music publishing interests and for writing a column for the BMI music memo known as "Platter-Chatter." At varying times, Block urged the broadcasters "to give preferential treatment to BMI-licensed music."

Once Block wrote:

. . . I think it is very important that all BMI affiliates know about the swell top tunes you own. . . . Having a financial interest in these tunes it seems only sensible to me that we should do everything in our power to promote their success and get back of any new songs cleared by BMI.

In a BMI pamphlet published in 1940, when the broadcasting interests were trying to get radio stations to buy BMI stock, this statement appeared: "Remember! . . . the public selects its favorites from the music which it hears and does not miss what it does not hear."

In a BMI music memo, there is a picture of a radio personality named Gregg Phillips, accompanied by this statement: "He uses the BMI pin-up sheet to guide him in building his programs with emphasis on the newcomers."

A raft of free services were offered to broadcasters. BMI distributed free sheet music and records to broadcasters featuring BMI popular music. At times it put out attractive television scrapbooks and a sketch-book with practical hints on how to use BMI tunes in video programs. It offered the broadcasters a "home away from home" when the broad-casters were in New York City. It sponsored program clinics. BMI's field men toured the nation's stations, said "Hello" to disc jockeys, and plumped for the virtues of BMI.

A small but active script department during the mid-fifties turned out a variety of programs. During my tenure a group of writers turned out such radio scripts as "Meet The Artist," "According To The Record," "Milestones," "Stories from The Sports Record." These scripts were free, and fantastically popular, even though sometimes it was a little forced to interrupt a tale of Babe Ruth hitting a home run to slip in a BMI tune.

The program I wrote, "According To The Record," was a popular five-minute, almanac-type program which recorded events day by day throughout history. Sample plugs from tag end of some programs: ". . . And here's a bouncy ditty that was popular one year ago at this time, the 1955 hit, 'No More,' given a rowdy-dow treatment by the DeJohn Sisters." ". . . And now let's dip into our musical almanac for a love song with a nautical touch, 'Walkin' by the River.' "

These scripts served a dual purpose: it was a valuable service to the broadcasters, and it built up performance credits for BMI materials, as opposed to ASCAP.

Of course, ASCAP competed with its own musical materials, program suggestions, and broadcasting aids. But the broadcasters knew that BMI represented them. Meanwhile, BMI got more aggressive. It en-ticed respected ASCAP publishers like E. B. Marks to leave ASCAP. This coup gave BMI entry into the rich Latin-American catalogue of Marks. BMI continued to subsidize musical personalities, disc jockeys, song pluggers. Result? To condense a long story, BMI whipped ASCAP in the popular music field. During the ascent to popularity of BMI, the popular music got worse, in terms of quality. During this era, there was the rise of cheap teen music, cheap rock 'n' roll, cheap teen-age idols, and the growth of "country pop."

If you grant the premise that there was an inundation of cheap music, did it get that way through the conscientious publicity of BMI or did it get that way naturally? Here experts and commentators differ. Gene Lees in *Hi Fi Stereo Review* traced the "decline of the American popular song" to the replacement of the bands by vocalists, as symbolized by young bow-tied Sinatra. "In climbing to fame," Lees wrote, "as an idol of adolescent girls, Sinatra opened a Pandora's box, from which was to eventually come some of the worst noises to be dignified by the name of music."

Writing in *Commonweal*, Nat Hentoff, in an article entitled "They're Playing Our Song," traces the low level of most popular music to the teenagers and their desires. He accuses the environment of the world teenagers live in with its corrosion of values, white-collar crime, the distortions of human relations. "It's not surprising then, that so many 'pop' song hits shake with formularized frenzy, emotions that cannot be directly expressed, that cannot be fulfilled, because frustration and day-dreaming are preferable for most of the young to take a chance, to be unique, let alone, uniquely wrong," he says.

He ascribes the cheap music not to any musical Mafia, but to the teenagers themselves. His authority is George Marek, head of RCA Victor, whom he quotes liberally. Marek said: "Rock 'n' roll is not a creation of payola. No form of entertainment can be artificially created. . . . Rock 'n' roll had something that made a fundamental appeal to its generation, just as 'Tea for Two' in its day. If 'the Rock' were an outgrowth of payola, why is it that in Japan Elvis Presley and Paul Anka are the most popular singers?"

First, Paul Anka is not a rock 'n' roll singer, as Marek should know since he records for RCA Victor. Anka does a lot of undistinguished songs, much of them of his own composition, but they are generally soft and ballady. So far as payola having no impact in the creation of taste, this is pure unwillingness to state the unhappy truth, particularly as it concerns impressionable teenagers. Marek himself, besides being a profound student of the opera, has long been a sturdy advocate of marketing, packaging, and promotion. Things do not often get sold by themselves. They have to be *pushed*. Payola played a not too inconsiderable role in the hotly competitive popular music world, where every turn of the disc jockey's turntable is important.

Of course, not everything that is publicized and promoted gets sold. But some of it rubs off. Some of it sticks. It comes down to a view of popular-taste formation. Either you accept the view that exploitation, publicity, and merchandising do have an impact, or you don't. Ascribing manufactured popular taste to social conditions is valid, but it does not explain nor give proper due to the forces behind the manufacturing of the taste.

Consider cigarette smoking. Millions find smoking pleasurable, relaxing in these tense days. However, much informed opinion says that excessive smoking leads to lung cancer. If people want to smoke, that is their own free choice. But one cannot deny that smoking is a habit that the tobacco industry encourages by costly and repetitive advertising in newspapers, magazines, radio, and TV. The industry is not an innocent bystander. Neither is BMI.

Of course, excessive listening to BMI "pop" songs doesn't cause lung cancer. However, BMI did promote rock 'n' roll and teenage mediocrities, and not because they made superior popular music. Many on the BMI staff grimaced at the material. The company backed the cheap music because its affiliated publishers and writers were involved in pushing it, and promoting it. It helped the process along, because it was *theirs*.

As to rock 'n' roll having a "fundamental appeal," this suggests that it was predestined that teenagers like rock 'n' roll. Why can't you have a "beat" with superior music and lyrics? Must rhythmic elements be tied to musical illiteracy? As to Presley's influence in the world, most cultural commentators have observed that in the postwar period, everything American was popular, including popular music. Presley's motion pictures also have helped his career in foreign countries.

Hentoff gives no credit to BMI in shaping taste or creating interest in certain musical materials. BMI begs to differ. In its official maroon-covered booklet *20 Years of Service to Music*, BMI states proudly:

> The expanded opportunity for new writers and publishers *created by* [my emphasis] BMI has sparked a continuing process of diversification, growth, and democratization of American music during the last two decades. New talents, particularly those from portions of our country outside of Tin Pan Alley and Hollywood have found an audience. New music has been able to gain a hearing. *New vitality* [my emphasis] has been brought to traditional forms of music.

Thus the cheap new music becomes "a process of diversification" and "democratization," laced with "new vitality." Hentoff even observed, as a footnote, that BMI cannot possibly be the giant ogre people make out, for it makes less money than ASCAP. This is another little-understood aspect concerning BMI.

BMI can perhaps make as much money as ASCAP. It chooses not to. All it has to do is raise its licensing fees for radio and TV stations. It has a good argument to ask for such an increase; look at the trade-

paper popularity charts, it is way ahead of ASCAP. But why would
BMI do that? The broadcasters own BMI. A board of directors composed of broadcasting interests (no songwriters or music publishers
are members) would not willingly vote for a proposition that would
cost them more money. Why pay $10 when you can pay $5 or $3 or $2?
So BMI is run as "a nonprofit" company. If it raised the rates, the
broadcasters wouldn't get it; perhaps the songwriters and music publishers and BMI staff people might get it.

The economics factor is tied to aesthetics. BMI put its money behind certain individuals and forces and plumped for the commercial
popularity of this music, which was largely rock 'n' roll, country and
western, and cheap "teen-pop." This is a matter of aesthetics.

The truth about BMI is this: Once you set in motion an organism,
finance it, subsidize it, baby it, nurse it, it can grow up quite strong.

Today's BMI has acquired status and respectability. Years ago its
ranks included largely unknown popular music writers and lyricists.
Today its ranks include many active jazz composers and arrangers
(Gil Evans, George Russell, Thelonius Monk, John Lewis), composer-
conductor-arrangers (Nelson Riddle), folk writers (Pete Seeger and
Lee Hays), and composers of classical music (Roger Sessions and William Schuman). It has moved into a new phase, where it has access
to talent.

A handful of its writers have cracked Broadway, notably Sheldon
Harnick and Jerry Bock, co-authors of the score for *Fiorello* and *She
Loves Me*. Because of tie-ups abroad, BMI has also speared the
licensing rights to *Stop the World, I Want to Get Off*, and *Oliver*. But
the composers and lyricists of those productions are, strictly speaking,
not really BMI-trained or shaped. The licensing agency also has un-
sung lyricists and composers who are on the literate side.

Truthfully, the success of BMI has astounded BMI, and ASCAP,
too. ASCAP is still preeminent in the musical theater and Hollywood.
Lately, it has taken more interest in modern jazz and country and
western music. Inside ASCAP there are still loud complaints that
younger writers do not get their proper due; that performance credits
for new songs should count more. There are cries that ASCAP is too
heavily weighted in the direction of the giant Hollywood-based music
publishing concerns; that TV theme music is given undue emphasis
in logging. Such views are expressed in meetings of ASCAP, whose
minutes sound like the log of a court-martial with its president, lyricist-
lawyer Stanley Adams on trial. Songwriters and music publishers are
very articulate.

At BMI the meetings are quiet as acoustic ceilings. There is hardly any voice-raising, losing of tempers, shouting for the chair's permission to speak. For the candid facts are that there is no democracy in BMI. It is complete captive of the broadcasters. There are no songwriters or music publishers on its board of directors, only representatives of radio stations. There are no meetings where the songwriters or music publishers can vote on the types of contracts they wish to sign with broadcasters or restaurants. They do not have the elementary right to formulate policy or set rates which affect their livelihood and their families.

BMI is completely management-dictated, a sort of Tin Pan Alley "company store." With all its bureaucratic weaknesses, ASCAP conceived in 1914 functions democratically. Members can fight for changes and do so. Membership meetings are held periodically. They elect officials and take votes on important and trivial issues.

The leopard has changed its spots. BMI is sleeker, more powerful, and as "hit" conscious as ever. It has whipped ASCAP, outlasted Congressional inquiries, and blocked laws to detach it from the broadcasters. Once a year, for example, it takes pride, expressed in full-page advertisements, to set forth the names of the popular music writers who have reached the pinnacle of success, best-sellerdom. These individuals are invited to a fancy ball or party, and given "Certificates of Achievement." To offer certificates of achievement to creators and purveyors of 95 per cent of these songs and themes is like awarding Jack the Ripper an award for brotherhood and community service.

Of course, the music-licensing agency is no complete hydra-headed devil. In publicity, in subsidy and promotion, it has done much to encourage contemporary classical music. It is to its credit that in its pin-up sheets there is a category devoted to new recordings of modern concert music. BMI has also encouraged modern jazz and folk music.

However, its biggest and perhaps most dominant influence has been in the field of popular music. Save for a handful of songs and themes such as "Lullabye of Birdland," "Sixteen Tons," "Young at Heart," "Never on Sunday," and "Too Close for Comfort," BMI has been intimately associated with the rise of teenage songs, rock 'n' roll, rhythm and blues, and "country-pop." In these four areas, it has been supreme.

Of course, the decline in popular music has multiple causes, the decline of the Broadway and Hollywood movie musicals, the payola scandals, the usage of the "top 40" in the trade-paper charts as a guide to radio programing, and unethical practices in the distribution and selling of records. And the weaknesses in our educational and social structure haven't helped either. Though the decline may be traced to these multiple causes, it does not lessen the crucial role of BMI.

BMI practices integration in its staff-hiring policies, and this is certainly good, but it needs to extend democracy to its own affiliated writers and music publishers. Also, it needs detachment from "Big Daddy," the broadcasters. Is it proper for one giant licensing agency to be owned by the chief means of exploitation? The BMI broadcaster relationship is a clear case of conflict of interests: the buyer of music (radio) is also the seller (radio, through the corporate mask of BMI). How can they bargain collectively?

The United States is big enough to have two large competitive licensing agencies—ASCAP and BMI. BMI should continue to function and operate, but as a fair competitor, without any ties to the broadcasters.

Looking back, there are several things that stick out in the BMI story. It did make it easier for young writers to break into the popular music field; it did shake up the logging practices of ASCAP, although this could have happened by internal dissent; and it made ASCAP more democratic and easier to join.

But Broadcast Music Inc. cannot be forgiven the rationalization of its aesthetics. It cannot be forgiven its opportunistic championship of the tasteless musical mediocrities. It cannot easily be forgiven the fact that certain patterns of writing prodded a certain pattern of amateurish performance, which still plagues us today. "The House on 48th Street" has helped nourish a lowered standard of craftsmanship, and this is audibly evident. Teenagers—and their parents—have spent millions of dollars on cheap BMI materials.

Of course, Broadcast Music, Inc. did not begin wanting to be associated with poor popular music. It got into the field at an odd historical moment. It attracted poor writers and money-hungry music publishers who would produce and "plug" anything.

Anxious for success, the BMI forces pushed and pushed. Some of the staff men there (musicians, lyricists, jazz enthusiasts, big-band devotees) knew better and winced at the product being turned out. But business is business.

As noted earlier, BMI has published a booklet saluting its *20 Years of Service to Music, 1940-1960*. So far as popular music is concerned, please save us from another twenty years of such "service."

17 · COUNTRY AND WESTERN MUSIC

> Nashville is Cashville as country music twangs its way into
> a nationwide boom.
>
> —*Show Business Illustrated*

> "The Dimple of the Universe," "The Protestant Vatican of the
> South," "The Athens of Dixie."
>
> —Nicknames associated with Nashville, cited by
> John Gunther, *Inside U.S.A.*

Since the 1950's the brand of urbanization has been strongly stamped
on the hide of country and western music. Today, much of the music
coming from Nashville, Tennessee, the "C & W" capital, can be characterized as "country-pop." Increasingly, the bland vacuities of Tin
Pan Alley (ill-fated love, triangle situations) are sung and recorded
with the "Nashville sound" by Bill Anderson, Brenda Lee, Skeeter
David, Eddy Arnold, and Elvis Presley. Country and western artists
have been caught up, perhaps irretrievably, in the process of twentieth-
century entertainment and exploitation.

With urbanization has come very unhomespun commercialism, and
with it also the struggle that continues with any music that has a folk
basis: the struggle to retain its integrity, honesty, and simplicity.

There is a photograph in a newly-published fan magazine, *Country
Music* [. . . . 101 Great Singers! Their Lives and Loves!], put out
by a northern publisher, Macfadden-Bartell Corporation, depicting
singer Webb Pierce, guitar in hand, sitting in his white Pontiac con-
vertible. The upholstery is "hand-tooled leather and unborn calf skin."
On the dashboard and around the car are a thousand silver dollars,
glued down. It is, perhaps, symbolic.

Today, country and western music is a formidable part of the
popular music and record business in the United States, Canada, and
abroad, particularly in Germany, Japan, and South Africa. Governor
Frank Clement of Tennessee once estimated that C & W music is a
$50-million-a-year industry. Nashville itself is the third largest music-
producing city in the country, ranking just below New York City and
Los Angeles.

A myriad group of subindustries have grown up in and around Nashville to service the needs of what is often called "Music City, U. S. A.," by its leather-booted boosters. There are countless music publishers, record-pressing plants, album manufacturers, printing plants, bookers and promoters of talent, and recording studios. Recently, Starday, founded in 1952, and a leading maker of country music recordings, started the Country Music Record Club of America.

Not long ago, the advertising trade magazine, *Sponsor*, ran an incandescent account of country music penetration into radio programing and advertising, titled, "The C & W Sound Captures the U. S. Heart and Purse." The subhead noted, "Over 1,400 stations beam country music to loyal fans, both urban and rural." Of course, the big headline is inaccurate. Lots of urban people dislike country music. There are show-music fanciers and jazz record fans who cannot take its repetitive melodies. And of course, many devotees of modern music, including twelve-tone and chance composition, shun it. They even think Wagner, Stravinsky, Cole Porter, and Gershwin are "old hat."

But it is an acceptable hyperbole. Recently, *Cash Box* (October 26, 1963) observed that there has been somewhat of a decline in the popularity of country music, but it reported these cardinal facts: "Nashville, its publishers, artists, recording companies and studios are directly involved with approximately 20 per cent of the nation's top fifty best-selling 'singles.'"

But the ruralism and homespun earthiness implicit in many country songs is fading under the impact of modernism in the United States generally, and in Nashville in particular. It is no hillbilly town, where people drink out of mason jugs and ride the range.

The country music citadel boasts of a new $35 million airport with runways long enough for jet aircraft. *Broadcasting* (June 17, 1963) describes the city this way:

Nashville has a hybrid municipal décor—a combination of contemporary structures and handsome landscaping blended with older architecture of a past generation or two or more. Downtown Nashville has two eye-capturing landmarks—the Life and Casualty Building just a few steps from the old site of historic Maxwell House and a Grecian Capitol surrounded by a half-circular park and driveway.

The population of Nashville is about 425,000, and there are nearly 600,000 within its commuting orbit. Some of its key industries are religious book and magazine publishing (2,000 employees, $57 million payroll), shoemaking (including Genesco, the fourth largest U. S.

shoemaker with 3,000 employees), components and appliances (Avco has 2,800 employees), glass (Ford with 2,300 employees), and textiles and plastics (DuPont employs 2,300).

Two of the principal life insurance companies in the United States are headquartered here, the National Life and Accident Insurance Co. and Life and Casualty Company. They have $10 billion worth of life insurance in force and employ 2,300 people. One of the interesting facts concerning National Life and Accident Insurance Co. is that it built and owns WSM, the electronic heart of country music, from which "Grand Ole Opry" broadcasts.

In the official 1961 *Grand Opry History-Picture Book*, there is this picture of the country and music industry in that city:

1100 professional musicians
Hundreds of amateur musicians
95 BMI publishers
16 ASCAP publishers
179 full-time BMI songwriters
20 full-time ASCAP songwriters
Untold thousands of would-be writers
15 recordings, two of which operate on a seven-day, around-the-clock basis
12 artists or booking agencies
Upward of 1,600 artists . . . singers, fiddlers, gospel quartets, and highly
  specialized soloists who may do nothing more than make the "background" noise in a recording session

Before going any further, it might be worth while to define, if possible, country and western music. It consists of old English ballads, cowboy songs, rural humor, sacred music, country blues, rhythm and blues, songs of unrequited love, topical songs (railroad wrecks to the story of President Kennedy's naval exploits in *PT 109*). It crosses into folk music and out of it. Elements of country style intermixed with rock 'n' roll (or rhythm and blues) became "rock-a-billy," exemplified by such early Elvis Presley records as "Hound Dog."

Nor is this all. Country music also is a way of singing, a way of instrumentation. The subject matter may vary, but you will rarely discover sophisticated lyrics, or a sophisticated form of singing engaged in by country and western singers. You cannot mistake a country and western singer for Frank Sinatra, George London, June Christy, or Joan Sutherland.

In 1904 the June issue of *Harper's* magazine ran an article by Emma Bell Miles titled, "Some Real American Music." The author objected to the then-common misconception that America had no distinctive folk music. She wrote, "But there is hidden among the mountains of Kentucky, Tennessee, and the Carolinas, a people of whose inner nature and its musical expression almost nothing has been said. The music of the southern mountaineer is not only peculiar, but like himself, peculiarly American."

But little was said or heard of this culture until, in the 1920's four things happened. (1) In the fall of 1925 the Nashville newspapers reported: "Construction of radio station here has begun." (2) Commercial recording men began to sit up and take notice. (3) Hollywood western movies became popular. (4) BMI (Broadcast Music Inc.) was organized.

The Nashville radio station, WSM (standing for "We Shield Millions") gave birth to a four-and-a-half-hour radio show that is, in the words of an official booklet, "The only radio program in the world that has never had a summer replacement, never had an intermission, never missed a performance since it started in 1925." The name of the show? "Grand Ole Opry."

Originally known as the "WSM Barn Dance," the show was originated by the station's first director, George D. Hay, who had been a newspaper man with the *Commercial Appeal* of Memphis, Tennessee. As a reporter he was assigned to cover the funeral of an Ozark World War I hero. Finishing his story there, he attended a hoedown in the area, where "lighted by a coal oil lamp in one corner" they "carried on until the crack o' dawn!" Mr. Hay says: "No one has ever had more fun than those Ozark mountaineers had that night. It stuck with me until the idea became the 'Grand Ole Opry' seven or eight years later."

Hay, himself, though only thirty years old, was on the show as "The Solemn Ole Judge" and the show's first and only artist on opening night was a bearded, eighty-year-old, "Uncle Jimmy" Thompson, who played the fiddle for an hour that first night saying, "a man can't hardly get warmed up in an hour."

The station had amazing response and "Uncle Jimmy" became a regular Saturday night performer. More amazing were the hordes of country musicians who began to pour into the station wanting to be in the show.

At first the show was instrumental, but in 1926 a singer known as the "Dixie Dewdrop" appeared, wearing a double-breasted waistcoat (always unbuttoned), a wide-brimmed black felt hat—summer or winter—and a "gates ajar collar." His name was "Uncle Dave" Macon, and for fifteen years he was the show's biggest attraction.

One observer credits WSM's "Grand Ole Opry" with the survival and renaissance of country music in modern times. Ralph Rinzler, manager of country talent, wrote recently in *Hootenanny:*

Whether the [record] companies could have continued to sell such records without the constant reinforcement of the radio is another question. It is not unlikely that urban dance music and popular song would have completely erased commercial country music had there not been jamborees [country music's version of the hootenanny] on the radio. . . . The program provided incentive and assured continuation of the vocal and instrumental traditions in rural areas. For years, it countered the urban "pop music" tradition of which it is now ironically an extension.

Perhaps WSM can't take all the kudos. Beginning in the 1930's country and western disc jockeys began to be heard, particularly in the South and the Midwest. Hundreds of hinterland stations from Tennessee to the West Coast and south to Texas and the banks of the Rio Grande transmitted a steady diet of C & W music.

In the late 1920's the pioneers of commercial recording began to beat the bushes to put country music on wax. They traveled by horse, by "tin Lizzie," on foot, and by mule.

When the Depression of the 30's hit the record business, it was found that country records still had a steady sale in the so-called "country market." In those days, if a country artist sold 10,000 records it was considered to be a smash hit. Money was rare, and one authority reported "farmers might only be able to afford one or two records a year."

Samuel B. Charters, in *The Country Blues* says, "The finest body of ethnic music material collected in the South was that collected by the commercial recording directors in the South in the late 1920's."

Outstanding among these first recording men was the late Ralph Peer, who worked both in country music and Negro music. He originated the term "race records," and he is credited with the discovery of Jimmy Rodgers. Equally noteworthy pioneer Country A & R men were Eli Oberstein, Frank Walker, Dave Kapp, Paul Cohen, Owen Bradley, and Don Law.

Record companies in the 20's, 30's, and 40's were building their country catalogues, but the sales were primarily to the country market. Consumer publications began to take some notice of country music but saw it as a source of comedy and ridicule, and often pictured the field as "freakish" and made up of suspendered gawks with guitars singing odd songs with nasal diction.

Also entering the picture in the 1930's was Hollywood's beloved perennial—the Western with music. These films gave birth to great popular singing stars like Gene Autry and Roy Rogers. Autry started his career with a fifteen-minute radio show on KVOO in Tulsa, back in 1928, and simultaneously began recording for Velvet Tone, then a subsidiary of Columbia Records. Autry, who now heads a business empire which includes five radio stations, two television stations, four hotels (including San Francisco's Mark Hopkins), and the Los Angeles Angels baseball team, recently told *Billboard:* "Even in those [early] days there were just as many so-called 'pop' fans who thoroughly enjoyed C & W music. I don't agree with the idea that there's a wider interest in C & W today than in the earlier years. I feel there always was a strong following for this music from all walks of life."

Autry's picture career began in 1934 with a twelve-chapter serial, *The Phantom Empire,* made for Mascot Films (forerunner of Republic Pictures). The following year he made his first full-length movie for Republic Pictures. It was called *Tumbling Tumbleweed* and in it he introduced the song of the same title. In each of the sixty pictures he made for Republic and the forty pictures he made for Columbia, Autry sang.

It was a wide audience that enjoyed cowboy films and Hollywood, always desiring to please, provided all kinds of "cowboys"—thus inspiring songs such as this humorous ditty:

> When I was just a little shaver back in Brooklyn
> I used to think that I would like to be a cowboy
> Because I loved to see 'em in the movin' pictures
> A-ridin and a-shootin' away.*

And a Johnny Mercer lyric that went:

> I'm an old cowhand
> From the Rio Grande
> But my legs ain't bowed
> And my cheeks ain't tanned
> I'm a cowboy who never saw a cow
> Never roped a steer, 'cause I don't know how
> And I sure ain't fixin' to start in now
> Yippee I O I A.**

These songs might be called "Eastern Westerns."

Western movies now have their video counterparts. In such TV programs as "Maverick" and "Bonanza," you hear a lot of so-called Western music, but these have been flattened out to become plain melodies with bursts of western color. One song from a Walt Disney show resulted in a national moppet craze. This was, of course, "The Ballad of Davy Crockett" by Hollywood-based writers a long way from Nashville.

The most recent important factor contributing to the growth of country music was the birth of BMI in 1940. Already established writers as well as up-and-coming ones, or writers with more sophisticated skills and taste, musically and lyrically, were inevitably drawn to ASCAP, the organization that includes in its roster every important name in musical theater. Broadcast Music Inc. had to have writers to function, and music to license, so they opened their doors to amateurs and also country writers. The music licensing agency was a "catalyst," according to *Billboard*. It gave "financial encouragement" to publishers and writers; "permitted them to make a living and spend more time at their craft; and the logging of country music performances—and the subsequent distribution of moneys as a result of those performances— was a welcome emolument."

Being wise to the ways of modern publicity, BMI also publicized country music on a national basis through its pin-up sheets, its trade-paper ads, and radio services.

Touching on the northern corporation's aid, Governor Frank Clement of Tennessee once fervently told a Nashville disc jockey: "You people well know, before BMI came into existence very few country music composers or publishers had any market for their musical wares. No market, no money—a simple economic formula."

Nashville is losing much of its folk-base, and becoming more Tin Pan Alley-ized. The lyrics, the sounds, the instrumentation have changed considerably from the old days of country music. The noted music educator and composer, Howard Hanson, has decried today's "hillbilly music," before a U. S. congressional committee: "The hillbilly music we hear on the radio is not really hillbilly music. It's a Madison Avenue version of hillbilly music. It's pretty doctored and a long way from the hills of Tennessee."

In a fascinating and encyclopedic special issue put out by *Billboard* and titled, "The World of Country Music" (November 2, 1963), Tex Ritter says: "Madison Avenue's ad agencies have yet to realize the full extent of country and western's appeal and harness it to their benefit."

Later, it is noted that special shows have been prepared to convince sales executives in the radio and broadcasting fields to use country music programs to sell products.

There is an apparent contradiction here. Hanson asserts that it is "Madison Avenue's version" of Tin Pan Alley which we hear of country music, and Ritter argues that Madison Avenue is not taking advantage of the potential of country music. In Hanson's case he means excessive commercialism, of which Madison Avenue is a synonym.

As noted earlier, much of the country and western music is even characterized by country A & R men, singers, and country-music executives as "country-pop," and this is what is landing up there on the best-seller record listings.

Trudy Stamper of WSM informs me: "You asked how the future of C & W music looked and I will have to answer, 'Terrific.' Although the distinction of C & W is becoming less and less. For instance, on the 'pop' charts today in the top 100 you will have 'Still' by Bill Anderson, 'Saving My Love' by Skeeter Davis, 'Abilene' by George Hamilton IV, and 'The Minute You're Gone' by Sonny James. These are 'Grand Ole Opry' stars—country and western singers."

"Still" sung and composed by Bill Anderson, is one of the most insipid "pop" tunes, lyrically, musically, and structurally. It is a cornucopia of corn, consisting of two short lyrics, interspersed by spoken dialogue that makes former soap-opera dialogue seem like T. S. Eliot:

Still

Still
Though you broke my heart
Still
Though we're far apart
   I love you still

Still
After all this time
Still
You're still on my mind
   I love you still

(Spoken): I've lost count of the hours and I've lost count of the days, in fact, I've lost just about everything since you went away. Everything, that is, except the memories you left me. And that's one thing no one can mar. I don't know who you're with, I don't even know where you've gone. My only hope is that someday you might hear this song and you'll know that I wrote it especially for you, and I love you wherever you are.*

One of the top C & W smashes in 1963, not noted by Miss Stamper was recorded by Skeeter Davis (RCA Victor), entitled "The End of the

*Copyright © 1963 Moss Rose Publications, Inc. Written by Bill Anderson.

World." It is the product of Tin Pan Alley up North—the Brill Building, to be precise. This, too, is in the style of grandiose slobbering and drippy sentiment that has to be scooped up with sugaring-off cans attached to maple trees.

End of the World

Why does the sun go on shining?
Why does the sea rush to shore
Don't they know it's the end of the world
'Cause you don't love me anymore

Why do the birds go on singing
Why do the stars glow above
Don't they know it's the end of the world
It ended when I lost your love.*

It is typical of Tin Pan Alley "mooncalfery." Also, there are a staggering number of "triangle love songs," one of "pop" music's oldest clichés. But now it is not puppy-love triangles, but marital infidelity. One country and western disc jockey, "Bashful Bobby" Wooten, KAYO, Seattle, a country and western disc jockey for thirteen years, recently wrote a tear-stained note to *Billboard:*

Look at the current C & W top 40. About 80 per cent of the songs have as their theme the triangle situation in which one or both of the central characters is married, and one or both sings about the tragedy and unhappiness of illicit love. Granted that this situation happens often enough in real life to make Dr. Kinsey blush, but even in these situations, surely there must be some happiness, at least at first.

The Tin Pan Alley influence on C & W is obvious. One rather recent album featured the country guitarist, Duane Eddy, recorded in RCA Victor's "Nashville sound" studio. In the LP Eddy plays all the new teen urban dances, allegedly popular in all the big cities. As the liner notes point out: "Here are the rhythms of the twist, and all the swinging dance variations that came out of the twist—the watusi, the hullygully, the mashed potato, the limbo, the popeye, and the twist with a Spanish touch, the loco-motion." There is a footnote on the album giving the address of this country star's fan club. Duane Eddy's Fan Club apparently is headquartered in New York City, P. O. Box 623, New York 19.

Of course, there is some country and western music which clings

*Copyright © 1963 Summit Music Corp. Written by Sylvia Dee and Arthur Kent.

to folk-based characteristics, such as topicality and comments on things happening in the country. One such composer-writer-singer is John Loudermilk. He composes all sorts of songs—teen songs, blues songs, and such modern-minded items as "He's a Scientist." In this, he touches on the heroes some Americans worship.

Here is an excerpt from "He's a Scientist":

> He don't play football, golf or guitar
> He's never been on Sullivan, Clark or Paar
> He's just not important 'cause he ain't a star
> He's just a scientist
> Oh, ho, just a scientist
> Hey, hey, just a scientist
> Mm, mm, just a scientist—that's all.
>
> Now all the dames are one for big and brawny halfbacks
> And Marshals find their rustlers by their horse's tracks
> But who is gonna take us to the moon and back?
> He'll be a scientist
> Hey, hey, just a scientist
> Oh, yeah, just a scientist
> Just a scientist—that's all.*

To cover himself, and perhaps make the song "commercial," Loudermilk resorts to the characteristics of rock 'n' roll lyrics such as "Oh, ho," "Hey, hey," "MM, mm" (a standby), and "Oh, yeah" (a *must*).

Country writers do not appear to be as socially adventurous as such folk writers as Bob Dylan, Lee Hays, and Pete Seeger, who are against "the bomb" and against bigotry. Hardly any of the Nashville-based writers deal with integration, perhaps out of fear that the C & W audience in the South won't stand for it. It is also true that some C & W recording artists do not resent segregation.

But the C & W writers haven't drawn away from social issues completely. There are a handful like Harland Howard who haven't accepted the fact that we are living in a country of pervading national affluence. Burl Ives sings this coal miner's lament, "Busted," written by Howard and in the Decca album called simply, "Burl."

> The bills are all due
> And my babies need shoes
> But I'm Busted
> We've had a hard time

*Copyright © 1961 by Acuff-Rose. Written by John Loudermilk. Used by permission.

> Since they closed down the mine
> We're Busted.
>
> Got a cow that's gone dry
> And a hen that won't lay
> A big stack of bills that gets bigger each day
> Tomorrow they'll haul our belongings away
> We're Busted
> Our friends are all leaving this old mining town
> They're Busted
> They're heading up North where there's work to be found
> And trusted.
> Lord, I hate to give up this acre of land
> It's been in the family since mining began
> But babies get hungry, they don't understand
> That they're Busted.
>
> I called Brother Bill, thought I'd ask for a loan
> —Busted.
> Lord I had to beg like a dog for a bone
> I'm Busted.
> But Bill lost his job and his rent's overdue
> His wife and his kids all are down with the flu
> He said, "I was thinking of calling on you."
> Busted.*

Sung to a rather typical country-type tune and the accompaniment of guitars and mixed chorus, the song goes on to say that poverty sometimes turns a man to crime, and it ends with the family selling their Guernsey and packing to head north. Musically there is no "bridge" or contrasting melody, simply a repetition of the one musical "paragraph" with new lyrics to further the story.

These lyrics are exceptions to the run-of-the-hill-country songs. Surrounded by an urban situation, advancing commercialism, and the twofold desire to put out "singles" that will appeal to teenagers and material that will appeal to the whole country, the C & W artists and writers have divided minds. A handful are battling to retain some of the heritage of honesty in country and western music. But it seems to be a losing battle. The situation is one of dilution, sweetening up, and distortion of the old C & W patterns. Such men as Loudermilk, Howard, Jimmy Driftwood, Merle Travis ("Sixteen Tons") are trying, but they are crying in the commercial wilderness.

Ralph Rinzler has observed: "In an effort to keep abreast of the times, the 'Opry' and those who follow its trends have allowed big business aspects of the industry to dictate its policies and dominate the scene."

The old-time country music is hard to come by any more. In a talk to C & W music disc jockeys in Nashville, Steve Sholes of RCA Victor, said that times have changed:

"Your older listeners who want old country music sounds are wonderful people, the backbone of this country, loyal radio listeners—when the kids aren't around—but they don't buy records—not enough to keep us in business, not enough to keep even the old-fashioned country artist in guitar strings. It's the kids who buy, and the kids want and buy the newer sounds."

It's a fast-moving world, he told the disc jockeys. "That's why old-fashioned country music is not created on a big scale any more. The people have been changing, the little red schoolhouse is no more. It has been replaced by the big rural centers, and when the kids start to cross geographical boundaries, they also begin to cross musical boundaries. Television, too, has had its impact, musical tastes have been broadened, *perhaps not for the better*. But that's the way it is."

The veteran country and western A & R man also noted these interesting changes in the music and the musicianship:

"The country artist [has] changed. Over the past ten years there's been a notable improvement in dignity and style in country singing. The country artist works much harder, rehearses more, and he's learning to read music at sight. In other words, he's become much more self-disciplined.

"There has also been a great improvement in the intonation and harmonic feeling between members of the vocal groups.

"The improvements in the solo and group country artists has, however, sometimes been overshadowed by the more obvious technical advances in instrument design and amplification, not to mention improvements in recording and broadcasting techniques.

"All these factors—greatest self-discipline on the part of the solo artist, a vast improvement in intonation and greater variety in harmonizing of the ensemble groups, plus the technical improvements in the instruments the country artist uses and refinements in sound reproduction—all these have freed the country *songwriter* from past limitations to express himself in more daring harmonics and imaginative lyrical ideas."

Added Sholes: "For instance, the instrumentation of 'pop' and rock 'n' roll music is much more closely allied today to country and western music than it is to anything else. Most 'pop' instrumentation nowadays features a rhythm section and a guitar, practically synonymous with country western music. Such vocal tricks long identified with country music as the yodel, tear in the voice, voice break, highly emotionalized expressions, are now standard for 'pop' music, too. For years, before country music changed them, 'pop' singers sang a song straight, pretty coldly, compared to country singers. Now, most of the 'pop' hit records are so souped up with emotion they could fire a rocket to the moon!"

Possibly nothing dramatizes the way country and western music has been bushwacked by commercialism than a recent ad by Custom Jingles of Nashville. In the advertisement, there is this headline:

HARNESSING THE FANTASTIC SELLING POWER OF COUNTRY MUSIC FOR THE ADVERTISING INDUSTRY

And on the right side of the ad, there is a face-portrait of C & W star, Eddy Arnold, a former Tennessee plowboy, with a personal message:

Nashville has long been famous for its fine musicians, singers, and great recording industry. Now comes something new to Nashville.

It's a company that specializes in singing commercials, and why not? If these musicians, singers, and recording studios can come up with hit after hit, selling their tales of love, troubles, and woe to the public, why can't they sell a product the same way?

The ad continued:

In *five* short months we have produced jingles with the famous Nashville Sound for the following advertisers: Pet Milk, Kroger, Gates Tires, Ford, Luzianne Coffee, Ballard Flour, Jones Homes, Pillsbury, Gunther Beer, Bubble-Up, Kayo Gas, TVA.

19 · FOLK MUSIC BOOM

America will have many folk song vendors in the next few years. Some city boys may take a short motor trip through our land and return to write the Song of the Prairies—others will be folk song authorities after reading in a public library for a few weeks. "And though we have no talents here for hiring, we'll hire the robe out anyhow." We'll have Folk Song Hot and Cold and in the Pot with whiskers on it.
—From article by Henry Cowell "Folk Song—American Big Business," in *Modern Music* (1940)

Not long ago, at a New York State summer resort, a teenaged youth counselor with long flowing black hair and white Bermuda shorts was seated on the concrete of the handball court, leading a group of equally recumbent children in the singing of a gentle classic of musical Americana, "Down by the Old Mill Stream." Toward the middle, she broke into the song abruptly, strummed a few chords and cried:

"Oh, the heck with that *Tin Pan Alley junk.*"

She returned to her purist ledge, "On Top of Old Smoky." Some of the folk music converts of the 1960's may be excessively cultist and narrow. But the folk music they champion is as wide as the world: church music, down-country blue grass, Elizabethan madrigals, African hunting songs, Negro folk-blues, cowboy songs, labor songs, integration songs, gambling songs, Israeli *horas*, children's songs, portraits of bordellos. Easy to satirize, the folk fever is healthy.

Since the 1950's, folk music has gained increasing importance within the popular-music-and-record structure, and within the vast range of show business in the United States and abroad. Though there were folk hit recordings in the days of bathtub gin and short-skirted girls, the modern folk music craze did not really begin until the mid-fifties. Then there appeared a handsome, coffee-colored West Indian, Harold ("Harry") Belafonte, Jr. From a short engagement at the Village Vanguard, he catapulted into a fabulous night club attraction, and later was signed by RCA Victor Records.

238

Time has offered this picture of Belafonte performing in the late 1950's.

Belafonte usually strides on stage in pitch blackness, stations himself by the microphone before the spotlight bursts on him—light blue, lavender or "upbeat pink," depending on the mood he is trying to convey. For his female fans the famed Belafonte costume—a tailored ($27) Indian cotton shirt partially open, snug black slacks, a seaman's belt buckled by two large interlocking curtain rings—combines the dashing elegance of a Valentino cape with the muscled fascination of a Brando T-shirt. The handsomely chiseled head is tipped slightly back, the eyes nearly closed. He is always backed by two guitars, a bass fiddle, and a conga drum to which may be added other instruments, or a full orchestra, or a twelve-man chorus.

One of the former pop singer's LP's, "Belafonte Sings of the Caribbean," became the first LP by a single artist to sell a million copies.

Belafonte brought sex appeal to folk music. In this he was more successful than earthier Josh White in his Greenwich Village days, who put an unlit cigarette atop his ear, and looking slightly evil, but not lascivious, sang, "I Gave My Love a Cherry," or "The House of the Rising Sun."

Along with the smoldering sex appeal of Belafonte (he always seemed to be angry) there came a sturdy push from the collegiate field, the advent of the smiling-faced Kingston Trio. The Kingston Trio didn't resort to theatrics, but they cultivated the college "image." They wore plain slacks, open-shirted, and ordinary leather moccasins. The Kingston Trio reflected in themselves the fabulous dormant audience for folk music—the young college crowd—as well as the young-married set and the brighter teenagers. In Belafonte and the Kingston Trio there was represented the ethnic base (folk songs) coated with urban showmanship, costumes (tailored shirts or the on-campus look) arrangements, lights, and pieces of "business." From then on, the dam burst.

The folk music boom is as big as dietetic foods. The Record Industry Association of America (RIAA) recently pinpointed this striking fact: "When Ben Gray Lumpkin compiled the first discography of folk music on records in America in 1950, he could find only 276 albums, most of them 78-rpm sets. A recent issue of Schwann's long-playing catalogue lists no less than 1953 folk music albums, with 697 of them devoted entirely to American folk music."

One of the U. S. A.'s earliest popular "folk singers" was the Irish tenor, John McCormack. Millions listened to him on those early cumbersome radio sets—the Fada, the Atwater-Kent, or the homemade crystal sets built with oatmeal boxes. He sang in what might be called a "semi-classical manner" such sturdy songs as "Molly Malone," "Molly Bawn," "The Foggy Dew," and "Macushla," which were best-sellers on RCA Victor Records in the so-called jazz age.

"During the 1920's," says Henry Brief of the Record Industry Association, "record companies began going out into the field to record for the first time. Studios set up in Nashville, Atlanta, or Memphis began sending back 'race' and 'country' records to the pressing plants—bluegrass music from the hill country of the South, Negro spirituals and folk music from Georgia and Louisiana, cowboy songs from Texas and Oklahoma. Although the records were intended for sale to members of the minority groups who had recorded them, record manufacturers suddenly found they were selling in the cities of the industrial Northeast as well—there were even sales on college campuses. Records drew the attention of scholars Charles Seeger, John A. Lomax, and others, who went into the field with their own recording equipment to bring back new folk songs and new folk singers."

Folk music has existed in America in myriad shapes and forms; it has never died. But today, folk music has become a part of the all-pervading American entertainment industry. You can hear it on radio programs, recordings, TV, juke boxes (the symbol of cheap urban entertainment). Along with it has arisen such magazines as *Sing Out*, *The Little Sandy Review*, and "fan magazines" such as *Hootenanny* and *ABC-TV Hootenanny*. Countless books on folk songs have poured out, as well as easy simplified collections of folk songs for voice, guitar, and piano. Besides these popular manifestations of folk-music popularity, there continues exhaustive researches into ethnic music, and survivals of the "pure" homemade music in every inaccessible area of the world. The taping of this pre-industrial age of music, the documentation of it, has become a minor industry, pioneered in by Cecil Sharp (Britain), Bela Bartok (Hungary), and the Lomaxes, John and Alan (United States). In the piney backwoods of the South and the cloistered academic milieu of the folk-music archives of the Library of Congress, ethnic musicologists, followists, and would-be singers listen and study.

There are even humorous LP's devoted to lampooning folk music clientele and singers such as the discs by the Smothers Four, "Think Ethnic" (Mercury), and Shel Silverstein's LP, "Inside Folk Songs" (Atlantic Records). A million-seller mining this vein was Allan Sherman's "My Son, the Folk Singer" (Warner Bros.). A flood of cartoons have also been pouring off illustration boards touching on all aspects of folk music—the pure ethnic performers, the "citybillies," the "folk-fakers," the often-affected folk audience, and the ethnic-musicologists.

Folk music in the context of modern mass media, night clubs, and television, is something a little wry, as if Peter Arno attempted to paint in the Brueghel manner. You have college-educated, conservatory-trained girls in calico gowns hugging long-necked banjos or guitars trying to be as rural as corn pone. There are folk-singing groups organized into corporations which own skyscrapers.

Some of the elements which have plunged into the folk-music "bit," are funny. A New York booker of exotics (stripteasers) has prepared touring folk-music units. TV cigarette commercials are sung to folk tunes associated with the good clean nicotine-free outdoors. Recently, Decca issued one of the howlers of recent years by releasing an album titled "Golden Folk Songs for Dancing," played by Guy Lombardo and his Canadians. Lombardo, a speedboat fancier and millionaire restaurauteur, plays hotel dance music associated with crystal chandeliers and potted rubber plants. His LP got a Billboard "Pop Special Merit" crest, and underneath the picture of the album was this quietly, quizzical evaluation: "Lombardo lovers are likely to go for most of anything the famed maestro picks out for a program, even if it's a collection of folk and neo-folk-songs which don't really lend themselves to the Lombardo scene particularly well." Songs included in the Lombardo "hootenanny": "Boll Weevil," "Goodnight, Irene," and "Molly Malone."

In the 1920's, as noted earlier, most of the authentic folk singers were regionally based; quite a few of them made recordings. Along with the Great Depression there came the voices of social protest, including Woody Guthrie, who sang in union halls and at Aid-to-the-Spanish Republic rallies. In the 1940's people began talking about reedy Richard Dyer-Bennett and his largely English-ballad repertoire, globular Burl Ives, Josh White, and Leadbelly.

As a callow young publicist, I worked for an office in the mid-forties which handled the Village Vanguard, a Greenwich Village nightclub, as an account. There I first heard the delicate light tenor of lean Richard Dyer-Bennett and his songs about foxes and geese, the keeper of the eddystone light, and "Greensleeves." There I first heard Leadbelly. He wore a regular business suit with a plain white shirt and jaunty bow-tie; and with his twelve-string guitar, he knocked urban audiences for a loop. They couldn't get enough of his gritty, guttural folk-blues sung with great whooping vitality (although frequently, you couldn't make out the words). One of the most popular numbers of this folk music giant was "Goodnight, Irene," which he and John Lomax are credited with writing. It later became a hit in 1950, almost a decade later, recorded by the Weavers.

I later participated in publicizing Dyer-Bennett's first Town Hall concert in New York City, produced by the late Ted Zittel, a rotund, fabulous character. Though all the leading folk singers of the period were popular—Dyer-Bennett, Leadbelly, Burl Ives, Josh White—none were anywhere near as popular as today's top folk singers.

In retrospect, the folk boom had to wait until the world was settled down peacefully, and until there appeared on the American scene a fairly substantial postwar college generation that had money to spend for recordings and concerts. It also had to wait until the recording industry—a pivotal element in national promotion—got bigger and more powerful. Folk music, too, became the morale builder and voice of the growing integration movement and "ban the bomb" demonstrations. When all these elements coalesced, folk music hit America like a thunderclap.

In the late 1950's folk music penetrated the broad mass of urban America, which had forgotten its folk past in favor of the manufactured dreams of Hollywood, radio, television, and slick fiction. Much of its success from the start came on the college campuses and the coffee-houses where the collegiate crowd and the urban sophisticates gathered to listen to folk songs in an atmosphere borrowed from Europe. The colleges ate up folk music, and they still do.

In one recent issue of a UCLA newspaper, *The Daily Bruin,* there were printed advertisements of three folk-music concerts. The ITA (International Talent Associates) reported in its house organ, *The Scene:* "Biggest Campus Season: 62-63." Some of the "acts" reported heavily in demand by colleges were Peter, Paul, and Mary, Odetta, the Limelighters, Bud and Travis, and the Phoenix Singers. The ITA "Scene" disclosed that "many of the folk groups also head up hoote-nannies on the campuses and perform in a variety of other formats besides the standard concert style."

These days, practically every record company is putting out hoote-nanny albums, and beating the bushes or the Ivy League college campuses for new versions of Joan Baez, Bob Dylan, or the Kingston Trio.

These artists are creating an unrivaled impress of folk music on every aspect of entertainment. They are as idolized as Frank Sinatra was in his Paramount Theater bobby-sox days, but in a more dignified and contemplative manner. Comparatively speaking, they have outdrawn the top "pop" and jazz artists in the past few years, particularly in the concert field.

The folk music boom in the early 60's has been successful in all forms: concerts, recordings, television appearances, and night clubs. It has even helped to put on the map a new type of American night club, replacing the old Babbitty commercial night club with its garish and gaudy settings. U. S. night clubs, once an important part of American show business, have been slowly headed toward extinction. But what has been fairly successful, and has provided launching pads to folk singers, are coffee-house-type clubs like the hungry i (San Francisco) and the Village Gate in Greenwich Village, on the site of the old Mills rooming house for down-and-outers.

The modern folk-music boom has shattered many dearly held convictions—that songs with a "message" do not sell, that you cannot write modern folk songs. Beyond this myth-breaking, the folk-music fever has shaken up the concert field, the night club field, and has changed the look of many comedy-variety TV programs. Entertainment is such a pervading interconnected force that should something become popular in one sphere, it reaches into every orbit of show business.

Cash Box, the remorseless hunter of commercial trends, has noted the unorthodox quality of the content of the songs. In an editorial on "The Message Song," it said: "At least two message songs have done the top 100 in major fashion. They are 'Where Have all the Flowers Gone?' by the Kingston Trio (written by Pete Seeger), and more currently, Peter, Paul and Mary have one of today's fastest rising efforts, 'Blowin' in the Wind.' The metaphors of the folk music do not hide the fact that these songs are taking stands on the vital issues of the day—the possibility of a global holocaust and racial discrimination here at home."

Later the trade paper said: "When a 'pop' hit can contribute to a better world, that's something."

One of the cardinal characteristics of today's folk-music fever is its social awareness.

On August 29, 1963, 200,000 persons—students, businessmen, shipping clerks, lawyers, railroad workers, social workers, psychiatrists, Hollywood actors and actresses—met in a gigantic Freedom March rally in Washington, D. C. One of the highpoints of this integration rally—perhaps the largest public assembly ever held in the United States—was the singing of "We Shall Overcome," a revised version of a Baptist hymn said to be around sixty-two years old.

> We shall overcome, we shall overcome
> We shall overcome some day.
> Oh, deep in my heart, I do believe,
> We shall overcome some day.

> We'll walk hand in hand some day
> Oh, deep in my heart, I do believe,
> We shall overcome someday.*

In Forest Hills Stadium, Queens, N. Y., site of the national tennis championships, baby-faced composer-singer Bob Dyan held a summer-time capacity crowd of 15,000 enthralled as he sang a song of his own composition, "A Hard Rain's a-Gonna Fall." It is about nuclear war and marrow-killing radioactive fallout. It is a desperate kind of song which he says he wrote during the Cuban missile crisis of October, 1962. "Every line in it is actually the start of a whole song. But when I wrote it, I thought I wouldn't have time alive to write all those songs, so I put all I could into this one."

Exciting Joan Baez, the "star" of the concert, who shared the im-promptu stage with Dylan, told the audience: "Bobby Dylan says what a lot of people my age feel, but cannot say."

The costumes folk singers wear differ. Twenty-two-year-old Bob Dylan is fond of sporting a Huck Finn type of corduroy cap that has become his trade-mark. Twenty-three-year-old Joan Baez (born in Staten Island, N. Y.) wears simple clothes on stage, no fancy Dior creations with hundreds of handsewn beads. Thirty-seven-year-old Harry Belafonte sticks to simple, but expensively tailored, shirt and slacks. Forty-four-year-old Pete Seeger, the Harvard-educated patri-arch of all the folk singers, goes on stage wearing thick-soled work shoes, purple socks, faded brown pants, a bright red shirt, and a yel-low tie.

But whatever the outer garb, they frequently sing folk materials filigreed with social consciousness, references subtle and unsubtle to integration, the bomb, and economic injustice. They sing happy, whimsical, gay, or roguish material, too. But they are very much in earnest about linking their art to their outlook.

These provocative folk songs are sung at civil rights rallies, "sit-ins," and on construction sites where pickets demonstrate against alleged job bias. And oddly enough, they are popular commercially, on rec-ords, in night clubs, and on TV. On a recent TV special, produced by the National Academy of Recording Arts and Sciences, "The Best on Records," one of the most touching moments was Peter, Paul and Mary doing a freshly written folk song concerning brotherhood, which went:

> If I had a hammer,
> I'd hammer in the morning,
> I'd hammer in the evening

*Copyright © 1963 by Ludlow Music Inc.

All over this land;
I'd hammer out danger
I'd hammer out a warning,
I'd hammer out love between my brothers and my sisters,
Oh-Oh, All over this land.*

Despite the occasional thrust of the censor's blue pencil, (The Chad Mitchell folk group could not sing a song satirizing the John Birch Society on the "Ed Sullivan Show," although Sullivan did not object) the folk singers have been fairly free to comment on modern times in words and music. In this way, they have given millions a taste of the folk heritage riches. Harry Belafonte sings about American chain gangs. The Clancy Brothers and Tommy Makem sing Irish rebellion songs. Theodore Bikel reinterprets Yiddish songs of freedom. Miriam Makeba brings us folk songs from Africa. The varying subject materials, musical styles, approaches to song are in resplendent abundance in today's folk boom.

Besides dipping into the past, the folk groups are singing new compositions by Pete Seeger, Lee Hays of the Weavers, and Bob Dylan. There are also scores of other folk-song writers who are beginning to get recorded and heard, and who show promise. Most do no more than state an editorial to an old tune. But there are others who have a feeling for striking imagery. Their leader and young Moses, of course, is young Bob Dylan, perhaps the most gifted folk-writer of our time. Samples of his work can be heard in two of his Columbia Records albums: "The Freewheelin' Bob Dylan" and "Bob Dylan."

Lately, even some of the popular music personalities have gotten into the act. Composer Jule Styne and lyricists Betty Comden and Adolph Green recently recast an Israeli freedom song, "Hava Nageela" into a civil rights rouser, "Now," recorded by Lena Horne on 20th Century Fox Records.

With one foot in show business and another in folk music, the folk scene is picaresque, like moonshine "corn likker" poured from a Swedish modern George Jensen decanter. There's giant Columbia Records, producers of Bob Dylan recordings, with its shiny polished white-formica air, and little Folkways Records, which is one-floor-up above a jewelry store, alongside a parking lot, with raw-wood shelves holding a marvelous collection of ethnic-folk music on West 47th Street. Guided by the emotional, bulky son of novelist Sholem Asch, Moses,

*Words and music by Lee Hays and Pete Seeger. Copyright © 1958 and 1962. Ludlow Music, Inc., New York. Used by permission.

this small record company has thousands of LP's of mountain songs, country songs, bluegrass, folk-blues, political songs, songs of the Spanish civil war. Asch is also associated with *Sing Out* magazine and *Oak Publications,* folk-music publisher and distributor.

On the folk-music scene are Sarah Lawrence College girls who have been analyzed, as well as field hands; "hip" folk-music connoisseurs like Lou Gottlieb of the Limeliters, as well as John Lee Hooker, folk-blues artist. An active participant, too, is diffident, unbusinesslike Israel Young of the Folklore Center in Greenwich Village, seller of folk-music recordings, books, and magazines. At the other end you find personal manager Harold Leventhal, the Sol Hurok of hootenannies, producer of countless folk-music soirées at New York's Town Hall and at the Lincoln Center of the Performing Arts. You will find countless other persons in the folk field, spreading the gospel in Chicago, Los Angeles, San Francisco—all types, all occupations, every strata.

There are folk-song writers who sit in Greenwich Village flats and compose. One of them is a *Playboy* magazine cartoonist, Shel Silverstein. Most are continuing in the path of fifty-one-year-old Woody Guthrie, hospitalized by a severe illness. Guthrie, a folk original, is the wiry Dylan Thomas of the Depression of the 1930's. His Swansea was the great dustbowl, the freight boxcars, the bed-bugged jails. But Guthrie didn't sour; he felt close to the land, and he saw its abundant possibilities. Guthrie has written words and music to more than five hundred songs, and according to Harold Leventhal, trustee of the Guthrie Children's Trust Fund, his most popular ones are "This Land Is Your Land," "Pastures of Plenty," "Hard Travellin'," and "So Long, It's Been Good to Know You." There are reportedly eight Guthrie albums available (Folkways). He is author of the autobiographical book, *Bound for Glory.*

The folk-music picture is very fluid and fractious. If it doesn't watch out, it may get to be as faction-ridden as jazz. Currently there are several principal tendencies. There is a continuing battle between the purists, the ethnic-folk devotees (exemplified by Leadbelly, Woody Guthrie, and anonymous folk bards) versus the popularizers (the Kingston Trio, Peter, Paul and Mary). There is also tremendous infighting on the part of many folk singers and folklorists who, by changing a word or two or a musical phrase, try to claim authorship to old folk songs for obvious commercial reasons. The ranks have also been invaded by amateurs, youngsters who are fond of folk music but who can hardly hold a tune. The Tin Pan Alley wing has also edged in, rather cautiously. A recent album by a good-looking Tin Pan Alley singer of romantic songs was just issued titled: "Gene Pitney Meets the

Fair Young Ladies of Folkland." There are also many jazz versions of folk favorites.

Musically, much of folk music is limited, and fits into certain musical categories—the talking blues, the English ballad, the *Hora,* the cowboy song. Even the new songs sound archaic, rather than freshly compelling. A popular music composer of scholarly bent, Philip Springer, has analyzed it this way:

"The songs have become popular because they're saying something. Like 'Blowing in the Wind' which talks about freedom and brotherhood. There's a message in the lyrics. I think their success is more in the lyrics. 'Pop' music is always based on 'I love you' or 'You don't love me.' One or the other. In folk music, the stories are very free and you can be quite imaginative and humorous. Which is rare in 'pop' music today. Imagination or humor.

"Folk music is simple. Their harmonic expressions are simple. Melodically speaking, they sing very diatonic melodies; that means very few sharps or flats. The form of expression is very emotional, a broad form rather than sophisticated or cerebral form."

American folk music will always be with us, for it is part of our courage, our weakness, our humor, our landscape. The words and music—and it is primarily a vocal music—document much of what has happened to our people—the good things, the bad things, the roistering joy, the grinding poverty. The new folk songs are continuing in that homespun tradition, except in an atomic milieu.

As the years go by, we will probably learn more of the world's folk music—from the Asian countries, the Balkans, Africa, Latin America. Whether the folk-music industry can sustain its fever-pitch popularity in a commercial sense is hard to predict.

Currently, there seems to be a superabundance of folk "acts." Not long ago, the Kingston Trio told the *Associated Press* that one folk group seems to be following another, Indian file, in city after city. But they said: "Nothing can kill folk music; it's too basic in the American consciousness. It won't be like calypso which went out of style because of overplaying. But the profusion of folk acts is bound to cut in on the business."

Cheerful, satirical, and muck-raking at the same time, Oscar Brand (who wears contact lenses when he performs and glasses offstage) feels that there isn't much of a "folk rage." He has asserted that it just appears that way. But he recently predicted in the *Toronto Daily Star* that much after the public moves to whatever new sound is being "mass produced by the music industry—Japanese popular songs, underwater music, or tape recorded animal mating cries" there will also be folk music. Its longevity, he wrote, will continue because people—and he has asked audiences the question—believe in a folk song's "meaningfulness."

"The folk song," wrote Brand, folk singer, writer, performer, radio folklorist, TV host, "sounds as if it has been sung by many others—it has the patina of history, of trouble that has been met before, of universals expressed in personal terms."

19 · JAZZ 'N' POPS

> Not a single human being on earth heard all the jazz records
> that were released in 1962 . . . [of these] a very small pro-
> portion deserve to be recorded.
>
> —Leonard Feather, *Down Beat*

Listeners hear jazz in coffee commercials and in coffee houses. There's
jazz in church services, Hollywood films and such Broadway musicals
as *West Side Story*. You can dial in on FM radio and hear jazz of all
types in every major city of the United States. Besides adult jazz recordings, there's an LP, "A Child's Introduction to Jazz." Steve Allen
and the "Tonight" NBC-TV program and educational television put on
jazz artists. Millions hear jazz in background scoring to TV mystery
stories, a technique pioneered in the adventures of the impeccably
dressed Brooks Brothers private eye, Peter Gunn, who was, sartorially,
a far cry from Dashiel Hammett.

In fact, the provocative jazz-flavored scoring by composer Henry
Mancini for "Peter Gunn" got so popular that TV producers of detective
epics sent out a call for jazz writers, which led a bard with a one-word
name, Bolof, to write in *Capitol Records Music Views*:

> The best composers now all try to
> Dream up music to die to.

Of course Bolof was loading the dice to suggest that the best writers
were engaging in that genre. But it is certainly no mystery that the
sound of jazz over the past decade has been no clandestine exotic sound.
What has been the impact of the enormous quantity of jazz upon popular music? Has jazz's own inner aesthetic drives been affected by the
popular music world?

Circumstantial evidence seems to indicate that contemporary jazz is
as commercialized a commodity as are the more obvious Tin Pan Alley

confections, replete with slick packaging, overstated album titles, (everybody's "a genius") and ridiculous, foot-thick liner notes.

Jazz liner notes, pianist-composer Andre Previn recently told *Down Beat* are:

. . . usually couched in terminology so serious that if the program notes of the Boston Symphony ever dared get that intellectual and stuffy, nobody would know what the hell the Boston Symphony was playing.

Yet I keep falling for them. I keep going to a record store and I pick up at random any one of the 750 releases that week by jazz artists, and I look on the liner notes, and somebody with a big reputation like Nat Hentoff, or somebody like that, will have written notes where I think this new artist and this new music has got to be a combination of Alban Berg, Mozart, Webern, and Schweitzer. And then I take it home, and they're playing the blues! So what the hell is *that* all about?

The only test, Previn stated, is in the music itself; play the record and listen to what the music says. "As soon as you have to distribute explanatory pamphlets for every track," he said, "you're in big trouble."

Jazz also owns a magnificent inferiority complex and a hunched suspicion that the world is against it, that you must stand up and be counted. It will not rest until there is a Secretary of Jazz in the Cabinet of the United States, with perhaps four Undersecretaries, one for New Orleans traditional jazz, one for the big-band devotees, one for the "funky-soul" group, and perhaps another representing the "third stream" and other modernistic experimenters, including those involved with electronic tape.

The jazz world and its precincts—night clubs to Newport to Carnegie Hall to recording studios—are roamed by money-hungry jazz promoters and jazz festival producers. For years they have produced countless jazz festivals, consisting mainly of quantity and speed. Their idea of a jazz festival has been to collect a hundred jazz artists and have them "play and run."

Resenting the night club milieu in which most of jazz seems to function, quite a few of jazz's creative elements—singers, bandleaders, instrumentalists—are no longer content to sing and play and record for a relatively small jazz market.

"Today, more and more jazz artists want 'pop' hits," says Bob Rolontz, editor of *Music Business* and one-time producer of jazz albums, including LP's of Charlie Mingus for RCA Victor.

No longer a folk music, modern jazz is split into as many factions as the Communist Internationale, each claiming it has the true direction, the true religion. But whatever its style or genre or method of composition, it is pummeled, pressured, pincered by the same forces that stifle popular music—corruption, opportunism, and banality. These are the conditions under which jazz operates—the musical and economic situation.

What saves jazz is its twin sources of strength: its form and its audience. As a form it allows for an exceptional amount of creativity, freedom in writing, performance, and arrangement. It is kept free, too, thanks to its fervent audience, minority though it may be. The jazz fan may be led to brackish saline waterholes to drink, but he is not afraid to sip new spring water from a brand new well. His ears are accustomed to new sounds. The length of the work may be unusual, the structure may be free of fixed keys, the jumps in range may be unheard of, but the jazz fan isn't afraid. He will buy it.

As to jazz's relationship to the popular music field, there is paradoxical and contradictory evidence. Since the 1950's there have been few original jazz works on records that have "made it large," as the saying goes, in the 45-rpm market. These include Dave Brubeck's "Take Five," Stan Getz's version of a South American importation, "Desafinado," and Jimmy Smith's version of "Hobo Flats." In the long-playing popular music charts, the showing is more impressive. Many jazz-flavored singers and movie sound tracks have made it on the charts.

As personalities and as recording artists, Ella Fitzgerald, Frank Sinatra, and Peggy Lee have been extraordinarily popular, and they represent the line where popular music and jazz converge. Equally popular among jazz *aficionados* and the broader "pop" market has been composer-conductor Henry Mancini, Elmer Bernstein, old-time veterans like Duke Ellington, Count Basie and Stan Kenton, and a newcomer, singer Jimmy Smith (Verve). Miles Davis sells well, but he doesn't come anywhere near the Sinatra-Mancini sales marks. Such jazz figures as Charlie Mingus, Charlie Parker, Ornette Coleman, John Coltrane, Horace Silver, Gil Evans, George Russell, the Modern Jazz Quartet, Sonny Rollins, Gerry Mulligan, and Thelonius Monk are hardly known in the "pop" market. It might be noted that some jazz devotees do not count Sinatra or Ella Fitzgerald or Peggy Lee as members of the "club."

Broadly speaking, however, contemporary jazz (and this term is being used to cover all of jazz's varied output) hasn't met with the popularity that swing did in the 1930's and 40's. But there is no doubt that jazz flavors have strongly penetrated movie background music, TV background music, popular recordings. Some of the top arrangers—Nelson Riddle, Billy May, Johnny Mandel—use the jazz language as a

French child uses French; it is perfectly natural. They are not "putting it on." Jazz has also had a subtle impact upon the singing styles and arranging styles of many singers, groups, and bands, which come nowhere near the orthodox jazz stream. Sometimes it is the way a note is bent, the final, crisp, whiplash ending to a tune.

On the other hand, jazz has experienced a total defeat in one crucial area—lyrics. Since the 1950's it has not come up with a body of good vocal music. It lacks jazz-oriented lyricists. Much of the creative excitements going on is in the sphere of instrumental works. This is a shame for a lot of early traditional jazz and rhythm and blues (when it was *really* rhythm and blues) gave birth to many superb songs.

It is quite astonishing that jazz does not do better in the popular marketplace, since there is an enormous amount of live performances of jazz going on in night clubs, colleges, festivals, and in concerts. And the recordings of jazz—which are reviewed widely in the nation's press— are so abundant that one critic has said: "It is now impossible for anybody to listen to all the jazz records being produced."

An Atlantic Records official recently estimated that there are about twenty to twenty-five record firms which release jazz works of all types on a fairly regular basis on 45 rpm, and on LP. They include: Pacific Jazz, Argo, Blue Note, Atlantic, Riverside, World Pacific, Roulette, Roost, Fantasy. Besides these small labels, there are large companies who are constantly issuing new material as well as repackaged material from the archives: RCA Victor, Columbia, Epic, Decca, Reprise, Mercury, United Artists, Verve, Capitol, and ABC-Paramount under its crest, Impulse! In addition, there are a few minor firms who specialize in issuing folk-blues and other subdivisions of jazz.

As to the jazz output, it is tremendous. *Billboard* recently disclosed that it reviewed, in 1962, 126 "singles" and 453 long-playing records in the jazz idiom. The trade paper noted that it only reviewed 90 per cent of the product issued. Most of these records were backed by some print and disc jockey promotion.

Of the "singles," quite a few find their way into juke boxes, interestingly enough, notably those chrome-flecked affairs in "hip" urban areas such as Greenwich Village or in campus shops in college towns. Incidentally, a good selling jazz "single" sells approximately 20,000 pieces, as one sales manager put it. A 50,000-seller is one "building into a hit."

The word is out that there is no reason why some of these "singles" cannot be sold to the teen market. But as yet, jazz firms haven't come up with the chemistry to tap the teenaged market. As to LP's, a big-selling jazz LP is that which sells 100,000. That is a smash. Million-selling jazz "singles" and jazz LP recordings that sell 250,000 are rarer than art films in drive-in theaters.

John Benson Brooks is a tall man with a bird-beak nose, a strong face, and humorous eyes. He lives in Greenwich Village, and on his door there are two cards: NOTHING MUSIC and TWINKLE PUBLICATIONS. Brooks is unique in many ways. He has been an arranger for such bands as those of Tommy Dorsey, Les Brown, and Randy Brooks. He has been a Tin Pan Alley figure, and spent many years there pursuing hit songs. And in the past decade, he has been engaged in exploring new paths in jazz, which have led him to the study of twelve-tone serial composition, and the study of electronic tape-music.

When he plays piano his right foot thumps, and he sings in a lusty, uninhibited way that is a pleasure to watch. Besides being a tremendous individualist, Brooks has seen the popular music and jazz scene from varying prisms, and therefore his impressions and thoughts are quite interesting. His two best known popular songs are "You've Come a Long Way from St. Louis" (with a superb, satirical lyric by Bob Russell) and "Where Flamingos Fly," based on an old folk-blues. I have know him for many years and recently I tape-recorded a talk with him. There is a multiple relationship between jazz and popular music, Brooks said.

"First there is the use that jazz men have made of popular music in connection with a base upon which to improvise. Much of the jazz men have learned from, and lean on the copyrights of the 20's, Gershwin and Kern. Jazz instrumentalists are rooted in popular songs for many of them learned the chords of popular songs and then developed into improvising.

Besides this, the composer sees jazz influences interacting everywhere in today's top tunes, the arrangements and singing styles. "I bought the 'top ten' [recordings] a couple of months ago. The daughter of a friend of mine was playing them, and I decided I'd like to listen to them for awhile. And I see a reflection of jazz in them, as well as in the less rhythmically free time values of the European scene. At least a couple of them are what you and I would call rhythm and blues artists whose style is very much in the jazz idiom, although it's the jazz of twenty or thirty years ago.

"Take even Hank Williams. Some of his work, you may not call them jazz, but they date from a kind of jazz that was extant in 1922, and I find it charming."

Told that one A & R man asserted that he couldn't detect any jazz influence in the "pop" field, Brooks replied: "I don't know what this fellow would mean when he said 'there wasn't any jazz.' Maybe he's thinking of a strict kind of jazz. Maybe he doesn't think of jazz as a free way of playing these phrases with the duration values and the syncopations. If he doesn't hear any jazz in it, well, this explains the A & R men to me."

Brooks finds "commercialism" in jazz as undeniable as a flatted fifth. "These jazz producers, they're like the Tin Pan Alley publishers. They've got their cigarette album covers and are pushing the things that are hot in the jazz field, just like the Tin Pan Alley guys. In a way they've got jazz bottled up the same way the publishers have songs bottled up. The tendency has been to concentrate on these things that have a past guarantee of success. If you have something fresh you got to be lucky that it happens.

"They are starting to come on just like the Tin Pan Alley guys come on. They're concerned with the sale of things, naturally, it's their function, primarily, and they disavow any interest in anything that isn't proved. So it's more or less the same as the Alley publisher who will tell you it's terrific, but it's too terrific. The commercialism isn't as strong, but the parallel makes one uncomfortable."

Not long ago, Brooks, who has been experimenting with twelve-tone, chance composition and electronic music, wrote a piece called "The Twelves." It runs about twenty minutes. It is a fusion of electronic tape materials, accompanied by alto sax and piano. Brooks played a tape of it made by the Voice of America at a Washington jazz festival for a jazz A & R man. The A & R man of one of the bigger companies said, "John, this has absolutely no commercial value."

John's reply was, "Thank you. Gee!"

Upon hearing another one of Brook's electronic compositions titled "Bird Meets Cage" (the "Cage" being John Cage, the mushroom expert and the prophet of chance composition), a jazz A & R man said, "Come back in the twenty-sixth century."

Besides the attitudes of the jazz A & R men, Brooks is a little chagrined at the gray-flannel suit attitudes developing in some quarters of jazz. Jazz artists used to be regarded as unregimented "natural men" who could play in honky tonks and on cigarette-stained uprights. Now some are infinitely more respectable. Brooks tells the story of the Jimmy Giuffre group which was to perform in a theater. "But Giuffre wouldn't go on because they only had an upright piano. He wouldn't play without a grand."

In a similar vein, the Modern Jazz Quartet was to play a third-stream work by Gunther Schuller with the Philharmonic Orchestra at Carnegie Hall. According to Brooks, "Milt Jackson appeared for the date or the rehearsal for the date with brown socks on. He was sent home, or fined by John Lewis (the Modern Jazz Quartet leader)." Brooks' comment: 'That's giving jazz a bad name, man!' "

John Brooks has produced two jazz LP's, neither of which is in print, "Folk Jazz" (on Vik, a one-time RCA Victor label), and "The Alabama Concerto" (Riverside). Both are based upon folk themes and materials. In the past few years, the composer, called a "prophet" by Don Heckman in *Down Beat,* has been studying chance composition and the theory underlying electronic composition with John Cage and Richard Maxfield at the New School for Social Research.

I once did an article on Richard Maxfield for the New York *Herald Tribune,* called, "Tomorrow's (Bach) May Be a Tape Recorder." In it, Maxfield expressed the belief that the sounds you can get on the piano, the clarinet, the trumpet, the violin, and the oboe are as old-fashioned as fringed lamp shades. Maxfield told about the virtues of tape: "On tape we can concoct a whole palette of sounds, instead of those produced on a few plucked, bowed, beaten, or blown limited devices. Electronic music is more creative, more daring, much more exciting than traditional music. It's less controlled. You get new timbres, new rhythms too complex or too rapid for performers to play. These new timbres you could only carve electronically."

Over a melted-cheese sandwich and coffee, which he prepared expertly, Brooks asserted that there are three basic compositional and creative forces operating in jazz today—the Free-Jazz Group (George Russell), the Third-Stream Group (putting jazz in classical forms) and the Funky-Soul Group (John Coltrane) which he characterized as the gospel-type, romantic, "soul" music. Brooks, in his tape experiments with jazz, is to the left of George Russell who still relies on human musicians.

The New England-born composer is aware that there aren't any jazz lyricists around, that is, "A Larry Hart with jazz feeling." Further, he added that the jazz composer's experiments with atonal music has widened the gulf between modern jazz and popular song music. "In the future," he told me during a previous discussion, "there may be lyrics which consist of cries and sounds instead of words."

The straightaway jazz writers are fairly alien to the theater, Brooks added, because of historical circumstance. "Jazz took the dance rhythm and the song in a package deal. It could provide an occasion for dancing and it could provide an occasion for singing and entertainment. Therefore, it found its way into utility in the culture."

However, Brooks envisaged a possible anthology-type modern opera, pieced together of the musical techniques that are available today. He thought aloud, as he sat on a couch which overlooks a wall covered with modernistic art. "Part of the score would be based on probability situations, chance operations; some parts would be serialized, other parts would be chromatic, still others would be in folk singing; all kinds of American speech and song, and sounds and kinds of music. You would require a form like the opera to meld all of the things together."

Mrs. Brooks, a book editor, and John Benson Brooks live in a very comfortable, imaginative apartment. It is filled with books, art objects, and with John's costly tape equipment, which consists of oscillators, (machines that can create synthetic sounds which are then tape-recorded and can be employed in compositions) and batteries of tape recorders. Brooks' studies are on the eclectic side, and you can find him reading works on astrology, numerology, folk music, poetry, as well as encyclopedias on science, mathematics, and physics. Some of the books on his study worktable bore these titles: *Dictionary of Scientific Terms, The Structure of Scientific Renditions,* and *The Concept of the Positron.*

In his mid-forties, Brooks is apparently searching for a way to use "systems," complex, ponderous, intellectual systems, as a methodology which would permit him to compose more provocative music. However, his eye and mind haven't left the field of popular music.

He sees hope for better songs emerging from the morass of the past decade. He asserts there is hope because there are about twenty-three jazz singers, "as I count them in this country who make LP's and work for jazz clubs. Perhaps they will do better material. I am sending around songs I wrote years ago. I wouldn't be surprised if I picked up a few records."

Once *Schwann's*, the excellent guide for record buyers and collectors, put out a catalogue titled, *Jazz 'n' Pops.* The linking of the two wasn't an accident, but hinted at the interweaving of both forces. There is a relationship between the two, but it is simultaneously obvious and covert, simple and complex.

In a business sense, jazz record firms are plagued by the same problems faced in popular music. The small jazz labels are in a profit squeeze, and quite a few are less than accurate in their royalties to artists. Because of the profit squeeze, its artists and A & R men are almost as commercial-minded as the popular music taste-makers.

Like many popular music figures, jazz artists are being touched by the world around them. Many of them have added the prestige of

their names to record albums issued to raise money for integration activities. Though there are pockets of anti-white hostility among some
jazz musicians, it is equally true that there is a good deal of warm,
affectionate, interracial feelings. Not all Negroes equate white "working joes" of jazz with the "white power structure" they assert is oppress-
ing 20,000,000 Black Americans. Many jazz artists are members of
CORE or of the National Association for the Advancement of Colored
People; and many contribute their talents to those organizations.

Speaking of talent, this is the most promising sphere in which jazz
will function within the larger spectrum of popular music. Each season
brings out a new flock of singers such as Terri Thornton, Nancy Wilson, and Nina Simone, who will add much to the popular music scene.
Besides singers, jazz-influenced arrangers, musicians, and A & R men
will provide the popular music fan with moments of great beauty as
they help interpret the best from Tin Pan Alley, Broadway, and Hollywood, and the more communicative elements of the modern elements
in the modern jazz wing. Jazz people have hundreds of repetitious
monotonous jazz clichés, as Joachim Berendt pointed out in *The New
Jazz Book,* but they also have taste, a sense of economy, and unsac-
charine dryness.

In terms of new work, repertoire that will be added to the over-all
output of popular music, this area remains in doubt. In the preceding
decade practically no "far out" atonal contemporary jazz has become
rooted within the popular music field. What has caught on has come
from Henry Mancini and Elmer Bernstein who have been active in media (TV and films) that demand strong communicative music; their
music is tonal and lyrical.

In checking with John Wilson, *New York Times* jazz writer, he could
think of only a few works that have become somewhat popular during
the past few years, which have emanated from the world of jazz. According to him, these were "Midnight Sun," based on a Lionel Hampton "riff," "Whisper Not" by Benny Golson, "Take Five" by Paul Desmond (the most popular), "Satin Doll" by Duke Ellington, and
"Django" from a foreign film, *One Never Knows.* "Take Five" is perhaps the only authentic "pop" hit, while the others have been recorded
and re-recorded.

Contrasted with the amount of new music poured out in jazz, this is
not a superb track record. In vocal music, of course, it is severely ham-
pered by the lack of any real fine lyricists. Jazz needs desperately to
penetrate into the musical theater; the genre would help it develop a
body of modern vocal music. But its creators are quite innocent of the
necessary skills involved—the selection of librettos, of shaping musical

materials from character, of how to make songs work, or the variety of moods necessary to sustain an evening in the musical theater. The fact is that jazz has been around more than half a century, and as yet no "pure" jazz writer (and you couldn't characterize many-sided Leonard Bernstein that way) from the jazz ranks has ever written a successful theater work. If jazz continues with experiments in chance composition and electronic music—jazz versions of John Cage and Karlheinz Stockhausen—it will have no impact on popular music.

Popular music, basically, is direct and easily communicative. If jazz is to make its contribution to popular music, chances are it won't do it in the twelve-tone atonal way either.

As Henry Pleasant puts it in his book *Death of a Music:*

As jazz gains in stature its composers will be less tempted to try symphonic writing as a bid for respectability. We may also hope that they will be less susceptible to the empty fashions of serious music's *avant-garde* reactionaries. There is no brighter future for the jazz musician in atonality and dodecaphony than there is for the serious composer. He may derive a semblance of vitality from the beat, but the beat alone is not enough.

What counts in any music is song. The jazz musician need only remember what the serious composer has long forgotten, namely, that the purpose of the musician is to sing, that the discipline within which he must work is his listeners' concept of song, and that his ultimate fulfillment is not just self-expression, which any fool can manage after a fashion, but rather the initiation of his listeners into an experience of the beautiful. This requires a knowledge and acceptance of the listeners' language. The objective of the musician's song is communication, and it cannot be accomplished without giving the listeners an even break.

20 · TIN PAN ALLEY 'ROUND THE WORLD

Under Langa Morka Vinterkvallar
(Our long, dark, winter evenings)

. . . Kvikker Vi Os Op Med Amerikansk Musik
(. . . are brightened by American music)
—From ad by EMI (Electrical Music Industries)

One U.S. music publisher, Ivan Mogull, even has a slogan, "Global Mo-gull." Hardly a day goes by without some recording star or popular music executive going to Kennedy Airport, en route to Italy, Germany, England or Scandinavia. The star may be Paul Anka, Louis Armstrong, Dave Brubeck, Connie Francis, or Jim Reeves, a country and western singer. (Country and western is pretty popular in Germany, South Africa, and Japan.)

In sun-baked South African villages, natives listen to Elvis Presley. In Marxist Rumania, saxophones honk as girls in beaded, shiny dresses do the twist. In Japan, it is not safe for Neil Sedaka, a nice Jewish boy, to appear among teenagers without a bodyguard. (Perhaps his name sounds Oriental.)

All of this adds up to the fact that more and more the U. S. popular music business—the record personalities, record companies, music pub-lishers, talent agencies—have become as internationally-minded as Rand McNally.

Such internationalism is based on sound economics. For the world record market—an audience for American popular music—has become in the words of one Tin Pan Alley executive, "simply fantastic." Perhaps $3 billion or more—there are no comprehensive, reliable statistics—spent in the form of pounds, kronen, marks, yen, francs, and lira are cascad-ing in from varied sources—U. S. recordings sold abroad, tours of U. S. stars, performers of U. S. music over radio and in night clubs, sale of sheet music, overseas theater productions, U. S.-originated TV musical programs, film grosses of musicals such as *Music Man, South Pacific, Oklahoma,* and *West Side Story.*

American popular music has always had modest roots in Europe, dating back to the 1920's when American musicians, entertainers, and servicemen, along with a sizable expatriate colony, established beach-heads. Jazz also has been winning adherents ever since World War I. In the 30's the popularity of U. S. music increased, and American music publishers started setting up offices in London, Paris, and Berlin; or they made arrangements with foreign music publishers for representation. But now, the gentle stream has become a booming river. And American popular music makers are splashing happily about, with side trips to the French Riviera's bikini-landscape, "on business."

Practically every U. S. record company of consequence has agreements with such firms as Philips, Pye, EMI, Polydor, Barclay, and Rifi to distribute its product abroad. Music publishers here have agreements with foreign music publishers—or have opened their own affiliates in key capitals. Practically every record company of stature has beefed-up International Departments covering sales and Artists and Repertoire. International A & R men keep a watchful eye on U. S. product that can be exported, and on what popular foreign-made recordings could possibly be imported with some chance of success.

Billboard delivers subscriptions to foreign music interests "by jet." Once a year, it puts out an exhaustive *International Music-Record Directory*, featuring market data, covering global record sales, country by country, and containing helpful lists of producers and distributors of records and sheet music throughout the world. Its rival, *Cash Box*, also casts its weekly eye on the foreign market, and also published a telephone-book-sized *World-Wide Directory*, which covers the popular music business from Argentina to Zanzibar. International copyright law and a knowledge of the inner workings of the popular music industry in all countries has become *de rigeur* for every music business attorney.

Unmistakably, the theme song of present-day Tin Pan Alley, to a considerable extent, is that cry of variety entertainers going into the next scene, "And now a little traveling music, please."

Hans Lengsfelder speaks English beautifully, but with traces of a *Mittel Europa* accent. A suburbanite, he lives in Scarsdale, New York and runs a record company (Request Records) and several music publishing companies from New Rochelle. He is active in ASCAP—some say too active—because he is a lively critic of some of its distribution procedures. A sometime playwright, he was one of the Continent's most active lyricists. Before being driven out by Hitler, Lengsfelder, who is Jewish, also published a music trade paper in Berlin.

"There's always a snobbish group that prefers foreign liquor, foreign-built cars," he said recently, without irritation, "and in the 1920's there was in Germany and in Europe a small group who liked American popular music. The only composer that was known, however, was Irving Berlin. Occasionally, there would be big hits from America. 'Yes, We Have No Bananas' was a very big hit all over Europe.

"Another big hit in the 1930's was 'Mama Inez.' I know, because I wrote the German and Czech lyrics, and I made a fortune. I also wrote the foreign lyrics for 'The Peanut Vendor,' a tremendous hit all over Europe.

"But American popular music was mostly occasional. Now it is dominant in Germany, Italy, Holland, Belgium. And it has even penetrated Japan.

"There are several contributing factors. After the war practically everything was destroyed. America came in with the Marshall Plan. It supplied everything—industrial machinery, building materials. Americans supplied many commodities, and one of the commodities they brought with them was their popular music. And the influence was not only felt in music. The whole life was Americanized—the format of radio shows, the refrigerators, the way teenagers dressed—and, of course, so far as the popular music was concerned, American interests exploited it, promoted it."

Walter Hofer, an activist in the International Records and Music Men's Club, is a good-looking, thirty-four-year-old music business attorney with extensive international connections. In his law offices in Manhattan he recently sketched in the anatomy of U. S. popular music abroad:

"I think the overseas market is bigger than the United States market," he said. "Take Germany. A big hit there will sell a million records as compared with all of the United States, where a big hit will sell a million only if you're very lucky. France can sell 300,000 copies of a record. I've just heard that Paul Anka's latest recording sold 800,-000 in Italy. So if you take the world market outside the United States, it is larger than the American market.

"At the same time, there has been a tendency in the last three years (some of this is very overt, and some is not) for countries to try to 'nationalize' their music. Years ago, American music could not be imitated easily. But about three years ago the imitation became very strong and very good. As a result, there are many countries where the local market and artists are much more important.

"If I were to pick up *Cash Box* today and look at Italy's charts, I would probably find, and I'm guessing, that seven out of ten of the records, or more, are Italian-originated. Three years ago, seven out of ten would be American-originated. It's gotten to the point where many American artists are now recording in the indigenous language, rather than be covered by the local artist. And these records are for local release within individual territories.

"When a U. S. record company or a music publisher develops a hit recording or hit copyright, they generally ask for steep advances from foreign producers or foreign music publishers. Today, if they bargain too much, they'll find themselves outflanked. If they do not place a song right away, if it looks like a potential hit, their version of it will never be released. A local artist will cover that record, or make an imitation of it very quickly. The same situation occurs with music publishing. In publishing, if the music is not placed immediately, you run into a problem because there will be an imitation of the arrangement. It will not be the same song, but the arrangement or type of music will be the same, although the melodic line will be different," the attorney said.

What about U. S. sheet music sales abroad? "It sells but not as well as it did at one time," stated Hofer. "It does sell much better than it does here. Sheets music is important for Spain. It is not so important for France. A major song in Germany could sell 30,000 or 40,000 copies; a big whopping hit may sell 200,000—a ballad type of thing. A rock 'n' roll or rhythm and blues number will not sell in any quantity whatsoever."

French music and record interests are the most vocal antagonists of the invasion of U. S. popular music. Recently there was an "actual meeting," according to Hofer, of French record companies and publishers to say "French for the French," and "Let's not use American product." And it is rather interesting because the American product does not sell in France, with the exception of Paul Anka and possibly a few other people," he said.

Though French consumers do not buy U. S. artists in quantity, throughout France you hear the "sound" of American popular music. Wherever you go, you hear rock 'n' roll, teenage-type confections, executed by French rock 'n' roll singers and vocal groups. This is pretty much true of England, too.

Of the countries where there is solid emotional involvement with U. S. record artists, Hofer named Israel, Sweden, Denmark, and Japan. "The best market for American music is Japan," said Hofer. "But again it works this way. The American song is covered by a Japanese artist. What they do is get a Japanese lyric and do it both in Japanese and in English. One chorus of each. Of the ten songs on the current Japanese charts, ten are American songs, but only one is the original record.

"All over, the country and western, Elvis Presley-type of material sells best. Connie Francis' type of material and the material of Paul Anka also is popular.

"Germany has popular disc jockeys. There's a young man named Mal Somdock. Mal is an American who was in the Army in Germany and was also with the Armed Forces Radio. While he was there, he decided to learn German. He learned it well enough so he became a local disc jockey on the local German stations. And has been fairly successful, not only as a disc jockey, but also a singing artist for Teldec (German recording company), as a producer for Deutsche Grammaphon as well as the German correspondent for *Cash Box*.

"But there are not too many disc jockeys around the world," he added. "Many areas have none because most radio is controlled by the government." Apparently, European radio broadcasting executives do not regard too highly the disc jockey format, which has become the staple of the American radio, nor do they relish excessive American cultural penetration."

There are varying restrictions, too. In some countries, American popular music can be played only one or two hours weekly. In one hour you can play about twenty records. In many countries there is simply no access to government radio, and the promotion that such airplay brings. Continued Hofer: "You have no control whatsoever. Because they will play what they desire."

However, there are some important outlets for exposure for U. S. popular music. There is Radio Luxembourg, a commercial radio station which transmits in three or four directions, and has German, French and Italian broadcasts. Fans of popular music take to it like the French do to *croissants*. On this station, which has enormous range, the record companies buy time.

"For example, EMI, I believe, has nine hours of time a week which they purchase. One hour would be devoted to MGM, one hour to Capitol, and so on."

Radio Luxembourg has an office in England, where their English disc jockeys may record the shows which are then broadcast from Luxembourg, a grand duchy (999 square miles, population 290,000) bordering on Belgium, and beamed back to England. It pivots largely on disc jockeys and the whirling turntables.

France has a tremendous number of disc jockey shows, and here, too, recording companies buy time on their shows. Not long ago there was a popular disc jockey program transmitted from a ship with a Pan-American registry anchored about three miles out of Stockholm. The station, conceived and run by two Americans, soon became the most popular station in Sweden. Eventually, the enraged government jammed the seaborne platter-spinners and the station signed off.

Japan is disc-jockey-prone too, and the disc jockeys there pattern themselves after their U. S. brethren. This is equally true of Australia and New Zealand, where they enjoy a popular vogue.

"The Latin American market is probably the most confused, disorganized market in the world. It is impossible to understand what they do," reports Hofer. American, English, and other foreign record companies have established themselves there, but the situation is most perplexing.

"In most cases, it's been a matter of distrust because royalties have not been paid, accountings have not been kept. It is a most difficult situation.

"The sluggish mails haven't helped," said Hofer. "I represent a company in Brazil. We made an agreement for a catalogue in December. The catalogue agreement required an advance of $2,000. The contract was consummated, finished in December, and as a precaution was sent by registered mail, return receipt requested. We did not want anybody to deny that they ever received it. It was mailed just before Christmas.

"It actually arrived in Brazil in April of the following year. Now this is the ordinary mail that I'm talking about. In the interim period, the American company was on one end screaming, 'these people are thieves' and the company in South America was doing the exact same thing."

The attorney asserted that there is tremendous anti-American feeling in South America, and this sour feeling rubs off on the phonograph and music publishing business. "It's our own fault," he says. "I think we've treated the South American countries so badly that the record business has to be affected as well as other business. But they still have certain U. S. artists who are very important, like Perry Como."

Speaking of royalties from sheet music and recordings, Hofer said that the foreign companies generally have gotten much more honest in their approach. Except for a few black sheep, the accountings are fairly straight, and the books verify themselves consistently.

However, hypertension is easier to get from the French than money, apparently. "My personal opinion has been that the French territory is the worst. It's between France and South America, and I would say France is worse," thought Hofer.

"I have gone into a French publisher's office and said to him, 'You owe me royalties on this and this account.'

"And he says, 'You're absolutely right.' This actually happened, and this was a Wednesday afternoon that I arrived in Paris and went to see him. He said, 'I'll have the statement for you tomorrow.'

"And I said, 'What do you think you owe my client?'

" 'Well, I think it's $2,000,' said the publisher. I came back the next day and he said, 'We have your statement for you. It's not written out, but we owe you $2,340. Could you come back tomorrow? I'll have the money and everything for you.'

"I said, 'Fine,' and came back the next day.

"He said, 'I'm terribly sorry, I still haven't had a chance to do it, but we owe you $1,462.34.' I said I'd come back the next day and pick up the statement. By this time it was Monday already, and I had been there five days. I returned to his office and he said, 'I'm terribly sorry, I just haven't had a chance to do it, but I know how much your royalties are. They're $6,340.'

"Every day the royalty changed. I sat down and said, 'Now you pay me right this minute. Make out the statement!'

"And he made it out, out of his head."

Lately, overseas fans have wanted American hits translated into their own idiom. In the interests of cultural internationalism herewith are reprinted some of the top U.S. hits and the foreign translations.

Hello, Mary Lou*

Hello, Mary Lou
Goodbye heart
Sweet Mary Lou
I'm so in love with you.

I knew, Mary Lou
We would never part
So, Hello, Mary Lou
Goodbye heart.

You passed me by one sunny day
Flashed those big brown eyes my way
And Oo I wanted you forever more.

Now I'm not one that gets around
I swear my feet's stuck to the ground
And though I never did meet you before

I said: (etc.)

Hello, Mary Lou (German)

Hello, Mary Lou
sieh mal an,
dein Kleid ist schick
und schick sind deine Schuh.

Und du, Mary Lou,
du lachst dazu
So wie ein donnenschein,
Mary Lou'.

Aus dem Hause vis-a-vis,
sieht man jeden Morgen fruh die
Mary Lou den weg zur Schule geh'n.

Und sie schaut so nett daher,
grubt so freundlich, bitte sehr,
das finden alle an ihr wunderschon!

Days of Wine and Roses*

The days of wine and roses
Laugh and run away
Like a child at play
Through the meadowland toward a closing door,
A door marked "Nevermore"

Vino e Rose (Italian)**

Perchè le rose e il vino,
or non hanno più,
no, non hanno più
il profumo di quei giorni che vorrei
rivivere con te.
Perchè? Tu sai perchè?
Perchè, le rose e il vino,
or non sanno più
no, non sanno più
d'aria, sole e primavera come te . . .
Sarà perchè non sei più con me.

This is a linguistic curiosa—The Madison Twist in Italian.

The Madison Twist*
(Meet Me at the Twistin' Place)

Man!
I sure wish I had somewhere to go.
I could go to the show
But that ain't no big thing.
I got it!

I.

There's a place that I know we could have a good time
(Over at the twistin' place)
There's a lot a girls there and the sho' is fine
(Over at the twistin' place)
So why don't you meet me
(Meet me at the twistin' place).
We're gonna have
(Gonna have us a ball today).
Over at the twistin' place
So why don't you meet me
(Meet me at the twistin' place)
We're gonna have (Gonna have us a ball today)
Over at the twistin' place.

Madison Twist (Italian version)

Ehi!
Non ci vengo al cinema, lo sai
e se dai retta a me
abbiamo di meglio.
su, su, dai! . . .

I.

Non discutere più: ti farò divertir . . .
(Il Madison t'insegnerò!)
Vieni fuori così non vestirti in blu
(Il Madison t'insegnerò!) Twist! . . .
Con due ingressi me la caverò . . .
(Il Madison t'insegnerò!)
Siamo a corto di lire ma il fiato c'e . . .
(Il Madison t'insegnerò!)
Non voglio la luna
(Madison Twi-ist)
Vorrei ballare
(Cosa vuoi, cosa vuoi lo sai,)
il Madison insieme a te.

Non voglio i tuoi baci,
(Madison Twi-ist)
per questa notte (Cosa vuoi, cosa vuoi lo sai)
il Madison mi basterà . . .

Since the craving for French lyrics by French "pop" fans and Italian lyrics by Italian consumers of popular music, U. S. singers have taken to translating their immortal best-sellers into foreign languages.

Earl Wilson, the syndicated columnist, is co-author of a song, based on the title of his column, "It Happened Last Night." Recently he told how Connie Francis met him in Al & Dick's, the music business hangout, and said: "I'm going to record your song in Japanese, Spanish, and Italian tomorrow night."

"All in one night?" asked Wilson, surprised.

"Sure!" said Connie.

This instant-Berlitz technique is also being employed in a new way. Increasingly, U. S. stars are going overseas and recording songs and material that are not released here. This has occurred with Paul Anka, Neil Sedaka, and even Peter, Paul and Mary, the folk singers. Not long ago, two brothers from Brownie, Kentucky, the Everly Brothers, stood before microphones in a Hamburg, Germany, studio and unlimbered German-language popular songs composed by German songwriters for the German-speaking market. The hillbilly accenting with the heavy Germanic sound must have been something. But is one of the newer anomalies of international "pop."

Some European cultural commentators and essayists are especially tart about the wholesale popularity of U. S. popular music, and tie it in with the "Coca-Cola-nization" of their culture.

Writing in the *New York Times* of November 11, 1957, the sociologist, Seymour Lipset, observed:

Many American intellectuals see in the supposedly greater dominance of "low-brow" popular culture in America as compared to Europe further evidence of the lower prestige of genuinely creative endeavor in this country.

Yet, in recent years, as Europe has become more like America in its economic and class structure, many European intellectuals, including a number of Leftists, have been in despair at the rapid increase of similar patterns of culture in their own countries. Perhaps the growth of mass culture in Europe is the result of the fact that for the first time the lower classes have enough money and time to make their own demands in the culture market felt.

That Tin Pan Alley is entrenched abroad is as obvious as the white-cliffs of Dover. It has spilled over in the form of photographic imitative-ness. Today, there are more and more European and Asian singers and musicians whose hair styles, singing styles, style of speech and idioms, and approach to lyrics have a made-in-America look.

One of the most popular European artists is the ardent rock 'n' roller, France's Johnny Hallyday. Britain's Cliff Richard is shaped in our image, too. Over there you will find countless vocal groups whose names seem to have that U. S. sound—the Swingin' Blue Jeans, the Violents. One Swedish singing group is called the Spotnicks.

A recent British musical film entitled *Play It Cool* tells the following story, according to a production sheet synopsis:

Billy Universe and the Satellites are a happy-go-lucky Rhythm and "Twist" group just off to Brussels to take part in a contest. They comprise Billy, Alvin, Joey, Freddy, and Ring-a-Ding. In the plane Billy gets talking to Ann and learns that she is being sent abroad for a holiday by her wealthy father, because of her infatuation for the disreputable "pop" singer, Larry Granger. The plane has to return to the airport owing to fog, and Billy and his friends persuade Ann to go back to the West End with them (as it is now too late for their Brussels visit), where they will help her find Granger. A whirlwind tour of some of London's night clubs follows, where Ann and the boys hope to find her boy friend, Granger. Stopping at "Rocco's," they are in time to hear Danny Williams sing the ballad "Who Can Say?" At the "Twist" club Shane Fenton and the Fentones are playing "It's Gonna Take Magic," while at the "Fountain" club they hear Jimmy Crawford sing "Take It Easy" as Lionel Blair and his Dancers perform a lively "Twist." Their tour finishes at the luxurious "Lotus Room" where Helen Shapiro sings "Cry My Heart Out" and "But I Don't Care" and it's here that Larry Granger is finally located— sitting with a pretty dancing girl named Yvonne.

The plot goes on and on until Ann, realizing her mistake, flies to Brussels to meet her father. As the plane takes off, Billy and the Satellites "sing one of their favorite numbers, 'Play It Cool.' "

This is American "pop culture" with a British accent. There are also a rash of U. S. style fan magazines: London's *New Musical Express,* and Belgium's *Juke Box,* which describes itself as the country's biggest musical magazine. "Every one in the music business, and every teenager in Belgium, reads *Juke Box,*" the magazine proclaims.

In 1963 a full-fledged rock 'n' roll, un-chic riot broke out in France. Apparently one of the foremost figures over there is a disc jockey, Daniel Filipacci. He organized a rock 'n' roll show, which he called, in a burst of Americana, "Musicorama," which was designed to publicize his magazine, *Salute Les Copians* ("Hi, Pals"). Twelve rock 'n' roll stars headlined the program, including a jazz band called *Les Chats Sauvages* ("The Wild Cats").

"Led by hoodlums known as *blousons noir* [because part of their standard uniform is black leather jackets]," *Newsweek* reported:

> . . . thousands of late arrivals pressed forward, assaulted the open-air stage as if it were a new bastille, and forced the performers to flee in a paddy wagon. The kids climbed trees, streetlights, balconies, and the Doric columns bearing the giant bronze statues of Kings Philippe Auguste and Saint Louis; they smashed car and shop windows, sacked apartments, and crashed into the homey Café des Colonnes. "It was an irresistible human wave," says the café's tousle-haired owner, Georges Bonnet.

The idiom of our "pseudo-hippies" is also copied abroad. For example, one German songwriter recently whipped up this beatnik ballad, "Die Mutter Ist Immer Dabei" (English translation, "I Can't Shake Mother").

The style of the American music business has become an overseas style, too. In England there are the Gold Disc Awards for sales in excess of 1,000,000 records. Of course, these resemble America's Golden Records Awards which are given, not for excellence, but also for 1,000,000 record sales. There are the remorseless charts. Payola has crept into the language there, and there is a great deal of wheeling and dealing and counterfeiting of records.

Altogether there has been a fabulous immersion in Tin Pan Alley folkways. Apparently, the level of music and lyric writing is equally downtrodden in the land of Shakespeare and Gilbert and Sullivan and John Gay.

In that piercing and delicious English film-musical, *Expresso Bongo* there is a song sung by a music publisher called "Nausea" which sums up what has been happening in its popular music marts. Here are excerpts:

> Call this music? What a scandal!
> In his grave is turning Handel
> Nausea! Nausea!
> Can't we have the Meistersingers in Expresso bars?
> All we get is shyster-singers
> Plucking muck on their guitars!

Just as Americans have taken to Italian clothes, German compacts, Japanese cameras, Swiss banks, and French films, they have also be-

°Nausea. Lyrics by Julian More. David Heneker, Monty Norman. Music by David Heneker and Monty Norman. Copyright © 1958 Robbins Music Corporation, Ltd., London. Rights for North and South America controlled by Robbins Music Corporation, New York. Used by permission.

come enamored of certain foreign popular artists and musical compositions. Some of the most popular imports have been: Acker Bilk (England), Cliff Richard (England), Anthony Newly (England), Georgia Brown (England), Kenny Ball (England), Domenico Modugno (Italy), Bert Kaempfert (Germany), Hadjidakis (Greece), Bent Fabric (Sweden). One of the biggest smashes in 1963 was boyish Kyo Sakomoto (Japan) with his 1,000,000-seller, "Sukiyaki" (Capitol) formerly called, *Ue O Muite Aruko* ("Walk With Your Chin Up").

Some of the songs and musical themes which have originated overseas and found favor here in the past decade have been:

"Mack the Knife"
"Never On Sunday"
"Stranger on the Shore"
"Al Di La"
"As Long As He Needs Me"
"Tie Me Kangaroo Down, Sport"
"What Kind of Fool Am I?"
"Desafinado"
"Midnight in Moscow"
"Alley Cat"
"Song from the Moulin Rouge"
"I Want to Hold Your Hand"

With the rise in the international record market for U. S. popular music and popular music personalities, there has been a rising cantata of complaints and problems. European music publishers are complaining bitterly about "exorbitant" royalties and advances to U. S. publishers of hit songs. There has been a growth of formula writing and jungle-like competition, similar to U. S. record business. The problem of getting your money, which is a continuing problem for U. S. record manufacturers who lease their hit records for sale abroad continues. (The same problem holds true for U. S. music publishers.) In *Cash Box* one Continental music publisher, Peter Plum Publications (Benelux) proclaimed its virtues in an ad thusly: "Statements in time and in . . . *full.*" Complaints are made by foreign music-licensing-rights societies that they are sending more money to the U. S. than either ASCAP or BMI is sending them.

Beyond these financial aspects, there is a transcending complaint of cultural domination. To many European cultural commentators, too much is too much. They believe "that it's gone beyond proportions that are necessary and healthy." To counter this, the European record makers and music publishers are combatting it—by imitation. More and more of the songwriters are copying U. S. music style, lyric themes. Continental singers and groups too are, as has been noted, notorious copy-catters of U. S. artists.

With the foreign music publishers and record manufacturers back on their feet, there is already a lessening of U. S. dominance in terms of importing U. S. popular songs and American musical personalities. But American-inspired popular music—the style of music, the "sound" of it—is being followed faithfully, just as better American clothes manufacturers copy Dior.

However, the U. S. recording star with pronounced distinction, or superb promotion will continue to make a splash along the Seine, the Thames, and elsewhere. For through independent radio stations, through the buying of air time, and the Armed Forces Radio network, young Europeans hear what we produce. And often they buy what they listen to.

The future of the overseas market for U. S. popular music seems fairly promising providing there is no thermonuclear war or economic depression. Right now, the European teenagers have money to buy clothes and recordings, and it reflects growing, though hardly affluent, economies.

Apart from all other economic and historical factors, it is perfectly natural for one country to know another through movies, shortwave radio, UN meetings, magazines, books, and the swapping of its most disarming direct and uncomplicated product—popular music.

Good popular music can even be a charming "ice breaker" on a high international level. In August, 1963, in the Kremlin, dignitaries and officials of many countries met to witness the signing of the limited test-ban treaty between the United States and Russia. Later, there was a glittering ball to celebrate the auspicious occasion, and *Time* magazine described how it began:

> . . . as Khrushchev, U. S. Secretary of State Dean Rusk and British Foreign Secretary Lord Home smilingly raised their glasses, a Soviet band struck up George Gershwin's 1938 hit, "Love Walked In."

But one thing cannot be sloughed over: much of what the United States popular music industry has sent over is far from Gershwin. The output of the past decade has been mostly horrendous. But the U. S. music merchandisers have exported it with glee, without any visible compunction or self-censorship. It has also exported poor singers and vocal groups, on records and in the flesh, to the rootless, tired teenagers of Europe, Asia, and Latin America. In this sense, a terrible disservice has been done, and hard-earned money has been wasted.

On the affirmative side, some of our better artists have toured widely—Louis Armstrong, Ella Fitzgerald, Dave Brubeck, Leonard Bernstein, Erroll Garner. They—and their records—do us proud. And throughout the world America's talented jazz artists have been heard. And brilliant theater productions such as *Porgy and Bess, My Fair Lady, South Pacific,* and *West Side Story*—"live," on records, and on film—have shown overseas audiences that there is a superb, gifted, imaginative side to our popular music culture.

So, the overseas popularity of American music abroad hasn't been completely a black situation. It has been an ambivalent picture. U. S. popular music makers—and the industry that succors them—can take comfort in having exported superior artists and musical materials. And they can cry a river of saccharine tears for having exported "aesthetic junk"—and for continuing to do so.

21 · WHO OWNS TIN PAN ALLEY?

> There's nothing surer
> The rich get rich
> And the poor get poorer
> — from "Ain't We Got Fun"

Economics, of course, demonstrably shape the character of popular music, and if there is any doubt, there are such expressions as "the money song," or "it's commercial"; there are the trade papers (*Cash Box, Music Vendor, Music Business*) and the best-selling record lists. And the biggest reward creators can acquire is a "golden record."

And as the popular music structures enters the '60's, there are signs of giantism, "pop-music" style. The individual enterpreneur isn't being replaced, but there are greater and greater concentrations of resources, money, manpower, and talent. "Bigness" is the style of modern Tin Pan Alley in recording, music publishing, exploitation, and talent. The word "acquisition"—borrowed from Wall Street—is not unknown. And there are all kinds of inbred, interwoven tie-ins with television and the movies, for mutual profit.

Oft voiced is the fact that there are countless record firms, and this is true. Yet, despite increasing competition most of the popular music recording business is concentrated among the "giants"—Columbia Records, RCA Victor, Capitol Records, and Decca Records.

A U. S. government survey of record sales for 1960 by the Federal Trade Commission revealed that bigness pays off. Here are figures for just three of the "big four," excluding Decca.

CBS, RCA, Capitol

(Aggregate)

All records	40%
All LP's	50%
Classical LP's	75%
Original cast LP's	90%
Subscription method LP's (clubs)	97%

Columbia Records is perhaps the largest record company in America. It is linked to a million-dollar corporate colossus, described by the January 1963 issue of the *Value Line Investment Survey* in this way:

Columbia Broadcasting System, composed of seven divisions, operates the world's largest radio and TV network through CBS Radio Division (206 affiliated stations) and CBS Television Division (254 stations). CBS Television Stations Division owns five TV stations in New York (CBS), Los Angeles (KNXT), Chicago (WBBM), St. Louis (KMOX), and Philadelphia (WCAU). News broadcasts are produced for both media by CBS News Division. Columbia Records Division (Columbia and Epic Labels) includes Columbia Record Club.

The analysis pointed out that collectively the divisions employ 16,000.

Columbia Records, of course, is an enormous and successful producer of "pop singles" and LP's, and has a potent talent list under contract. Its record club is the world's largest, with approximately 1,750,000 members. Its advertising and promotion is sleek, well-managed. It spends a lot of money to merchandise its wares. In 1960, CBS Records net sales of records amounted to more than $54 million; it spent $2,-156,406 on advertising and sales promotion, according to a government study. This expenditure was independent of the money spent for advertising its record club. This is more money than most independent record companies gross a year in sales.

RCA Victor Records is one of the oldest and proudest names in the record business, from the earliest days of the birth of the phonograph record. It is owned, of course, by the Radio Corporation of America. In a booklet given to employees of this electronic giant, *You and RCA*, the company is pictured as "the world leader in radio, television, and electronics." A mere listing of what RCA Records is connected to is flabbergasting:

Astro-Electronic Products Division
RCA Laboratories
Surface Communications Division
Airborne Systems Division
Missile Electronics and Controls Division
Moorestown Missile and Surface Radar Division
West Coast Missile and Surface Radar Division
Communications and IEP Operations Division
Industrial, Automation and Aviation
Broadcasting and Television Equipment Division
Electronic Data Processing Division
RCA Communications, Inc.

RCA Electron Tube Division
RCA Semiconductor and Materials Division
RCA International Division
RCA International Service Corporation
RCA Victor Home Instruments
RCA Sales Corporation
RCA Purchasing Corporation
RCA Service Company, Division
RCA Institutes, Inc.
RCA Victor Distributing Corp.
National Broadcasting Company, Inc.
California National Productions, Inc.
RCA Staff

As can be seen, the "Little Nipper" (the famed pup that is the logo of RCA Victor Records) is no homeless stray. Victor owns Camden Records (low-priced subsidiary), a record club, in association with the *Reader's Digest*, and also owns tremendous record-manufacturing facilities in Camden, New Jersey, and Indianapolis, Indiana. Like Columbia, RCA Victor is very strong internationally, a leading producer and distributor of records in cities from Rome to Rio. It has, for example, magnificent recording studios in Rome—RCA Victor Italiana. Today the RCA Victor Record Division sells millions of dollars worth of discs of all types. In its first year of operation, the Victor Talking Machine Company reportedly earned $500.

The third of the "majors" is Capitol Records. It, too, is a multimillion-dollar company with its own record club (Capitol Record Club). It has a wholly-owned classical division, Angel Records. Based on the West Coast, Capitol has a strong talent list, including the Kingston Trio, Nat "King" Cole, Nancy Wilson, Stan Kenton, and Tennessee Ernie Ford. Though originating as a U. S. record company, Capitol is owned by EMI, Electric and Musical Industries, Ltd. of Great Britain, which puts out ads claiming that it sells one-quarter of all the records sold in the world. More about foreign control of U. S. record companies later.

A great deal of the "pop-record" business is done by Decca Records, organized in the mid 30's. It is now part of a multimillion-dollar combine that resembles a General Motors of show business. Formerly perhaps the largest talent agency in the world, the old MCA (Music Corporation of America) headed by Jules Stein has shucked its flesh-peddling and has ribbed together in one "umbrella" the following: Decca Records, Revue Productions (maker of many TV series), Universal Pictures (motion pictures), and a Midwest bank with assets of approximately $90 million.

Recently, Murray Schumach of the *New York Times* reported MCA's latest "epic."

The tallest structure ever built at a movie studio was "topped out today" at Universal City when a steel beam was hoisted fourteen stories after a brief ceremony.

The building, known as MCA Tower, will be the world headquarters of MCA Inc., the billion-dollar corporation. . . . Universal City, which covers 410 acres, is the largest studio in the world. It has thirty-two sound stages and is now working at such a pitch that all stages are in use, and more space has to be rented at Paramount."

Of the MCA film division, Budd Schulberg wrote in *Life's* special issue on the movies: "Everything is bigger and better at MCA-Revue. It is the film factory of the future."

The MCA colossus is already planning to invest in Broadway productions, including musicals. In this way, they might perhaps acquire the rights to cast albums of Broadway musicals, the movie rights, and a possible spin-off for a TV series. At the tag end of 1963, MCA put money in a musical version of *What Makes Sammy Run*, ironically based on Schulberg's novel.

Decca, the recording division, produces recordings under its own name, and also issues discs under its sister logos, Coral, Brunswick, and Compo of Canada. It also manufactures phonographs, owns music publishing firms, and conducts an active custom-record department which presses commercial records for other companies, such as Caedmon Records, famed for the spoken word.

"Bigness" and corporate thinking are as evident in the popular music and record structure as the radio tower in an airport. In the giant record companies, management experts cast astringent eyes on the supposedly compulsive, carefree sector of show business. In 1960, Capitol Records announced that it had hired Bruce Rozet, "well-known Southern California management consultant" for the "newly created post of Administrator, Management Planning."

In his new job, Rozet, Capitol said, "will supervise the Administration and Finance Division's Organization Planning Department, which includes the former Systems & Procedures Department; the Profit-Planning Department; and a new activity, the Management Review and Development Department. Under the new organization, Rozet's department will provide specialized management services to all managers in Capitol Records, Inc., and its subsidiaries."

In the big record companies, there are premium experts who busy themselves selling whopping record premium tie-ins with oil companies or shampoo manufacturers ("Buy the shampoo, get this record for $1"). Educators are also hired to take the company's catalogue, and recast it in academic terms and categories to stimulate the sale of the company's records to the growing audio-visual school market for recordings.

Hollywood, too, has taken greater interest in the popular music industry. The film capital has always been interested in popular music, from the silent movie days when music was composed for pianists to play during the running of a silent film. With the advent of sound films, it sired many publishing houses and/or acquired existing publishing firms such as the MGM purchase of Robbins, Feist and Miller. From music publishing interests, though, Hollywood has gone deeper and deeper in the recording industry.

MGM Pictures started the move back in 1947 when it created MGM Records with the aid of the late Frank Walker, a pioneering record executive. Later MGM bought Verve for $2.6 million which gave it status in the jazz and humor (Shelley Berman) market.

In 1947 Paramount Pictures bought Dot Records for a reported $3 million. In the 1950's Warner Bros. created Warner Brothers Records; in 1963 it purchased Reprise Records from Frank Sinatra. Not too long ago, United Artists, which subsidizes the making of many motion pictures in return for distribution rights, created its own record wing—United Artists Records. At the same time it began its own music publishing firms, Unart and United Artists Music.

Columbia Pictures, not to be left behind, established Colpix Records. To beef up its record operation it acquired a Tin Pan Alley powerhouse called Nevins-Kirschner, which consisted of a group of music publishing companies, for a reported $2 million. It also bought the "pop savvy" of Don Kirschner, a brood of songwriters under contract, such recording artists as Little Eva, and a record label, Dimension Records. The entire *modus operandi* now functions as a wholly owned division of Columbia Pictures.

20th Century Fox is no nonconformist, and it, too, owns a record company, 20th Century Fox Records, which recently had a sizable hit with its movie sound track of the film, *Cleopatra*.

Behind the movie companies accelerated interest in the recording field are many subtly connected reasons: (1) it simplifies the making of promotion records for their own motion pictures; (2) they have an inside track on sound tracks and original-cast albums of movie musicals;

(3) they can build teen stars who may have movie possibilities, and (4) it satisfies the need to diversify. They have watched with beady-eyed, thin-lipped interest the shrinking nature of movie box-office (from ninety million persons weekly to about forty-four million weekly) and the enormous expansion of the record-buying, home-entertainment market.

There is another new phase in the multimillion-dollar popular music structure which also reflects a sense of bigness: absentee ownership. Two British concerns today own two important U. S. record companies—Capitol Records and Mercury Records. EMI controls Capitol. As noted earlier, it is a gigantic corporation with enormous interest in making records and marketing them through the world, from England to the Orient.

And, recently, Philips (corporately known as Philips Lamp Works), a Dutch company, bought a U. S. company founded in 1945—Mercury. A Chicago-based firm, Mercury has grown a lot in the past few years. It seems to be getting bigger, and it has two lusty subsidiary labels— Smash and Philips. The world-wide connections of Philips can pay off in new "product." Perhaps Mercury's most powerful successes in 1963 didn't originate in the United States, but were foreign importations from European affiliates. They were two instant long-playing hits, "The Singing Nun" and "Bach's Greatest Hits" done in a jazz manner. A 45-rpm band, "Dominique," from "The Singing Nun" also led the best-selling charts.

Foreign recording interests want to tap the rich U. S. market. They have apparently found it better to buy into an American company which has native taproots in marketing, distribution, and exploitation, than to try to sell their own output from abroad, through licensing or some other arrangement.

There is a shaking out, and merging of music publishers, too. Small music publishers, who once had their own little shops, are now employees of larger music publishing firms. Increasingly, as noted earlier, record companies and independent A & R producers now have their own music publishing enterprises, thus cutting in on the small, independent publisher. The independent music publisher is riding on a wing and a prayer, and the struts are loose. Consolidation is in the wind. This is unmistakably true in the distribution and retailing of recordings as well.

What does all this bigness and concentration of power in the popular music and record business mean? For one thing, the bigger record companies can pluck off popular artists developed by the smaller companies. Bobby Darin, for example, switched from Atlantic Records to Capitol. Paul Anka moved from ABC-Paramount, which brought him to stardom, to RCA Victor. Steve Lawrence and Eydie Gorme departed from United Artists to Columbia Records. Perhaps the most astonishing coup of the decade, which nobody could predict at the time, was the buy-out of the contract of a young Mississippi singer, Elvis Presley, for $30,000 from a hillbilly company, Sun Records, by RCA Victor. Sun Records could not resist the ready cash.

The young artists gravitate toward the larger record companies for prestige reasons, these firms are looked up to, and the "majors" have greater financial resources and greater strength in advertising and distribution. And they know that if they connect with a series of hits, the "majors" will pay them record royalties.

With millions of dollars in resources, the big record companies can acquire original Broadway cast albums, which often means buying into a show, and this can cost $100,000, $200,000, or $300,000. The smaller firms cannot stand such financial risk. Those firms connected with Hollywood production have natural access to the original movie sound tracks; for example, Decca controls products of Universal Pictures, MGM Records has the pick of MGM sound tracks, and Warner Brothers Records works closely with Warner Brothers Pictures.

The "big boys" can spend a little more on packaging, too, in-store promotion, and field-promotion men. And as employers, the larger record companies are more generous, and they can build a more stable staff. Staff workers—publicists, A & R men, salesmen, production experts—are attracted to them by a measure of security, health, and welfare benefits and pension plans.

The "indies" still exert a powerful voice in the music and record business, in terms of economics and aesthetics. But they are being squeezed and pushed by the majors who can out-advertise them, out-exploit them, and have more focused marketing skills.

A noted music industry trade-paper editor recently told me over a brandy: "The 'indies' are suffering. At the height of rock 'n' roll it was possible for an 'indie' to exist from single hit to single hit. But today 'singles' don't sell as much. And they cannot develop that album image. Pure independents of substance are becoming rarer and rarer."

Many independents cannot pay their bills on time, if at all. There is a piggy-back concept among suppliers of little record companies (the men who supply the record album jackets, the 45-rpm record sleeves, and the actual recordings). They carry many of the marshmallow "companies," because, who knows, that company may have a smash single hit or LP soon.

A Wall Street analyst, Charles S. Dayian of *Moody's Investors'*

Service, has made this analysis of the difference between the big and small firms in the popular music and record business:

The industry seems to be divided into two segments, the majors and the minors or smaller companies. The majors are characterized by high-priced merchandise, strong distribution organizations, their own manufacturing facilities, large inventories of records, established artists under fairly long-term contracts, adequate finances for advertising purposes and the organization of record clubs. Currently, a few of the major record companies are instrumental in producing Broadway musicals so that they will control the rights to the music. In some cases, the rights to the entire musical show can be sold to the motion picture studios or filmed by the record company itself through its other subsidiaries.

The minor companies, on the other hand, have practically none of these various characteristics. A few do have some popular singers under contract, but the companies are strongly dependent on these performers and if their popularity wanes, the companies suffer accordingly.

Bigness has a built-in advantage in record distribution. The larger record companies usually possess wholly-owned distributors in the key consumer markets, and they can focus all their energies upon the product of the *one* company. The independent record companies have a regional network of distributors, many of whom may handle the product of ten to twenty rival record companies. The question is: Can any one distributor with myriad interests match the single-minded devotion of the company-owned distributorship?

Chances are they cannot. Equally important is the fact that the majors have more substantial funds to withstand the vicissitudes of today's record-retailing picture, which has been described by one insider in *Fortune* this way: "It's murder."

For the past few years there have been anxious groans by many in the recording industry by what Dave Kapp, one of the "deans" of the industry and head of Kapp Records, terms "profitless prosperity." Price-cutting, discounting, and "special deals" have put the record manufacturer in a profit-squeeze. Yet, if they do not maintain a certain price, they can not make any money. But some big-volume outlets (discount chains, department stores, rack merchandisers) want recordings for less than it costs the manufacturer to produce them.

In free enterprise, the manufacturer must make a profit or go under. This is elemental, but for years the "swinging 'indie' labels" have been so anxious to sell records that they have neglected the fact that profits are essential to healthy growth and stability. There is a counter-move on now to restore some sanity in pricing, and some effort to curb "deals."

With the abnormal profit picture, can the independents compete against the major power blocs? Perhaps. But they will need to rely upon superior and more imaginative recordings, greater flexibility in putting out material geared to a rapidly changing fickle market, a sales manager who does not give records away in order to show astronomical sales, clever publicity and promotion, and excellent use of art work—album covers, promotion pieces, catalogues, or throwaways. Provocative, authoritative liner-note copy is increasingly important, too.

The peanut-sized record companies have to rely, too, upon the aesthetic mistakes of the larger companies. For big firms make costly bobbles. Recently, for example, Columbia Records took a tremendous flier, backed by lavish, expensive ballyhoo and press parties, into the realm of "gospel-pop." Scores of 45-rpm records and LP's were released carrying that music. The sacrilegious musical abortion—gospel music done in a sweetened "pop music" manner with touches of "showmanship"—proved to be a tremendous flop. But Columbia is big enough to absorb such losses. The independents, working with limited capital, have to be more cautious.

In the zigzagging evaluation of the big versus the small, it should be noted that the big four—Columbia, Capitol, Decca, RCA Victor—are not newcomers to the record field. Their very longevity gives them an edge. They have in their vaults all sorts of material which can be repackaged into selling merchandise. This is true of RCA Victor with its successful reissues of deluxe Glenn Miller albums, Decca with its Judy Garland albums and early show music albums, Columbia with its jazz archives. Some of the swinging "indies" do this, too. They put out what they call the "goodies" and the "oldies"—the rock 'n' roll hits of the 1950's.

The independents lose in another way. They do not own their pressing plants, as do Columbia, Victor, Decca, and Capitol. These larger record firms manufacture their own product, and thus achieve a "price break." In addition, most of them turn a handsome extra-curricular profit turning out recordings for small independents. Thus, if a rival record company produces a runaway hit, chances are that the "majors" benefit by making a profit on the pressing of the hit.

The word "independent" has been used frequently, and it might be worthwhile to define it more precisely. In the record industry, an independent refers to any company not in the "major-label" class. Under such an interpretation, 20th Century Records may be considered an independent. However, the term is used here in the dictionary sense and in economic implication. The true independent is defined as having two or more of these syndrome-lacks: (1) it has no record manufacturing facilities of its own; (2) it has few wholly-owned distributors; (3) it is not connected to any parent corporation; (4) it does not own film companies or TV or radio stations.

Those independent record companies, often with less than fifteen employees, who specialize in producing the blues, modern jazz, ethnic-music, and spoken-word will probably survive the economic pressure of the power blocs. The "indie pop-music" record manufacturer will need all the imagination he can muster because his basic product has little or no distinction.

What has happened in the popular music field since 1950 has happened to every U. S. industry: bigness. Clearly, the thirty-two-bar tunes have got a corporate tiger by the coda.

Popular music devotees and record fans have a stake in the independents' survival. These firms have made sturdy contributions in terms of artists, material, album concepts, mechanical improvements, superior art. Before being bought out by Philips, Mercury reportedly introduced plastic lamination of LP jackets, which protect albums. The provocative folk singer, Joan Baez, was nurtured by Vanguard. During the McCarthy era, when big firms got buttery knees about recording Pete Seeger because of his political views, Folkways produced his recordings. Atlantic Records is noted for its excursions into modern jazz. Audio Fidelity, which is a record "reprint" house for previously established "standards," pushed the record world into the stereo LP.

The record goliaths are beset with problems. They suffer from bureaucracy, power politics, internal feuds, a fat overhead, and a powerful organism so arranged as to produce albums and 45-rpm "singles" that have no aesthetic reason for being produced except to live up to a "release schedule." They act as if possessed by C. Northcote Parkinson's humorous law, "Work expands so as to fill the time available for its completion." A record company needs recordings to produce income and accounts receivable. But the question is: does it have anything worth recording?

Though there are power blocs dominating the popular music scene it is doubtful that complete monopoly can ever be maintained. Mostly this is because of the economics of recording. It costs $1,000 to $2,000 to put out 5,000 45's, and that brings about a situation where anybody can enter and can put his ideas on the firing line.

But the big power structure can tempt the young artists developed by the independent companies, can buy into Broadway musicals, can run full page ads in the *New York Times*. The economic power that it wields, its strong "catalogue image," and its merchandising and marketing knowledge puts it out in front.

Does the growing giantism have an aesthetic impact? The aesthetic ideology that emerges from growing big business can't help becoming tinctured with a marketing psychology. It tends to propel the big company to produce what sells, to stick to what is "commercial."

In a speech by Steve Sholes (read by Jack Burgess), head of the Artists and Repertoire Department of RCA Victor to a convention in Nashville, this idea is stated candidly:

"It would be nice to have art for art's sake, but you can't eat art, stockholders won't take unsold records in exchange for dividends, employees like to be paid regularly, and you can't do any of these practical things without being very practical about art."

However, if the creative figures at the top are powerful enough, and have enough "status," they can resist these pressures and produce maverick materials that deserve to be done. Columbia's President Goddard Lieberson, for example, has done some marvelous recordings of early Broadway musicals, even though the possibilities of their being successful, given the expenditure of making such albums, were slim.

The fact that the large companies are getting larger scarcely means that they have all the imagination, talent, or sensitivity to words, music, talent or exploitation wizardry. They just have a lot of "muscle."

Not long ago, a marketing observer, E. B. Weiss of Doyle, Dane, Bernbach, Inc., told an assembled audience of musical instrument makers and home entertainment retailers in Chicago that "It's time for the music industry to get out of Tin Pan Alley." He added, "In an age in which cultural progress is in a stage of explosive growth, you continue to live, think, and function within the brassy, irresponsible tradition of Tin Pan Alley."

Increasingly, Tin Pan Alley concepts are giving way under social and economic pressure. Certainly the brassiness is still there, but apparently not enough gold. And the voice of big business is becoming the opposite of pianissimo.

22 · BROADWAY: THE GAY WHITE WAY?

Theater attendance for 1944-45 was 11,500,000. By 1960-61 it was 3,000,000 less.

—*New York Times*

In the 1953 musical, *Me And Juliet*, the Rodgers and Hammerstein portrait of life behind the painted flats, pulley-cords, and orchestra pit of a musical show, there is a scene that throws a pin spot on theatergoers. During this "intermission scene" a group of gossipy patrons lament that the theater is "dying," and that the financial investors in Broadway productions are taking a "shellacking."

More than a decade later, The Fabulous Invalid has more crimson ink flowing through his veins than ever. He continues to walk around, put on make-up, sing and dance. But he is a hobbling invalid with high blood-pressure, poached-egg eyes, and a heart murmur as noisy as an old World War I De Haviland bi-plane.

And this is a pity. Much of the quality American popular music comes from the Broadway musical theater. Shubert Alley may be crass, inbred, and pushy, yet somehow from the curved, cramped pits hugging the Broadway stages has come the best contemporary popular music in the world; music that doesn't stop at thirty-two bars, or usual forms; words of wit and literary value commonly eyed with distrust by Tin Pan Alley and the "pop-singles" record business.

Through prohibition, depression, recession, and rock 'n' roll, Broadway musical shows have brought forth something rather new: a popular music rooted in contemporary colloquial language; poetic in a non-esoteric, non-rhetorical manner, and matched with irresistible and varied melodies, rhythms, and harmonies. The works of Jerome Kern, George Gershwin, Richard Rodgers, Irving Berlin, Oscar Hammerstein, Cole Porter, Larry Hart, Alan Jay Lerner, Leonard Bernstein have been, as *Theatre Arts* once expressed it, "something to cheer about."

It is still something to cheer about, but now those cheers are mixed with music as sad as Mozart's "Requiem." Broadway may be one of the healthiest components in the popular music and record structure, but it is very sick, and everybody knows it. In countless seminars, speeches, interviews, conferences, producers, college professors, and theatrical accountants have related the same tale of chronic woe.

There may be some minor quibbling on the extent of the woe and what is an authentic profit-and-loss statement for any given twelve-month season. In the theater, disasters are fairly easy to compute. When a show shuts down, it is easy to compute the loss on a calendar basis. But a hit musical show, for example, earns money for decades from productions in this country and abroad, cast albums, single 45-rpm recordings, and sheet music. *Oklahoma!* still makes a handsome stipend though it was first produced in 1943, more than two decades ago. Do you figure the annual profit of *Oklahoma!* into the profit-and-loss statement of every succeeding theater season?

These rejiggered figures would probably give Broadway a happier face. But you would have to be an accountant steeped in the optimism of Dr. Pangloss of *Candide* (who saw good things in all disasters) to ignore the warning bells sounding over Shubert Alley.

There are only a handful of musical productions each year, contrasted to the cornucopia of musicals in the 1920's and 1930's. Destructive, too, is the high cost of productions, which now hovers around the $350,000 to $400,000 mark. The rate of theatrical casualties are so heavy that one veteran theatrical "angel," Marguerite Cullman, told *Show Business:* "We need a complete revolution in the method of financing and producing, and if we don't get it soon, we're going to find we're pouring all our money into England, rather than Broadway."

Modern musicals, because of steep theater prices, cast albums and royalty-structures are great money-makers. Columnist Leonard Lyons once reported a conversation between Ira Gershwin and Fritz Loewe, in which the lyricist said that his two-year royalties from *Oh, Kay* weren't as much as Loewe received from *My Fair Lady* in one week. But while good musicals have kept making money for a quarter of a century, they are also catastrophic money-burners. In one season alone, five musical flops can drop $2 million. The spectacular costs of musical productions have also prodded into being merchandising pattern indigenous to the toothpaste industry.

One famed musical comedy librettist-lyricist has noted: "It is not a musical or theater business. It's like everything else—a packaging business. With a $400,000 or $500,000 proposition, the producer has to worry not about the play itself, and not about the music and lyrics, but who is going to be in it that will attract the Hadassah and the other theater parties, and everybody is catering to the box office, to the gimmick that will attract the theater parties."

And the high costs of theater tickets has led to a situation where the closest many get to theater attractions is mooning over the bright, dazzling ads in the theater section of Sunday's *New York Times*. More people talk theater than go to the theater, and the reason is largely pocketbook. If a boy and girl go out on a date, it may cost them $8 to $10 just for theater tickets. If a New York City married couple go to the theater, they have to add the expense of a baby-sitter. Those living outside of New York City are triply pressed. If they take a train to and from the theater, that's expensive; if they take the family car, there are murderous toll costs and garage-parking fees. These factors, to put it mildly, undercut a larger theater attendance and help bring about a corrupted, hit-crazy audience.

As one theatrical investor-accountant, J. S. Seidman, told the Harvard Business School Club: "It's perfectly natural for patrons to confine themselves to hit shows. This means that unless a show is a hit, it dies fast."

Such crushing logic means that music and straight plays that have some merit, some accomplishment, cannot make their money back, even if the entire cast goes on Equity minimum and the authors and producers voluntarily relinquish their royalty arrangements. And that is not good for popular music, which needs all the help it can get from a functioning, healthy theatrical sector.

For those ten or twelve blocks of playhouse on Manhattan Island which take in the Imperial Theatre, the Majestic, the Winter Garden, the 46th Street Theatre, and the Lunt-Fontanne are the few outposts of nonteen-directed music. A retarded thirteen-year-old mentality is not its focus. Good show scores—lots of them—have a cumulative impact; they provide adults with something they love; the music and words are given air play, and juke-box exposure. They tend to counterattack the trash that is pushed out from the single-record business, and the teen LP artists.

So the more musicals, the bigger the counterforce. The music and record business sucks on the concrete bosom of Broadway for much of its mature substance. Economically, too. A 1,000,000-selling original-cast album will gross $3 million to $4 million, even under discount-conditions. Record shops also ingratiate more people into sampling their wares by displaying the latest Broadway cast albums in the window. Discount houses (an interesting description) and department stores feature cast albums at reduced prices as economic lures to bring customers into their precinct with the noble aim of selling them washing machines and color TV sets.

Recently, Stern's, a New York department store, was mobbed by record buyers. One of the baits was the RCA Victor cast recording of

Oliver, on sale at $1.47. There are many merchandising ramifications for a Broadway musical triumph (it provides the record industry with highly-publicized new stars), for a big musical is really a sociocultural event.

Broadway is also popular music's aesthetic conscience. (Yes, Virginia, popular music *does* have a conscience). For in show music, you can write up, musically and lyrically, and that makes Shubert Alley and Tin Pan Alley a world apart, even though they are blocks apart.

Today, the relationship of the Broadway musical theater to the popular music and record business is roughly that of a Phi Beta Kappa to somebody who has a reading problem. The "pop music" writers who function in the individual single song and instrumental market look up to show writers as minor gods. Their ideals are the Shubert Alley marquées of musicals.

The Broadway writer's position is revered. For he is relatively untrammeled. He is pretty much a creative spirit. Of course, he is not completely free. He is controlled by the concepts, the characters, the texture of his "book" (the source of the musical), the producers, the director, the choreographer. And the creators often have to contend with the "stars" who are chosen for box-office potential, rather than for their ability to fit a certain role.

But on Broadway, even during the dark days of the 1950's, craftsmanship has been allowed to breathe. The writers do not always succeed. But they do not have to answer to an A & R man or a music publisher or some callow young recording star on the artistic quality of their work; nor do they have to be beaten down by the savage words: "It's not commercial."

And the paradox is this: being unencumbered by the imprisoning theories of record company experts and music publishing experts, show writers have come up with fabulous individual hits as well as best-selling cast albums. Here are just a few titles: "Make Someone Happy" *(Do Re Mi),* "I Could Have Danced All Night" *(My Fair Lady),* "What Kind of Fool Am I?" *(Stop the World, I Want to Get Off),* "Standing on the Corner" *(Most Happy Fella).*

Besides these large individual song successes, there have been countless "quiet hits." These are musical theater compositions which often do not reach the teen-oriented hallowed best-selling charts in flamboyant rocket-like fashion. Yet, they are recorded, re-recorded, and heard on AM and FM, and in the better night clubs. They make money on performances on radio and TV. There are dozens of these unspectacular, money-making hits, including Frank Loesser's "I Believe in You" *(How to Succeed in Business without Really Trying),* Harold

Arlen's "Sleepin' Bee" *(House of Flowers)*, Lerner and Loewe's "Come to Me, Bend to Me" *(Brigadoon)*. There are even remarkably alive songs from off-Broadway shows which do not reach the popularity charts. According to Chappell Music, the haunting "Try to Remember" from *The Fantasticks* has so far been recorded by the following artists: Harry Belafonte, the Kingston Trio, Jerry Ohrbach, and Mabel Mercer.

Tin Pan Alley finds it hard to maintain its rationalization of cheap songs by saying that is what the public hungers for, when royalty statements indicate that better-quality music and words make more money in the long run than the mediocre kind.

Throughout these peculiarly Stygian days of popular music, the few Benday notes have come from the Broadway musical theater. Since the early 50's there have been many 45-rpm "singles" and albums of show music; anthologies of show music, show music in varying styles; big band, small combo, Latin American style; show music in the form of instrumentals as mood music; show music in a percussive manner. Teenage singers hoping to move out of the tadpole stage try to appear adult by singing "show songs." Rock 'n' roll singers have (unfortunately) discovered show songs. Jazz artists lean on Broadway as do the better popular singers. Everybody from Arthur Fiedler and the Boston "Pops" Orchestra to country and western singers have interpreted the output of Broadway over the past two decades. They have put millions of record buyers "on the aisle."

To come to the "argument"—the old fashioned term for a musical plot—show music is one of the formidable components in popular music. But pancake make-up cannot hide the fact that its health is seriously imperiled; it may even be a terminal case.

In the depression era of the 1930's, the opening number of one revue was a tribute to the show's financial bird-dog, producer, Max Gordon. It was called "Max Gordon Raised The Money." Since the 1950's, money has hardly been that tight. A quasi-national affluence had made venture capital available to sponsor shows. But theatrical investors are getting noticeably restless over the stratospheric costs of productions and the declining rate of profit. One intangible factor that keeps many enmeshed in putting up money in Broadway musicals is "culture status." Broadway press agent Harvey Sabinson says: "If an investor invests in stocks, or even a movie, there's no glamour connected with it. But if you're an angel for a Broadway show, you're looked up to."

The word "angel" is very apt for musical shows because costs seem to be heading over the moon. In a booklet, interestingly entitled *Crisis in the Free World Theatre*, by John F. Wharton and published by the

League of New York Theatres, Inc., the jump in costs of mounting a production are set down clearly:

1949	*South Pacific*	$225,000
1950	*Gentlemen Prefer Blondes*	$160,000
1956	*Bells Are Ringing*	$360,000
1956	*My Fair Lady*	$400,000
1960	*Camelot*	$600,000

Such rising costs have helped cut down the number of musicals being put on. In 1927-28, there were 264 shows produced on Broadway. Even in 1930, the beginning of tin-roofed Hoovervilles, more than 233 productions got on the boards. During those years, 40 to 50 "book shows," musical revues, musical entertainments, operettas were put into rehearsal and produced annually. From 1951-60, Broadway saw an average of 62 productions, of which 10 or 12 were musicals.

Speaking of rising costs, composer Jule Styne produced a lavish revival of *My Pal Joey* in 1951 for $125,000. It was rather opulent, with many sets designed by Oliver Smith and costumes by Miles White. "To duplicate the same production today," he wrote not long ago in the *Herald Tribune*, "would cost $400,000."

Profits, too, are hard to come by these days. Writing in *Playbill*, Gerald M. Loeb, a senior partner in Wall Street's E. F. Hutton & Co., asserted that in the 1930's, "there were shows that paid as much as $25 to $30 for every $1 invested." He said that today if you invest $1 in a hit, the return is $3. If it's a smash hit, the return jumps to $10."

The melancholy truth, according to Loeb, is that backers of Broadway productions—musicals and dramas—can expect to lose about $5 million a year.

All these factors have led to a situation fraught with black connotations. The *Wall Street Journal*, the omnivorous student of the financial aspects of regional planning, shopping centers, washing machines, and Elvis Presley, published a survey recently (September 11, 1963), concerning the Broadway Theater. Its headline observed:

RELUCTANT ANGELS
           Broadway Producers
           Encounter More Snags
           in Raising Show Funds

           Flops and Rising Costs Deter Some Investors:
           New York Probes Financing Methods.

The article noted that a handful of producers do not find trouble raising money. The producers with a streak of previous successes—what smart Broadwayites call "a good track record"—such as David Merrick and Harold Prince—have a body of loyal backers who won't cavil at whatever these gentlemen want to put on.

However, even so-called "name producers" like Herman Levin, producer of *My Fair Lady,* found it difficult raising $400,000 for the Broadway production, *The Girl who Came to Supper,* with a score by Noel Coward and book by Harry Kurnitz. "We went through hell to raise the $450,000," he said. "A couple of years ago I'd have raised the money in a week." Noel Coward's previous Broadway failure, *Sail Away,* probably frightened off money, too.

The *Wall St. Journal* adds:

What often makes or breaks a show is its weekly operating costs—or "nut" as it's known in the business. The basic bills that constitute the "nut" include salaries; a big chunk of the gross receipts—often 28%—for the theater, with a minimum rent guaranteed; and small percentages of receipts for the director, the playwright, the composer, the choreographer, the producer, and perhaps several others.

The "small percentages" paid to stars and directors are often not that minor. Some stars take 10 per cent off the gross; some take more. Knowing their box-office power (and the impact of their names to theater parties) the "names" take extraordinary percentages of the box office.

In a recent painstaking probe in New York State, Attorney General Louis Lefkowitz has exposed the existence of a multimillion-dollar theater-ticket scandal known as "ice." "Ice" is under-the-counter-premium on tickets for hit Broadway shows, mostly musicals. He also uncovered "kickbacks" from costume-makers to producers, "peculiar" financing, and improper accounting methods. Off-Broadway, some producers kept nonexistent "books." Lefkowitz reported that the hearings would develop "needed reforms and legislation," particularly in the realm of limited partnerships to protect investors from unbusinesslike and unethical producers.

The distress signals are flying high on the ramparts of Shubert Alley, at Sardi's East and Sardi's West. Howard Lindsay, co-author of the libretto for *Sound of Music,* says: "I don't know what is wrong with the theater, except it is very sick." David Merrick, during negotiations aimed at reducing dramatists' royalty structure, said: "We're in a big, leaky boat—dramatists and actors as well as producers."

But the most alarming note has been voiced by John F. Wharton in *The Crisis in the Free World Theatre.* He observed:

In order to have a sufficient number [of theater productions] there must be a sufficient number of entrepreneurs [who, in the theater, are the producers] who can bring together the talent, and the capital necessary for a production. The money, in the theater, is of unusual importance, for every production of a play is a new venture calling for venture capital, the most difficult kind of capital to obtain. Fortunately, the theater has had an instrinsic fascination for many venture capitalists, but it has, *up to now*, also offered a chance for reward commensurate with the risks.

Later, he sighed:

Let us repeat once more—if the Creative Core is to continue as part of a free enterprise system, it must attract venture capital. Every factor which the venture capitalist scrutinizes is shifting toward the negative. The trend cannot continue indefinitely, or the theater will require subsidy, or cease to exist.

Artistically, where is the Broadway musical theater going? Is it imprisoned by the so-called "integrated idea" in which songs—music and lyrics—express and shape the musical? (And is there any dramatically sound alternative?) Are lesser talented men taking the integrated idea and providing dialogue set to music, rather than songs which can be lifted out bodily from the show (Rodgers and Hammerstein's great genius) as well as move the story along? And if there isn't too much production, how can the veteran show writers as well as the younger talents develop and sharpen their talents and individual styles?

Since the 1950's, there seem to be two principal tendencies in the American musical theater: (1) the traditional approach, which is finding a pre-made, pretested, property (book, play, or short story) and crafting it into a musical comedy or play; (2) a more free, more *avant-garde* approach, represented by *The Fantasticks* and *Stop the World, I Want to Get Off*, which tell their stories unnaturalistically.

The philosophy of the traditional approach possibly was best expressed by a remark of Irving Berlin's. Not long ago, he told a newspaper interviewer that *My Fair Lady* was the best musical theater show he had ever seen. And it proved to him that "You don't have to be different to be good." Weeks later, in his Broadway offices, I asked the remarkable bouncy, seventy-six-year-old composer-lyricist about the statement he had made. He jumped up from his couch and said: "I will add to that. You don't have to be different to be good. And if you're *good*, you're different."

There is actually nothing new in form in *My Fair Lady*. It moves beautifully and fairly naturally from the first word uttered by dirt-streaked Eliza outside of the Royal Opera House—"Aaaoooowww"—to its close in the parlor of Professor Higgins. But, and this is the formidable but, the songs, the lyrics, the craftsmanship, the continuity, the sense of characterization and style are beautifully wrought.

Stop the World, I Want to Get Off, produced and written in Britain, is another kind of musical, freer in form. It leans heavily on the revue, and on pantomime. Its songs hardly match that of *My Fair Lady*. However, it represents a certain creative and poetical tendency.

Throughout the history of musical theater, it has been eclectic. In music and lyrics and in stagecraft, it has drawn upon the English musical hall, vaudeville, opera *bouffe*, Viennese operettas, burlesque, tap dancing, modern dancing, eccentric dancing, the revue, Gilbert and Sullivan, the comic monologue, and other genres. For "books" it has reached into everything—plays, published novels, stories, motion pictures, as well as upon original concepts.

Since the 1950's, the emphasis on having a successful literary or theatrical "property" as a basis for a musical has become less an idea and more of an ideology. All types of writing are now eligible for musicalization, even such "nonbooks" as the original "novel" by Shepherd Mead, a poorly written humorous sketch, which is the source of *How to Succeed in Business Without Really Trying*.

The trend is partly aesthetic, partly economic. Actually, there are few librettists, in this country or elsewhere. Creative writers seem to be attracted to the novel, the short story, the straight play, because in those forms they can control the work's destiny, and do not have to rely upon a composer or lyricist to bring it to life. Also, the dark mood of the twentieth century does not seem to evoke a light, satirical touch in them. Thus, composers, lyricists, comedy writers, "constructionists" who love the form have been attracted to musical-libretto writing. The work of the more serious writers, with its deeper probings, leads to more complex musical plays, in which the Broadway backer is still reluctant to invest. It may be doubtful, too, if the "creative writers" could easily master the grammar and rhetoric of musical theater, which may seem simple and artless but is one of the most difficult forms: the writing has to be economical and yet penetrate to the core of character and situation in a few quick lines. In a novel, a writer can go on and on. In the theater he cannot, and he must know how to write in such a way that the music and the lyrics "star." This is not easy for the professional literary workman to do, and accept.

The choosing of pre-made properties is also an economic factor, for if an initial piece of writing is successful, the authors and producers feel that they have some box-office insurance, that it should "go" again.

Regardless of the reasons, the trend toward precast properties displeases talented composer-lyricist Stephen Sondheim. Though a product of an Ivy League prep school and college (Williams) he produced the pungent lyrics for the switchblade masterpiece, *West Side Story*. On his own, he has also written the music and lyrics for *A Funny Thing Happened on My Way to the Forum*. So far, Sondheim has been connected with three successful musicals, all of which were "pre-made" in varying ways: *West Side Story*, a twentieth-century adaptation of *Romeo and Juliet;* "Gypsy" (for which he wrote the lyrics), based upon the memoirs of Gypsy Rose Lee; and *A Funny Thing*, the product of a third-century B.C. Roman dramatist, Plautus.

In his brownstone, ground-floor duplex on the East Side of Manhattan, packed with art objects, American board games, and a rare-hunting bow, Sondheim argued for a change in preformed libretto material. He asserted that the formula has had a viselike grip on American musical comedy for too long.

"What is commonly referred to as the Golden Age of Songwriting, when Gershwin and Kern and Rodgers were active, was an age of absolute formula. Formula always exists, and the theater is always in a state of transition, and if it isn't, then I think it's stagnated and dead. I hope that era never arrives.

"There's a great deal being done today that's formula-thought. Rodgers and Hammerstein introduced a concept with *Oklahoma*, and people are still writing Rodgers and Hammerstein musicals. I find this a rut. Instead of writers using what Rodgers and Hammerstein had to offer and inventing on top of it, and adding to it, and expanding it, they have been copying, and that seems to be a great mistake, a waste of time, and unlikely to be successful.

"They're choosing well-made properties, putting them on the stage, and adding some songs. I don't think that's the way musical theater is going to stay alive.

"Again that's copying the Rodgers and Hammerstein approach, to take a story with some seriousness, or at least some tone—usually a play—and pepper it with songs, instead of trying to see whether it should have music or not. Usually they take anything that looks as if it has song possibilities and they adapt it, and that's it. I find that boring."

Conceding that there is a dearth of librettists, Sondheim believes that it is easier to create original musicals with original stories. He said that writing an adaptation is just as hard as writing an original, perhaps harder. "You're stuck with certain preconceptions, some of which are voluntary and some involuntary. There are certain obligatory moments in all ready-written work, whereas in an unwritten work there are none. You proceed along in an unchartered path, and if an obligatory scene or song is coming up that you don't think is good or right, or that you don't like, you can take another path. Which is why I am more interested in originals or very loose adaptations of non-theater works. There's more of a chance of turning out a good, fresh, or exciting musical if you deal with original material, or material that is not so preformed that freedom is lost."

As to subject matter, Sondheim believes that *West Side Story* eased the barrier against certain themes, yet he warned that the barriers are never down. "There are always people, like there are always music publishers, who say this is too this, or too that. There are always producers and backers who will say this, too; those who will not judge it on its own terms but in terms of what they think the commercial market wants. David Merrick, at the moment, is of the opinion that what the public wants is experiment in musicals, which is an interesting turn of events. But it's one of the reasons he produced *Stop the World.*

"The public is anxious for out-of-the-ordinary musicals. The barriers are going down in both subject matter and form. That is what makes it a period of transition."

The boyish, black-haired composer-lyricist, an expert at word-games, also believes in "fiddling around with forms, varying forms of musical patterns, dramatic techniques, the handling of sung-speech. Most theater-composers do, because unless you do, boredom can set in during an evening."

Sondheim cited the example of the Jerome Kern song, "They Didn't Believe Me," which dates back to 1914. Its structure is the orthodox thirty-two bars, "but actually in a very subtle and not so subtle way, it's quite a departure. I don't know any other song that's ever been written that way, with that form. The phrases recur in different orders in the song. The second half of the song, what seems like the second half, is really quite a variation on the first half. A phrase is left out, another phrase is interpolated. It's very strange. Kern, who's written as many 'standards' as anybody, was always fiddling around with forms. But I don't think he fiddled around with forms consciously, and said 'O.K., I'm going to write thirty-four bars instead of thirty-two.' Again it was the musical content that dictated it. And that's why his songs sound constantly fresh," Sondheim said.

There have also been successful experiments with twelve-tone in the Broadway musical theater, according to Sondheim. "The whole development section of 'Cool' in *West Side Story* is based on a twelve-tone row, and is, in fact a twelve-tone fughetto, and people accept it easily. They don't even know it's there, which is exactly the mark of its success. But dissonant songwriting has already been used in theater, and I don't see any reason why it shouldn't move on to twelve-tone songwriting. Most of the score of *West Side Story* is dissonant.

"Everybody said that they couldn't hum the score of *West Side Story* when it first came out. The only reason that it is 'melodic' now, or 'hummable' is that they have been exposed to it over and over again, so that it's come into their consciousness with some ease. There were no song hits from the show until the movie came out three years later, and then the repeated hearings made people like the songs."

Sondheim believes that twelve-tone atonal system and electronic music have not yet been explored in the American musical theater. "There's quarter-tone music, too. And experimentation doesn't always consist of new systems. It consists of new ways of exploiting old systems. Experimentation with form, so to speak; short songs, songs with no refrains, sung pieces without an orchestra going on. Sung speech, all sorts of things, an amalgamation of ancient techniques used in new and fresh ways."

Though many of Broadway's most important composers, lyricists, and producers would disagree, Sondheim fears music that is "too accessible." Said he: "I'm often suspicious of songs that are immediately hummable and memorable because it usually means it's reminiscent of something else; that's one reason they're immediately hummable. Fresh melodies take a good deal of rehearing before they seep into the consciousness enough to make you go around whistling it all day long.

"And that has happened in much less pretentious cases than *West Side Story*. For example, take 'Bewitched, Bothered and Bewildered.' Rodgers writes very fresh and odd melodies, some of which take years to catch on. The reason this is so is that they don't fall immediately on the ear with a sense of attraction or grace, not right away. They're odd and they strike strange poses and they hit very peculiar notes and they startle people. And quite often they take a long time to catch on."

Because the Broadway theater writer is aware that he's in a "hit-or-miss" market, it has thrust a lot of pressure on him that has had an impact on his inner world. It "prevents a certain amount of spontaneity, and a certain amount of joy, and even takes longer to put on because of that. Everything is more carefully looked at."

In the off-Broadway playhouses, near the handmade space-shoes shops, the pottery outlets, the sit and sit *espresso* coffee houses, the same problems that plague Broadway exists off-Broadway, in a miniaturized state. Ticket prices are high, and it is difficult to see any off-Broadway musical for less than $3. Orchestra seats to most of them are $4.60. Production costs are not inexpensive. The *Fantasticks* cost

$16,500 to produce. But a recent off-Broadway musical version of *The Scarlet Pimpernel* was just announced for production with a $40,000 budget. Also, and very much more to the point, few off-Broadway productions ever make any money.

Approximately half-a-dozen musical productions (bookshows and revues) reach off-Broadway annually, representing about $120,000 to $150,000 capitalization. Most budgets for off-Broadway musicals run from a lean $10,000 up to $45,000.

There are many bumbling singers, and doe-eyed ingenues off-Broadway, and there are dancers whose huffing and puffing make the audience tired. But off-Broadway has also provided a vehicle for talented young people—singers, dancers, choreographers, backstage technicians, producers—to perfect their craft. Producers have to learn, too, otherwise where are the future entrepreneurs going to come from? Off-Broadway, too, has put on musical productions that might never have been produced on gay, calculating Shubert Alley.

Since the 1950's, the off-Broadway musical picture has been brightened, at this writing, by few real top-drawer musicals. Two of quality come to mind. One is in its fourth year, *The Fantasticks*, a sort of free-form musical, with a fine though frequently derivative score by Harvey Schmidt and Tom Jones. The other, *Riverwind*, whose words and music by John Jennings are far superior to the middle-class soap-opera theme of the woman who tries to bring romance back into her marriage by having her husband and herself return to their "honeymoon cottage." A commercially successful show, but far less creative, was the full-length, out-and-out parody of operettas, *Little Mary Sunshine*, by Rick Besoyan. (Ordinarily, parody of this sort turns up in a musical sketch in a revue.)

The maverick and experimental sides of off-Broadway's drama tradition is not equaled in its musical productions so far. Most of the musical productions have been rather standardized. It has done its best job as a source for "revivals," giving audiences a glimpse of the evolution of musical theater, through such productions as *Leave It to Jane* (Kern-Bolton-Wodehouse), *Best Foot Forward*, and *The Boys from Syracuse*. One of its most successful revivals was Kurt Weill's and Brecht's *The Threepenny Opera* with an English translation of lyrics by Marc Blitzstein.

There has also been a revue explosion off-Broadway. Revues have been pouring out of Greenwich Village and elsewhere in Manhattan, and in Chicago. But they do not have much musicality. These shows are mostly sketch- and blackout-oriented. The music they employ is largely of a parody type. Years ago, some of the greatest songs came out of revues, notably Irving Berlin's *Music Box Revues* and Schwartz and Dietz's *The Bandwagon*. Today's revues are largely impoverished in terms of music and lyrics of quality. Word-heavy light verse overcomes any sense of song structure.

However, young writing talents have gotten a chance to develop off-Broadway. Composer-lyricist Jerry Herman, who later produced *Milk and Honey*, first made a splash in off-Broadway revues, including a show called *Parade*. And several *Shoe-String* revues, produced by Ben Bagley, nourished such writers as Sheldon Harnick, lyricist Lee Adams, and Composer Charles Strouse. Adams and Strouse later created the score for *Bye Bye Birdie*. Also, Jay Thompson, who composed two well-received one-acters, had his days in the sun off-Broadway. Thus, off-Broadway, while not being an outstanding source of exciting new musicals, has provided an apprentice training school, a sort of postgraduate High School of Music and Art and musical comedy Juilliard.

Campus theaters and theaters in civic cultural centers have not made important contributions as yet to American musical theater. For off-Broadway and Broadway there are some workshop writing seminars conducted by ASCAP and Broadcast Music Inc. that have made writers conscious of the techniques of musical theater.

Few of the outstanding creative talents of Broadway are drawn to off-Broadway. One noted Broadway lyricist decries off-Broadway and calls it "degenerate." He said: "I won't go off-Broadway. It's degenerate. You have to run around pipes. The actors are paid starvation wages—$40 or $50 a week. You have to skimp on artistic effects. Why should I, as an artist, have to skimp on artistic effects? It's humiliating and degrading."

There are simple, inexpensive methods to pare down production costs of Broadway musicals. You can put on no musicals which have more than two pianos and one set, preferably a suggestive and abstract set, capable of being fabricated from corrugated cardboard remnants. Costumes should be fashioned from multi-colored burlap or twenty-cent-a-yard dime store cotton. The singers, of course, should double as dancers, and perhaps the same person would be the choreographer-director. Better still, eliminate the singers and dancers and use puppets. Or forget the theater completely and do "concert versions" of all the new musicals with a bare stage and a lectern. A narrator could narrate the story, and two singers might interpret the score played by the composer on one of the two upright pianos (they're cheaper to rent than massive grand pianos).

Failing these cut-to-the-bone economies, can anything less drastic be done to pare the half-million and higher budgets represented by a Broadway musical? Producer Leland Hayward has actually suggested that playwrights visualize their conceptions with as few "sets" as possible. Some assert that "stars" and the creative elements (composers-lyricists) take less money. Some believe that producers should be as thrifty as a New England housewife. Some believe the ball game is lost, though the lights are bright in Sardi's and the attractive girls, crewcut producers, and the show merchandisers buzz with theater-talk. Some are cutting costs by cutting out-of-town try-outs, which is practically suicide in the case of a big musical. Recently, the producers have championed another money-maker—bars in theaters.

As to current theatrical financing, there are contradictory trends. Venture capital is not venturing out so easily. Private investors are increasingly wary. But there has been some fresh money poured into the Broadway scene by the record companies. Increasingly, record companies are backing Broadway musicals in return for the rights to cast albums of the productions. Not long ago, ABC-Paramount Theaters, in association with AM-Par Records, its recording wing, put aside a $1,000,000 fund for composer-entrepreneur Jule Styne to help produce three musicals. MCA, since its takeover of Decca Records and Universal Pictures, may decide to back Broadway musicals, for its corporate label, Decca, and also the right to make a film musical out of the production. Other record companies may also invest, depending on the show, the producer's background, stature of writers and director.

As matters stand there is fresh "venture capital" readily available—if the script, score, cast, producing auspices are considered strong—by three leading firms, RCA Victor, Capitol Records, and Columbia. Decca in recent years hasn't been too active in the theater sector, although with MCA behind it perhaps it may join in subsidizing musical shows in return for original-cast-album rights. So far the smaller firms find the financial aspects too heady, too risky, although one or two have taken a slight flier, such as Kapp Records with *Once Upon A Mattress,* and *Donnybrook!*

The reluctance of the smaller firms to venture forth on the Gay White Way is based upon the initial big-money investment in the show and the $25,000 to $30,000 budget required to record the cast album. And if the morning-after reviews are bad, you cannot *give* the album away.

There doesn't seem to be any orthodox way of meeting two ingrained problems of modern musical theater: high costs and shrinking profits. And you cannot eliminate failure. Many shows do not succeed. It is impossible to fabricate hit formulas, out of obeisance either to the late Oscar Hammerstein, the theater of the absurd, the "smart talk" of Broadway ticket brokers, or any other theory.

Can anything else be done besides shaving costs and concept-miniaturization? One way out would be to appeal to *Cosa Nostra;* they seem to have illicit millions laying around. After all, prohibition gangsters did put money into musicals in the 1920's. Another thought might be to detach Manhattan's theater district, set up a new government, headed perhaps by restaurateur Vincent Sardi, and he might graciously become a recipient of foreign aid, just like any South American country.

There are cultural foundation funds, and those nasty words, "government subsidy," which could supplement private theater-producing. A government-subsidized theater flourishes throughout Europe. Towns vie with one another for the best theater and the best theater company.

August Heckscher, formerly special consultant on the arts to the late President Kennedy, pinpointed the problem in a statement launching an inquiry into the performing arts, sponsored by the Twentieth Century Fund and the Rockefeller Brothers Fund: "In the end, the individual artist is what counts, but the individual artist, without the support of a sound economic substructure, is not able to reach his audience, or to attain the fulfillment of his talents."

Famed drama critic Kenneth Tynan is literary manager of the British National Theater. Recently he told a symposium on culture in New York City that if subsidy is a concept that bothers people, they should try to remember that we all subsidize the art around us: "Who pays for the vast advertising campaigns launched on behalf of 'pop' movies, 'pop' records, 'pop' magazines? We—the consumers—do. Eventually, it is always the consumer who pays."

The United States is not against the theory of government subsidy. In the New Deal days the Federal Theater Project produced countless productions of the classics, journalistic "living newspaper" shows, Gilbert and Sullivan, and children's shows. Admission was minimal. Today, we are making baby steps toward the same type of civic approach. Increasingly, state and city municipalities are subsidizing touring productions of Shakespeare, in association with school boards of education.

The government today provides subsidies for the farmer; sponsors scientific and medical research; helps education; buys books, filmstrips, and recordings for schools under the National Defense Act. It may be just a matter of time before Congress does pass bills involving some theater subsidy, which would divorce art from money-making.

If this occurs, paradise won't be attained. There are certain problems involved in government subsidy of the theater that cannot be

glossed over, and swept under the marble corridors of the Capitol—
problems of bureaucracy, the expression of unpopular ideas, and the
freedom to experiment in new styles and forms. Yet, the production
of plays and musicals through venture and "status capital" has resulted
in its own unlikable forms and stultifying attitudes. There is a "packaging approach," a theater-party approach in casting, and a prodigious
"be safe" approach in content and form.

And the prices should come way down, too, with a nonprofit subsidy
approach. Right now, theatrical economics dictates a heavy price structure, which could be worse. Theater-going has actually become off-
limits for most Americans and their families, except on special holidays
or anniversaries. Several large blocs of our people can no longer afford
to go on any regular basis—the teenager, the "unemployed" college
student, and the older people on Social Security whose fixed income
does not permit them the luxury. Civil-service workers and those in
the lower-income brackets cannot afford Broadway's prices. Consequently, Broadway shows have become a theater-party affair, an ex-
pense-account venture, looked up to as a form of middle-and-upper-
class pleasure.

The risky nature of producing Broadway musicals and the high prices
consumers have to pay to see them are lamentable. And depressing as
these facts seem (and they cannot be sweetened or puréed) still Broadway musical theater continues as though there'll always be a tomorrow.
And the Broadway musical shows still carry a heavyweight punch in
the popular music scene.

Millions see musicals in New York City, including many out-of-
towners. And they spread the ideas, standards, and music everywhere.
Also, road companies of the successful musicals tour the country, and
thousands of college and community groups put on their own homemade productions of the best musicals. Thus they have become a living
heritage of the best urban writing. During the summer, the musical
tents from coast to coast play the big musicals under the big canvas
tops. The tents reach millions, and they provide the people with repertory musicals at fairly inexpensive prices.

Practically all of this is created by the fabulous invalid. The fabulous
invalid wears a wrinkled stare, an anxious brow. But he still sings and
dances, and his standards are perhaps the best in the world. And his
impact is not to be denied as an exciting form—loose, free, fluid,
colorful.

Musicals are as frothy as a *charlotte russe,* but they can also contain images of importance, comments upon the world in which we live.
Some repeat the cliché that musicals somehow are picturesque retreats

from the world, dressed up with music and pretty girls in dancers' leotards, or less. Yet *Finian's Rainbow* wittily told the story of a white southern senator who turned black, and through the metamorphosis got to know something of what prejudice is. *South Pacific,* one of the musical theater's all-time hits, displayed Nellie Forbush's acceptance of Emile's native children. And although *My Fair Lady* didn't propagandize, ingrained in the transformation of the flower girl into a lady is the Shavian sociological theory that one can grow and expand one's talents, given good environment and training.

The late Oscar Hammerstein was a man of great moral fervor, and he compressed his beliefs of what the theater can do in a song from *Me and Juliet,* in which he characterized an audience as a "giant."

The Big Black Giant*

One night it's a laughing giant,
Another night a weeping giant,
One night it's a coughing giant,
Another night a sleeping giant.
Every night you fight the giant
And maybe, if you win,
You send him out a nicer giant
Than he was when he came in

*Copyright © 1953 by Richard Rodgers and Oscar Hammerstein II. Williamson Music, Inc. New York, N.Y. owner of publication and allied rights.

23 · FROM THE HOLLYWOOD SOUND TRACKS

"Top Hat"
"Cheek to Cheek"
"The Trolley Song"
"Lullabye of Broadway"
"I Only Have Eyes for You"
"A Foggy Day in London Town"
"Let's Call the Whole Thing Off"

Remember when millions sat in darkened movie houses and heard such songs sung by Dick Powell, Judy Garland, and Fred Astaire, and they watched the leggy, twinkling dance routines of Ruby Keeler and Eleanor Powell? And can you recall the visual splendor of chorus girls— enough of them for a full-time Peace Corps—twining in and out of crystalline formations devised by those West Pointers of choreography, Busby Berkely and Hermes Pan?

Lyricist Larry Hart once satirized the cinemography of some of these musicals. "You saw," wrote Hart in *Theatre Arts*, "overhead shots of coryphees forming a star, or the keys of a typewriter; and the crooners singing to an open fire-lance, in which shimmering over the flames is the face of the girl you can't forget."

For approximately twenty years, from the time Al Jolson opened up his vocal cords on October 6, 1927 in *The Jazz Singer* to the early 1950's, movie musicals spun off the Hollywood production line with the regularity of the Sante Fe leaving from Chicago to Los Angeles. Singers were under contract, and they worked regularly. Songwriters—platoons of them—were under contract, and they produced over three hundred songs a year, many of which moved from the sound tracks into the mainstream of U. S. popular music.

A few statistics tell the story. In 1947-48, a *Billboard* survey disclosed that the following musical pictures were released:

35 straightaway musicals
20 films with songs interpolated
7 Westerns with music
8 musical short subjects

In 1962, a year-end review in the magazine, *Film Review,* noted that

303

there were only two pictures with original scores: *The World of the Brothers Grimm* (music and lyrics by Bob Merrill) and *Gay Purree* (Harold Arlen and E. Y. Harburg), a cartoon musical with songs sung by Judy Garland and Robert Goulet. There were also adaptations of Broadway musical hits—*West Side Story, Gypsy, The Music Man, State Fair* and *Jumbo*. For *State Fair*, Richard Rodgers conceived some additional material. 20th Century Fox also turned out an item called *Swinging Along*, which contained some previously recorded songs by Ray Charles that were inserted into the sound track to enliven the picture. Another musical came from Hal Wallis, an Elvis Presley item called *Girls, Girls, Girls*.

It is perhaps symbolic that in recent years the most active star in Hollywood musicals is recording star Elvis Presley. He has appeared in and sung in more than eight musical films, all of which contain handcrafted Elvis Presley-type songs; the sound tracks of these films are dutifully issued by RCA Victor. The films include: *King Creole, G. I. Blues, Blue Hawaii, Love Me Tender, Kid Galahad,* and *Fun in Acapulco*.

The muting of the motion picture musical has silenced many Hollywood sound stages, and this, of course, is a pity, for it has meant that a major genre for quality songs has been laid low. Years ago, there were countless musicals of all kinds—original screen musicals, catch-all revue-type musicals, screen biographies, operettas, remakes of Broadway musicals, and films built around a musical comedy star. Specific vehicles were built and prepared for the singing and dancing of Ginger Rogers and Fred Astaire.

Many were backstage musicals like *Broadway Melody*. There were countless armed service and college musicals. *Meet Me in St. Louis* portrayed the charming Americana of yesteryear and *Little Miss Marker*, with Shirley Temple, caught the sentimental "mug-land" of Damon Runyon's Broadway. Occasionally, there would be a maverick socially conscious musical. One of them had a joyous title, *Hallelujah, I'm a Bum*, with music by Richard Rodgers and words by Larry Hart. From this score came the beautiful ballad, "You Are Too Beautiful."

As a celluloid footnote, there were also all-Negro musicals. Mantan Moreland, a character actor who achieved modest fame as the stereotyped saucer-eyed butler in "Charlie Chan" detective films, tells of Negro musicals produced during the 1930's in twenty-one days for little more than $25,000. These were shown in segregated theaters down South, and in the Negro neighborhoods in the North. One such film musical was a satirical cowboy saga with songs, entitled *Harlem on the Prairie*. "I was the right-hand man to the sheriff," he says.

The film musicals of yesteryear were very popular, despite the fact that many were largely *papier mâché* and ascending staircases. Many contained such unfortunate staging as the sequence in one film in which Frank Sinatra, in shimmering white tie and tails, and standing atop a ramp, sang "Ol' Man River." The Hammerstein-Kern song is, of course, a work-song with lyrics suggestive of grimy, dirt-caked, back-breaking toil. Frequently, too, the arrangers concocted elaborate Graustarkian treatments for silly little tunes.

And yet from these musicals came a superb collection of songs: rhythm songs ("Forty-second Street," "Lullabye of Broadway"), straw hat gaiety ("Mimi"), dance-type ("The Carioca," "Top Hat," "Cheek to Cheek"), amusing songs for the moppet set ("Who's Afraid of the Big Bad Wolf?," "Swingin' on a Star"), ballads ("Long Ago and Far Away," "Love Walked Right In"), witty duets ("Baby, It's Cold Outside").

The screen musicals provided a vehicle for Rodgers and Hart, Jerome Kern, Cole Porter, George and Ira Gershwin, Arthur Schwartz, Al Dubin and Harry Warren, Harold Arlen, Johnny Mercer, Jule Styne, Gordon and Revel, E. Y. Harburg. It gave countless other composers and lyricists a chance to grow, and to develop a popular music approach that the rest of the world is still trying to attain: a way of using colloquial words and music in poetic, witty, and touching ways, in combination with dance and story.

Save for remakes of Broadway shows, the original film musical has been hard to find. Today's movie-goers do see a few new "musicals," featuring the voices of teenage idols, and they have to listen to a level of writing in music and lyrics that will make adults—who remember the George and Ira Gershwin scores, the Harold Arlen scores—hold their heads. A mighty popular art has been gutted, and denigrated to the teen-musical, or the exploitation-type of musical built around a record personality.

Do audiences miss the old movie musicals? An editorial, "Let's Bring Back the Movie Musical," which ran in *Show*, the publication founded by A & P heir, Huntington Hartford, and the grocery shoppers of America, observed that there is "great hunger for good songs, good dances and good wholesome comedy, the sort of thing that abounded for some reason in the movies of the threadbare Thirties and the dazed Forties and which now have withered and utterly dropped away, leaving the field to pallid recaps of Broadway hits. . . . But if not truly great, these movies required high spirits (in a desperate time) and high skill, and although we wouldn't give up Ingmar Bergman for the world, we do wish the old formula which made these movies so infinitely enjoyable would be reemployed."

There are four principal reasons given why the Hollywood community does not make original movie musicals on a fairly regular basis as part of the year's product: (1) They are too expensive to make in contrast to a straightaway dramatic or comedy film. (2) They do not do well in the foreign market. (3) It is quite difficult to find original stories for musicals. (4) The actual filming of a musical picture is harder because of the studio break-up, and the dismantling of the musical departments of most studios.

Perhaps the most crucial reason is economic. Since television, the U. S. movie box office has shrunk. According to the New York Motion Picture Association of America, in 1962 American film studios earned more money abroad than they did in this country. Foreign returns brought in 54.6 per cent of the world gross receipts. It was estimated that in 1962, American films earned approximately $310 million abroad. Ralph Hetzel, of the association, reported that about 15,000 persons were employed to handle distribution in foreign lands, and that United States film "occupy 60 per cent of the screen time in theaters of the free world."

In other words, U. S. film-makers eye every production with a global look. And abroad, the musicals, with some exceptions, have not done well. Frank Leyendecker, editor of *Box Office* says: "The Europeans don't like our musicals. They don't understand them. They can't dub the songs easily. The Germans are still writing operettas and making movies of them. But we don't like operettas, and the movies are never booked here. *West Side Story* is the exception. They just seemed to like it." Similarly, Arthur Mayer, the film observer, has noted that our musicals have never been as popular outside the United States as other types of musicals.

The void left by the Hollywood movie musical has been plaguing the popular music and record business. Hollywood's movie songs, written largely for the broad gamut of movie-goers (young people, middle-aged people, young marrieds, old folks) brought about a more adult lyric, a more mature brand of music. And each score contained eight to twelve songs, which were plugged hard by movie firms. Moreover, the near-extinction of the movie musical left more air time, and more air play, and more attention to the poverty-stricken inanities and burps concocted by amateurs, mediocrities, and musical hacks. One of the key threads in the decline of popular music has been the gradual obliteration of the original Hollywood musical.

"Musicals are a mystery," lyricist-librettist E. Y. (Yip) Harburg said, his round face tanned by a summer at Cape Cod.

"Most people don't know anything about them. They pretend to, but they don't. The modern musical play is a highly complex art form, since it involves the coordination of the libretto, lyrics, music, choreography, and orchestration with performers who must not only be singers and dancers, but also actors.

"You could have all sorts of beautiful ideas in film musicals. And you could make wonderful money. But nobody is interested. With whatever success I've had—certainly my name opens doors—I've tried many times. I'm just sick of it. I won't do it any more."

Harburg sat in his Fifth Avenue offices that he shares with his attorneys. He wore a gray-flannel sports jacket and gray-flannel slacks. With his feet planted firmly on the desk and the winter sun streaming in on him, he reminisced about the days of the Hollywood musicals.

Youthful and perceptive, though gray-haired and in his sixties, E. Y. Harburg has spent most of his mature years as a lyricist and librettist on Broadway, shaping such shows as *Bloomer Girl, Flahooley, The Happiest Girl in the World,* and, of course, *Finian's Rainbow.*

However, he was, as the phrase goes, "gainfully employed" by Hollywood during the 1930's and 40's and turned out songs for Hollywood musicals—sometimes as a contract writer, sometimes as a writer for a specific film musical. Together with Harold Arlen, he won the Academy Award for the single song, "Over the Rainbow." Actually, the entire score, and production scheme of *The Wizard of Oz* (1939), from which "Over the Rainbow" came, represents one of the most memorable musical achievements ever written directly for the screen anywhere in the world. It is one of the few musicals in which there is a continuity of style, and in which the succession of warm, witty, humorous, fantastic songs actually tell the story, with a minimum of straight dialogue, much like a Broadway musical.

Why aren't there more film musicals? The lyricist again stressed the economic hurdles. Hollywood, like the stage, is working for the box-office smash—for what is "sure-fire." In such a climate innovation cannot flourish.

"Who is the average Hollywood producer? Is he an originator? Is he a creative mind? No, he's a businessman. And a businessman is a man who looks at his ledgers and balance sheets and says, 'Well, if *Love in a Bathtub* made money, let's make another version of it.' That's how the big executive keeps his job. There are a few who have creative minds and free spirits, but no free money. Since everything depends on the big-name star, and the big-name star depends on big money, the maverick producer with the fresh ideas is out of luck.

"My co-authors and I can't even get *Finian's Rainbow* done as a movie. Certainly 'Finian's' is one of the top-ranking shows of all time according to Tams-Witmark, the largest musical comedy library in the business. *Finian's Rainbow* is more often revived throughout the United States than any other musical. It plays in amateur, and professional companies including colleges, schools, etc., week in and week out, and has grossed about $20 million since its Broadway opening. And yet, because of its off-beat quality, Hollywood has shied clear of it."

Returning to the so-called "Golden Age of Film Musicals," the 1930's and 40's, which were a wild and happy time for American songwriters: "We used to work a good part of a year on a picture and we nursed it. Among songwriters there was a great, friendly, though competitive spirit, a camaraderie, and a pride of craftsmanship. By and large, they were a tribe with a lot of good feeling and respect for each other. We couldn't wait for a score to come along so we could play it at the piano, study it, admire it, see its fine points and learn from it.

"Many nights, at the Gershwin's, when George was alive, all the fine writers would gather several times a week, and play their new songs. It was invigorating and inspiring. We went home stimulated with new ideas and the urge for further expression."

This was an especially productive period for American popular music, according to the veteran lyricist. "The songwriters really knew their business, and they were writing memorable songs, most of which are now the backbone of all our radio and television programs."

Harburg went to Hollywood in 1934 at the age of thirty-two, after turning from contributions of light verse in F.P.A.'s newspaper column to concocting revue material for such shows as *Earl Carroll's Vanities* (with Jack Benny and Jimmy Savo), *Americana, Ballyhoo,* (Bob Hope's first show), *Walk a Little Faster* (with Beatrice Lillie) and *Ziegfeld Follies* (Fanny Brice).

In Hollywood, he says, there was a frontier spirit in the air. "It was not only one of competition, but of each wanting to add a little originality and quality. Such flowering periods seem to recur in different cultural eras. Why was the Elizabethan era such a great one?

"What sets it off? That is a question for sociologists. As far as America goes, the 20's, 30's, and a part of the 40's saw an outpouring of excellent songs. It has been America's finest contribution to that part of world culture. In fact we really started sophisticated songwriting. American songwriters went many steps beyond the simple folk and naïve light operetta songs to a more dimensional melody and lyric that captured people everywhere.

"If you were a Jerome Kern or a Gershwin you could elect to work at home, though you always had an office to go to. If you were one of the lesser writers at Warner Brothers, you were expected to punch the clock, and get in and out on organization-man time. They thought it helped the creative process. It didn't. Because you could do more on the fly, late midnight or early dawn, than you could sitting in an office. Inspiration comes swifter on Cloud Nine than in Studio Nine. MGM recognized that you could work anywhere. In an automobile, for instance. Harold Arlen and I always worked at home or in the garden. In fact we wrote 'The Wizard of Oz' in the swimming pool."

Some of the motion pictures that Harburg wrote for were the early Warner Brothers "Goldigger" pictures, *Stage Struck* and *The Singing Fool* for Al Jolson.

Harburg explained the economics of Hollywood songwriting: "The good songwriters were paid per picture. Some were on a yearly salary. Because it was a year-in, year-out industry, they could afford to do that. Lots of lyric and music writers were signed up for several years on annual contracts, which ranged from $300 or $500 a week to $2,500 or $3,000.

"On a picture basis, it was a flat sum usually. You'd get $40,000 or $50,000 a picture. For *The Wizard of Oz* I think we got $40,000, which was not high at the time. Some of the big teams of songwriters were paid $75,000 to $100,000 per film. Later on, a chosen few got percentages of the picture. These were the prices and patterns through the 30's until the war, and the rise of television."

Even during those years, the title-song field was active. According to Harburg, the price for a title song was negotiable—$5,000, $10,000, $15,000, sometimes as low as $500. "It would depend," he says, "on your ability, on your status in the business, and your standing. Writers usually had agents. William Morris was very active. And Louis Shurr was big at the time. And then there were a lot of smaller agents around. They were as ubiquitous as used car lots.

"Most of the Hollywood studios paid its help much like any large industrial firm. You went to the cashier's window, and got your paycheck. But Warner Brothers apparently was fond of delivering weekly salaries to some of its select people. Every week, a courier on a motorcycle would zoom up and hand Harold Arlen and me an envelope. I still have memories of a scooter coming to a halt outside our workshop home."

Save for a hiatus in the late 1920's, when people suddenly tired of the words-and-music extravaganzas, Hollywood musicals were produced on a mass-production basis. Production schedules called for a certain number of musicals along with dramas, comedies, biographies.

As Harburg put it: "This was a great rolling thing. Like a steel mill with so much output every year. They knew where they were going, for their product was pre-sold via the blessings of block booking. The days of mass movie production are gone. It is now in the hands of television, delivered free, but added to your milk bill and aspirin bill."

Of *The Wizard of Oz*, he disclosed a few interesting behind-the-scenes facts concerning the musicalization of the Frank Baum classic. First, many felt that the musical would be a "prestige picture," not necessarily commercial. Many at MGM were against its making. The director tossed out "Over the Rainbow" three times. He claimed it "slowed up the film." Only fantastic in-fighting by Arthur Freed, Arlen, and Harburg saved the song and sequence (one of the world's most famous celluloid moments) from the cutting room floor.

Further, Harburg revealed that he himself, though credited as the lyricist, wrote some of the scenes where song cues were necessary. "I wrote the scenes in which the Tin Man gets a heart and the Scarecrow gets a brain, which the book never resolved. I think the book gave them pills. But I thought it would be more enlightening to have the Wizard give the Scarecrow a diploma for a brain, the Tin Man a watch for a heart, and the Cowardly Lion a medal for courage. It was a satiric commentary on our whole 'Image Culture.' I think it added not only stature to the book, but a resolution which it lacked."

The film, starring Judy Garland, Ray Bolger, Frank Morgan, and Jack Haley, was begun in 1937 and released in 1939. It cost $3 million to produce, a lot of money at that time, for the country was still in the midst of the depression. It has since become a screen classic—and a profitable one—and it is now frequently shown on TV as an annual "spectacular."

Harburg conceded that many of the screen musicals were third-rate in story ("mono-dimensional"), staging, and approach. "Once people became accustomed to the big parade and the routines and the inane dancing, and nothing to offer in content, why the thing became 'old-hat.' Now television has come in and is offering the public for free, the same inanities and dance routines that the Hollywood musicals gave them."

But one thing television isn't doing is producing popular music as good and as plentiful as that produced during these two decades of the twentieth century—the 1930's and the 40's in Hollywood. It could do so again, or at least that is the view of this experienced Broadway and Hollywood lyricist.

But just like Nelson Eddy appearing in the masculine red-and-blue uniform of the Canadian Mounties to rescue the virginal lady in distress, Jeanette MacDonald, in those filmed operettas, there is always Sigmund Romberg—and hope. And the hope has come from an unlikely source: movie sound tracks.

A liner note to a United Artists album of the film music of *McClintock*, starring John Wayne, states: "In the late 20's, sound revolutionized the motion picture—first the stars talking, then singing, and gradually background music became paramount in assisting the Director to enrich and vitalize the story being filmed. Today the composer-conductor entrusted with the creating of the musical score for a picture is screened as carefully for his assignment as the star and the director."

This is not precisely accurate. But these days, great care is lavished on movie sound tracks, for they have become, surprisingly enough, money-makers on LP's, and key movie themes have developed into important musical copyrights.

A listing of an omnibus collection "Original Sound Tracks and Music from the Great Motion Pictures (United Artists Records) demonstrates that very little film music is left unrecorded.

Side One
    Theme from *The V.I.P.'s*—Leroy Holmes Orch. (M. Rozsa)
    More (From *Mondo Cane*—Riz Ortolani Orch. (Ortolani-Olivero–Newell)
    "Lawrence of Arabia"—Ferrante & Teicher Orch. (M. Jarre)
    "How the West Was Won"—The Hollywood Sound Stage Orch. (Darby–Newman)
    "Never on Sunday"—Moras Hadjidakis Orch. (M. Hadjidakis)
    "The Wishing Star" (From *Taras Bulba*)—Frank Waxman Orch. (F. Waxman—M. David)
    "James Bond Theme" (From *Dr. No*)—Leroy Holmes Orch.
    Theme from *The Apartment*—The Hollywood Sound Stage Orch. (C. Williams)
Side Two
    Theme from *Irma La Douce*—Andre Previn Orch. (Langdon & Previn)
    Love theme from *Phaedra*—Mikis Theodorakis Orch. (Theodorakis)
    March from the Film "The Great Escape"—Elmer Bernstein Orch. (Bernstein)
    Caesar and Cleopatra theme (from "Cleopatra") Ferrante & Teicher Orch. (A. North)
    "Song of Love" (from *Divorce Italian Style*) Carlo Rustichelli Orch. (C. Rustichelli)
    Theme from *Mutiny on the Bounty*—Ferrante & Teicher Orch. (B. Kaper)
    Theme from *Exodus*—The Hollywood Sound Stage Orch. (E. Gold)

The original Hollywood "song musical" may be temporarily extinct but the movie sound track has changed its celluloid spots, and its status. Once movie background music was looked upon as a utilitarian brand of music, of importance only within the context of the film. It was eyed and dismissed as a form of music necessary to point up story climaxes, and to be expressive of changing moods and unsaid emotions. But as the years went by Hollywood decided to take the themes—the most melodic, the most memorable—and get them on record, mainly as a form of promotion for the film.

Through the years some of these themes became extraordinarily popular on radio and on single records—"The Tara Theme" from *Gone With the Wind,* Charlie Chaplin's "Terry Theme" from *Limelight.* Later on, with the birth of the LP, film producers went further, and with record producers they released the complete tracks on long-playing records. Record collectors apparently welcomed music from the films. Subsequently, a new type of long-playing album appeared—the film music anthology. Now there are hundreds of film-music collections played in every conceivable style from big-band swing and quiet jazz combos, to the sweet-voiced zither.

At the same time, the movie music sound tracks from a single production have become very important in the popular music structure. During the week of November 30, 1963, the following Hollywood albums (primarily nonvocal) were on the best selling lists:

Mondo Cane—Sound Track (UA)
Lawrence of Arabia—Sound Track (Colpix)
How the West Was Won—Sound Track-MGM (contains vocal music also)
The Great Escape—Sound Track (UA)
Cleopatra—Sound Track (20th Century Fox)

Hollywood has always employed talented composers to write film scores: Max Steiner, Miklas Rozsa, Dmitri Tiomkin, and Alex North. But what they composed wasn't considered vital, except as dramatic contribution to the film. Now the cardinal themes from motion pictures—and the complete sound track itself—have become "commercial." And, of course, even if they are not profitable, the publicity they get for motion pictures is, as they used to say in the happier, optimistic days of Hollywood, "colossal."

Sid Rechetnik in *Fame,* a Hollywood trade publication, once pointed out the bread-and-butter side of motion picture music exploitation. He described the activity of Arnold Maxim, head of MGM Records, to promote films produced by the parent company, MGM Films.

Rechetnik wrote: "A record of this type (a single plucked from a movie sound track) receives 10,000 to 15,000 performances daily by disc jockeys across the country over the nation's 7,000 radio stations."

He quoted Maxim as follows: "Imagine, the promotional impact of having a film title mentioned many thousands of times every day across the nation, weeks before the release of the picture."

For this reason, the movie-connected record companies are ecstatic about movie sound tracks. Practically every important new film is generally covered by the release of a theme from the film by the top instrumental combinations under contract to the record company; and the release of the sound track. Film publicists also collaborate with record publicists to achieve the maximum exposure over the air. For the few thousand dollars that it costs them to produce a recording from the sound track, the film company receives a million dollars worth of publicity.

Popular themes which have enormously helped films include the theme from *Never on Sunday* (More than 400 recordings of the main theme have been released); the theme from *The Apartment;* "Song of the Moulin Rouge," the "Marching Song," from *Bridge on the River Kwai,* "The Third Man Theme"; "The Man With the Golden Arm Theme."

The flurry of movie music put on records has helped popular music a great deal during its darkest hours. For this music composed for motion pictures has been—by and large—superior music, performed by gifted musicians. The quality of each score may differ, and there can be fiery debates on the true aesthetic worth of the movie sound tracks, yet, they are the products of musically gifted minds. You can't have a teenage innocent faking a movie-background score.

In his book, *The Death of Music,* the provocative music critic, Henry Pleasants, wrote that many of the jazz-flavored sound tracks—Elmer Bernstein's score for *The Man With the Golden Arm,* Johnny Mandel's score for *I Want to Live,* and Henry Mancini's scores for the television detective series "Peter Gunn" may be portents of a new kind of musical theater. He says, "exciting hints of what may lie ahead in this new kind of musical theater have come, not from the motion picture musical, but from straight films."

One thing that silent movies had in common with sound films was, oddly enough, the "title song." Though Hollywood has been deficient in song musicals, it hasn't lost sight of the promotional power of the title song which dates back to the earliest days of movie-making. According to Edward Jabolonski, writing in *Film Review* on "Filmusicals" (February 1955): "Movies have always been associated with song ever since the days of the nickelodeon, when a singer and a slide combination was used. A recording of 'The Perfect Song,' later the theme of Amos 'n' Andy, provided the background music for *The Birth of a Nation* in 1915."

One of the top hits during the Hollywood silent era was the song called "Charmaine," which Erno Rappee and Lew Pollack wrote for the 1926 film, *What Price Glory*. The pair later matched the feat by providing "Diane," for the 1927 film of life among Parisian "sewer rats" titled *Seventh Heaven*.

From those hand-cranked camera days to the space age, the title song in essentially nonmusical pictures has flourished. Some students of film box offices say that a "hit song can sometimes make a hit film," and they point to the rather rich box-office propulsion provided by such title songs as "Tammy," "Three Coins in the Fountain," "Gigi," and "Love Is a Many Splendored Thing."

Because of the success of these and other title songs, some producers have encouraged songwriters to somehow squeeze out these exploitation-geared songs against all the rules of reason and singability. Some of the outlandish by-products are such movie-title songs as:

"3:10 TO YUMA"	"THE MOLE PEOPLE"
"DON'T GO NEAR THE WATER"	"VERTIGO"
"MADBALL"	"GIDGET"
"IMITATION OF LIFE"	"HAVE ROCKET, WILL TRAVEL"
"THE SEVEN HILLS OF ROME"	"SINK THE BISMARK!"
"THE 4-D MAN"	

Try these on your rhyming dictionary.

Such ill-conceived commercialism has led some to claim that title songs are a racket. But they needn't be. Some of the work concocted by James Van Heusen and Sammy Cahn have resulted in some attractive words and music, including "All the Way," and "The Tender Trap." One recent title-song from a Hal Wallis comedy also had quality "Wives and Lovers," a good tune, and well-fabricated lyrics. And of course, one of the most famous was a synthetic folk song, moving and effective, Dmitri Tiomkin and Ned Washington's "High Noon," which heightened that moment of decision when Gary Cooper had to face the gang of cowboy hoodlums, alone at high noon.

The better quality title songs have been practically the only outlet for Hollywood's famous songwriters who have been pretty much technologically unemployed in the past decade. One cannot completely cavil at songs within dramatic properties, for the technique of adding songs to material is as old as Shakespeare, and, in fact, predates the good Bard.

When Hollywood discovered its "voice" the result was a fruitful and reciprocal relationship between popular music and the film art. Popular music had acquired another dimension. Through the big 35-mm. camera—in black and white and color, with all its techniques (close-ups, cross-cutting, production largesse) came popular music with a visual appeal it couldn't have as a disembodied voice coming out of a record, or radio, or even in the theater. The ancient art of making music was thus linked to the offspring of modern technology; and one enhanced and enriched the other.

As the years went by and Hollywood musicals were accepted and became part of the film scene, it revealed schizoid tendencies. It gave aesthetic traumas to many who were depressed to see banal songs given "colossal" production in clichéd stories. But there was a sunnier side.

Hammered out under studio mass-production methods, the original Hollywood musicals produced an enormous cavalcade of songs that were poignant, witty, sentimental, and full of warmth, from about 1930 to the 1950's. Many of today's standards are from that period, and a listing of them would cover pages of fine print such as the type employed for stock-market listings. Since the 1950's, the genre has been practically extinct.

From time to time, there are flashes of activity. A *Gigi* gets made. A Broadway musical is transferred to the screen. *My Fair Lady* will shortly be shown to millions, and Irving Berlin is reportedly putting together a score (new songs and some of his previous work) for a mammoth, $4 million MGM musical, tentatively titled, *Say It with Music*.

Still in evidence are the quick, inexpensive, "exploitation-type" musicals. Hollywood wants to attract the teenage audience into the movie theaters and to do this they have turned to teen stars. As a result, Elvis Presley, Connie Francis, Chubby Checker, Joey Dee, Fabian, Frankie Avalon, and Bobby Rydell have all been pressed into service. None of them are abundantly gifted in acting. And with them on the nation's marquées, the film sound tracks have been pouring out rock 'n' roll, the twist, teenage ditties. With the folk music boom at its height, MGM recently took up the guitar and put out *Hootenanny Hoot*. By repeating the title twice, the film moguls probably thought it would double the box-office gross.

Consider Annette. She got her start on the Walt Disney TV "Mouseketeer" program which propelled millions of little ones to stand at attention and sing the mouseketeer theme at the start and the end of the show. Remember little Annette wearing a black skull cap with little cloth ears intoning:

> Now it's time to say goodbye to all our company
> M-I-C-K-E-Y M-O-U-S-E.

Annette, a big girl now, wore a bikini no larger than a black skull cap in the musical film, *Beach Party*. A splashy bit of celluloid flotsam and jetsam, produced by American International, which called it a "spectacular surfing film," it had a score consisting of such water-logged epics as "Beach Party," "Sweet Surfin' Spot," "Swingin' and Surfin'," and something called "Pineapple Princess." Along with Annette there appeared Frankie Avalon, Dick Dale, and the Del Tones, three recording personalities, two vocalists, and a singing group.

Obviously, this was a teen-slanted film to capitalize on the West Coast surfing sport. The bathing suits were nice to look at, but there were the thirty-two-bar intrusions.

The movie sound tracks are prospering, and will probably continue to do so, outside the film in which they are heard, in the form of recordings, and performed music by bands and instrumental groups. Composer Elmer Bernstein (*The Man With a Golden Arm, A Walk on the Wild Side, The Ten Commandments*) once pointed out in an interview with *Variety* some fascinating statistics: that more than 40,000 minutes of music are composed each year for the sound tracks of more than 1,000 motion pictures throughout the world. "This is one of the most important arenas for modern music," he asserted.

This is undeniably true, but there is no substitute for vocal music. In a musical, the music is the star, the main dish, not the *aperitif*. In a motion picture the score plays a secondary role. Few people today place the motion picture sound track musicals on a lordly plain, because of its episodic character, and sometimes it consists of arranged bits of music from other sources for "color." However, it cannot be denied that the movie music composers, sans lyricists, have made an outstanding contribution to popular music.

As to the future of movie musicals, it cannot be considered good. Over a period of two decades a promising popular art form, the original movie musical has been gulled into comparative inactivity because ostensibly it doesn't "pay." Yet *West Side Story* was a box-office winner throughout the world, so the answer is partly economic, and partly failure of imagination.

The mass production of movie musicals as a steady source of vocal music seems, at present, to be as extinct as the hand-cranked camera and the gigantic studios. Which is a shame, for as Gene Kelly once told the Columbia University Oral Research Center inquiry into entertainment: "In motion pictures we are the only nation that can put on a musical in the movies and make it work. This has been a slow growth. Rapid, if you say 'just a couple of decades,' but when I say slowly I meant it didn't happen with one musical or one thing."

Whether words and music pictures come back in full cinematic bloom, nobody can foretell. Meanwhile, there are few, if any, sound stages where you can hear the modern-day counterparts of Judy Garland, Fred Astaire, Ginger Rogers, Bing Crosby, sing and dance in modern musicals by the finest popular composers and lyricists in the land, in film musicals involving excellent choreographers and skilled librettists.

Let us shed a quiet, nostalgic tear, just as NBC-TV did recently in a documentary, *The Fabulous Musicals*. Against music culled from famous song-and-dance films, the narrator, Joesph Cotten, observed: "These [the 30's] were the exciting years, when the sound of music and the sight of countless beautiful girls brought to the screen a new and spectacular type of entertainment . . . lavish, absurd, enchanting . . . a memorable legacy—these are the fabulous musicals."

24 · SOMEWHERE OVER THE RAINBOW

> I look forward to an America which will steadily raise the
> standards of artistic accomplishment and which will steadily
> enlarge cultural opportunities for all our citizens.
> —President John Kennedy in an address at Amherst College

George Bernard Shaw has a marvelous first act curtain line in his
thoughtful comedy, *Too True to Be Good*, which goes: "The play is
now virtually over; but the characters will discuss it at great length
for two acts more. The exit doors are all in order. Goodnight."

Goodnight.

For those staying up to hear the final *dénouement*, there are some important trends, tendencies, and patterns that need underscoring, insofar
as the future of the vast popular music business is concerned.

Broadway may be in turbulent waters financially, and Hollywood
movie musicals may be infrequent, but the recording business, around
which most of the popular music industry pivots, is heading toward
greater consumer acceptance. *Billboard's* Thomas Noonan, director of
research, has predicted a $800 million volume in 1966, and he does not
see why recordings do not become a billion-dollar industry by 1970.
Of course, this is a projection for all types of recordings; new versions
of *Der Rosenkavalier* and Beethoven's Fifth Symphony, as well as the
broad spectrum of popular music.

Equally important is the anticipated growth of leisure. Automation
and new labor union contracts are expected to pare the work-week
down from forty hours to thirty-five, and perhaps to thirty. This, of
course, ties in with an earlier forecast of more people buying more recordings. In an ad showing an analysis of entertainment industry stocks,
a Wall Street market firm headlined it this way: EXPECTED RISE IN
SPENDABLE INCOME FOR LEISURE PURSUITS."

What about television's impact? Television's impact on popular music
has been simultaneously substantial, skimpy, and sketchy. Mostly TV
has functioned as a medium for the exposure of previously established
songs and artists. The electronic miracle, now going into its second
decade of business, had led a rather thin creative existence as far as

popular music is concerned. The musical comedy-variety shows of Perry Como, Ed Sullivan, and Garry Moore stick to predictable and dull formats: a star sings old "standards" or new "hits." Little new music is exposed on video, new musical films—such as one-act musicals or revues with original music (not parodies), or modern ballets. The excitement of really hearing provocative new materials is rarely experienced by those who watch.

Some TV musicals have been especially prepared for the small screen: Rodgers and Hammerstein's *Cinderella,* Cole Porter's version of *Aladdin,* Jule Styne's dramatization of *Ruggles of Red Gap,* and Richard Adler's musical adaptations of *Gift of the Magi* and *Little Women.* Perhaps the most successful was a TV version of Thornton Wilder's *Our Town* by Sammy Cahn and Jimmy Van Heusen from which came the very popular song, "Love and Marriage." This tack needs to be explored on a more systematic, continuous basis.

In a creative sense, TV has done best in the background scoring department. From TV has come the lyrical jazz of "Peter Gunn" and some catchy instrumental themes. The little moppets, of course, were delighted wtih the homogenized, sugared-up buckskin tune, "The Ballad of Davy Crockett," which emerged from the Walt Disney television programs.

In a promotional sense, TV has been quite effective with those "dance parties," popularized by Dick Clark. There is a curious footnote, perhaps explainable only by a Krafft-Ebbing, a Wilheim Reich, or an Al Capp, concerning adults who are fond of watching these teenaged video dance parties. Vito Genovese, named by Joe Valachi in United States Congressional hearings as the No. 1 leader in the national *Cosa Nostra* crime syndicate, used to live in Atlantic Highlands, New Jersey. A neighbor once told the New York *Post* that Genovese would frequently phone him around seven P.M., and say:

" 'C'mon over Jerry, have something to eat, or watch TV.' I'd go over and we'd sit around drinking beer, and watching TV. His favorite was Ted Steele's Dance Party."

Some other trends hovering over the world of popular music are intensifications of present tendencies; the growth of "bigness" in recording and publishing to record distribution and record retailing; continued growth of the record clubs; continued wheeling and dealing with the cost of records to consumers; expansion of international show business with more U. S. stars traveling abroad; and foreign popular artists visiting here. And the way popular artists have entered the battle over civil rights suggests they will increasingly lend their talents, prestige, and organizing ability to other than show business ventures.

The popular music industry will function on a larger base, too. By 1975, census experts expect that in the United States alone, the population will reach 230 million, and in that year there is to be a bumper crop of teenagers.

Looked at in historical perspective, the crass, money-hungry world of popular music has given much beauty to millions in the United States and the world; our best writers are the best in the world, and their words and music are sung, hummed, danced to, broadcast, recorded, and imitated everywhere, including Russia. (Of course, U. S. "junk music" is equally audible from here to Calcutta). Our schizoid record industry had put in the grooves what the Record Industry Association of America has rightly called "a wonderful world of records."

Walk into a good record shop and you can find high fidelity and stereo recordings of the best popular music from Tin Pan Alley; show tunes, Hollywood materials, folk music, country music, jazz. Easily accessible are the works of George Gershwin, Jerome Kern, Harold Arlen, Richard Rodgers, Oscar Hammerstein; the voices of Louis Armstrong, Judy Garland, Bing Crosby, Frank Sinatra, Mary Martin, Billie Holiday, Ella Fitzgerald, Joan Baez. Tonight at 8:30 you can go to the theater, without leaving your home, and listen to such musical theater gems as *Show Boat, Porgy and Bess, Carousel, Guys and Dolls,* and *West Side Story,* on cast albums.

In other words, much of the tradition of craftsmanship, in the writing and performance of popular music, is now permanently transcribed. A living archive has been built up on recordings, as well as on sheet music and motion pictures. There is objective criteria on twelve-inch, long-playing discs containing the brilliance of American popular music, with which we can match current creativity.

And this is the heart of the matter. There is such a thing as quality in all music—including popular music. In a striking passage in the *Oxford Companion to Music,* Percy Scholes, the noted critic, writes that there are several characteristics of "quality" in music: Vitality, Originality, Workmanship, Proportion, Fitness, Feeling, the Element of Personal Taste, the Test of Time.

"As to the 'goodness' or 'badness,'" writes Scholes, "in music [to say nothing of the 'goodness' or 'badness' of particular compositions] there have probably always been debates—and probably always will be. There are even people who deny that 'goodness' and 'badness' exist, thinking it to be a mere matter of taste; but in that case music would stand alone as the one thing in the world not possessing quality, and, anyhow, there is no musical person of experience who does not assert the existence of grades of value in the musical repertory. The thoughtless division of music into 'what I like' and 'what I don't like' is too easy-going. Music, like everything else, has its standards."

Much of the newer popular music has been a revolt against quality and craftsmanship, and much of it has revolted millions of Americans.

Even the intelligent American cannot escape from the long reach of cheap music. He may privately choose the best show music, the best jazz, the best popular singers for listening to on recordings or on FM, but modern Americans cannot escape cheap, tawdry, teen-oriented pop music. It covers the country like a tarpaulin. It runs after people in restaurants, in car radios, transistor radios, in garages, on TV.

The cheap music pushed at intelligent Americans is a reminder of how commercial forces can twist the youngsters, and sell them inferior materials. It is a reminder of how the commercial forces can take advantage of the airwaves, the movies, the very social life of growing young people. The cheap music creates a kind of crazy-mixed-up honky-tonk milieu that colors and cheapens the quality of American life.

And what is ironic about it is this odd fact: only 500,000 teenagers buying a certain record can saturate the atmosphere of 180,000,000 people. A minority can make the majority a "captive audience." In most cases the public—that is, the adult public—hate these songs.

Like screaming billboards, shrieking advertisements on TV, and singing commercials, music clothes Americans in cheapness. It is another link in the bastardization of Walt Whitman's cry, "I hear America singing/The varied carols I hear."

The battle for taste and quality in popular music goes on, often unseen, in the hearts and minds of composers, lyricists, theater producers, press agents, record producers, singers, instrumental groups, arrangers, critics, radio station program managers, disc jockeys, jazz and folk music makers. There are always choices, directions, decisions. Even record retailers and record salesmen have a certain role to play. The fight for better material, keener discernment of quality products, and the promotion and merchandising of superior products is ceaseless.

Of course, the music business professionals cannot win the battle alone. Much of what has been going on is linked to a total social and cultural situation. While there has been retrogression in popular music, there has been a rise in cultural paper-back publishing. More than $500 million is being spent to build some one hundred new American cultural centers, according to a Manhattan School of Music survey. Attendance is also up in art films and art museums. Classical music records sales are high. All this is encouraging.

President John Kennedy was fond of show business and the better popular artists and writers. His favorite musical, according to Mrs.

Jacqueline Kennedy, was *Camelot* (a vision of a warless world) and his favorite folk song was "Greensleeves." He once observed: "If art is to nourish the roots of our culture, society must set the artist free to follow his vision where it takes him."

This vision is being obscured by the pragmatic marketeer, the merchandiser, the dollars-and-cents man who is deeply embedded in the popular music culture, as he is in all phases of the entertainment industry, films, television, radio. He is the technician in the billion-dollar cultural apparatus. The cultural technicians in all fields have several attitudes in common: they have more regard for sales, trade-paper listings, box-office, ratings, cost per thousand, than they have for the innate cultural worth of a recording, motion picture, or a television show.

C. Wright Mills caught the attitudes of these men in an essay on "The Cultural Apparatus":

The virtual dominance of commercial culture is the immediate ground of America's cultural scope, confusion, banality, excitement, sterility. In this overdeveloped society, the mass production, the mass sale, the mass consumption of goods has become The Fetish of both work and leisure.

Elsewhere, the sociologist noted:

There is, of course, a widespread idea, often and carefully repeated, that on the market for leisure, the consumers determine the products, that people get childish fare because that is what they really want. We should not be misled by this naive and mistaken "democracy of taste," in the name of which merchants of amusement reinforce the prevailing low levels of experience in America. What a man does with his leisure is determined by the leisure experiences that are most readily available to him and by his sensibilities and tastes. But what has happened is this:

As the hours of nonwork have increased, the mass means of communication and entertainment have trained the sensibilities and tastes of a generation or more of Americans. For levels of sensibility are, in fact, largely acquired, by atmosphere and by training.

On the other hand, there are quite a few who are culturally aware in the music and record business, who are sensitive to the whirligig that is show business and musical culture at the same time. Many think the popular product is awful, but they are frequently boxed in, since they have to make a living. Still there is a maturing aesthetic conscience in the popular-music complex, which leafs together all the entertainment media. It is perhaps best expressed by the statement of principles adopted by the National Academy for Recording Arts and Sciences

(NARAS). The academy—the recording industry's equivalent of Hollywood's Motion Picture Academy of Arts and Sciences—often makes some compromising awards in its yearly citation, such as an award for the "best rock 'n' roll recording." But the approach that it has taken represents a growing number of participants in the popular music industry, and it is illuminating and encouraging. Its credo is as follows:

Sales and mass popularity are the yardsticks of the record business. They are not the yardsticks of this Academy. We are concerned with the phonograph record as an art form. If the record industry is to grow, not decline in stature, if it is to foster a greater striving for excellence in its own field, if it is to discourage mediocrity and encourage greatness, we—as its spokesmen—can accept no other credo.

This is the kind of uncommercial heresy that may help us change our decade of musical mediocrity, where hacks and puffed-up adolescents, teenage idols, and their shrewd, calculating personal managers and booking agencies have held dominion. If they are dislodged, and the attitudes which they accept are defeated, perhaps popular music will gain new heights and bring us a sane musical milieu that will do honor to this country, and its people.

The sacred word is "excellence."

INDEX

325